D1496260

ANVIL OF VICTORY

Studies of the East Asian Institute—Columbia University

ANVIL OF VICTORY

THE COMMUNIST REVOLUTION IN MANCHURIA, 1945–1948

STEVEN I. LEVINE

COLUMBIA UNIVERSITY PRESS

New York   1987

The Andrew W. Mellon Foundation, through a special grant, has
assisted the Press in publishing this volume.

Library of Congress Cataloging-in-Publication Data

Levine, Steven I.
  Anvil of victory.

  (Studies of the East Asian Institute, Columbia
University)
  Based on the author's thesis (Ph.D)—Harvard
University)
  Bibliography: p.
  Includes index.
  1. China—History—Civil war, 1945–1949, 2. Manchuria
(China)—History. I. Title. II. Series: Studies of the
East Asian Institute.
DS777.5425.M36L48   1987   951'.8042   86-19821
ISBN 0-231-06436-5

Columbia University Press
New York   Guildford, Surrey
Copyright © 1987 Columbia University Press
Printed in the United States of America
This book is Smyth-sewn.

Book design by J. S. Roberts

For DOROTHY BORG

CONTENTS

ACKNOWLEDGMENTS

THIS book originated long ago as a doctoral dissertation at Harvard University under the Olympian direction of Benjamin I. Schwartz, a wise and modest mentor. It acquired much of whatever intellectual coherence it now possesses during my association with Columbia University, first as a Junior Fellow at what was then the Research Institute on Communist Affairs, and later as a teacher and Research Associate at the East Asian Institute. I shall always treasure the memories of my colleagues, students, and friends there whose encouragement sustained me in my work. The book was completed at the American University in Washington, D.C. There my friend the late Charles Heimsath welcomed a newcomer with his generous spirit and my colleagues in the School of International Service provided a stimulating intellectual environment.

The ritualized list of gratitude which all of us scrutinize, I suppose, has special meaning for the author alone. My parents, Julius and Eda G. Levine, taught me in their own way to savor the Confucian truth that, "To learn and at due times to repeat what one has learnt, is that not after all a pleasure." The late I. Milton Sacks, my teacher at Brandeis University, first opened the door for me to the study of Asia. I would like to record my thanks to the following persons who helped my work along its tortuous way, some by critical readings of the manuscript, others by providing references, encouragement, and fellowship: the late M. Searle Bates, Robert L. Beckman, Thomas P. Bernstein, Dorothy Borg, Maura Brennan, Philip Bridgham, Bruce Cumings, David Egler, John K. Fairbank, Austin Fulton, Donald Gillin, Steven M. Goldstein, Roy Hofheinz, Kenichiro Hirano, Michael H. Hunt, Chong-Sik Lee, Madeline G. Levine, Edwin Martinique, James W. Morley, Andrew J. Nathan, Douglas Reynolds, James Reardon-Anderson, Shaw Yu-ming, Frank Joseph Shulman, Ezra F. Vogel, Allen S. Whiting, Edwin A. Winckler, C. Martin Wilbur, and Eugene Wu. Ricky Ch'an and Daniel Kiang provided valuable research assistance at a relatively early stage of my work. Xiaoxiong Yi helped me in the critical final stages.

Among this list four names must be emphasized. Andrew J. Nathan as colleague, Dutch uncle, and close comrade-in-arms gave generously of his cold intellect and warm heart. Where I saw only problems he saw *problematik*. His encouragement and support were indispensable. Robert L. Beckman has been a friend and brother to me. His intellectual companionship has sustained me through years of commuting between North Carolina and Washington. He has tended my sometimes battered psyche, generously ladling out the spiritual chicken soup which I could not have done without. He is indeed *amicus usque ad aras*—a friend to the last degree. Madeline G. Levine has been my rudder and stabilizer. She has wielded an expert editor's pen on all my work. We inhabit each other's writings and we savor a rare partnership. Finally, Dorothy Borg has embodied for me an ideal of scholarship and fellowship that I despair of ever attaining myself. She has been my muse and my counselor. Without her inspiration this book would never have been completed. Rather than attempting to describe those virtues of wisdom, Socratic modesty, and tough-minded empathy which all who know her treasure, I dedicate this book to her.

The lengthy gestation period of this book had less to do with the intrinsic difficulty of the subject than with the fact that I am easily distracted. Over a period of many years, I methodically deferred working on the manuscript in order to play with my children (Elaine and Daniel), dig in my garden, pluck my banjo, share joy and sorrow with the friends whom I love,

and engage in other life-affirming diversions. Quite without design, such procrastination facilitated the sluggish metamorphosis
of a jejune dissertation authored by a 1960s-era graduate student
into a somber graybeard's opus.

Financial support for my work has been provided over
the years by the Foreign Area Fellowship Program of the SSRC,
the Research Institute on Communist Affairs, Columbia University, and the Joint Committee on Contemporary China.

Lest anyone suspect that I have churlishly omitted
expressing gratitude to my typists, let it be recorded that the
manuscript in its numerous incarnations has been typed by the
author himself using a modified hunt and peck method, a feat
that may have added several years to its gestation period.

Finally, I would like to express my thanks to Ian Von
Essen for preparing the maps and to Alan Adzherian for redrawing
the graphics from the barely discernible originals in the *Tung-pei
jih-pao*.

A great revolution must go through a civil war. This is a rule. And to see the ills of war but not its benefits is a one-sided view. It is of no use to the people's revolution to speak one-sidedly of the destructiveness of war.

—Mao Tse-tung.
Reading Notes on the Soviet Text
Political Economy

 At the end of an historic era abstract concepts always stink like rotten fish.

—Osip Mandelstam.
The Noise of Time

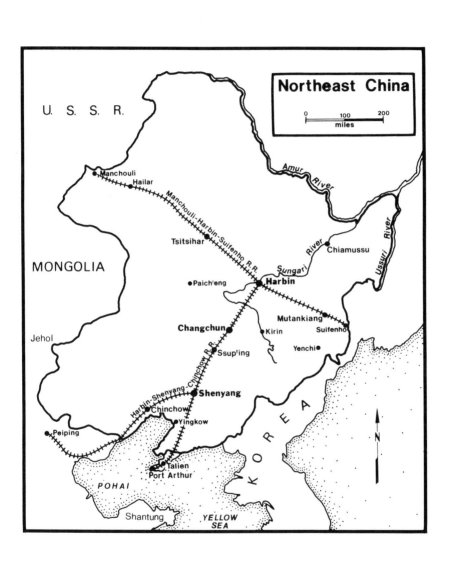

Northeast China

0   100   200
miles

U. S. S. R.

MONGOLIA

Jehol

Manchouli
Hailar
Manchouli-Harbin-Suifenho R.R.
Tsitsihar
Amur River
Sungari River
Chiamussu
Ussuri River
Paich'eng
Harbin
Mutankiang
Changchun
Kirin
Suifenho
Ssup'ing
Yenchi
Harbin-Shenyang-Chinchow R.R.
Shenyang
Chinchow
Yingkow
Peiping
KOREA
Talien
Port Arthur
POHAI
Shantung
YELLOW SEA

N

INTRODUCTION

IN mid-November 1948, thousands of rampaging Chinese Nationalist troops stormed through the North China metropolis of Tientsin. Cold, hungry, and demoralized, they looted Chinese homes, shook down shopkeepers, and raised the level of tension in a city that was already anxiously awaiting the imminent collapse of Nationalist power. These disorganized soldiers were all that remained of the crack, American-trained armies Chiang Kai-shek had sent to Manchuria in the fall of 1945 to reestablish Chinese power after fourteen years of Japanese colonial rule. In a brilliant seven-week campaign commencing in September 1948, a campaign that brought an end to three years of civil war, the Communists' Northeast People's Liberation Army (NEPLA), commanded by Lin Piao, completed the destruction of the once-powerful Nationalist forces. The NEPLA capped its offensive with the occupation of Shenyang, Manchuria's largest city, on November 2, 1948.

Within days of the Communist victory, the United States Ambassador to China, J. Leighton Stuart, gloomily cabled Washington: "We reluctantly reach conclusion, therefore, that early fall present Nationalist Government is inevitable . . ."[1] Stuart knew that the Nationalist commander in North China, Fu Tso-i, would be unable to resist the massive forces that Lin Piao was now positioning for an assault on the region. Indeed, on January 15, 1949, the Communists forced the surrender of Nationalist troops in Tientsin after bitter fighting. Just sixteen days later, Fu Tso-i peacefully yielded Peiping to the fur-hatted peasant troops from Manchuria. Lin's forces continued their triumphant southward procession. In mid-October 1949, with a new People's Republic already proclaimed in Peking, they liberated Canton and stood at the southernmost land frontier of China. This brief chronicle clearly establishes the direct connection between the Communists' military victory in Manchuria and their conquest of all of China.

To most students of the Chinese Communist movement, the revolutionary civil war of 1946–1949, which brought the Chinese Communist Party to power, remains virtually terra incognita. The paucity of work on this period suggests that most scholars assume Communist victory in the civil war was foreordained by developments in the preceding decades. Such a view is untenable. The leaders of the CCP themselves, despite their revolutionary optimism, were under no illusions that the task they faced at the end of the anti-Japanese war in 1945 was merely to ring down the curtain on a play whose action was virtually completed. They believed that they faced a long and difficult military and political struggle against an enemy who surpassed them not only in military power but in domestic political authority and external support as well. In retrospect, of course, the Nationalist collapse occurred with astonishing rapidity.

This study attempts to provide part of the answer to the question of why the Communists won the civil war in China. It is grounded in the assumption that in order to understand why and how the CCP came to power one must examine the civil war period, for this is precisely the time when the Party achieved victory. This is a commonsense assertion, but it is by no means a commonplace. In seeking to understand so protean and profound a phenomenon as the Chinese revolution, scholars have been drawn inevitably to broad-gauged explanations rooted in intellectual history, political sociology, theories of organizational behavior, ideology, peasant revolution, and the like. These investigations have honed our understanding of the revolutionary process in

China. Explanations of the CCP's success have tapped deeply into the rich soil of the Chinese past.

While students of the Chinese Communist movement have differed substantially in their interpretations of the CCP's victory, the very fact of that victory has had an influence on how they have looked at the Communist rise to power.[2] When Edgar Snow published his classic *Red Star Over China* in 1937, it was visionary to suggest that the Chinese Communists would one day govern all of China. But once Mao Tse-tung and his colleagues were securely installed in the Forbidden City, their very possession of power retrospectively conferred an aura of inevitability on their victory. Except for a minority who persisted in viewing communism in China as an exogenous force brought to power through some sort of conspiracy (Kremlin machinations or U.S. State Department treason), most scholars equated the Communist revolutionary victory in China with the much broader phenomenon of the Chinese revolution itself. Hence, the identification of Chinese communism as the embodiment and logical culmination of nationalism, anti-imperialism, agrarian revolution, and so forth. This cast of mind imparts a distinctly teleological flavor to many studies of the Chinese Communist movement, whose history in this view becomes a kind of long learning curve sweeping upward to Mao's annunciation of the People's Republic on October 1, 1949.

In this progression, the anti-Japanese war period (1937–1945) is often accorded a special significance as the time when Chinese communism matured into a powerful military-political force with an effective program, an experienced leadership, an efficient organization, and an appealing ideology. It is certainly true that from Yenan, "the cradle of revolution" where the Communist movement was reborn, the CCP spread its organization and ideology throughout the hills of the northwest and the plains of northern China. Over the course of a stormy decade, what had been a marginal and struggling political party in 1936 grew into a powerful contender for national leadership.

Nevertheless, as the Japanese expeditionary forces stacked their arms in the late summer of 1945, the decisive struggle for power in China was just getting under way. In retrospect, of course, it seems logical to conclude that during the war years the always tenuous foundations of Chiang Kai-shek's rule had eroded almost beyond hope of repair.[3] But this is wisdom after the fact. At the time, few observers possessed sufficient clairvoyance to predict either the rapidity or the totality of the CCP victory.

In 1945, Chinese Communist leaders, inspired by Marxist faith and quite possibly by their knowledge of the rise of new dynasties, looked to the future with considerable hope tempered by the realization that the Nationalists' strength exceeded their own. Mao's concern that Chiang Kai-shek might wrest the fruits of victory over Japan from the hands of the people (read CCP) attests to his anxiety that a sustained Nationalist military-political offensive might reverse the gains made by the CCP between 1937 and 1945.[4] Such indeed was Chiang's own calculation. However, between 1945 and 1948 Chiang Kai-shek's anticipation of victory evaporated while Mao's bounded optimism was validated beyond expectation. In these few years, the CCP recruited and supplied vast armies, trained a large number of civilian and military cadres, created effective and cohesive organizations, and transformed the structures of economic power, the social order, and the political system in countless villages, towns, and cities.

The revolutionary civil war of 1946–1949 was the period of decisive victory for the CCP. Any attempt to explain the success of the Chinese Communist movement that slights the culminating phase of its development can only be partial at best. Of course, the civil war cannot be viewed in isolation from the preceding stages of CCP history. My point here is simply to draw attention to the importance of a generally neglected period in CCP history that needs to be studied in detail. Naturally, the civil war is connected as well with the succeeding decades and, as will be suggested in the conclusion of this study, the imprint of Party practices and policies from the civil war period may be discerned in the post-1949 history of China. Such a conclusion echoes David Wilkinson's observation that "revolutionary civil war is characteristically a parenthesis within a revolution: an episode marked by wide and intense violence in the form of an organized and polarized two-sided struggle ended by a victory and autocratic rule."[5] The CCP's victory was much more than the first step in a journey of ten thousand *li*, as Mao Tse-tung described it, but it was by no means the termination of the Communist revolution. The impulse toward revolutionary change was not exhausted by the conquest of power. Nevertheless, victory transformed the Communists from rebels into rulers. It freed them from the need of pretending to fight for democracy, and it enabled some of the leaders of the CCP—Mao Tse-tung in the first instance—to indulge with impunity their penchant for radical experimentation.

The would-be student of the civil war at once confronts the fundamental condition of Chinese politics in the first half of the twentieth century—political disunity—and its accompanying profusion of political actors, regional and local regimes, and competing ideologies. Fortunately, this very condition facilitates a kind of economy of analysis by legitimizing a focus on just one of the loosely interconnected geographical areas of Chinese politics during the era of disintegration. The present study focuses on Northeast China (Manchuria) during the civil war years of 1945–1948.[6] The struggle for the Northeast was a critical component of the CCP's successful contest against the Nationalists (Kuomintang) for control of all of China. Both parties realized that the outcome of this struggle would be crucial to the resolution of the overall conflict and they invested political and military resources in the region accordingly.

How does the contest for Manchuria fit into the overall contours of the civil war? This is a question that cannot yet be answered fully because of the dearth of detailed empirical studies of other regions during this period. A general history of the civil war should analyze the various regional actors and trace the dynamic connections between sectors in both political and military terms.[7] It is likely that additional studies of the civil war period will reveal significant regional and local variations in the pattern of Communist victory.

One point is obvious and has already been suggested. The Communist triumph in the Northeast accelerated the timetable of victory on a nation-wide scale by producing a kind of internal domino effect. The achievement of victory there made available Communist military resources which were quickly concentrated on the next target. On the Nationalist side, administrative chaos, civilian demoralization, general panic, and psychological collapse induced by Communist military victory in one region prepared the ground for Nationalist defeat in the ensuing engagements. The PLA rolled up China like a mat from north to south.

A study of the civil war in Northeast China, then, transcends local history or regional history. In fact, during revolutionary civil wars the boundaries between regional and national history collapse. The absence of an effective central government produces a centrifugal effect on politics. Key decisions that affect the outcome of nation-wide issues are often made by regional leaders. The process of reconstituting a central decision-making apparatus may occur more or less simultaneously in several regions. In China, the high command of the Chinese Communist Party as represented by its Central Committee and top military commanders was widely dispersed during the civil war years. After the Nationalist capture of Yenan in April 1947, even the central core of the Party's leadership was split into two separate groups with no fixed residence. During this time Party Chairman Mao Tse-tung and Commander-in-Chief Chu Teh provided symbolic and diffuse leadership to the Communist movement rather than effective day-by-day control over its disparate activities. The close working relations within the central elite achieved during the anti-Japanese war period enabled the CCP to combine ideological and programmatic unity with operational flexibility. Effective integration was achieved without excessive centralization.

Just as revolutionary civil wars erase the boundaries between regional and national politics, so they further blur the already indistinct dividing line between domestic and international politics. The contending parties in an internal (civil war) often solicit the intervention of external actors to tip the balance of power in their favor.[8] The likelihood of intervention increases during periods of bipolarism in the international system, particularly if the civil war is in a contested area that does not clearly fall within one or the other of the two major powers' spheres of control. The Chinese civil war of the late 1940s is a case in point since it coincided with the emergence of the Soviet-American Cold War. Both Moscow and Washington were deeply suspicious of each other's motives and policies in China. American fears that the Soviet Union was seeking to dominate Manchuria prompted the dispatch of General George C. Marshall to China with the mission of bringing about a peaceful solution to the Chinese internal conflict. Such an outcome was intended to close off the avenues of Soviet influence. For its part, the Soviet Union covertly supplied intermittent political, economic, and military support to the CCP, but it also maintained contacts with and tried to influence Chiang Kai-shek and the Nationalists. In sum, the Chinese civil war and the contest in Manchuria in particular were affected by the international politics of the early Cold War era. This study of the Northeast civil war, then, links regional and national history, domestic and international politics.

In addressing the central question of why the Chinese Communists won the civil war, one must constantly bear in mind these complex, overlapping levels of domestic and international politics. It is this very complexity and multiplicity of elements that casts doubt on any explanation of the Communist victory which is predicated predominantly on a single factor. A central theme of this study is that the CCP's triumph in Manchuria resulted from the intersection of many factors in the domestic China *and* international political environments of the late 1940s. Far from being the ineluctable outcome of underlying socioeconomic forces, the Communist triumph was a contingent victory, very much dependent upon a variety of political, military, and organizational factors peculiar to the conflict in the Northeast. The decisive character of the Communists' Northeast victory in the fall of 1948 creates a misleading impression about the course of the three-year struggle in the region. Even after two years of intense fighting (1945–1947), the CCP's position in Manchuria was far from secure, and its margin of victory in the civil war was thinner than it might appear to have been. Had the Nationalists been only somewhat better organized and better led, they might have fought the Communists to a standstill in the region.

Turning to the international environment of the conflict, it was one of the anomalies of the early Cold War that the United States, although ostensibly embarked on a global anti-Communist crusade, declined to bail out Chiang Kai-shek's faltering effort to combat communism in China. The traditional primacy of Europe in U.S. foreign policy, the widespread conviction that the Nationalist regime was not worth saving, and the belief that China just did not count for much in the global balance of power outweighed the pleadings of the Asia-firsters and the fundamentalist anti-Communist ideologues.[9] In essence, the limited U.S. assistance to Chiang Kai-shek no more than roughly balanced out the covert aid that Stalin gave to Mao. The general effect of the tacit Soviet-American agreement to limit their involvement in the Chinese civil war was to emphasize the primacy of internal factors in deciding its outcome.

Such a conclusion, however, should not blind us to the importance of the international environment in contributing to the Communist victory. Many scholars have echoed Secretary of State Dean Acheson's assertion in his Letter of Transmittal accompanying the State Department's China White Paper (July 30, 1949) that "the ominous result of the civil war in China was beyond the *control* of the government of the United States. Nothing that this country did or could have done *within the reasonable limits of its capabilities* could have changed that result."[10] To such a carefully qualified statement one can hardly take exception. Certainly, from the perspective of July 1949, the momentum of Communist victory appeared enormous. Yet at an earlier stage of the civil war, before the onset of rapid Nationalist military and political decline, it is not inconceivable that a direct U.S. role in the war on the side of Chiang Kai-shek might, at a minimum, have greatly delayed the Communist victory if not actually changing the outcome.

Let me hasten to clarify this point. I am not retrospectively advocating an American armed intervention in the Chinese civil war as an earlier student of this period has done in effect.[11] The historical and human tragedy which U.S. intervention compounded in Vietnam makes one appreciate the wisdom and restraint of Truman and Marshall in comparison with Lyndon Johnson, Dean Rusk, et al. Nor am I arguing that the United States *in fact* could have reversed the outcome of the Chinese civil war, that it could have overcome the enormous domestic advantages of the CCP. That seems highly unlikely, to say the least. What I am suggesting is that the unwillingness and inability of the United States to attempt a sustained armed counterrevolutionary intervention such as it mounted later in Korea and Vietnam created a favorable international environment for the Chinese Communist revolution. Given the disparity in power between the United States and the Soviet Union in the early postwar period, it is unlikely that Stalin would have directly countered an American effort to block a Chinese Communist victory. Thus, notwithstanding their diatribes concerning American imperialism during the civil war era, the Chinese Communists could consider themselves fortunate that they carried out their revolution before the United States had fully learned its imperial role.

The civil war was an era of revolution in China, a decisive phase in a revolutionary process that is one of the major strands of modern Chinese history. Any student of China in the 1940s must confront as a central question the role of the agrarian revolution in the Communist victory. Some scholars have described the Chinese Communists as the natural heirs to the age-old tradition of peasant rebellion in China, and the Communist revolution, in essence, as a species of peasant revolution, albeit led by a modern-style political organization. Others have seen the CCP as taking advantage of peasant rebelliousness and discontent for their own aim of attaining power. Both views assume the existence of an innately restive peasantry waiting for the proper leadership to liberate its pent-up fury. Yet a third view interprets the revolution as an autonomous, self-generated expression of peasants whose politics was a quest for social justice and suggests that the CCP was assimilated into this tradition.[12]

This study points to a different reality. In Manchuria, as elsewhere in China, it is true that a massive rural revolution accompanied the transfer of power. In the predominantly rural counties from which the CCP drew most of its strength, a vast army of peasant lads was recruited to the Communist banners, sustained by the surplus of the agricultural sector, and led to victory in battle. In the village and county seats of the Northeast, political, economic, and military power passed in a series of often violent struggles from the hands of the old elite into the hands of a new leadership of political activists, cadres, and Party workers.

It is my contention that no part of this revolution would have occurred without the strong and forceful presence of the Communist party and the military forces at its disposal. In Manchuria, the Communist party did not simply lead the rural revolution to victory, the Communist party created that revolution. It did so in an atmosphere where most peasants and other rural dwellers were initially quiescent, politically passive, and not inclined toward rebelliousness. The resort to rural revolution was a conscious choice, a deliberate political strategy for the CCP in its quest for power. The implementation of a strategy of rural revolution enabled the CCP to organize its territories in northern Manchuria in order to fight a civil war. Without the Communist armies, which initially entered the Northeast from outside, and the Communist political organization, which successfully mobilized rural and urban dwellers for political-military conflict, there would have been no more than scattered unrest and the usual low level of violence in postwar Manchuria. Communist organization, both political and military, spelled the difference between the survival of the old order and the creation of the new.

From this one may conclude that an emphasis on the agrarian revolution as the primary avenue to understanding the Communist victory in the Northeast would be misplaced. This is not to deny the importance of comprehending how the rural transformation was effected and, even more, of examining what benefits the Communists derived from this transformation. But for Manchuria, at least, *the rural revolution must be viewed within the context of the civil war itself*. The central organizing principle of this study is the idea that with respect to Communist policy, all political, economic, social, and other transformations must be viewed within the context of the war. Revolution was a means—the most important means—of fighting the war.

I also do not mean to imply that the CCP was not genuinely committed to the revolutionary transformation it effected. That it was committed as a matter of principle seems to me beyond question. But that is not my point. In the civil war period, as in any revolution, the fundamental question was "To whom the power?" In 1945–1946 the Communists participated in abortive negotiations to avert civil war and to establish a coalition government of national unity from within which they might have competed for power through peaceful means. It seems reasonable to suppose that had these negotiations succeeded and the Communists become junior partners in a regime still dominated by Chiang Kai-shek's Nationalists, they would have eschewed radical policies of social upheaval in favor of more moderate appeals and slogans, at least temporarily. But the failure of a negotiated solution to China's civil conflict pushed Communist policy in a more radical direction as civil war became more imminent.

The CCP enunciated a program of radical land reform in the spring of 1946, denounced the "illusion" of peaceful accommodation within Party ranks, and established a separate government for Northeast China in August 1946. In foreign policy, beginning in mid-1946 the CCP, no longer impelled to assuage the United States, sharply attacked American imperialism and condemned the duplicity of the Truman administration for supporting Chiang Kai-shek while supposedly engaged in impartial negotiation.[13] In short, a series of measures was taken to prepare the Party and to mobilize the population as soon as it became clear that war would decide the question of who would rule in China.

Although revolution in the countryside was a means to help the Communists fight the civil war rather than simply an end in itself, an agrarian revolution was not enough to ensure victory. The widespread notion that in the Communist revolution the revolutionary countryside surrounded and defeated the passive Nationalist-controlled cities is belied by the reality of the Northeast civil war. Possession of a strong urban base in northern Manchuria was an important factor in the Communist victory.

In his analysis of the anti-Japanese war period, Tetsuya Kataoka has argued that the CCP's wartime strategy of the second united front combined elements of a peasant revolution approach with elements of an essentially urban anti-imperialist approach.[14] Suppression of the radical peasant associations in 1927 and the defeat of the Kiangsi soviet in 1934 had earlier demonstrated the weakness of a revolutionary strategy based solely on the countryside and had shown the superiority of military power based on control of the cities. The neutralization of the Nationalists' urban-based power by the Japanese occupation, Kataoka argues, was the essential precondition for the success of the CCP's rural revolution.[15] Kataoka's thesis is extremely suggestive, and I would like to carry forward his analysis into the civil war period.

At the Seventh Congress of the CCP (April–June 1945), Mao Tse-tung declared that the Communist Party must acquire control of cities in the next stage of the revolutionary struggle.[16] Towards the end of the anti-Japanese war, Communist troops positioned themselves to seize major cities in north and east China, but, aided by the United States, Chiang Kai-shek quickly occupied major cities along the coast as well as in the interior. For a variety of reasons, however, the Nationalists were unable to convert their control of the urban centers into a decisive strategic asset during the civil war. The Nationalists' apparent dependence upon the United States coupled with their reluctance to confront the USSR enabled the Communists to pose as the champions of anti-imperialist nationalism. Repressive but ineffectual Nationalist tactics for dealing with intellectual and particularly student opposition to the civil war cost them support among these largely urban groups. Financial mismanagement, rampant inflation, and incompetent bureaucracy, among other reasons, compounded the Nationalists' difficulty in using the cities to their advantage.[17] In any case, the Communist armies had grown beyond the point where the encirclement and eradication strategy applied by the Nationalists in the early 1930s could be effective. The cities could no longer surround and suppress the countryside!

It is clear that the cities continued to exert a powerful attraction upon the Communists despite their disappointment at not being able to occupy any of the major urban prizes in 1945. In Northeast China, for example, the Communist leadership expended significant military resources in the spring of 1946 in a futile attempt to hold onto central Manchurian cities such as Changchun which had fallen into their hands when the Soviet Red Army withdrew from the region. In northern Manchuria, the Communists occupied and retained control throughout the civil war of Harbin, the largest city in the north, as well as of the medium-sized cities of Mutankiang, Chiamussu, Tsitsihar, and others. These cities proved to be vital assets. They functioned as administrative centers and military headquarters, and were used for cadre training and education and for cultural, industrial, financial, and commercial activity.

In addition, control of the Northeast cities may have had an important psychological impact on the leaders of the CCP. It reassured them that their long march to power was nearing completion. In this connection, it should be noted that very few if any of the CCP's central elite, even those from peasant backgrounds, could legitimately lay claim to being considered leaders of the peasantry or even of the countryside. During their metamorphosis into Communist leaders, they had all acquired in varying degrees a modern, cosmopolitan orientation, either through residence in China's major cities, study, work, or travel abroad, intellectual training, and ideological conviction. Mao Tse-tung, for example, despite his occasional pose as an earthy, simple son of the soil, fitted this mold no less than the suave Chou En-lai or the urban apparatchik Liu Shao-ch'i. It is true, of course, that the Communists had learned to speak the language of the peasants and had become adept at organizing peasants and other rural dwellers during the long years of their rural diaspora. But they retained their identity as a political organization with an internationalist ideology, a closed central leadership, and, above all, a determination to rule China from its modern cities.

The Communists were an *urban nucleus* sojourning in the countryside until such time as they could return to the urban power centers as victors. Communist leaders in the Northeast established their headquarters in Harbin—the communications, transportation, industrial, commercial, cultural, and financial hub of northern Manchuria—not in some remote county seat. And the capture of Shenyang, the region's largest city, was an appropriate symbolic as well as actual conclusion to the civil war in the region. When feasible, then, the Communist leaders made full use of the cities under their control as they were able, even though not all of the middle-ranking cadres understood how to administer urban areas. In sum, Communist strategy in the Northeast civil war combined centralized urban-based organization with an induced peasant revolution. The result was an amalgam that produced victory.

CHAPTER ONE

POLITICAL CONFLICT IN CHINA: THE ORIGINS OF CIVIL WAR

ON August 20, 1945, twelve days after the USSR attacked the Japanese Army in Manchuria, some 225 Soviet paratroopers jumped over Shenyang and quickly seized control of this largest city in the region.[1] Major-General A. I. Kovtun-Stankevich, the newly appointed Red Army garrison commander in Shenyang, immediately found himself the target of numerous clamoring Chinese—indigenous representatives of the Kuomintang and the Chinese Communist Party, local notables, and many others—all seeking to promote their own or their parties' interests in the city.[2] Kovtun-Stankevich, who had stormed the bastions of Budapest and Vienna in Central Europe, was initially baffled in Shenyang, uncertain what to do. Soon, however, taking the advice of newly arrived Chinese Communist cadres, he appointed Chang Hsüeh-ssu (younger brother of the former Manchurian warlord) as governor of Liaoning province in which Shenyang is located, and also installed a CCP-approved mayor and police chief in the city itself, much to the chagrin of the Nationalist supporters.[3] With the war against Japan barely over, the struggle for power in Northeast China had already begun.

The Historical Setting

The revolutionary civil war in Manchuria occurred in a region whose history distinguished it from intramural China in many ways. For centuries Northeast China had been a sparsely settled frontier region. During the late Ch'ing period, when restrictions on Han Chinese migration into the Northeast were lifted, the trickle of settlers swelled into a torrent. The railroad and the steamship—instruments of Western and Japanese imperialism—hastened the destruction of the historic equilibrium between the older agricultural settlements and the frontier. Freight cars and steerage compartments disgorged millions of migrants from the crowded provinces of Chihli (Hopei) and Shantung onto the virgin soils of central and northern Manchuria, and linked the rich interior plains and valleys with Chinese and foreign markets. New towns like Harbin sprang up to serve as the economic ganglia of a burgeoning industrial and commercial economy closely tied to the world market in soybeans, that miracle crop that provided man with bean curd and soy sauce for his table, fodder for his cattle, explosives for his wars, and varnish for his coffins.

The statistics of regional growth indicate an increase in population from 8.1 million in 1891 to about 18 million in 1910 and 44.6 million by 1940.[4] Between 1910 and 1930 the cultivated area expanded nearly two-thirds from 8 million to 13 million hectares and by 1940 to 18 million hectares. Most of the increase was in market-oriented crops such as soybeans, kaoliang, and wheat.[5]

In the first decade of intensive migration, the influx of settlers was basically a hegira of the dispossessed set into motion by natural disasters, population pressure on the land, and civil war. Later on, in the 1920s and 1930s, as the pace of regional economic development increased, a labor shortage in Manchuria acted as a magnet for manpower needed to build the roads and railways, fell the timber, and toil in the factories and mines.[6] The most enterprising of migrants might parlay their savings into modest fortunes enabling them to return to their ancestral North China villages and invest in land. Those migrants who permanently settled in Manchuria endured a harsh life at first as the road to prosperity was not an easy one, but eventually most of the migrants were able to improve their economic and social status. Economic and social mobility in Manchuria was quite high.[7]

After the passing of the Ch'ing dynasty in 1911, what had been a trend toward increasingly centralized control over Manchuria's administration was reversed. The long-gowned scholars once more yielded the reins of power to the men on horseback. In the late teens and twenties, Chang Tso-lin, a man of humble origins, became the de facto ruler of Manchuria, and used the region as an autonomous base from which he tried with sporadic success to extend his grasp into North China. However, the virtual autonomy of Manchuria in the 1920s did not mean that the region was cut off from intramural Chinese developments. On the contrary, the most important political fact of the twenty years between the end of the Manchu dynasty and the Japanese conquest was that Manchuria failed to produce a significant political movement with a separatist program or ideology that might have transformed the autonomy of the militarist period into a permanent separation. The region continued to be an important square on the chessboard of Chinese politics, giving its possessor control of rich agricultural, industrial, and financial resources as well as access to the North China plain and Peking.

During the period between 1911 and the Japanese invasion of 1931, Northeast politics was dominated by a narrow oligarchy of large landowners, merchants, militarists, and government officials. Politics consisted of the rivalry and competition of civilian and military cliques within the oligarchy.[8] The Northeast was certainly not sealed off from the turmoil of intramural China during these revolutionary years, but only an echo of the reverberations reached beyond the Great Wall rather than the shock waves of the revolutionary explosions.

Japan's efforts to promote a sense of Manchurian nationalism in the puppet state of Manchukuo (established in 1932) had little effect. During the fourteen years of Japanese de facto colonial rule, however, the economic infrastructure of an industrially developed country was created in the Northeast. Among the accomplishments of this period were the improvement of the transportation and communications systems, the development of industry and mining, and the creation of a modern tax structure, banking system, and a unified currency.

Soon after the Japanese occupation of Manchuria, a serious internal security problem developed in the new state of Manchukuo. Elsewhere, particularly in North China after 1937, anti-Japanese resistance movements became an important vehicle for Communist mobilization, enabling the CCP to expand its influence and control rapidly and setting the stage for the Communist victory in the ensuing civil war against the Nationalists.[9] In Manchuria, too, both the Kuomintang and the CCP tried to organize guerrilla resistance to Japanese rule, but their initial successes simply provoked increased Japanese efforts to suppress them. By the time the war ended in 1945, the KMT and the CCP had virtually no organization or supporters in the region to show for their efforts. A brief look at the failure of this strategy of guerrilla resistance may help us understand the tasks the two parties confronted at the beginning of the revolutionary civil war in the Northeast.

The policy of nonresistance which Nanking had urged upon the regional leader of the Northeast, Chang Hsüeh-liang, was unpopular among young Chinese Nationalists in Manchuria, many of whom were the modern-educated offspring of the regional elite. Using their family ties and traditional patron-client relationships, these young Nationalists organized a large number of local resistance forces which loosely coalesced into what came to be known as the I Yung Chün (Volunteer Army). As many as 300,000 men may have participated in the non-Communist resistance in 1932, but by 1935 the I Yung Chün had succumbed, a victim of effective Japanese counterinsurgency and of insufficient support both from within the region and from intramural China. Nationalist efforts to sustain underground political organizations in Manchuria were equally unsuccessful.[10] Little if anything survived of these efforts on which the Nationalists could build in the postwar struggle for power.

The Japanese occupation of Manchuria presented the CCP with an unparalleled opportunity to broaden and deepen its hitherto feeble organizational efforts in the Northeast. During the 1920s, Communist activity in Manchuria was highly fragmented along ethnic lines. Expatriate Korean Communists in the districts abutting Korea were more successful than their Chinese comrades in the region, but even their activity was politically marginal.

During the years when the Communist movement was burgeoning in intramural China, the CCP in Manchuria was stagnating.
The reasons for this are not hard to find. The Manchurian Provincial Committee (MPC) of the CCP directed its organization
efforts at urban workers and intellectuals, making itself an easy
target for the police who effectively controlled the cities. Second,
the MPC pursued an insurrectionist, anti-nationalist, and nar-
rowly sectarian line.[11]

At the time of the Manchurian Incident, the MPC was
still groping for a successful strategy. Between 1931 and 1936, the
Communist International in Moscow made several attempts to
breathe life into the moribund Communist movement in Manchuria, but without lasting results. Hawk-eyed Japanese police
repeatedly arrested successive leaders of the MPC and effectively
disrupted its functioning. Meanwhile, the MPC itself, torn between competing strategies emanating from the Comintern in
Moscow and the CCP Central Committee in intramural China,
contributed to its own demise through internecine conflict between its Han Chinese and ethnic Korean members.[12]

While the urban-oriented MPC disintegrated under
Japanese pressure, a rural-based Communist-led guerrilla resistance briefly flourished between 1934 and 1936, but it too eventually succumbed, leaving little trace upon the region's later history. What distinguished the Communist-led guerrillas from their
urban comrades was their much earlier willingness to combine
with other anti-Japanese forces in coordinated or even united
resistance activity. By early 1936, the Communist forces were
joined together as the Northeast Anti-Japanese United Army
(NEAJUA) headed by the veteran Honanese Communist Yang
Ching-yu. The program of the NEAJUA proclaimed an anti-Japanese patriotism leavened with Northeast regionalist sentiment.[13]

The NEAJUA engaged in extensive guerrilla opera-
tions in the rural hinterlands throughout the Northeast, but it was
in the traditional bandit base areas such as the frontier districts of
eastern Kirin that they were most successful, combining a program
of economic and social reform with their patriotic anti-Japanese
message. The period 1935–1937 was the highwater mark of Communist-led anti-Japanese guerrilla warfare in the Northeast. But
once the Sino-Japanese War broke out in 1937, the Japanese

intensified their efforts to suppress the Manchurian resistance in
order to secure their main rear supply base. The Communists were
unable to bear up against the unremitting and ruthless Japanese
pressure. By February 1940, when Commander-in-Chief Yang
Ching-yu was hunted down and killed, the NEAJUA had been
reduced to a couple of hundred widely dispersed and nearly de-
fenseless men. The Manchurian chapter of the saga of resistance
had ended ingloriously.

In considering the causes for the failure of Communist
guerrilla resistance in Manchuria (a striking contrast to the CCP's
successes in North China) several factors stand out. First, because
the Japanese had long seen Manchuria as a vital region, Tokyo
invested greater military resources in garrisoning and controlling
the region. Harried in the towns and hunted in the countryside,
the Manchurian Communists could find no refuge. Second, organizational weakness rather than programmatic or ideological
deficiencies help explain the Communist failure in the Northeast.
The Chinese Communist leadership viewed Manchuria as a back-
water far removed from the center of Chinese political struggle.
Accordingly, they invested very few resources in the Northeast.
Third, the Communist movement was gravely weakened from
within by ethnic strife between Han Chinese and Korean Communists, and exhibited the self-destructive paranoid behavior of
an organization under stress.

Perhaps most importantly, social conditions in Manchuria did not generally favor the creation of a wide-scale resistance. Except for a thin stratum of officials, the regional and local
elites were not seriously threatened by Japanese rule in the region.
In the crisis of the Japanese invasion, most of the local elite opted
to preserve its property under Japanese rule. In most rural areas,
there was apparently little change in the distribution of power
from pre-Manchukuo days, and thus no opportunity for Communists to fill a void.

At the mass level, a different problem existed. The very
character of the Chinese migration into the Northeast may have
fostered a negative predisposition toward participation in or even
support of resistance movements.[14] It is likely that few farmers
shared the intelligentsia's sense of aggrieved nationalism even
though they bore the brunt of Japanese taxation and labor service.
Indeed, much, if not most, of the rural population probably even

lacked a strong sense of local identification. Although most of the migrants sought out settlements of *landsleit* from their native villages or county, there may not have been enough time for the creation of that web of kin, friend, and neighbor relations to develop to the point where they might serve as the basis for political and military organization. Manchuria, China's frontier of commercialized agriculture and capitalist development, supplied a poor soil for the primordial sentiments that quickened village radicalism elsewhere in China.[15]

In sum, Japanese rule in the Northeast brought new hardships as well as new economic opportunities, but it did not bring social or political upheavals, at least not right away. Consequently, even a more experienced, better manned, and more wisely guided regional Communist organization than the MPC might not have been able to sustain a viable resistance organization in the face of the Japanese juggernaut.

Despite the failure of the Manchurian resistance, the Manchukuo interlude played a crucial role in preparing the soil for the civil war. Japan's occupation quickly accomplished what a decade of nationalist agitation had barely begun to effect. By posing the issue of Chinese national survival in the starkest terms possible, it forced Chinese on both sides of the Great Wall divide to make a fateful choice. Those in Manchuria who chose to fight were comparatively few in number and in the end they were defeated, but their message of resistance whetted the thirst for national revenge. Manchurians, who had lagged behind in the nationalist struggles of the 1920s, now stood in the forefront of those Chinese who insisted upon a decisive victory over Japan. Frustration and defeat had brought Manchuria to center stage in Chinese politics, and in the postwar struggle for power neither the KMT nor the CCP could afford to ignore the region any longer.

The Political Situation in China at the End of the War

The prospects for a peaceful resolution of the political conflict in China between the KMT and the CCP did not look bright in this late summer of 1945. Knowledgeable observers, both foreign and

Chinese, expected that Japan's defeat would rekindle the flames of civil war. The awkward cohabitation of the KMT and the CCP in the wartime united front beginning in 1937 had not worked out well, and by 1940 the two ill-matched partners had separated. The Kuomintang survived the war in its southwestern bastion, while the CCP cultivated its power in the northwest and behind enemy lines in North China. Tentative efforts to develop genuine political and military cooperation between the two sides had failed. The New Fourth Army Incident of January 1941 was the most serious indication among many of open conflict.[16]

The underlying cause of the breakdown of the united front was really quite simple. Each side deemed itself uniquely qualified to lead China through war and reconstruction and believed that the other was not only illegitimate but also destined to defeat. In other words, they shared no long-term interests beyond the struggle against Japan. Within the CCP in particular, a bitter intraparty struggle over how to define the contents of the united front had been won by Mao Tse-tung and his adherents. The Soviet-leaning "internationalists" like Wang Ming believed in urban mobilization and vigorously supported genuine cooperation between the CCP and the KMT in order to prosecute the war against Japan more effectively. In contrast, Mao fought to maintain maximum independence within the united front so that the CCP could mobilize peasants and use the war to expand its army and territory.[17] The resolution of the Sixth CC Plenum (October–November 1938) that addressed the issue of the united front ratified Mao's position, and the *cheng-feng* (rectification) campaign of 1942–1944 discredited Wang Ming and his supporters who retained their Party positions thereafter only through Mao's cynical generosity. In 1944 the Japanese ICHIGO offensive devastated Nationalist positions in central and southwest China and even threatened the security of Chungking. At this time, the CCP made a key strategic decision to expand southward in the wake of the Japanese armies even though such action jeopardized its parallel attempt to establish a relationship with the United States grounded in military cooperation.[18]

These developments were still of only peripheral interest to the Soviet Union, whose military efforts and political concerns were centered in Europe. The United States, however, which was bearing the brunt of the war against Japan, viewed the renewal of Nationalist-Communist conflict with alarm because it sapped the Chinese war effort and threatened postwar hopes of using China as an anchor for stability in Asia and the Western Pacific.[19] That most implausible of diplomats, Patrick Hurley, who became the U.S. envoy to China after the recall of General Stilwell and Ambassador Gauss, tried with little luck and less finesse to resolve the KMT-CCP conflict in 1944–1945.[20] As the war against Japan moved toward its successful climax, the likelihood of postwar civil conflict in China increased.

     Communists and Nationalists agreed that control of Manchuria was a vital element in their struggle for power. They also realized that this could be accomplished only with the cooperation of the Americans or the Soviets, whose political influence in postwar China might prove decisive. But given their different assets and liabilities the two Chinese parties faced different tasks in seeking to achieve hegemony in the Northeast.

     The Chinese Nationalists' situation was not unique. The abruptness of the Japanese collapse imperiled the restoration of the prewar status quo in several Asian countries as political initiative passed into the hands of local opposition groups including Communist-led resistance forces. In China, the "legitimists," as represented by the Nationalist government, were similarly disadvantaged. Even before the war, the Nanking government had been little more than a regional regime whose authority was restricted even within many of the provinces that it nominally controlled.[21] Once it lost its base in east-central China, its position worsened considerably. Confined to its southwestern refuge, the Nationalist government, although still based on Chinese soil, became in effect a government-in-exile, facing a task of far greater magnitude than that of most of the European governments-in-exile.[22] Yet Chiang Kai-shek's outlook was by no means entirely bleak. In the provinces affected by the war (for example, Szechwan, Sinkiang, Yunnan, Kweichow) militarist power had been weakened and central power extended.[23] Before the war, Chiang had faced multiple internal enemies. Now, like a man consolidating his debts by taking out another loan, Chiang had only one major problem to contend with—the Communists.

     The recovery of the key region of Manchuria was part

of a larger problem. In September 1945, much of intramural China remained in the hands of undefeated enemy troops, while the government's partly U.S.-trained elite forces were deployed in the southwest, Burma, and India, far from the urban, industrial, and communications centers of East, North, and Northeast China.[24] By contrast, Communist forces were just outside the urban centers of North and East China and within striking distance of Manchuria, then occupied by the Soviet Red Army. Therefore, in the Northeast, as in intramural China, the Nationalists became critically dependent upon external support to expedite their recovery effort. Here, as during the war, Chiang's legitimist status conferred a great advantage enabling his government to be the main recipient of foreign aid and support.

The CCP faced a different problem. During the war years the Chinese Communist movement had come of age. By the time of the Seventh Congress of the CCP (April–June 1945), the Party claimed a membership of 1.2 million, an army of almost a million, and dominion over a population of 90 million persons scattered throughout an archipelago of so-called "liberated areas" in the sea of the Japanese occupation.[25] The CCP had passed through the *cheng-feng* (rectification) movement of 1942–1944 which decisively established the personal authority of Mao Tse-tung as Party chairman and confirmed his strategy as the Party's compass to future victory. Techniques of mass mobilization, administrative parsimony, political education, and economic self-sufficiency had been tested and refined in the course of struggle.[26]

Despite these impressive wartime gains, particularly in North China, the postwar balance of domestic military forces still seemed heavily weighted against the Communists. A successful Nationalist takeover of all the people, resources, and territory held by the Japanese would have further disadvantaged the CCP. Thus, for the Communists merely to hold onto and consolidate their gains would have been to suffer a loss in the rapidly evolving political situation. This consideration, coupled with their long-term aim of achieving power, dictated an active policy of expansion in the postwar period. Despite this imperative, Mao Tse-tung shrewdly adopted a defensive posture. He warned that civil war was almost inevitable because Chiang Kai-shek would try "to rob the people" of the fruits of their wartime resistance.[27]

At this time, it seems likely that broad agreement existed within the CCP leadership on the need to test the option of peaceful political struggle in postwar China, although important differences in emphasis may well have existed on tactical issues.[28] More important even than international pressures was the existence within the Party as well as among the Chinese people in general of hopes for a peaceful future which the CCP leadership could have ignored only at great peril.[29] At the end of the war both Mao and his chief lieutenant, Liu Shao-ch'i, voiced confidence that a peaceful settlement was possible through Kuomintang-Communist negotiations.[30] On the eve of his departure in late August 1945 for talks with Chiang Kai-shek in Chungking, Mao expressed his readiness to make concessions in the forthcoming negotiations as long as these did not damage "the fundamental interests" of the people, meaning retention of the Communist areas and sufficient troops to defend them.[31] In public interviews in China's wartime capital in September, Mao promised "to exert every effort to achieve peace" and repeated his belief that a long-lasting rather than merely a temporary agreement between the CCP and the KMT could be achieved through negotiations.[32] Although Mao's private view may have been different, at the very least he was contributing to those "peaceful illusions" for which Liu Shao-ch'i was later condemned during the Cultural Revolution. As Mao departed for Chungking, leaving Liu in Yenan as Acting Party Chairman, Communist troops moved out vigorously to expand the area under the Party's control. In late August 1945 Communist troops were first entering the Northeast. The region still lay outside "the fundamental interests" that Mao swore not to concede, but Manchuria was the prime target of opportunity in Communist postwar strategy. Because of its great intrinsic importance, at no point was the CCP ready to cede control of it to the Nationalist Government.

Two basic reasons underlay the Communists' eagerness to control the Northeast. The first and most important was that Manchuria represented precisely that combination of urban industrial power and agricultural surplus that the CCP required in order to mount a successful drive to power. The main Shen-Kan-Ning base and its capital Yenan, like the other bases, was desperately poor.[33] While a rigorous program of self-help combined with bare-bones frugality had sufficed to sustain limited guerrilla warfare against Japan, the CCP could not advance toward national power from such weak bases alone. Mao recognized this clearly. In a speech to delegates attending the Seventh Party Congress,

Mao said that the CCP could not continue to rely solely upon the peasantry and its village base, but must invest a major effort in the urban areas in order to become "masters of the cities."[34] Thus almost four years before his famóus call at the Second Plenum (March 1949) to shift the center of Party work to the cities, Mao was already expressing the need to acquire an urban base. Northeast China with its concentration of heavy and light industry and its advanced communication systems could, in Communist hands, become a formidable counterweight to the East China industrial region centered on Shanghai which the Nationalists were sure to reacquire. Mao's political sagacity consisted in his recognition of the potential of a peasant base for the Communist revolution, but it would be wrong to suppose that the CCP under his leadership was oblivious to the advantages of urban industrial centers. While Yenan was a fine place to sit out the war against Japan, it had little to offer as a launching place toward revolutionary victory. Later in 1945, and thereafter to be sure, when it became clear that the CCP still lacked the power to contest the cities (in part because of U.S. intervention), Mao's public attitude toward the cities shifted again, but by then it was clearly a case of sour grapes.

Manchuria's second great advantage was its proximity to the USSR. Despite the difficult relations between Moscow and Yenan, CCP leaders correctly anticipated that if Soviet forces invaded Manchuria they would cooperate with any Chinese Communist forces they encountered in the region. Yenan fully intended to be in a position to reap the benefits of such assistance. As the CCP's hopes for establishing a satisfactory working relationship with the United States receded in the spring of 1945, it became increasingly imperative to strengthen links with Moscow. How could this be accomplished? A discussion of Soviet-CCP relations must begin with a consideration of what were the major Soviet interests in China at this time.

Soviet-American Rivalry in China and the Cold War

By the end of World War II, the emerging confrontation between the United States and the Soviet Union was already promising to become the most important single factor determining the structure of postwar international politics in East Asia as well as in Europe. Although in the first postwar years the United States was easily able to rebuff intermittent Soviet attempts to share in the occupation of Japan, Soviet-American competition for power and influence in China became a major factor affecting that nation's internal power struggles. International and domestic conflicts became linked in a complex pattern in the Chinese arena.

In the summer of 1945, the new international system was still coming into being; the marks of transition were visible everywhere. The disintegration of the wartime Grand Alliance was a gradual process. Within the industrial democracies, it was partly slowed by individuals and groups that pressed for policies of accommodation and bargaining rather than confrontation in dealing with the Soviets.[35] Even as the Cold War consensus was taking shape in Washington in the latter half of 1945, the Truman administration continued to test the possibilities of partial accommodation with the Russians.

In Moscow, a similar mood of ambivalence prevailed. On the one hand, Stalin reasserted Leninist orthodoxy about the inevitability of war, but almost simultaneously he expounded the possibilities of peaceful coexistence and prospects for parliamentary transition to socialism.[36] However, this ambivalent mood in Moscow and Washington was essentially evanescent, the fading image of a dissolved partnership. In the concrete actions that established the framework of the postwar international order, the fear of conflict rather than the possibility of cooperation was the touchstone of decision.

In the Soviet and American interest in China, Communist and Nationalist Chinese saw opportunities for advancing their own goals. Great power competition for influence enhanced the competitive bargaining position of the Chinese parties to the point where they could bid for concessions as well as beg for favors.[37] This competition was part of an even more complicated process in which the Soviets and the Americans likewise were trying to alter the behavior of the Chinese antagonists to serve their own ends. This multilevel pattern of complex competition is the framework of our analysis.

What, then, were Soviet aims in China at the end of the war? Emerging from the conflict as one of the two major world powers, the USSR expanded the range of its interests and demanded certain traditional great power prerogatives. However, following his enormous wartime gains in East and East-Central Europe, Stalin prepared for a period of consolidation. The basic reason for this was the hollowness of Soviet power in the aftermath of war and the enormous job of reconstructing a devastated nation.

An important corollary that Stalin derived was the necessity to act prudently with respect to support of foreign revolutions. Only in East and East-Central Europe, where Soviet arms helped enforce a transformation from above, was Stalin a revolutionary at this time. Elsewhere he was not ready to hazard the inherent high risks of supporting foreign revolutions in a period of superior Western strength.[38] He preferred to opt for a kind of rough and ready coexistence, a recognition of the new balance of forces, although without a commitment to maintain that balance indefinitely. Stalin was eager to delineate spheres of influence within which the great powers might exercise their dominion in relative isolation from each other.[39]

This prudence did not imply any weakening of Stalin's control over the international Communist movement. Rather, in return for a free hand in his sphere of influence, Stalin was ready to command his foreign followers to engage in peaceful political struggle, the orthodoxy of the immediate postwar period. He had no compunctions about sacrificing the interests of local Communists if they interpreted their interests differently than he did or even in allowing their destruction as in Greece in 1944–45.[40] This is not to suggest that Stalin was indifferent to the fate of Communism in Europe or Asia, but he continued to define the interests of the Communist movement in terms of its subordination to the USSR and to his own power.[41]

Where did China fit into this sphere-of-influence conception of the world? In 1945 China's role in the postwar international order was still uncertain. Touted by the United States as one of the great powers, China, in fact, again lay open to the countervailing pressures of her senior allies. As Soviet-American tensions mounted during 1945, Stalin, cognizant of American wartime support of China notwithstanding the frictions between Washington and Chungking, had to consider the potential effect of China's probable adherence to an emerging American bloc which he viewed as his future adversary. What Stalin would apparently not countenance was the implicit American assumption that China fell within an American sphere of influence.[42] Therefore, Soviet policy sought to reverse the wartime tendency by formally acknowledging American influence in China in the short run while actually seeking to undermine it as rapidly as possible.

Primary Soviet interests in Asia were concentrated in the northern border regions of Manchuria, Mongolia, and Sinkiang. In Sinkiang, where Soviet influence had peaked in the 1930s, Moscow supported an indigenous revolt beginning in November 1944, aimed at establishing an Eastern Turkestan Republic. But Moscow, leery of provoking an American response, backed off and settled for only partial gains when the Chinese Nationalists threatened to make a larger international issue of the affair.[43] In Mongolia, Soviet influence had been paramount since the early 1920s. But in Manchuria, Russia's position had steadily eroded since the time of the Russo-Japanese War. In 1935, the USSR sold the Chinese Eastern Railway to Manchukuo, and through the Soviet-Japanese Neutrality Pact of 1941 recognized Japan's puppet state.[44] But in anticipation of Japan's defeat, as early as 1943 Stalin indicated his desire to reestablish the Soviet position in this key region of Northeast Asia. U.S. anxiety to ensure Soviet participation in the war against Japan, as manifested in the Yalta Agreement on the Far East, simplified Stalin's task and led directly to the Sino-Soviet Treaty of 1945.

At Yalta, Stalin pledged to enter the Pacific War three months after the end of the war in Europe and gained U.S. and British acquiescence to a restoration of the tsarist position in Manchuria as of 1904, including the leasehold of the Port Arthur naval base, Sino-Soviet condominium over the Chinese Eastern and South Manchurian Railways, recognition of the USSR's "preeminent interests" in an internationalized commercial port at Talien, and maintenance of the status quo in Outer Mongolia (the Mongolian People's Republic).[45] In return, the Soviet Union pledged to respect Chinese sovereignty in Manchuria and "to conclude with the National Government of China a pact of friendship and alliance between the USSR and China in order to render assistance to China with its armed forces for the purpose of liberating China from the Japanese yoke."[46]

After prolonged hard bargaining in Moscow, T. V. Soong and Wang Shih-chieh (who succeeded Soong as Foreign Minister during the negotiations) concluded a Treaty of Friendship and Alliance with Stalin on August 14, 1945.[47] During the negotiations, U.S. Ambassador Harriman kept in close contact with Soong and, by his own account, encouraged the Chinese diplomat to stand firm against Stalin's efforts to stretch the terms of the Yalta Agreement. But Harriman failed to get Washington's authorization for anything but a very weak diplomatic intervention on China's behalf and succeeded only in angering Stalin.[48] When Wang Shih-chieh pressed Stalin for a specific pledge that Soviet aid would go only to the Nationalist government, Stalin supposedly bristled and responded, "What do you want me to do? To fight against Mao?"[49] In fact, the treaty and the exchange of notes that accompanied it contained just such a pledge of exclusive Soviet support and aid to the National Government, but Stalin, of course, would not "fight against Mao."[50] Furthermore, as a U.S. intelligence report noted at the time, "There is nothing in the treaty which specifically obligates the Soviets to exclude the Chinese Communists from Manchuria."[51]

The Soviet Union had reason to be satisfied with the treaty, but it is certain that Stalin harbored no illusions about the long-term community of interests between the USSR and China. In fact, not only in 1945, but even after the Communists triumphed in China, Stalin pursued what might be termed a "weak neighbor policy"—a powerless China would be most amenable to Soviet influence. Failing that, he preferred a strong but dependent China.[52] By playing his cards shrewdly, Stalin might even be able to minimize the risk that China might lend itself to the hostile purposes of more potent enemies of the USSR such as the United States or a resurgent Japan.

The treaty secured Soviet interests in Mongolia and Manchuria. By obtaining Chinese recognition of its client state in Outer Mongolia, Soviet diplomacy guaranteed a vast buffer zone protecting strategically exposed eastern Siberia. The reestablishment of Russia's old position in Manchuria eased Soviet fears that the region might become an industrial and strategic base harnessed to an American threat to the Soviet Far East. But this was not enough. Subsequently, through a series of threats and promises,

Stalin sought to establish his control over the Northeast economy and to lure Chiang Kai-shek away from his pro-American orientation. In short, the USSR pursued a policy of counter-containment, designed to check the expansion of the United States at key points along the periphery of the Soviet Union.

In accordance with his generally low-risk approach to international politics, Stalin chose to deal primarily with Chiang Kai-shek's government as the more powerful of the competing Chinese forces and the one likely to remain in at least nominal control of China for the foreseeable future. Dubious about the prospects for armed Communist revolution in 1945, Stalin urged the Chinese Communists to enter into a coalition with the Nationalists.[53] Stalin's appraisal of the competing Chinese forces is readily understandable. All the measures by which he was likely to judge pointed to continued Nationalist hegemony. Chiang's vast army was being stiffened with American-trained and - equipped divisions. Control of China's cities with their industry, finance, commerce, foreign trade, skilled workers, and educated elite was his or soon would be. In addition, Chiang could count on American aid. Against this, Mao's guerrilla armies, rural dominion, and primitive technology bulked small indeed. In other words, Stalin shared a Western technocratic sense of power as deriving from the urban, industrialized, and technological—in short, the modernized sectors of society. From this perspective (quite normal for a Western Marxist), the Kuomintang, despite its inner weakness, looked comparatively strong and the Chinese Communist Party weak. Stalin may have thought that at most the Communists could retain control of parts of North China under the nominal jurisdiction of a coalition government in which the Kuomintang would be the senior partner.

An additional effect of Stalin's overall posture was its anticipated effect on his relations with the United States. To a certain extent, the proximate goals and methods of Soviet and American policies in China coincided. Soviet recognition of Chiang, desire to avoid a civil war in China, support for the goal of a coalition government, and willingness to cede to the United States the dominant role in mediating China's political conflict raised hopes in Washington that China might avoid becoming a contentious issue in postwar Soviet-American relations.[54] However, like two trains with different destinations running for a time along parallel tracks, the ultimate divergence of Soviet and American policies in China was temporarily obscured. Had Stalin succeeded either in detaching Chiang from his American protector or in his bolder aim of substituting a Soviet for an American presence, the repercussions from the United States would have been enormous, as indeed they were when the Sino-Soviet alliance came into being in 1950! For this reason, a large measure of dissemblance was needed in order to reassure the United States that Soviet and American purposes were compatible. This was done by reiterating Soviet support for Chiang Kai-shek in talks with top-level American officials and fostering the widespread American illusion that the Chinese Communists were not real Marxist-Leninists but rather "margarine Communists" as Ambassador Hurley was told.[55] In reality, if the Soviets viewed the CCP as composed of "margarine Communists" it was not because of its moderate wartime program (this, after all, was the orthodoxy of the united front period), but because as independent national leaders, Mao and his associates were ultimately insubordinate in Stalin's view of international Communism. The policy of reassurance was primarily intended to minimize the extent of American interference in Sino-Soviet relations. In seeking to preserve the exclusively bilateral character of their relationship with the Nationalists, the Soviets knew that the lopsided distribution of power would greatly facilitate the attainment of their objectives. Chiang also knew this only too well.

Stalin's decision to deal with the Nationalists did not by any means exclude a relationship with the CCP as well. In fact, the continued existence of a strong Communist party in China afforded Stalin additional freedom to maneuver. In Manchuria, where the Nationalists became critically dependent upon the degree and quality of cooperation extended by the Soviet occupation authorities, this became extremely important. The Communist challenge to the goal of Nationalist hegemony in Manchuria transformed the character of Soviet-Chinese Nationalist relations and further strengthened the Soviet hand. The open or implicit threat to switch their support to the CCP was a potent lever for extracting further concessions, particularly in Manchuria. The limiting factor in exploiting the threat, however, was the possibility that the Nationalists might succeed in eliciting an American reaction.

Beyond this, of course, the Soviets recognized that the Communists did control a significant portion of Chinese population, territory, and resources. Hence it would have been imprudent (as well as unfraternal) not to have cultivated ties with the CCP.

These various considerations shaped a Soviet China policy that was in essence flexible. Its most consistent characteristic was a determination to keep all options open and to avoid too close identification with one side or the other. In short, the Soviets engaged in that duality of tactics that was as old as their China policy itself.[56] Support for the revolutionary side was balanced by support for the status quo. Like a rich patron at the racetrack, Stalin bet on all the horses to be sure of a winner.

U.S. China Policy
in Soviet-American Focus

Until shortly before the surrender of Germany, the dominant American conception of the postwar world was that a concert of the major powers working through the United Nations would be able to secure the peace and deter any would-be aggressors. As intractable problems emerged with respect to political arrangements in the occupied and liberated countries of Europe, the mood in Washington changed. The sentimentalized view of Stalin's Russia as a staunch and reliable ally was gradually replaced by a sober realization that the Soviet Union's concept of European and world security was incompatible with the American view, and that Russia was a rival and even a potential enemy of the United States.

Obviously, the strength of this conviction varied. When on May 19, 1945, Acting Secretary of State Joseph Grew wrote in a private note that "a future war with Soviet Russia is as certain as anything in the world," he was penning a thought that most persons in Washington would likely have rejected at the time.[57] More prevalent was the view that the only way to deal with the Soviets was through tough, no-nonsense tactics using all

the diplomatic, military, and economic power the United States
could muster. Men sharing this view surrounded Harry Truman
upon his accession to the presidency. In brief, the adversary view
of Soviet-American relations that lay at the heart of the Cold War
existed from at least the spring of 1945.[58]

The United States asserted its interests in global terms,
but in view of the emerging confrontation with the USSR, American leaders viewed Europe as their top foreign policy priority. By
comparison, throughout the postwar period, China was seen as a
secondary arena, although there were moments when important
U.S. interests there were presumed to exist. In this respect, Truman
proved an apt pupil of President Roosevelt. Toward the end of the
war, Roosevelt tended to view China more as a potential irritant
in postwar Soviet-American relations than as an independent
issue. Therefore, he sought to encourage Sino-Soviet cooperation
as a means of providing the USSR with the security it sought and
to work toward a peaceful resolution of the KMT-CCP conflict
that threatened to draw the United States and the Soviet Union
into opposing camps of a civil war.[59]

After Truman's assumption of the presidency, Soviet-
American relations continued to be the primary prism through
which China was viewed. Even then, it was only when anxiety
over Soviet intentions mounted, as in the fall of 1945 and the
winter of 1946, that China became a subject for cabinet-level
discussions. This crisis-generated interest in China may be seen,
for example, in the diaries of Secretary of the Navy Forrestal, who
otherwise paid no attention to China.[60] Insofar as China policy
concerned the traditional pursuit of American commercial interests and even the traditional political goal of fostering the growth
of a strong China, it was a matter left to the State Department's
Far Eastern experts. It was only when China policy moved across
the field of Soviet-American relations that it engaged the attention
of the President and his closest advisers.

China's significance as a factor in the Soviet-American
relationship was obscured somewhat by the legacy of traditional
policy, one element of which was the promotion of a strong and
united China friendly to the United States. This by itself might
serve American efforts to help bring about a peaceful resolution
of China's political problems. Moreover, the United States initially

viewed China as an integral strategic link in an Asian and Pacific security system designed to check the reemergence of a bellicose Japan. Thus, despite the accumulated evidence of Nationalist weakness, these were strong reasons for continuing American mediation in China.[61] A second traditional element was concern for securing the commercial Open Door. However, very few of the top policymakers were interested in this question. Ambassador Harriman and Secretary of War Stimson feared that Soviet hegemony in Manchuria might shut the door in an area that had long attracted U.S. commercial and financial interests, but Truman brushed them off.[62] The real importance of the Open Door was not in the realm of foreign economic policy at all. A perusal of the American diplomatic documents of the time suggests that for most officials the Open Door was much more an inherited language or residual framework for discussing China policy than it was an active concern. Even when the issues under discussion related to national security and realpolitik, the language of expression tended to be the old Open Door formula.

In the postwar period, the traditional concern for China's territorial integrity became part of an American strategy of denial motivated not by vague feelings of "friendship" for China but rooted in the developing Soviet-American rivalry. Again the key region was Manchuria.[63] As U.S. policy shifted from a focus on preventing the renascence of Japanese militarism to a preoccupation with the Soviet threat, the salience of Manchuria increased. Only a unified China that included Manchuria could act as a partial counterweight to the expansionist designs of the USSR in East Asia.[64]

Viewing China policy through a Soviet-American prism did not necessarily determine the direction of that policy itself. If the USSR was a potential antagonist, the central question Washington faced was how should the United States act in China so as to maximize constraints upon the Soviet Union? Answering this question involved judgments about the probable course of Soviet policy itself, the strength and viability of the Chinese Nationalists and the strength and international orientation of the Chinese Communists. Baldly stated, there were two main options. The first was exclusive support for Chiang's government (with or without pressure upon it to reform) in order to buttress its control domestically and strengthen its pro-American orientation. The alternative was to implement a de facto two-China policy (like that adopted by the Soviets) by seeking to develop a working relationship with the Chinese Communists despite Chiang Kai-shek's opposition. As is so often the case in foreign policy questions, what might have been a great debate on this issue occurred only in fractured form.

As is well-known, a number of Foreign Service Officers in China strongly recommended that U.S. policy take into account the rising strength of the Chinese Communists, for as one of them—John Paton Davies—predicted, "China's destiny is not Chiang's but theirs."[65] On the basis of soundings from Mao and other Communist leaders, the diplomats concluded that the Chinese Communists were not presently wedded to a pro-Soviet orientation, but that U.S. inaction would likely drive the CCP into dependency upon the Russians. Davies' hope was that "preemptive collaboration" between Washington and Yenan would be expressed in joint military efforts directed against the Japanese in North China and would have the effect of barring the USSR from that region and reducing its influence in Manchuria.[66] Even if a KMT-CCP coalition government failed to materialize, the United States would have relations not only with Chiang Kai-shek, but also with Mao, whose forces Davies expected to control North and Northeast China.[67] The critical insight which Davies, John Service, and the others supplied was that a competitive situation existed in which both the Americans and the Russians could bid for influence in and over the CCP. They believed that unlike most other Communist parties in this era, the CCP was not a Bolshevized political force looking submissively to Moscow for leadership and direction.[68] An important corollary of this perspective was that the United States need no longer pussyfoot in its dealings with Chiang, who had lost the aura of the indispensable man.

The U.S. Ambassador to China, Patrick Hurley, angrily rejected this realistic but heretical perspective on China policy and, in March 1945, having gained President Roosevelt's renewed support, engineered the transfer from China of the men he felt were obstructing his policy of unqualified support for the Nationalist government.[69] Thereafter, "ideological thinking" replaced political realism.[70] An orthodox view of the Chinese Communists as instruments of Russian expansionism triumphed in Washington and every scrap of evidence that tended to confirm this was carefully gathered and collated. Knowledge about relations between the USSR and European Communist parties was mechanically transferred to China. Communist proffers of cooperation and appeals for U.S. nonintervention were spurned. Thus, well before the race between the CCP and the KMT began, the United States had put its money and its hopes on Chiang Kai-shek.

Bridging the Gap—U.S. Intervention in North China

American and Soviet forces entered China in order to hasten the defeat of the common enemy, Japan. Both Washington and Moscow proclaimed their intention to remain aloof from the developing internal conflict, but neither was able to adhere to this position. The temptation to use military force to shape political outcomes proved irresistible. This was especially so since the United States and the Soviet Union were already competing in other areas along the periphery of the USSR, most significantly in Europe. American intervention in North China and Soviet activity in Manchuria arose simultaneously, but even after the USSR withdrew from the Northeast in late spring 1946, the United States continued its doomed efforts to mediate the Chinese civil conflict.

The conjunction between American policy in North China and Soviet policy in Manchuria demonstrated the close politico-strategic link between the two regions which the later course of the civil war amply confirmed. The two powers were partly responsible for the structure of conflict that emerged from the Nationalist takeover of North China and the Communist seizure of a toehold in the Northeast. As the Red Army crushed Japanese resistance in the last days of the war, Chinese Communist troops raced toward Manchuria. Meanwhile, the United States directly intervened on the Nationalist side in the impending civil war.

In mid-August the CCP claimed the right to participate in accepting the Japanese surrender and Commander-in-Chief

Chu Teh appealed for strict U.S. neutrality in Chinese internal affairs.[71] But Washington like Chungking was determined to check Communist expansion into the territories being surrendered by the Japanese. It realized that a hands off policy would allow the Communists to occupy major portions of North and East China, including key cities, and to acquire substantial stocks of Japanese arms and equipment. General Order No. 1, issued by General Douglas MacArthur, therefore, directed Japanese commanders (with the exception of those in Manchuria) to surrender only to Chiang Kai-shek, and a message from MacArthur to Japanese Imperial Headquarters underlined the importance of this directive.[72]

The restoration of Nationalist authority in North China, particularly Hopeh and Shantung, was an indispensable precondition for mounting an effective effort to recover control of Northeast China. The prominent role played by U.S. troops in North China was to have important repercussions in the Manchurian arena. Thus foreign troops—the defeated Japanese and the victorious Americans—shouldered the chief burden in the North China recovery campaign with the ironical aim of helping the hapless Nationalists to resume the position of master in their own house.

Three means were employed. Japanese troops were directed to maintain order in the areas they were garrisoning pending receipt of instructions to surrender from the Nationalist government.[73] In other words, the undefeated Japanese Army was told to hold the ring for the Nationalists against the Communists. By their wholehearted cooperation, the Japanese turned out to be exemplary allies for this purpose.[74] Second, the United States landed some 50,000 Marines of the III Autonomous Corps in Hopeh and Shantung to accept the Japanese surrender on Chiang's behalf, repatriate Japanese soldiers, and perform local garrison duties. Finally, the United States provided the Nationalists with the logistical support—the aircraft and the shipping—to transport their armies from the distant south to North and East China.[75]

The War Department directive of August 10, 1945, to the U.S. Commander of the China Theater, Lt. Gen. Albert C. Wedemeyer, cautioned: "All of its provisions apply insofar as action in accordance therewith does not prejudice the basic U.S. principle that the United States will not support the Central Government of China in fratricidal warfare."[76] Wedemeyer's reply pointed out the difficulties and contradictions in his mission, and concluded that "it must be recognized that the movement of Central Government troops to key areas may be construed as a deceptive maneuver designed primarily to cope with the Communists."[77] In fact, the measures authorized by the War Department constituted unmistakable intervention in China's civil conflict.

When American Marines began to land in North China, Communist military dominance there was unquestioned. According to an official American estimate, "Communist regular forces in Hopei and Shantung totaled 170,000 troops . . . disposed near the big cities garrisoned by the Japanese" while "Nationalist strength in the two provinces was negligible . . ."[78] Marine forces landed in Hopei and Shantung in the first days of October 1945 and quickly fanned out to secure their main objectives. The leathernecks garrisoned the main cities of the two provinces and preserved "law and order." They guarded the Peiping-Mukden rail line against Communist attempts to disrupt it. Marine aircraft patrolled the rail lines and flew reconnaissance missions over Shantung and Hopeh spying the location and movement of Communist troops as well as junk traffic in the Gulf of Chihli. The Americans spurned Communist attempts to cooperate in the disarming of Japanese troops. Over and above the actual duties they performed on duty in North China, the Marine Corps presence served as a constant reminder of U.S. power to intervene in Chinese affairs if its interests were threatened. Despite their ostensible neutrality, the Marines acted as upholders of the status quo and slowed the process of political change.[79] Because of Japanese cooperation it soon became evident that only a very small number of U.S. troops was needed to supervise the Japanese repatriation program, the official reason for U.S. Marine presence in North China. In fact, for some time Nationalist reluctance to release Japanese troops guarding the rail lines (as well as civilian technicians) was the chief factor in slowing down the repatriation process.[80]

The expressed American intention in North China had

been to facilitate Nationalist recovery of the region without getting involved in the civil war. This proved to be impossible. As the Marine Corps official history notes:

The very presence of the Marines in North China holding open the major ports of entry, the coal mines, and the railroads was an incalculably strong military asset to the Central Government. And the fact that the U.S. had provided a good part of the arms of the troops scheduled to take over North China and Manchuria made the situation even more explosive.[81]

Let us take a closer look at the relationship between these events in North China and the Northeast takeover problem. Nationalist control of North China was a necessary though not sufficient precondition for the success of the KMT recovery effort in the Northeast. Without bases in North China and secure lines of communication and supply, the Chinese Nationalists simply could not have extended their power into Manchuria. But even if a combination of American logistical support and Soviet Assistance had enabled the Nationalists to leapfrog from the far south directly to the Northeast, the resultant position would have been completely untenable. Isolated and exposed Nationalist garrisons would have become sitting ducks exposed to Communist attacks. (This is what happened in 1947–48.) Lacking organized support within Manchuria itself and without a system to procure supplies, military recruits, and food, the Nationalists could sustain control over Manchuria only if the crucial overland communications and supply links with North China were in their own hands. (Shipping and air transport alone were far from sufficient to meet Nationalist needs in Manchuria.) Without American support, not only would North China and Manchuria have been beyond Nationalist reach, but the lower Yangtze valley center of Kuomintang strength would have become vulnerable to Communist military-political attack at a much earlier time. With U.S. troops garrisoning North China cities, securing railroads and ports, and generally keeping the CCP out of urban North China, Nationalist troops were freed to concentrate on the task of recovering Manchuria. The continued presence of the Marines in China in 1946 derived largely from U.S. recognition that the chances for Kuomintang success in Manchuria rested upon the stabilization of the North China arena.

Nevertheless, the game was lost because the CCP moved more quickly into Manchuria and benefited from Soviet support in the first crucial stage of the struggle.

Soviet-Chinese Communist Relations and Manchuria

Americans as well as Chinese Nationalist officials hoped that the Sino-Soviet Treaty of August 1945 would reduce the CCP threat to Manchuria by denying them Soviet aid. Communist leaders had long pondered the probable effects of Soviet entry into Manchuria, and nurtured the hope that the Red Army would collaborate with the CCP's armies if contact could be effected in Manchuria.[82] After a long interview with Mao Tse-tung in the spring of 1945, John Service reported that the Chinese Communists were confident of gaining control of Manchuria through linking their forces with the Red Army.[83] In fact, Yenan greeted Soviet entry into the Pacific War with obvious satisfaction, and Mao published a brief article in *Chieh-fang jih-pao* entitled "The Last Round with the Japanese Invader."[84] On August 11, Chu Teh ordered a general offensive against the Japanese with the explicit purpose of effecting a link-up with the Red Army and bolstering the Communist claim to receive the surrender of Japanese troops. Forces under the command of Generals Lü Cheng-tsao, Chang Hsueh-ssu, Wan I, and Li Yun-chang advanced toward Manchuria from positions in North China.[85]

Just at this time, however, Mao's hope of receiving support from the Russians was dealt a rude blow with the signing of the Sino-Soviet Treaty of August 14, 1945. Apparently, among Party leaders as well as the rank and file, resentment toward the Soviet Union and suspicion of its intentions swelled.[86] Nevertheless, CCP leaders still pursued their strategy of seeking Soviet aid. *Chieh-fang jih-pao* called the agreement "the first equal treaty in the history of our country with a foreign government," and pledged to "make still greater efforts to consolidate and develop the success of this treaty."[87] But this at best tepid endorsement glided over the effect of the treaty on revolutionary prospects in

China. Putting a bolder face on the matter, an inner-party document from this period justified the treaty in terms of the overriding importance of Soviet-American relations:

The signing of the Soviet-Chinese Treaty has eliminated the possibility of conflict between the USSR and the USA on the Chinese question and has made open intervention by the USA on the side of the Kuomintang against the Chinese Communist Party more difficult. This is very important.[88]

Was this anything more than a hope?

About this time, a top level strategy meeting between Stalin and a CCP delegation headed by Liu Shao-ch'i and Kao Kang took place in Moscow.[89] This was apparently the occasion when the Soviet leader counseled the CCP to seek a coalition with the Kuomintang because the prospects for armed revolution in China were dim.[90] Unfortunately, we do not know the details of this meeting which may have been critically important in defining how Soviet policy in postwar China would be applied in practice. Specifically, it would be interesting to know whether Stalin gave any assurances or made any arrangements for defining the relations between the Red Army and the Chinese Communist troops when they met in the field.[91] Whatever may have occurred within the Kremlin walls, the Soviets publicly indicated continued support for their Chinese comrades. On August 31, 1945, *Pravda* reported without comment the contents of the CCP Central Committee declaration of six days earlier which stressed that democratization and the creation of a coalition government were the essence of the Party's program.[92] *Pravda's* publication of this program constituted an indirect endorsement of the CCP's position. Appearing soon after the publication of the Sino-Soviet Treaty, it served to indicate that the Soviets were not abandoning the CCP, and further suggested that Soviet support of the Nationalist government in China would depend, in part, on the degree to which Chiang was willing to transform his regime to accommodate the Communist proposals. In other words, the August treaty was far from a blanket endorsement of the Nationalists. Manchuria quickly became the test case of Soviet policy.

The CCP launched its effort to seize control of the Northeast in August 1945 by dispatching large numbers of troops and cadres from North China into the region. This attempt to transform Manchuria into a revolutionary base area was greatly facilitated by Soviet diplomatic and military efforts which implicitly favored the Communists until the middle of October 1945. By this time, just two months after Japan's surrender, the race between the Nationalists and the Communists to recover territory was well underway. This competition had already become linked to divergent American and Soviet interests in China which were part of an emerging pattern of global rivalry. The consequences of great power involvement in the Chinese struggle could not yet be fully discerned, but the outlines were unmistakable. In the short run, American support for the Nationalists had facilitated their recovery of urban North China; the Communists, meanwhile, were using the Soviet presence in Manchuria to establish their own claim on the region. The effect was to bring the two sides into closer proximity and hasten their inevitable conflict. Moreover, like much about the early Cold War, later developments reenforced rather than altered this early pattern.

CHAPTER TWO

SOVIET-AMERICAN RIVALRY IN MANCHURIA AND THE COLD WAR

ON March 9, 1946, Major-General Kovtun-Stankevich, Commandant of the Red Army garrison in Shenyang since August 1945, unexpectedly received orders to pull his troops out of the city. He was directed to relinquish control within forty-eight hours to Chinese Nationalist officials who had nominally held office in Shenyang since December 26, 1945.[1] Two days later, the chief Soviet liaison officer in the lengthy negotiations with the Chinese Nationalists summoned his Chinese counterpart to a hastily called meeting and announced that the withdrawal of Soviet troops, already underway by then, would be completed by March 15.[2] No formal ceremony marking the transfer of power would be held.

Paul Frillman, a United States Information Service official, arrived in Shenyang just in time to witness the last Soviet soldiers departing with their motley war booty.

Healthy, dirty boys they seemed, and they were cheerfully loading their trucks and boxcars with weird loot, the dregs of the city's debris. I remember filthy, torn mattresses, bags of worn-out overshoes, garlands of frayed suspenders, boxes of buttons. Then they were gone . . .[3]

With the Russians on their way out, conditions seemed favorable for a return to normality. A Scottish Presbyterian minister, Dr. John Stewart, returning to Shenyang just a few weeks later, vividly recorded his impressions.

We passed into Manchuria through the Great Wall in the remains of a third-class carriage with broken windows and incomplete wooden seats. . . . Most of the stations were wrecked and many of the bridges had been blown up and insecurely repaired. The places we passed through seemed half-dead. As we drove in ramshackle carriages through Moukden [Shenyang] it looked even more than half-dead . . . the streets had the traffic of a small country town. There was no electricity and therefore no trams and no lights at night. There was little petrol and therefore no buses. There were no goods to sell and therefore the shops were shut.[4]

In this south Manchurian metropolis with a population of a million and a half, transportation was furnished by Russian-style droshkies pulled by diminutive ponies which clattered along the streets after the curfew was lifted at 6 A.M. Sharp winds blowing off the desolate Jehol plains turned the horse droppings into an acrid powder that permeated everything.[5] "Mukden," wrote Paul Frillman, "struck us as a stage set of a modern Western city with nothing behind the painted facades and glassless windows except barbaric poverty and deprivation."[6]

In this springtide of revolution, Shenyang and the other urban centers of Northeast China were slowly expiring. Though the civil war had barely begun, the forces of war and revolution were already rapidly gathering strength. Communists and Nationalists had spent the preceding months in feverish efforts to build up their positions in the Northeast. And while Soviet occupation forces pursued a complicated strategy of political maneuver, the American envoy General George C. Marshall pursued his doomed mission of negotiating a peaceful settlement of the ineluctable conflict.

The Nationalist Recovery
Effort in Manchuria

Chiang Kai-shek's government was ill-prepared to shoulder the heavy burden of taking over the Northeast from Japanese control.

During the war years little high-level attention had been given to the problem of the postwar administration of the Northeast. A Northeast Investigation Committee of the Central Planning Board (Chung-yang she-chi chü tung-pei tiao-ch'a wei-yuan-hui) collected a massive amount of material on conditions in Manchukuo which it published in March 1945.[7] Meanwhile, a committee of the Executive Yuan charged with the task of dealing with provincial demarcations suggested redividing the traditional three provinces of the region into nine.[8] The obvious purpose was to avert the reemergence of regionalism by fragmenting Manchuria into units too small to permit the aggregation of power by ambitious regional figures such as Chang Tso-lin.[9]

Japan's precipitate surrender in mid-August 1945 found the Nationalists without any political structure in place to take over the Northeast. Chiang Kai-shek hastily improvised an organization to administer the region. He was determined to exclude the pre-1931 regional elite from positions of authority within Manchuria because he did not trust them fully.[10] Instead, the prize was awarded to leading members of the Political Science group within the Nationalist Party. On August 31, 1945, Chairman Chiang established the Northeast Headquarters (Tung-pei hsing-ying) of the Military Affairs Commission and appointed Hsiung Shih-hui to serve as its director and concurrently as chairman of its Political Affairs Committee.[11] At the same time, Chang Kiangau was tapped to serve as chairman of the Economic Affairs Committee. General Hsiung, a native of Kiangsi, had been Secretary General of the Central Planning Board (responsible for wartime and postwar reconstruction) among other high-level posts. Chang, a leading modern banker, had served in cabinet-level positions and achieved a reputation for probity and competence.[12] Chiang Kai-shek also assigned his eldest son Chiang Ching-kuo to the Northeast as Special Commissioner of the Ministry of Foreign Affairs, presumably to make use of his twelve years of experience in the Soviet Union. (The younger Chiang had first gone to Moscow as a student in 1925, and, after the KMT-CCP split in 1927, he was detained in the USSR and given a variety of assignments before finally being allowed to return to China in 1937.)[13]

As soon as it became clear that the National Government would have to fight its way into the Northeast, Chiang Kai-shek appointed General Tu Yu-ming, one of his trusted lieutenants, as head of the Northeast Combat Command with operational military authority in the region.

This initial arrangement proved less than satisfactory. Friction soon developed between Generals Hsiung and Tu and grew worse as the regional politico-military situation deteriorated beginning in late 1946.[14] As the Nationalist position rapidly eroded in the latter half of 1947 and the early months of 1948, Chiang Kai-shek cashiered Hsiung Shih-hui (in late August 1947) and appointed Chief-of-Staff Ch'en Ch'eng to serve concurrently as director of the Northeast headquarters. By that time, Ch'en, in ill health and facing an impossible task, was unable to turn the tide.[15] Just a few months later, in January 1948, General Wei Li-huang was named commander of the newly established Northeast Bandit Suppression Headquarters, which first coexisted with and then entirely supplanted the Northeast headquarters in June 1948, by which time almost nothing remained of the Nationalist position in Manchuria. This juggling of administrative personnel produced nothing positive for Chiang Kai-shek and his cause.

All these troubles, of course, lay shrouded in the future. From the vantage point of August 1945, as Communist troops poured into the Northeast by land and sea, the National Government sought to cash in the promissory note of Soviet cooperation which the Sino-Soviet Treaty appeared to embody. One concern dominated Nationalist thinking on Manchuria. It was to move its armed forces into the region as quickly as possible so that a real Nationalist power component could be introduced into the developing Northeast equation of forces. An army would provide a shield and a sword for the administrative apparatus which had already been created on paper and provide a means for countering CCP growth. Delay might be fatal. Unless Nationalist forces were in place before the Soviet withdrawal from the Northeast, the entire region might pass into Communist hands by default. Lacking their own transport, the Nationalists received assurances that U.S. ships would be available to carry Government troops to the Northeast.[16]

In early October, Soviet Ambassador A. A. Petrov notified the Chinese Government that the Red Army would soon commence its withdrawal from the Northeast. He coupled this with a warning to Chungking that the USSR would not allow the

Nationalists to land troops at Talien because of its status as a commercial port, nor at Lushunkou (Port Arthur), which was a naval base.[17] The Nationalists objected to this high-handed and unwarranted interpretation of the Sino-Soviet treaty, but Petrov responded that all questions should be negotiated with the Soviet command in Changchun.[18] For this purpose an advance group of Chiang Kai-shek's Northeast headquarters led by Hsiung Shih-hui, Chiang's regional viceroy, arrived in Changchun on October 12.[19]

The first meeting with Soviet representatives revealed the pattern of nominal cooperation and actual obstruction which characterized the Soviet attitude over the succeeding months. The Soviet commander Marshal Malinovsky was generous in his assurances of aid, but niggardly in transforming his promises into specific agreements that the Nationalists sought.[20] Repeating the Soviet refusal to allow the use of Talien and Lushunkou, Malinovsky agreed that several smaller Manchurian ports could be used, but he would not assign Soviet forces to guarantee a secure landing. When Chinese Communist troops turned up in control of Hulutao and Yingkow, American naval officers in charge of the Nationalist troop convoy decided not to risk armed conflict and diverted the ships to Chinwangtao in eastern Hopei.[21] Parallel efforts to move in Nationalist troops via land and air routes were also obstructed by the Soviet side. In addition, the Soviets balked at Chinese requests for permission to organize peace preservation forces in cities garrisoned by the Red Army, refused to allow a Chinese representative into Talien, tolerated Communist political activity in the Northeast, appointed a Communist as mayor of Changchun, and stood aside as the physical safety of the Nationalist representatives was endangered by Communist crowds.[22]

Meanwhile, Soviet economic advisor M. I. Sladkovsky, representative of the Far Eastern Department of the Ministry of Foreign Trade, presented Chang Kia-ngau, head of the Northeast Economic Committee, with demands that all major industrial and mining enterprises come under control of joint Sino-Soviet management. When Chang countered that he could not discuss economic issues until political questions were settled, Sladkovsky hinted darkly that prior agreement on economic cooperation might facilitate a solution of the political impasse.[23]

In short, by mid-November the Nationalists' hopes for Soviet cooperation in the takeover of Manchuria had been punctured. Mindful of the escalation of local armed conflicts, especially in North China, and probably informed by General Wedemeyer that an American policy reevaluation was then underway, Chiang Kai-shek attempted to regain mastery of the Northeast situation by a change of tactics.

At first Chiang sought to approach Stalin directly, but the Soviet dictator would not then receive his emissary.[24] Chairman Chiang thereupon decided to withdraw his advance mission from Changchun.[25] Chiang was again resorting to a well-worn strategy. He knew that in the sphere of bilateral Sino-Soviet relations, China, lacking sufficient power, had nothing to fall back upon in resisting Soviet demands except appeals to Soviet good faith and moderation—commodities in scarce supply. Therefore, Chiang frequently tried to redefine Sino-Soviet questions as broader issues involving the United States as well. If he could successfully substitute multilateral for bilateral arrangements, he could force Stalin to consider an entire new range of factors in his policymaking. Chiang's strategy was an application of the old ploy of the fox trying to borrow the authority of the tiger, as a Chinese saying goes. American strength would compensate for Chinese weakness.

On November 17, the main body of the Changchun headquarters group withdrew to Peiping, but a military liaison team remained in Changchun. In order to avoid inflaming anti-Soviet sentiment, the Northeast mission personnel were ordered to maintain a discreet silence, but the pullback of the Changchun mission was an unmistakable signal to both Moscow and Washington.[26] Chiang sought to secure a more helpful Soviet attitude by eliciting the support of the United States, which favored the Nationalist takeover of Manchuria. Meanwhile, Chiang readied his forces for an assault on his Communist enemies in the Northeast.

The immediate Soviet reaction to Chiang's tactic of withdrawal was consternation followed by a rapid reversal of attitude.[27] Proffering apologies for past difficulties, the Soviet authorities in Changchun pledged to assist the Nationalist takeover of the Northeast. Indeed, in rapid succession they ousted the Communist mayor of Changchun, banned public criticism of the National Government, promised to guarantee the security of the

Northeast headquarters, and offered to postpone their troop withdrawal so that the Nationalists could recover Manchuria in accordance with the Sino-Soviet Treaty.[28] In the workmanlike atmosphere of the renewed negotiations in Changchun, agreement was soon reached on the transport of Government troops to Manchuria via land and air. The Soviet side also agreed to disarm local armed forces which were not recognized by Chungking. Chiang's government requested that the Soviet withdrawal be delayed until the beginning of February 1946.[29]

In the following weeks the Nationalist takeover program shifted into high gear. Municipal administrations were established for the major cities of Changchun, Shenyang, Harbin, Tsitsihar, and Ssup'ing, and a number of provincial governments came into being.[30] Nationalist troop movements into south Manchuria accelerated and a limited airlift of forces to Changchun was carried out. But throughout this period (mid-November 1945 to mid-January 1946) Nationalist control in central and northern Manchuria rested not upon the Government's own power but on the essentially unstable foundation of cooperation with the Soviet Union. The Red Army retained responsibility for order and security in the Nationalist-administered cities while the Government's armies waited on the sidelines. Meanwhile, Communist forces continued to entrench themselves in the hinterlands.

Even in this high-water mark period of Soviet-Nationalist relations unresolved questions persisted. Malinovsky and Sladkovsky continued to press for the conclusion of Sino-Soviet economic agreements on the basis of extensive Soviet co-ownership of Northeast industry.[31] Whether the Red Army would provide liaison personnel to facilitate Nationalist takeover of the vast area outside the major cities also remained in doubt. Still, on balance there were grounds for Nationalist optimism. Chiang's pressure tactics appeared to have worked.

The Marshall Mission
and Manchuria

The apparent change in Soviet policy came too late to affect the high-level discussions of China policy in Washington which culminated in the Marshall mission. By late 1945 the U.S. policy of

promoting a strong and stable China to anchor America's postwar
hegemony in Asia was foundering badly. Nowhere was this more
evident than in Northeast China. U.S. logistical support had enabled the Nationalists to recover much of North and East China,
but a direct U.S. role in the recovery of Manchuria was precluded
by the presence there of Soviet occupation forces as well as by the
impending liquidation of the China theater. In sum, Washington
was deeply troubled by the drift of events in China, particularly
by the Soviets' apparent inclination to take maximum advantage
of their military presence in the Northeast. Casting about for a
course of action, the Truman administration asked its men in the
field for counsel.

In response to queries from Washington, Lt. General
Albert C. Wedemeyer, commander of American forces in China,
stated in a message of November 14, 1945, that "the Chinese
Central Government is completely unprepared for occupation of
Manchuria against Communist opposition." The general believed
that the Soviets were indirectly aiding the expansion of the
Chinese Communists, but he advised Chiang Kai-shek to consolidate his hold on North China before tackling Manchuria, saying
that "arrangements to reoccupy Manchuria from the Russians was
a purely Chinese-Russian problem." Wedemeyer warned his su-
periors that a U.S.policy of seeking the unification of China and
Manchuria under Nationalist control not only risked involvement
in the Chinese civil war but conflict with the USSR as well. Simultaneously, American diplomats in North China were expressing fears that an early withdrawal of U.S. forces would jeopardize
the fragile stability of that area.[32]

In Washington these pessimistic analyses were viewed
not as grounds for an American retreat in the face of incalculable
future difficulties but rather as a reason for expanded American
involvement designed to rescue the original objectives of America's China policy. In mid-November, Everett Drumwright, director
of the State Department's Division of Chinese Affairs, argued that
the United States should help the Nationalists recover Manchuria
in order to preclude the creation of a Soviet-dominated puppet
regime which would "sow the seeds for a fundamental cleavage
between the U.S. and the USSR."[33]

The unfolding strategic contest with the Soviet Union

informed the discussions within the powerful interagency State, War, Navy Coordinating Committee (SWNCC) and seemed to dictate the necessity of devising a policy that would rescue the vital Northeast from Communist control and restore it to the Nationalist government.[34] At a November 27, 1945, meeting, SWNCC gave initial approval to a new policy outline including retention of United States Marines in China, transport of additional Nationalist troops to North China and Manchuria, and an effort to arrange a political settlement and truce. President Truman told his cabinet that a strong American stand on China was necessary to prevent Russia from replacing Japan as a threat to the peace. Reacting swiftly to Ambassador Patrick Hurley's unexpected resignation from his posting to Chungking, Truman appointed General George C. Marshall, just retired as Army chief-of-staff, as special ambassador to execute this new policy.[35] For over a year, from mid-December 1945 through early January 1947, General Marshall made a valiant but ultimately futile effort to compose the differences between the Nationalists and their Chinese Communist foes.

The principle underlying what came to be known as the Marshall mission was the judicious use of pressure to extract concessions from both the Communists and the Nationalists in order to arrange a political and military settlement through peaceful means.[36] But Washington's instructions did not envision Marshall as the even-handed dispenser of justice. The reinforcement of the Nationalists' position in Northeast China was deemed too vital to be made an object of diplomatic maneuver. Marshall was given wide discretionary powers to tailor his promises of military and economic support for the Nationalists to the rate of progress toward a political settlement, but he could not withhold American transport and supply of Manchuria-bound Nationalist troops.[37] A further indication of the asymmetry of U.S. policy was Truman's verbal instruction to Marshall that if Nationalist rather than Communist obduracy blocked the attainment of a political settlement, the United States would not abandon Chiang but would continue to move his troops into North China.[38] As an inducement for Chiang's cooperation, Washington held out the promise of additional military and economic aid to a unified and democratic China.

During the war, Marshall, as chief-of-staff, had been a strong supporter of General Joseph Stilwell, commander of U.S. forces in the China-Burma-India theater, and he was sympathetic to Stilwell's caustic view of Chiang Kai-shek and the Nationalist war effort. He had few illusions and little respect for the Nationalist leader.[39] However, on the eve of his departure for China, Marshall was eager to facilitate Chiang's control over Manchuria, fearful that the Chinese Communist delaying tactics would result in Soviet control.[40] Given the autumn's events and the political climate prevailing in Washington, it is no wonder that Marshall set off in this frame of mind.

In his public statement of U.S. China policy (December 15, 1945), President Truman referred to the cost of American efforts "to restore the peace which was first broken by Japanese aggression in Manchuria," and he underlined the commitment of the United States and its allies to "the liberation of China, including the return of Manchuria to Chinese control."[41] General Marshall was to learn all too soon how many complexities these simple-sounding phrases concealed.

As already noted, Marshall's mission to China commenced at a time of growing U.S. concern about Soviet intentions in China, particularly in Manchuria. Apart from the State Department's China hands, who were committed intellectually and emotionally to averting a civil war in China, Washington policymakers were primarily interested in heading off conflict so that a weak and divided China would not fall victim to a predatory Russia. This concern informed Truman's instructions to Marshall and guided the latter's course throughout the following year. Toward the end of Marshall's China mission, Undersecretary of State Dean Acheson clearly restated the administration's interest in China in a message to the general:

As you know, one of our principal concerns, if not our principal concern, in endeavoring to bring about peace and unity in China, has been to forestall China's becoming a serious irritant in our relations with Russia. . . . the principal problem is adjustment of our relations there with the Russians without prejudice to our legitimate interests. It has been our hope, and we know that it has been yours, that a peaceful settlement of China's internal problems would be conducive to such an adjustment.[42]

Although never spelled out explicitly, America was presumed to have a "legitimate interest" in the continued existence of a Chinese government that would side with the United States on international political issues, be friendly to American financial, commercial, industrial, cultural, and religious interests, and cooperate in barring the USSR from intruding into Chinese affairs.

Like his Washington colleagues, Marshall was ever alert for signs of Soviet assertiveness in China. Before launching any new initiative to expand the American role in China, he carefully weighed the possibility that such an initiative might prompt the Soviets to seek a parallel role for themselves. In fact, anticipated Soviet reaction became a major constraint upon American willingness to support the Nationalists. Washington's underlying premise was that Moscow would intervene directly rather than permit the Nationalists to wipe out the Communists with all-out U.S. support. In order to sustain this fear Moscow had merely to emit a few growls from time to time.

American apprehension about Soviet intentions in China was linked to U.S. perceptions of the CCP. Despite repeated efforts by Chou En-lai to convince him otherwise, Marshall believed that the CCP, like other Communist parties, was not an autonomous political organization but a stalking horse for Soviet power. Political instability in China encouraged the Soviets to support Communist expansion in areas such as Manchuria. In this light, the American policy objective of promoting a unified and stable China was based primarily on the desire to exclude Soviet influence. The administrative and territorial integrity of China that the United States supported was not a rhetorical flourish or a vestige from the days of John Hay. It was seen in Washington as a means toward a strategic objective—averting a dangerous concentration of Soviet power. In midsummer 1946 a State Department paper warned that

our exclusion from China would probably result, within the next generation, in an expansion of Soviet influence over the manpower, raw materials and industrial power of Manchuria and China. The U.S. and the world might then be faced in the China Sea and southward with a Soviet power analogous to that of the Japanese in 1941, but with the difference that the Soviets could be perhaps overwhelmingly strong in Europe and the Middle East as well.[43]

This geopolitical nightmare was distilled from the experience of men who had just fought the first truly global war in history. The neglect of Chinese nationalism obviously implied in such an assessment was to have disastrous consequences for post-1949 U.S. policy toward China when sober men believed that their nightmare had become a reality. Washington's short-term concern was that an expansionist USSR working through its loyal surrogates— the Chinese Communist Party—would effectively divide China and bind the northern half (including Manchuria) to the burgeoning Soviet empire.

Negotiations in Moscow

The Soviet Union had reacted to Truman's announcement of the Marshall mission by intensifying its propaganda attacks on the role of U.S. troops in China. Several articles in the central Soviet press during late November and early December 1945 sought to divert world attention away from Soviet behavior in Manchuria to the American role in North China.[44] One such article in *Pravda* on the eve of the Moscow Foreign Ministers' Conference in late December stated that the task of the Chinese government was "democratization" and consolidation. This should be done by eliciting the cooperation of "democratic elements" (meaning primarily the CCP). Charging that the presence of U.S. troops in China damaged the prospects for a political solution by inspiring Chinese reactionaries, *Pravda* asserted that Soviet security interests in Manchuria, a territory adjacent to the USSR, justified the continued presence there of the Red Army. The article concluded ominously that "there would be a much greater basis for retaining Soviet troops in Manchuria for a certain period than for retaining foreign troops of any kind in North China."[45]

In discussions with Molotov in Moscow during the foreign ministers' meeting, Secretary of State Byrnes parried the Soviet foreign minister's attempt to link the issue of U.S. troops in North China with the Red Army presence in the Northeast. To his justifiably skeptical Soviet counterpart, Byrnes blandly repeated the transparent fiction that U.S. troops were needed to disarm and repatriate the Japanese. He rejected Molotov's proposal that a specific date—January 15, 1946—be set for the simultaneous withdrawal of American and Soviet troops from Chinese soil.[46] Since Moscow had just promised Chungking to withdraw the Red Army in early February without any American quid pro quo, Molotov's proposal had little to commend it. A precipitate American withdrawal would have jeopardized the National Government's position in North China and a parallel Red Army pullout might have strengthened the Communist hand in Manchuria because Chiang's troops were not yet present in sufficient numbers to take over the region.

Stalin did not press the issue in his own talks with Byrnes, stating disingenuously that he did not object to U.S. troops in China and musing that Chiang Kai-shek's position might be weakened because of his reliance on foreign troops.[47] The final communique of the Foreign Ministers' Conference weakly linked the two issues by stating "complete accord as to the desirability of withdrawal of Soviet and American forces from China at the earliest practical moment consistent with the discharge of their obligations and responsibilities."[48] These weasel words bound no one to do anything. Byrnes, who had gone to Moscow seeking support of America's China policy, came away with nothing but Stalin's lulling affirmation of faith in General Marshall and his equally dubious statement of support for Chiang Kai-shek.[49] In fact, Soviet policy at this time had not forsaken its basic posture of shifting support back and forth between Chungking and Yenan.

That Soviet suspicion of U.S. policy in China had been fueled by the Marshall mission was the message Chiang Ching-kuo, Chairman Chiang's Russian-educated eldest son and trusted personal envoy, received in Moscow in early January. (At this time, incidentally, CCP leader Liu Shao-ch'i's eldest son Liu Yung-p'in was a student in Moscow along with the children of other top Communist leaders.) Warning that the United States would sacrifice Chinese interests, Stalin proposed exchanging Soviet industrial technology for Chinese mineral and agricultural exports as a stable basis for Sino-Soviet relations. His primary aim, he told Chiang, was to secure a Chinese pledge that American troops would not be stationed on Chinese soil.[50] Stalin now invited the elder Chiang to a summit meeting on these issues, but this invitation was declined. In accordance with his earlier position, Chiang Kai-shek sought to avoid bilateral Sino-Soviet negotiations in preference for multilateral diplomacy in which American support might compensate for Chinese weakness.

Conflicting Demands
Over Manchuria

As General Marshall's mediation effort got underway, the elements of conflict were already in place in Northeast China. While Nationalist officials resumed their efforts to elicit Soviet assistance, Chiang's armies, thus far denied access to the Northeast via Talien and other ports, launched an overland assault against an estimated 30,000 Communist troops at Shanhaikuan.[51] Contrary to expectations, the Communists offered little resistance, and the Nationalist drive continued up the Peiping-Shenyang (Peining) railroad, swiftly capturing a number of railroad towns and pausing within easy distance of Shenyang to await developments in the Sino-Soviet negotiations.[52] General Tu Yu-ming, directing the Northeast China Command, brashly predicted the collapse of the enemy's military resistance within two months.[53] This was neither the first nor certainly the last of a long line of Nationalist military misjudgments.

The announcement of General Marshall's mission shifted attention in China from military to political problems. By the last quarter of 1945, in addition to rushing troops into the Northeast and commencing political organizing, the CCP had already articulated its initial political demands for the region. In the Chungking talks between Mao and Chiang, the latter had brushed aside Communist demands to participate in the government of the Northeast.[54] Shortly after Tu Yu-ming began his drive up the Liaohsi corridor, the Communist military leader Chu Teh stated that the CCP did not in principle oppose the movement of Government troops to Changchun by rail, but that until accord was reached on the status of the Communist liberated areas, there must be a mutual agreement on troop transfers in order to avoid open conflict. He charged that the Government had acted arbitrarily in moving troops through the Chi-Je-Liao liberated area and in suppressing the people's democratic rights in the name of "bandit suppression." Chu proposed that as a step toward a united, democratic coalition government the National Government accord legal recognition to the local governments which the CCP was in the process of hastily establishing in the Northeast.[55] Predictably, the Government rejected this demand.

As Marshall's mediation effort commenced, the CCP issued another challenge to the legitimacy of the Northeast regional power structure established by Chiang Kai-shek. On New Year's Day of 1946, Lin Feng, a leading member of the CCP's Northeast Bureau, clarified his party's demands. Branding Chiang's Northeast regional administration an example of one-party rule, Lin called for the abolition of the Northeast headquarters and its replacement by an executive committee representing nonparty persons as well as all of the anti-Japanese political parties. Within the framework of a national coalition government, democratic provincial, district, and local organs of power enjoying broad autonomy should be chosen through popular elections. Finally, Lin sought legal recognition of the Communists forces in the Northeast and their incorporation as the main component of the Northeast Peace Preservation Corps.[56] Between these sweeping demands and the Government's grudging concessions lay too wide a gap for General Marshall or any other mediator to bridge.

Truman's China policy initiative elicited divergent responses within both the CCP and the Kuomintang. Broadly speaking, the basic cleavage in each party was between those who viewed Marshall's mission as an opportunity and those who saw it as a threat to their own position. In both Chinese parties the foremost leaders—Mao and Chiang—threw their weight initially on the scales of those favoring Marshall's mediation but encountered stiff intraparty opposition to any attempts at reconciliation. The ascendancy of the "irreconcilables" in both the CCP and the Kuomintang eventually led to the frustration of Marshall's efforts and to the civil war itself.

Yenan had welcomed the appointment of General Marshall as special ambassador because this seemed to presage a U.S. policy less partial to the Kuomintang.[57] Until the middle of November, Soviet policy had facilitated Communist expansion into the Northeast, but the reverse curve of Soviet policy produced by Chiang's withdrawal of the Northeast mission from Changchun threatened CCP gains in the region and forced Yenan to back down from a military confrontation with Tu Yu-ming's armies. Now it appeared that the new American policy enunciated by President Truman might enable the CCP to achieve its objectives of a standstill cease-fire and participation in a democratized national government.[58]

Alarm over Soviet machinations in Manchuria had helped launch Marshall's mission, so it is not surprising that in his very first meeting with chief CCP negotiator Chou En-lai, Marshall flatly stated that "the U.S. Government is committed to the movement of [Nationalist] troops into Manchuria."[59] Chou maneuvered unsuccessfully to hedge in the movement of Chiang's troops to the Northeast as Marshall upheld the Nationalists' insistence on their unrestricted right to recover Manchuria. The standstill cease-fire that Chou signed with Nationalist negotiator Chang Ch'ün on January 10, 1946, exempted the movement of Nationalist troops to the Northeast.[60] American ships continued to transport the crack troops of Chiang's army into southern Manchuria.

Communist leaders in Yenan must have calculated that the political benefits they might derive from Marshall's mediation outweighed the threat of unimpeded movement of Nationalist troops into the region. On December 25, 1945, Mao issued a directive on policy for the Northeast.[61] Its exhortation to build base areas in the rural counties and district towns over a period of two to three years was a tacit admission that the previous strategy of seizing urban Manchuria had failed because of American pressure and Soviet ambivalence toward the CCP.

Marshall's arrival in China on December 21, 1945, signaled the beginning of a period of high expectation concerning the prospects for a peaceful resolution of the political stalemate. The January 10 cease-fire that Marshall was instrumental in arranging was quickly followed by the resolutions of the Political Consultative Conference (PCC) that brought together representatives of the Kuomintang, the CCP, and other groups. These resolutions augured the end of Kuomintang one-party rule and looked toward the creation of a democratic coalition government, the central demand of Mao's transitional program. Moreover, the Communists found support in the PCC resolutions for their insistence on broad local autonomy.[62] Pending a final settlement, the resolutions stated that "in those areas where the local government is under dispute, the status quo shall be maintained." The principles supporting a final settlement were local self-government through popular elections, and a "fair distribution of powers" between the central and the local governments.[63] If these principles were honored in an atmosphere free of coercion, the CCP's superior organization might prove decisive in the ensuing political conflict with the Kuomintang.

Party Chairman Mao Tse-tung hailed the PCC resolutions as "a great historic victory of the Chinese democratic revolution."[64] In a February 1, 1946, speech, his chief deputy Liu Shao-ch'i echoed Mao's view and spelled out the Party's forthcoming tasks. Liu stressed the necessity for Party cadres to learn new skills in order to operate successfully in a democratic political system where multiparty competition might persist for a long time. Henceforth, he suggested, the Party would have to expand its work into the cities, the factories, and the villages. He saw the main danger in left sectarianism ("closed doorism"); that is, the reluctance of Party members accustomed to guerrilla struggle to adapt themselves to new forms of conflict for which they were unprepared either by experience or temperament.[65]

Liu was raising a critical issue. Could an underground illegal party accustomed to armed struggle adapt itself to legal conditions of peaceful political competition? Although every Leninist party was supposed to possess this dual capacity, such flexibility was not easy to achieve in practice. Despite its skill in mobilization and its popular rural programs, the CCP, no less than the Kuomintang, lacked the experience of open, quasi-democratic politics.[66] Liu believed that such adaptation could be successful only if the Party leadership consciously impressed upon the rank and file the importance of the new tasks at hand. At the Seventh Party Congress (April–June 1945), Mao himself had acknowledged this point. Where Liu may have differed from Mao was in the vigor with which he defended the projected "nationalization" of the CCP's army as a necessary concession in return for the Kuomintang's political concessions, and his further insistence that

this critical step actually be implemented.[67] But there is no contemporary evidence to support the Cultural Revolution charge
that a fundamental divergence between the two leaders existed at
this time.

There can be no doubt, however, that by agreeing to
the Chungking-Washington demand for unrestricted Nationalist
troop movement to Manchuria, Chou En-lai and Mao Tse-tung
had jeopardized the position of their comrades in the Northeast.
Moreover, the two leaders subsequently went out of their way to
convey their party's appreciation for Marshall's role in the tripartite negotiations. Earlier Communist efforts during 1944–45 to
secure American assistance had foundered in part on Washington's conviction that the CCP was still basically an extension of
the Kremlin. Now, in a meeting with Marshall on January 31,
1946, Chou sought once more to secure the elusive "American
connection" by laying to rest U.S. fears of Chinese Communism.

Chairman Mao instructed me to communicate to you in particular that
he regards the attitude you assumed in handling the truce problem being
[sic] fair and just, and the Chinese Communist Party is prepared to
cooperate with the United States in matters both of a local and national
character on the basis as embodied in your aforementioned attitude. We
believe that the democracy to be initiated in China should follow the
American pattern. Since in present-day China, the conditions necessary
to the introduction of socialism do not exist, we Chinese Communists,
who theoretically advocate socialism as our ultimate goal, do not mean,
nor deem it possible, to carry it into effect in the immediate future. In
saying that we should pursue the American path, we mean to acquire
U.S. styled democracy and science, and specifically to introduce to this
country agricultural reform, industrialization, free enterprise and development of individuality so that we may build an independent, free and
prosperous China.[68]

This, then, was Mao's New Democracy for an official
American audience that was not expected to see in it the familiar
contours of a Communist-led bourgeois-democratic revolution
such as Lenin had outlined thirty years earlier. Knowing that the
United States viewed the CCP as an instrument of Soviet expansionism, Chou and Mao tried to alter American perceptions
through a series of reassurances. On repeated occasions over the

next several months, Chou En-lai explicitly dissociated the CCP from Soviet goals and policies in China.

Mao's personal leadership of the CCP had been buttressed at the Seventh Party Congress, but his policies were not yet immune to criticism from within the ranks of the Party elite. It appears that some Communist leaders in Yenan and the Northeast may have doubted the wisdom of courting the Americans and preferred to rely upon the USSR. In mid-February an unidentified spokesman for the CCP Central Committee stiffened the Party's demands concerning Manchuria. Repeating what were by now long-standing Communist demands for reorganization of the Northeast headquarters and recognition of the local democratic governments and Communist armies, he added the important demand that the number of Nationalist troops sent to Manchuria be limited in view of the absence of a foreign threat, the existence of the cease-fire, and the need to lighten the people's burden. Such a demand ran directly counter to the January 10 cease-fire. At the same time, he linked the delay in Soviet troop withdrawal to the CCP's political demands. Asserting that "Russia's unwillingness to quit Manchuria is a direct result of the Government's demands that Soviet forces disarm local Manchurian troops and Communists," the Yenan spokesman continued, "the Russians will be able to pull out of Manchuria as soon as the Government agrees to recognize local Manchurian troops and assents to a peaceful discussion of the Manchurian problem."[69]

Unfortunately, there is no direct evidence to confirm the implication that Soviet-oriented CCP leaders and the Russians had reached an understanding over Northeast China. However, it is clear that by retaining its army in Manchuria beyond the stipulated February 1 deadline for withdrawal and thus delaying the Nationalist recovery of the region, the USSR was reenforcing Communist pressures for a de facto regional coalition government. In early March 1946 Raymond Ludden, who was monitoring CCP-Soviet relations from within the U.S. embassy in Chungking, noted that the CCP was echoing the Soviet line on international affairs more closely than usual, particularly since the February 14 statement on Manchuria. Ludden reported that Po Ku (Ch'in Pang-hsien), prominent Soviet-oriented editor of the *Liberation Daily*, had stated that Soviet evacuation of Manchuria could not be expected while the United States maintained bases in continental Asia and the Pacific islands.[70] If there was a group in Yenan that looked toward Moscow for assistance in the Northeast, it was most likely supported by CCP leaders in the region itself. The rapid buildup of Communist forces in the Northeast strengthened the position of leaders such as P'eng Chen and Lin Piao and gave them an opportunity to press their views in party councils, which they appear to have done. In March and April 1946, when the Communists were running up a string of military victories in Manchuria, Chou En-lai's freedom to negotiate in Chungking was seriously curtailed. He frequently consulted Yenan which, in turn, apparently looked to its field commanders in the Northeast before making any decisions.[71]

The split within the Kuomintang over the question of how much to cooperate with General Marshall's mediation effort became visible only in the context of the frustrated Nationalist attempts to elicit Soviet aid in the takeover of Manchuria. In the wake of the PCC resolutions and the January 10 cease-fire, the situation in the Northeast remained tense. In principled terms, the crux of the unresolved Manchurian problem was the contradiction between the Communist-supported PCC principle of maintaining the status quo in disputed areas and the National Government's legalistic insistence on "recovering Chinese sovereignty in Manchuria" by establishing its own administration throughout the region backed by military power. Consequently, while an uneasy truce took hold in intramural China following the January 10 cease-fire, in the Northeast the Government's attempts to dislodge Communist forces from their local strongholds resulted in frequent clashes.[72] Worried that the continuing turmoil in Manchuria might unravel the entire cease-fire, Marshall proposed that tripartite truce teams of the Peiping Executive Headquarters—an institution established to monitor the truce—be dispatched to Manchuria.[73] His proposal was accepted by Chou En-lai and by Mao. However, Chiang Kai-shek rejected the idea, ostensibly to avoid inciting Soviet displeasure, but more likely because the general effect of truce team activity was to preserve the status quo. In Manchuria this would have meant confirming the Communists' local control in all but the largest cities.[74]

The Soviets Postpone
Their Withdrawal

As the February 1, 1946, target date for the Red Army's evacuation
from Manchuria approached, new difficulties arose to frustrate
the National Government's hopes of completing its takeover of
the region. Although Chiang Kai-shek and his representatives in
Changchun privately laid responsibility for these difficulties upon
the Soviets, the underlying reason was the strengthening position
of the Chinese Communists in the Northeast. In the late autumn
of 1945, as Nationalist troops advanced into southern Manchuria,
the Communists withdrew from the cities they had occupied and
avoided frontal battles. They began to entrench themselves in
northern Manchuria and to buttress their positions in the district
towns and rural areas in accordance with Mao Tse-tung's directive
of December 1945 (see below, pp. 00–00). Unable for the time
being to dislodge the Communists through their own efforts, the
Nationalists again turned to the Soviets for assistance.

In detailed discussions with their Soviet Red Army
counterparts in Changchun, Chinese military liaison officials
sought aid and cooperation in four interrelated spheres: (1) providing liaison and military support for local takeovers; (2) suppressing and disarming non-Government armed forces; (3) facil-
itating the transport by rail of Nationalist troops to central and
northern Manchuria; and (4) coordinating the Soviet evacuation
with the Nationalist military advance.[75]

There can be little doubt that had the Russians com-
plied with these requests, in the short run, at least, the Nationalists
would have been able to extend and consolidate their control over
much though not all of Northeast China. But this would have
signified an abandonment of the Soviets' dual policy and resulted
in the thorough alienation of the CCP. It is not surprising, therefore, that through May 1946 Moscow's policy continued to be
cooperation by halves.

By January 1946 it was becoming evident that the
Nationalists would encounter determined resistance in their attempts to occupy the county seats and their surrounding districts
where Communist-sponsored local administrations governed under the protection of their own military forces. In Liaopei province

in mid-January, for example, local officials in Changtu and Lishu rebuffed Nationalist takeover personnel, and not long after an identical reception occurred in Chiut'ai north of Changchun.[76] In these cases, Soviet liaison personnel accompanied the Nationalists, but the Soviets were often unwilling to provide even this limited service. Even when the Russians agreed to send liaison personnel they refused to provide any troops to aid the Nationalist takeover on the grounds that such action would constitute intervention in Chinese internal affairs.[77] This became the chief point of contention between the Soviets and the Chinese government. Nationalist spokesmen asserted that for the duration of the Soviet occupation of Manchuria the Red Army was responsible for guaranteeing local order and security in places where a formal transfer of defense responsibilities to the Chinese government had not yet occurred. However, if local Communist officials resisted Nationalist takeovers, then the Soviets should use force to ensure compliance. Nationalist officials repeatedly requested the Red Army to dispatch troops in order to escort Nationalist civilian officials and disperse "illegal" armed forces which were disturbing public order and obstructing the takeover. They also called upon the Russians to guard the vital rail lines against harassment and disruption, but the Soviets regularly turned down these requests.[78]

The limits of Soviet assistance to the Nationalist government emerged very clearly with respect to the issue of irregular armed forces in Manchuria. In the aftermath of war, Manchuria once again became honeycombed with local armed forces as it had been prior to the Japanese conquest of 1931–32. This was by no means simply a reflection of the Nationalist-Communist conflict. It represented rather the flourishing of banditry in a time of political uncertainty and social disarray and the revival of village and other local self-defense forces seeking to protect their autonomy and security. Finally, the disbandment of the several hundred thousand strong Manchukuo Army set loose in the countryside large numbers of armed men with uncertain loyalties whose major objective must have been the survival of their own primary groups. Many of these ex-soldiers sought to have their units recognized and reorganized into the Government's army or local Peace Preservation Forces.

Both the Chinese government and the Soviet occupation authorities were concerned by the activities of irregular military forces, and negotiations revealed apparent agreement on the need to suppress and disarm such forces. It soon became clear, however, that the two sides were defining the objectives of their supposed concern in very different ways. The Chinese government was seeking Soviet aid in order to eliminate the local and irregular Communist troops which were protecting the Communist-spon-sored governments and resisting Nationalist takeover efforts. However, the Russians generally viewed these as legitimate self-defense formations and left them alone. However, as an occupying power, the Red Army was concerned with the wide variety of military units in the region whose anarchic activity threatened the security of Soviet troops and their lines of communication. As early as the end of October 1945, Marshal Malinovsky complained that the Red Army had already suffered 200 casualties in the Northeast since the occupation began.[79] In practice, the Russians apparently cracked down on unofficial armed groups which sup-ported or sought recognition from the National Government, and on occasion even disarmed and interned security forces organized by the Northeast headquarters and provincial Nationalist authorities.[80]

Given the divergent aims of the two sides, the prox-imity of their military forces, and the wide variety of other armed units (including Communists) in the Northeast, it is no wonder that numerous incidents broke out for which each side blamed the other. From the Nationalist perspective, the most serious of these was the murder in January 1946 of Chang Hsing-fu, an engineer sent to survey the Fushun coal mines. The Soviets ex-pressed their regrets but disclaimed responsibility for his protec-tion.[81] The Soviets in turn sought to blame the National Govern-ment for the sporadic attacks on its soldiers. However, hostility to the unpopular Soviet troops is a more likely explanation for such incidents, since the Nationalists were carefully pursuing a policy of negotiations short of appeasement and stressing to their own people the importance of Sino-Soviet friendship. Nevertheless, following a series of anti-Soviet demonstrations in February 1946, Soviet authorities openly accused Kuomintang supporters in the Northeast of colluding with remnant enemy forces to attack the Red Army and organize underground armed detachments.[82]

As Sino-Soviet talks continued, signs accumulated that the Soviet withdrawal from the Northeast would be delayed beyond the February 1 deadline. In early January, General Trotsynko hinted that the harsh winter weather and severe fuel shortage on the railroad might delay the troop pullout. Thereafter, he refused to provide a firm schedule of withdrawal dates from specific areas.[83] February 1 passed and the Red Army remained in the Northeast. This time the delay was unilateral.

Economic Issues
in the Northeast

Chief among the unresolved bilateral issues between the Chinese and Soviet governments at this time was that of economic cooperation in the Northeast. How important a factor was this in delaying the Soviet withdrawal?

An answer to this question must begin with a brief review of the Soviet industrial despoliation of Manchuria starting in the fall of 1945, which in turn was rooted in larger problems. A major objective of Soviet immediate postwar economic policy was to compensate for Germany's vast destruction of Soviet industrial plant and equipment by seizing control of enemy assets with little attention paid to the legal niceties. In their discussions with Britain and the United States on reparations policy, Soviet leaders had idiosyncratically defined war booty as all property which had been used to support the Axis war effort including industrial plants, machinery, and mines.[84] (The standard definition used by the United States was "finished equipment and supplies produced for and belonging to the German armed forces.")[85] Without waiting for Allied agreement, the Soviets undertook the large-scale physical removal of German industrial plants and equipment from their zone of occupation. Such unilateral Soviet action soon led to a breakdown of the Allied reparations discussions and the adoption of a zonal approach which granted a free hand for each occupying power in its own zone to take what it would.[86]

The outcome of the German reparations discussions

convinced the Russians that they could expect little if any reparations from Japan unless they acted unilaterally. Again employing their very broad definition of war booty, the Soviets staked a claim to a large proportion of industry in Manchuria on the grounds that it had served the Japanese war effort. Soon after the end of their Manchurian military campaign, Soviet special personnel began to dismantle and remove industrial machinery, raw material stockpiles, and inventories of finished products from Japanese factories and mines in the Northeast on a vast scale. An American investigation commission headed by reparations commissioner Edwin Pauley estimated in 1946 that U.S. $895 million in direct damage or $2 billion in production loss and replacement costs had been sustained.[87] Soviet estimates of the worth of the so-called "industrial trophies" were only $95 million, which probably reflects the drastically diminished value of the goods and equipment after transport to new sites.[88] Whatever the precise dollar value, it is clear that within weeks of the end of the war much of Manchuria's industrial wealth had been destroyed. The economy of China, the USSR's putative ally, had been ravished as thoroughly as that of the German enemy.

Certain specific features of Soviet policy in Manchuria during the autumn of 1945 may be partially explained by the exigencies of industrial removal. Soviet refusal to allow the debarkation of Nationalist troops at Talien may have stemmed from the fact that the port was a key point for shipping out industrial equipment. One of the reasons for obstructing the Nationalist takeover may have been to facilitate implementation of the industrial removal policy without the embarrassing presence of Chinese government officials. Rather than being a subtle or devious attempt to influence the outcome of political competition in Manchuria (as some authors have suggested), industrial removals should probably be understood as part of the Soviet effort to rebuild the USSR's industrial economy as rapidly as possible in the context of an uncertain world.[89] In view of the potentially damaging effect of industrial removals on economic and political stability in occupied areas, it seems likely that in Manchuria, as in Germany, military occupation authorities came into conflict with the officials directly responsible for enforcing the removal directives even though the actual dismantling was done by military

forces. Economic ministries responsible for postwar recovery in
the USSR implemented industrial removal policy within a grant
of authority coming from the top levels of the Soviet government.[90]
Once the procedure had been drawn up and personnel selected
and trained, organizational imperatives rather than rational cal-
culations for specific cases likely governed policy implementation.
To the men carrying out the policy of industrial removals in Manchuria, the Nationalist-Communist conflict may have been very
far from their minds indeed.

November 1945 brought a new Soviet line on the
Manchurian economy. When Sino-Soviet negotiations resumed
in Changchun in an improved atmosphere, the Soviet side presented a proposal for extensive Sino-Soviet economic cooperation
in the Northeast. Economic advisor M. I. Sladkovsky presented a
long list of industrial enterprises to Northeast Economic Committee Chairman Chang Kia-ngau which the Soviet government
wanted to have placed under joint Sino-Soviet management. The
list included most of the heavy industrial enterprises in the fields
of power production, metallurgy, chemicals, machine-building,
and cement.[91] It has been suggested that the Soviet proposals for
joint management of industrial enterprises in Manchuria were
part of an alternate strategy for postwar Soviet economic recovery
pushed by a CPSU group headed by Andrei Zhdanov, A. I. Mikoyan, and N. A. Voznesenskii which hoped to use the industrial
output of plants remaining in place to restore the USSR's economy.[92] While this may have been the case, Soviet policymakers
considering China policy as a whole may have realized that an
alteration in the policy of industrial removals was warranted on
several grounds. The Chinese government remained committed
to developing the Northeast as the industrial center for the postwar
modernization of China, but lacking adequate supplies of capital,
skilled labor, and technology, China would have to look abroad
for assistance and the United States was the most logical source
for such aid.[93] Washington had repeatedly expressed its economic
interest in Manchuria through its efforts to secure the Open Door;
now Moscow, having ravished much of Manchuria's economic
base, faced the possibility that U.S. economic power would be
drawn into the area following the Soviet evacuation. The Soviets
may have sought to preclude such an outcome by pressing for

joint Sino-Soviet management of Manchuria's industrial economy while the Red Army was still in place to lend weight to such a demand. Had the Chinese government acquiesced, Moscow would have grasped a vital lever of control and Manchuria's economy might have been integrated into that of the Soviet Union as were the economies of the East European client states after World War II.

Initially the Chinese government responded to Soviet economic demands by saying that in order to avoid the appearance of negotiating under duress any such proposals could be considered only after completion of the Soviet troop withdrawal.[94] But since the Soviets continued to insist on an economic cooperation agreement, a divergence of opinion apparently developed within the Nationalist leadership. T. V. Soong and Foreign Minister Wang Shih-chieh expressed the view of those who opposed any Sino-Soviet economic agreement on the grounds that it would give the USSR a permanent economic interest in the region and compromise Chinese sovereignty.[95] But Chiang Kai-shek and Chang Kia-ngau, among others, hoped that by making some concessions they could dispose of the war trophies issue and gain Soviet military cooperation in the Northeast.[96] Acting on Chungking's instructions, Chinese representatives in Changchun began secret negotiations on the question of economic cooperation. They sought to offer compromise proposals which would be acceptable to the Russians without sacrificing China's economic sovereignty, but the Soviet side would not accept the Chinese offers.[97] After the Soviets pared their original lengthy list of enterprises slated for joint management, it appears that Chang Kia-ngau urged his government to accept the truncated list as a basis for friendly relations, but Chiang Kai-shek hesitated until the public outcry against the Soviet demands, which in the meantime had become known, no longer made their acceptance politically feasible.[98]

The Soviet commander in Manchuria, Marshal Malinovsky, repeatedly warned that a solution to the problem of economic cooperation would have to be found before his troops would leave the region.[99] As noted, Stalin himself, in talks with Chiang Ching-kuo in early January 1946, stressed that the issue of economic cooperation was closely linked in his mind to the Soviet-American strategic rivalry in China. Stalin's offer of assistance for the industrialization of China (particularly Manchuria and Sinkiang) was linked to his demand that China stay clear of an American military entanglement.

Kuomintang Politics
and the Soviet Troop Issue

By prolonging the Red Army's occupation of Manchuria, Stalin exerted pressure on Chungking to yield the economic concessions he desired while at the same time keeping Washington edgy about Soviet intentions. He may also have been trying to influence political developments within China.

As the deadline for Soviet troop withdrawal passed, the political situation in the Northeast remained extremely volatile. The continuing inflow of Nationalist forces into Manchuria as well as movement within the region (permitted by the cease-fire) challenged Communist control over many districts. The fate of the Communist armies and local governments remained uncertain. Local clashes erupted frequently as both sides jockeyed for position.[100]

While the retention of Soviet troops in Manchuria emboldened the CCP, the effect within the Kuomintang was to question the wisdom of Chiang Kai-shek's strategy of quiet diplomacy. Although Chiang himself saw no way out of the impasse other than to continue negotiating with the Russians on the tangle of unresolved issues, there were persons within the Kuomintang (frequently identified with the right-wing CC clique) who for some time had been dissatisfied with Chairman Chiang's approach to Manchuria. (These were part of the Ko-hsin or Renovationist movement in the KMT, an ideologically oriented coalition of CC and Whampoa clique members who were trying to reanimate the party through idealistic appeals.)[101] More important, they were extremely hostile to the Marshall mediation effort. The unilateral Soviet delay and the popular disquiet it provoked, coupled with the prolonged agony of the government's takeover effort, presented this group with an opportunity to take the offensive. Moreover, since the top government officials in the Northeast were associated with the rival Political Science clique, an attack on their handling of the situation in the Northeast provided an opportunity to strike at factional rivals.

In the last week of February 1946, large well-organized student demonstrations in Chungking and other cities demanded the immediate evacuation of Soviet troops from Manchuria, expressed opposition to all new Soviet economic demands, and called for the dissolution of the CCP's Northeast Democratic United Army and the Party-sponsored local governments in Manchuria. Small groups of rioters sacked the Chungking offices of the Communist *Hsinhua jih-pao* (New China Daily) and the Democratic League's *Min-chu jih-pao* (Democratic Daily).[102] The strategy of the Kuomintang intraparty opposition was to link the Communists in Manchuria with the unpopular Soviet occupation in order to create pressure for change in the government's policy of negotiating with the Russians and the CCP.[103] The Northeast, a region in which the conciliation approach had thus far failed, could lead to the unraveling of the PCC agreements.[104]

The sharpest attacks on the government's handling of the Manchurian problem were launched within the Kuomintang Central Executive Committee at its March 1946 meeting. Critics condemned the government's reliance on negotiations with the USSR and accused Foreign Minister Wang Shih-chieh as well as the top officials in the Northeast, Hsiung Shih-hui and Chang Kiangau, of bungling and incompetence. A resolution calling for the dismissal and censure of the latter two officials elicited cheers. Chiang Kai-shek responded to these attacks by assuming personal responsibility for the policy and urging unity and mutual trust upon his irate colleagues.[105] He sought and received more time to proceed with the negotiations and to see through the Soviet evacuation. Nevertheless, the critics' attacks were not without consequence. By offering a foretaste of the anti-Russian public sentiment that could be mobilized on the Manchurian issue, they effectively precluded government concessions on the economic issues. In addition, they elicited bitter Soviet reactions and contributed to a drastic deterioration in the negotiating climate.[106]

In response to the anti-Soviet demonstrations and Chinese public criticism of Chungking's policies in Manchuria, Soviet Red Army headquarters in Changchun issued a belligerent statement on the withdrawal issue. While correctly asserting that the Soviet evacuation had been delayed twice previously at the request of the Chinese government, General Trotsynko blamed harsh weather and the inability of Chungking to move its troops into the districts garrisoned by the Red Army as major causes of the newest delay. In addition, he again linked the withdrawal of Soviet troops with the issue of American forces in China.[107] By not providing a schedule for Soviet withdrawal, he bolstered the pessimistic expectation in Nationalist circles that the Red Army was settling in for a prolonged occupation in Manchuria. In fact, on March 5, 1946, Soviet Marshal Malinovsky, commander of Red Army forces in the Northeast, had told his garrison commander in Shenyang to prepare for a long stay.[108]

Marshall's Attempt to Force a Northeast Truce

The continuing Soviet occupation of Manchuria and Moscow's demands for economic concessions there provoked mounting American concern. A U.S. diplomatic note to the USSR on February 11, 1946, protested Soviet economic demands on China, claiming that they were unjustified by the terms of the 1945 Sino-Soviet treaty and that they threatened American commercial interests in Manchuria. Molotov dismissed these charges abruptly.[109] In Chungking General Marshall was even more concerned. On February 9 he cabled President Truman that "it is clear to me that the survival of much of what has been accomplished in China this past month will depend to an important degree on an early disposition of the festering situation in Manchuria."[110]

Marshall's anxiety was grounded in his belief that China's security was imperiled by the linked threat of the Soviet Union acting from without and the CCP acting from within the country. Believing that until the government was reorganized, China would be "very vulnerable to low-level Russian infiltration methods," Marshall counselled the Chinese government to "proceed with her projected unification at the fastest possible pace so as to eliminate her present vulnerability to Soviet undercover attack, which exists so long as there remains a separate Communist Government and a separate Communist Army in China."[111] Clearly, Mao's protestations of interest in "the American path" had not allayed Marshall's suspicion of CCP-Soviet collusion. Marshall's strategy was to neutralize the CCP-Moscow connection by bringing international pressure to bear on the USSR to withdraw from Manchuria and by involving the CCP in a national coalition government. Such a government would command the loyalty of a depoliticized army no longer subject to party control.

    Marshall's expectation that CCP political behavior would be radically altered if it entered into a coalition government was apparently rooted in a deep-seated conviction about the transformative powers of constitutional democracy. John Carter Vincent, director of the Office of Far Eastern Affairs in the State Department, expressed the American hope most succinctly and most cynically in stating that "a reduction in the influence of the Communists might be more readily achieved if the Government 'took them in' (in more senses than one) on a minority basis rather than try to shoot them all."[112] American hope was misplaced, and in this respect one must agree with the conventional wisdom that the thinking underlying the Marshall mission was naive. U.S. pressure on Chiang to accept the substance as well as the form of a coalition government was certainly not based on any sympathy with the Communists' political objectives as right-wing U.S. critics subsequently charged.[113] Rather, Marshall was struggling "to convince some of these people [i.e., Nationalist leaders] that acceptance of the Communists in a constitutional government doesn't mean the end of everything."[114]

    The difference between the American and Chinese political perspectives is best demonstrated by the fact that both Communists' and Nationalists' views on coalition differed substantially from that of the United States. Of the Communist leaders, perhaps only Liu Shao-ch'i with his long-time experience in the urban "white areas" viewed coalition as a challenge for the Party to sharpen its political skills in free competition for political leadership. Other leaders, especially the Communist military, most likely saw coalition government as at best a detour on the road to total power, and in the short run as a threat to their existing power. Chiang Kai-shek and the Nationalists viewed coalition as an opening to Communist "infiltration" of their government under Marshall's unwitting protection.[115] In his autopsy of the civil war published in Taiwan, Chiang alleged that a coalition government was precisely what Stalin was seeking in China because it represented a vital step in "Moscow's scheme of 'peaceful transformation' for China."[116] In short, neither side viewed coalition government as a means toward the establishment of a functioning democratic state, which was Marshall's hope. Chiang and the Communist generals shared the fear that it might obstruct their quest for power while Liu Shao-ch'i, in proper Leninist fashion, saw it as a stage on the road to power.

Despite these underlying divergences of perspective, by the end of February 1946 Marshall had apparently worked three miracles. The January 10 cease-fire had basically ended the fighting in intramural China; the PCC resolutions contained the blueprint for a government of national union—a coalition government which would steer China onto the road of constitutional democracy; and a military reorganization agreement of February 25 provided for the abolition of "party armies" and their integration into a nonpartisan force under the command of a professional bureaucracy above the passion of party.[117] Yet one element eluded Marshall's grasp. The "festering situation in Manchuria" urgently required a solution lest the continued fighting there undo what had thus far been accomplished.

Characteristically, Marshall responded to this problem by attempting to expand his own authority and that of the Peiping Executive Headquarters, an instrument designed by the Committee of Three (Marshall, Chou En-lai, and Chang Ch'ün) to implement and monitor the truce. He sought specifically to extend the operation of the three-man truce teams into Manchuria in order to bring a halt to the fighting there. Since the general effect of truce team activity was to freeze the politico-military status quo, the Communists, holding the upper hand in the region, at first favored Marshall's initiative. The Nationalists opposed it, ostensibly on the grounds that it might complicate their dealings with Moscow, but more likely because they feared their freedom of movement into and within Manchuria might be curtailed.[118]

By mid-March, when Marshall returned to Washington for consultations, Communist enthusiasm for the dispatch of truce teams to the Northeast had visibly wilted. The Party sensed the opportunity for even greater gains through vigorous politico-military activity in the wake of the Soviet Red Army withdrawal. To Lt. General Alvan C. Gillem, his deputy on the Committee of Three, Marshall cabled, "You will have to force an agreement quickly regarding entry of teams into Manchuria. . . . We cannot delay any longer." Two weeks later, when the teams were in the field at long last but accomplishing nothing, Marshall again cabled Gillem urging him to go to Manchuria in person to enforce compliance with the cease-fire. "The teams are there and the trouble is there and we can't just sit back and let the affair stew. You will have to use strong measures to bring about a sufficient understanding to go ahead," Marshall wrote with ill-concealed impatience.[119]

Marshall's determination "to force an agreement" betrayed his fear that his accomplishments were falling apart while he was in Washington. He may have felt that if only he were there in person, rather than his ineffectual subordinate, a workable agreement could be attained. In his anxiety to resolve the Manchurian imbroglio, Marshall abandoned his normal caution and tried to force the issue rather than pursue the path of multilateral cooperation which was the only effective means available to him. He had no chance of succeeding. Although his Chinese partners were too tactful to break off the negotiations, it is quite obvious that from mid-March through mid-May the deliberations of the Committee of Three were peripheral to the developing politico-military situation. The reason for this new state of affairs was not difficult to determine.

The Pattern and Consequences of Soviet Withdrawal

On March 11, without prior warning, the Chinese government received notice that the withdrawal of the Red Army from Manchuria was underway. Both sides had been waiting for this signal. Almost immediately the Chinese Communists increased their military pressure on the vulnerable government positions north of Shenyang such as Ssup'ingchieh and K'aiyuan.[120] Nationalist officials in central and northern Manchuria, lacking adequate defense forces, withdrew to the safety of Shenyang and Chinchow to await reinforcements.

Why did the Russians, who had just given several indications of further prolonging their occupation of Manchuria, suddenly resume their evacuation at this time? Several possible reasons may be suggested.

Soviet pressure on Chiang to wrest economic concessions in the Northeast had failed. The continued Red Army occupation had succeeded only in arousing a wave of patriotic indignation in China which stiffened the government's resolve to yield no further. The Soviet occupation was also diminishing the chances for a political settlement in China via a coalition government and the sharing of power between Communists and Nationalists in the Northeast. The presence of an unwanted foreign army on Chinese soil seemed to validate the Nationalist claim that the principal issue in the Northeast was the recovery of national sovereignty, and strengthened the Nationalist tendency to seek a military solution in the Northeast. The Soviets thus risked completely alienating Chiang Kai-shek.

Moreover, as the Soviet occupation dragged on, U.S. willingness to defer to Moscow in the Northeast was wearing thin. On March 9, 1946, the State Department announced the dispatch of a note to Moscow protesting the protracted occupation of the Northeast. Almost simultaneously, General Wedemeyer claimed that Manchuria fell within his command jurisdiction as chief of the U.S. China Theater, and he added that the United States might soon commence a program of repatriating Japanese from the region.[121] It is likely that Moscow also viewed Marshall's efforts to dispatch truce teams to Manchuria as another unwelcome sign of American resolve to bolster its position in China. Stalin's objective of accelerating the liquidation of the American military presence in China seemed to be receding.[122] Ironically, Marshall himself favored termination of the China Theater and removal of U.S. Marines from North China in order to reduce American vulnerability to Soviet charges of intervention. The steps he proposed the better to do battle with the Soviets were precisely those that would have allayed Moscow's suspicions! But Marshall's views on this point were not accepted in Washington.[123]

Perhaps most important in triggering the Soviet withdrawal was Stalin's realization that the Red Army's presence in
Manchuria was fast becoming an important political liability in
the larger arena of world politics. This late winter of 1945–46 was
a crucial period in the maturation of the Cold War. In a widely
noted election speech on February 9, 1946, Stalin had reasserted
the Leninist orthodoxy about the inevitability of war and stressed
the need for Soviet preparation.[124] On March 5, with President
Truman by his side, Winston Churchill delivered his famous Iron
Curtain speech at Fulton College proposing the formation of an
Anglo-American alliance directed against the Soviet Union. Soviet
obduracy and the Red Army's failure to withdraw on schedule
from Manchuria as well as Iran were widely included in bills of
particulars concerning Soviet expansionism.[125] In these circumstances, Stalin apparently sought to reduce the threat of a hostile
coalition forming against him by withdrawing his forces from
Manchuria and Iran, the dangerously exposed salients of his political position.[126] Thus, seen in its international context, the Soviet
withdrawal from Manchuria was a conciliatory move regardless
of its impact upon the internal Chinese power struggle. This was
not long in coming.

The resumption of the long-delayed Soviet withdrawal
signaled the beginning of a full-scale CCP attempt to seize control
of the Northeast quickly by military means, circumventing Mao's
long-term strategy of building rural bases.

The CCP's military initiative was quickly reflected at
the negotiating table in Chungking. From mid-March through
mid-May Chou En-lai, while keeping lines of communication
open to the United States, effectively blocked any progress in the
negotiations over Manchurian issues. He sought to limit the number of Nationalist troops sent into the Northeast, control the conditions under which the Nationalists might take over locations
evacuated by the Red Army, and to link Communist military
concessions in the Northeast to the transformation of the Northeast
regional government, a step that Chiang had long resisted. In this
period, Chou appears to have been deprived of much of his authority to negotiate. He frequently pleaded his need to seek instructions from Yenan which, in turn, he claimed, was dependent
upon information from the field in the Northeast.[127] Marshall, for

his part, believed that the Communist generals were having their day and that Chou was unable to restrain them.

On March 26, Marshall's long-sought agreement regarding the entry of truce teams into Manchuria was signed in Chungking. It stipulated that the teams operate within territory controlled by the Nationalists or the Communists (but not where Soviet troops were still in control) in order to effect a cease-fire.[128] Chou En-lai's demand for linking military and political questions in Manchuria was covered by the vague assurance that "as to political matters in Manchuria separate discussions will be held with a view to reaching an early settlement."[129]

When the first truce teams were finally sent to the field, it quickly became evident that the Communists as well as the Nationalists had no intention of allowing their work to succeed. Military men on both sides placed one impediment after another in their path.[130] Thus Marshall's instrument for forcing a Northeast truce proved completely ineffectual.

While public attention focused on the Chungking negotiations, more vital discussions were taking place in Changchun between Nationalist representatives and the Soviet Red Army command. The mode of the Red Army's withdrawal from the Northeast might determine whether the Nationalists or the Communists gained a decisive short-term advantage in the struggle for Manchuria. The Chinese government redoubled its efforts to gain Soviet support for its takeover, but again failed to achieve the desired degree of cooperation.

In central and northern Manchuria the simmering crisis which the government had been experiencing in its takeover came to a boil as the Soviet withdrawal proceeded. In many county seats in the provinces of Heilungkiang, Hokiang, Sungkiang, Liaopei, and Nunkiang Nationalist forces were stymied as local Communist-sponsored administrations refused to relinquish their power. Soviet authorities turned aside Nationalist requests for assistance to clear away these obstacles.[131] General Trotsynko stated that if Government troops failed to arrive in a locality by the date of the scheduled Soviet withdrawal, the Red Army would turn over defense of the area to the local forces. No alterations would be made in the schedule to accommodate Chungking.[132]

The maintenance of Government control in the towns

and districts where its administration was already established depended on bolstering the local garrisons to withstand attacks from
the encircling Communist armies. In this connection, the problem
of coordinating the arrival of Government forces with the evacuation schedule of the Red Army was crucial, for once the Soviets
withdrew from a town its immunity from Communist attack was
ended.[133] Soviet withdrawal in mid-March from Shenyang and
the towns lying north along the railroad to Changchun had been
carried out with scant prior notice. Consequently, Communist
forces attacked and captured such cities as K'aiyuan, Changtu,
and Ssup'ingchieh.

Despite their steady military buildup in Manchuria
(aided by continuing U.S. logistical support), as of mid-March
Nationalist troops were still largely confined to the Liaohsi corridor
and the environs of Shenyang. Nationalist generals needed to
transport large numbers of troops along the Chinese-Changchun
railroad, but the Soviets, citing their own need for fuel and rolling
stock, provided no assistance. The Nationalists thereupon concluded an agreement with the Soviet director of the railroad to
transport their troops using Peining (Peiping-Shenyang) railway
equipment and their own fuel supply, but the Soviet side failed to
implement the agreement adequately.[134] The Nationalists were
also unable to secure Soviet assistance in moving troops over the
Manchouli-Suifenho axis of the rail route which the Russians had
converted to their own wide gauge in September-October 1945.[135]

Taking advantage of the Soviet position, Chinese Communist troops methodically destroyed bridges on the line to
Changchun and harried the Nationalists' lines of communications. They succeeded in delaying Nationalist troop movements
as they built up their own strength for a positional battle at
Ssup'ingchieh.[136]

During the final weeks of the Soviet occupation, Nationalist officials pleaded for advance information concerning the
evacuation schedule and sought to elicit a Soviet commitment to
relinquish control to the Chinese government alone through a
formal transfer of command responsibilities (the Chinese term is
chieh fang).[137] By obligating the Russians to await the arrival of
regular Nationalist garrison troops to accept the transfer of command, the Nationalists sought to eliminate the hiatus between the

Soviet departure and their own arrival when Communist forces stepped in and seized power. However, the Russians refused to make any adjustments in their withdrawal schedule. As they had from the very outset, they declined to shoulder any part of the burden for the Nationalist takeover bid.[138]

The short-term effect of Soviet policy was to crush Nationalist hopes for recovering control of the Northeast. In the last two weeks of April, as Lin Piao's troops blocked the Nationalist advance at the rail junction of Ssup'ingchieh, their comrades seized power in Changchun, Harbin, Tsitsihar, and elsewhere. By the time the last Red Army units crossed back into Soviet territory in early May, most of Northeast China lay in Communist hands. Emboldened by their military successes, Communist leaders increased their claims in any final settlement for the region. However, far from being chastened by defeat, especially the loss of the regional capital at Changchun, Chiang Kai-shek and his commanders became even more determined to press their military campaign toward success and eliminate the hated Communists. Once more, in a mood of winner take all, leaders on both sides trusted to the hazards of war.

The Shifting Military Balance in Manchuria April-June

Political charge and countercharge volleyed between Chungking and Yenan as their troops struggled to wrest control from the departing Red Army troops in the Northeast. In an angry speech to the People's Political Council on April 1, Chiang Kai-shek sharply rejected Communist demands for a reorganization of his Northeast regional administration and recognition of their local governments and military forces.[139] At the same time, a Communist effort to establish a de facto coalition government in Liaopei province as a pattern for all of Manchuria was brushed aside by government leaders.[140] Responding to Chiang's rejection of their demands, the Communists charged that the Government had reneged on its agreement to discuss Northeast political problems. Mao personally penned a blistering response to the Government's position.[141]

Judging by how easily the CCP took over many of the areas evacuated by the Red Army, American officials in China were more than ever convinced that "direct contact and coordination [of] strategy exists between the Communists in Manchuria and the Russians."[142]

When Marshall returned to China after a month's absence in Washington, he found that neither side was willing to compromise its position on the Northeast. While privately blaming Nationalist intransigence, which he felt had led up to the present predicament, Marshall sought to convince both sides that a military solution in Manchuria was impossible. Acting on the apparent belief that the United States, and he in particular, held the key to the peace, Marshall attempted to revitalize the Committee of Three by drafting various plans for a Northeast cease-fire. However, the Nationalists refused to consider any plan until Communist forces evacuated Changchun, which they had seized on April 18, while the CCP, riding the crest of military victory, refused to comply. Chou En-lai bluntly criticized American policy for transporting Nationalist troops to Manchuria while simultaneously trying to arrange a peaceful settlement. At this juncture Marshall wrote to Truman that "the successful Communist generals in the Changchun area . . . are now, I feel sure, dominating the negotiations of their representatives." Yet he entertained the chimerical notion that he might induce Chou and possibly Mao as well to go to Manchuria and convince their stiff-necked military leaders of the need to compromise.[143] Finally, a change in the battlefield situation again proved decisive.

In the third week of May the lengthy Nationalist siege of Changchun ended with a Communist defeat. Shortly after Government troops occupied the city, a subdued Chou En-lai returned to the negotiating table seeking a Northeast truce. While a Communist wind had been blowing on the Northeast battlefield, Chou's diplomacy had not been needed. Once that wind had shifted, he was summoned to salvage what he could from the wrecked hopes of a quick military victory. It was now the Government's turn to be obdurate as Chiang Kai-shek encouraged his field commanders to follow up their victory.

Even before the Nationalist drive against Changchun, Marshall had warned Chiang against dreaming of a military victory in the Northeast, which he believed was well beyond the

Government's military capability. But as the Communist armies fled northward across the Sungari and their commander Lin Piao prepared to evacuate Harbin, Marshall's warnings sounded womanish to Chairman Chiang's ears. Implicitly admonishing Marshall for sheltering the faltering enemy, Chiang asserted that the CCP would accept the harsh terms he now offered them if only Marshall supported the Government's position. Marshall was adamant, however, and threatened to withdraw his services as mediator if Chiang's military offensive continued. Behind Marshall's threat stood the possible loss of American military assistance and economic aid that Chiang needed badly. Thus on June 6 the Chinese leader agreed to a fifteen-day truce in Manchuria, but he warned Marshall that "this would be his final effort at doing business with the Communists . . . all-out war would be preferable."[144]

In the labyrinthine negotiations that dragged on through the remainder of June during the extended truce, Marshall failed to bridge the gap between the Government's stiff demands and the Communists' bounded willingness to compromise. The latter feared that Chiang would not be satisfied with a harsh peace, but would try to use it to launch a final extermination drive against the Communists in the Northeast.[145] In fact, the Nationalist commander in the Northeast, General Tu Yu-ming, undoubtedly reflecting Chairman Chiang's mood, confidently predicted a complete rout of Lin Piao's armies once the truce expired.[146] Chou En-lai's proposals for a permanent end to the fighting reflected the CCP's desire to consolidate its weakened position within a northern Manchurian redoubt. When the extended truce expired on June 30 without an agreement on the tangled skein of issues, the Marshall mediation effort expired with it, despite the desultory rounds of inconclusive negotiations that dragged on over the next six months.

Conclusion

The final chapter of this book will address the larger question of the significance of international factors in the Chinese Communists' revolutionary victory. Here some interim observations on

Dreams and Reality: Nationalist General Tu Yu-ming dreams of capturing Harbin within ten days. Defeated Nationalist troops are welcomed to Harbin. *Tung-pei jih-pao*. March 26, 1947.

American and Soviet policy, particularly relating to the Northeast, may be in order.

　　Measured by the conventional yardstick, General Marshall's mediation effort not only failed to bring about a government of national union in China, but earned him and the United States the enmity of both Chinese antagonists. However, to wield such a yardstick is to confuse the instruments of the Marshall mission with its primary objectives which were to remove China as a node of conflict in Soviet-American relations and to keep Soviet political influence and control there to a minimum. From this perspective, what seems most worth noting is the fact that at a time when actual and incipient Soviet-American crisis points were popping up all over like a case of measles, China was not a contentious issue between the two powers from mid-1946 to 1950. The Marshall mission contributed indirectly to this.

　　In contrast to the dominant American view of the

Marshall mission as a failure, Soviet writers exalt the presumed
triumphs of Soviet statecraft, claiming that the Soviet Union both
adhered to a *principled* policy of nonintervention and that the USSR
made a decisive contribution to the CCP's victory in Manchuria.[147]
Despite their provenance, I believe one must examine seriously
Soviet claims concerning Moscow's contribution to the CCP
victory.

   As I have already observed, the Soviet leadership pursued a dualistic policy characterized by political maneuvering
designed to keep open Soviet options and to maintain Soviet
influence whatever the political outcome in China. Pursuing their
overlapping and sometimes contradictory interests in Manchuria,
the Soviets on balance facilitated the initial Communist efforts to
establish an organizational and, especially, a military presence in
the region, and frustrated Nationalist takeover efforts. Soon after
the Red Army withdrew from Manchuria in May 1946, the CCP
quickly experienced a sharp reversal of fortunes. But the Chinese
Communists never lost the toehold that Soviet assistance had
helped them gain in northern Manchuria. It is not too much to
suggest that Soviet assistance to the CCP, concentrated in the
initial phase of the struggle for the Northeast, may indeed have
spelled the difference *at that time* between success and failure. That
the Soviets were consciously following a policy designed to promote the country-wide victory of the CCP is at present an unsup-
portable proposition that can be tested only when and if Soviet
archives are opened to serious scholars. It seems more likely that
the Soviet preference accorded the CCP was an effect of the tortuous but essentially simple Soviet pursuit of national self-interest
rather than the conscious intent of that policy. As it happened,
the superior resources the CCP was able to mobilize for its struggle
against the Nationalists obviated the need for all-out Soviet support which Moscow's prudence would have denied the Communists in any case.

CHAPTER THREE

BUILDING A STRUCTURE OF COMMUNIST POWER IN MANCHURIA

THE fate of the Communist revolution in China was decided in large measure on the political and military battlefields of the Northeast. It is true that the crumbling of Nationalist power between 1945 and 1949 occurred more or less simultaneously nearly everywhere in China, but the Communist victory in Manchuria—the first region to come under total Communist control—provided the military and psychological momentum for the nation-wide Communist triumph. From early 1947 on, the steady flow of dismal reports from the Northeast chronicling the encirclement and defeat of Chiang Kai-shek's crack U.S.-trained troops helped to accelerate the demoralization of the Nationalist army and bureaucracy and speeded the disaffection of the urban middle classes and the intelligentsia. The occupation of Shenyang (Mukden) on November 2, 1948, by Lin Piao's Northeast People's Liberation Army after the Liaoshen campaign—one of the three great strategic Communist victories of the civil war—tolled the death knell for Nationalist China.

How did this happen? How could the Communist Party, which had virtually no supporters in Manchuria in 1945, win such a resounding victory in view of its previous record in the region of failure and defeat? That the CCP first completed its march to power in Manchuria is surely the central paradox of the revolutionary civil war.

The Communist Party came to power in Manchuria through a vast civil war in which massive regular armies confronted each other in large-scale conventional warfare. The antagonists in this civil war had sharply opposed conceptions of how to fight the conflict as well as of the kind of social order they wished to create. Chiang Kai-shek and the Nationalists enjoyed international recognition and support, especially from the United States. Confident of their military superiority over their Communist foe, they hoped to achieve a genuine integration of the Northeast into a Chinese state free from the canker of Manchurian regionalism. The Nationalist civilian bureaucracy and armies were grafted onto Northeast China. Remarkably little effort was ever made to secure a broad base of local support or to recruit troops from within the region. Even when the politico-military situation was deteriorating rapidly, Chiang Kai-shek resisted the importuning of pro-Nationalist Manchurians to release Chang Hsüeh-liang from captivity. The perpetrator of the Sian Incident and the prime symbol of Manchurian regionalism, Chang might conceivably have been able to rally non-Communist forces in the region. True to form, the Nationalists made virtually no effort to organize the countryside as a potential base of their power. Plagued by conflicts within their regional leadership and saddled with inept military commanders, the Nationalists ended up in their besieged cities surrounded by a hostile or indifferent countryside awaiting the final coups de grace. Their strategy of achieving victory in the Northeast through the use of unalloyed military power appears in retrospect to have had only slight chance of succeeding.

The Communists, too, of course, were very much dependent upon military power. And at first their forces were also transplanted from outside the region. Eventually, however, the Communist victory emerged from the connection established between the political and military organizations of the CCP, based in the cities of northern Manchuria, and the revolution in the Northeast countryside which these self-same organizations initiated and thereafter kept in motion. The restructuring of the social, economic, and political order in rural Manchuria enabled the

Communists to tap the sources of manpower and supplies which they needed to wage conventional war against the Nationalist armies. At the same time, the beneficiaries of change in the countryside—particularly the poor and the landless—moved slowly from a position of hostility or indifference toward a position of acceptance or support of the Communist revolution.

This process of securing allegiance and building power occurred within the context of an ongoing military conflict that imposed its own severe demands upon the Communist leadership. Pressed to the limits of their trained manpower, and desperate for supplies of every sort, what the Communists lacked most of all in Manchuria was time. To effect a revolutionary transformation of a rural society where they lacked local roots, the CCP needed time to recruit village activists, train cadres, organize local peasant associations, and attack local elites. But the exigencies of war required that the Communists swiftly recruit and provision an army or face defeat. Thus, the entire timetable of revolution had to be accelerated. This speedup imposed considerable strain on the relations between the Communist party and the rural and urban folk to whom the Party was appealing for support. But by relying upon the organizational superiority they had developed through years of work in intramural China, the Chinese Communists hastily brought into being new structures of power and rapidly organized revolution in the rural areas as well as the cities in order to harness the support needed to win the civil war.

During the first year after Japan's surrender, the Communists rebuilt their Party structure in the Northeast, organized a system of governments from the local up through the regional level, and, operating on unfamiliar terrain, groped their way toward a viable strategy.

The Political Setting
in the Northeast

After a prolonged struggle in the 1930s, the colonial regime of Manchukuo had imposed a harsh peace on Northeast China by suppressing all Chinese political and military organizations that threatened Japanese control. A long and bitter winter descended over the political life of the region. Japan's surrender in August 1945 signaled the beginning of a tumultuous period in which numerous organizations sprang up on Manchurian soil in a kind of primordial anarchy. With no effective centralized political authority to turn to, local communities reverted to their own time-tested ways of survival. In the aftermath of war, there were an abundance of demobilized soldiers; weapons were widely available. Bandits and gunslingers, political adventurers and predators, had a field day. For a brief moment before the imposition of a new Communist order, the wide-open life of the old Manchurian frontier revived in a final luxuriant display of chaos.

Japanese rule had undermined the oligarchic political system of Manchuria. The crisis of 1931–32 had splintered the old regional elite. Those who remained in the Northeast were politically compromised by their collaboration with the Japanese. Others, who followed the Nationalists to Chungking, lost their regional power base and failed to develop a cohesive factional organization within the Kuomintang that might have competed for power. The Northeast Army had been dispersed following the Sian Incident. At the regional level, then, Japan's surrender cleared the stage for a new group of actors.

Lower down the administrative hierarchy, however, particularly at the county and village levels, the most striking feature of politics was the continuity and tenacity of local elites. Buffeted by political currents from the outside, local elites mobilized their considerable skills and resources and waged desperate but ultimately unsuccessful struggles to retain their power and privilege. It is no exaggeration to say that the outcome of the civil war in the Northeast hinged in large measure on the ability of the Communists to break the power of the local elites and thereby gain mastery of the countryside.

In short, it was far from a political vacuum that the Communists and Nationalists were entering in the Northeast. What was missing, however, from the constellation of military and political forces were organizations that could function effectively on a region-wide or even a provincial plane. In the immediate postwar period, politics in the Northeast had not only been decapitated by the removal of the regional elite, but fragmented—

reduced to a congeries of micro-level political processes. There were no groups or movements within the region capable of reintegrating the fractured polity; hence the initiative for political reconstruction would have to come from the outside.

This fragmentation presented both an opportunity and a problem for the CCP. Before the war, the Party had failed to secure a foothold in the Northeast; it had competed from a position of great weakness against much more powerful adversaries who disposed of regional political and military networks and additional resources that could be brought to bear from outside Manchuria. The prewar CCP had proved incapable of sustaining either urban political organizing or rural guerrilla warfare against relatively well-integrated, coordinated, and determined Chinese militarists and Japanese imperialists. However, by 1945 the CCP's wartime growth in North China enabled it to dispatch to the Northeast a sizable military and political nucleus which could join the competition for power.

The fragmentation of opposition to the establishment of Communist power meant that, especially in the political dimension of the struggle, the CCP had to engage in numerous local struggles, each with its own peculiar features. At this most basic level the CCP was initially quite weak. Its corps of transplanted cadres was unfamiliar with the varied local circumstances they daily encountered, uncertain as to who were their friends and potential allies, shut out from the informal networks of power and authority, and frequently deceived by their local adversaries as to the true situation within a given locality. In small-scale military engagements as well, the Communist local forces, usually recruited from peasants with little or no prior military training, were often inferior to the assorted irregular armed detachments they encountered. What gave the Communists a decisive advantage in both the political and military dimensions of their struggles against local adversaries were the regional and main forces that could be pressed into service to combat those enemies. These were deployed alongside local militia or county public security forces. These combined Communist forces proved more powerful than any of the local troops arrayed against them.

This margin of military superiority was also a kind of insurance policy against the commission of political errors. Within the base areas established by the CCP in northern Manchuria in the early stages of the civil war, the Communists enjoyed a certain latitude to experiment with policies. Because the Party's control remained secured by military power, they could even afford to engage in periodic bouts of ultra-leftism even though they thereby alienated middle peasants and other centrist elements. Communist armed forces played a vital role in the political alliances that Party cadres constructed at the local levels. In effecting change at village and county levels, Party work teams sought to build alliances with such local leaders and groups who were willing to respond favorably, neutralize those who would not commit themselves, and attack only those forces which resisted the revolutionary transfer of power. It is reasonable to suppose that local leaders adapted their behavior in recognition of the balance of local coercive forces when deciding whether to align with or resist the CCP. The effect of the local military preponderance was to facilitate the CCP's political task by predisposing local elites to acquiesce in Communist-directed change in order to preserve what they could of their position within the emerging new order.

In short, the political environment in the Northeast on the eve of the civil war had contained a multitude of military-cum-political forces whose sum was less than the total of their parts because they lacked both horizontal and vertical integrating links. Even in its relatively weak initial form, the CCP in the Northeast contained the potential for rapid development precisely because it was an integrated political organization that could coordinate and control both political and military action on a scale sufficiently larger than any of its local opponents.

If the CCP's local enemies lacked the capacity to coordinate their disparate forces at levels above the village or county, the Nationalists suffered from the opposite weakness. They proved unable to make their presence felt at these crucial lower levels. Like the Communists, the Kuomintang had never been a strong organization in prewar Manchuria, and their illegal underground urban apparatus had also been all but destroyed by the Japanese. The National Government's efforts to establish its power in the Northeast from the fall of 1945 through the spring of 1946 were seriously impeded by Soviet occupation policy. Yet even after the Red Army withdrew and the Communists had been pushed north

of the Sungari River, the Nationalists did not extend their organization much beyond the larger cities and their hinterlands. Like
the Japanese before them, the Nationalists channeled their military assets into the task of controlling the urban areas and the
modern communications/transportation system, and neglected
the power potential of the smaller cities, the county seats, and the
countryside itself. The result was that a crucial gap opened up
between the Nationalists at the apex of the hierarchy of urban
places and their potential supporters at lower levels of the system.
The Communist-armed work teams entered through this gap,
followed by the mobile armed forces of the Northeast People's
Liberation Army. Not until it was already much too late did Nanking make even half-hearted efforts to enlist the human and material resources of the Northeast in the struggle against the Communists. By then the tide of battle had already shifted. With the
strategic initiative in the hands of Lin Piao's forces, the beleaguered
Nationalist urban garrisons numbly awaited defeat.

Evolution of a Regional Strategy

Communist civil war strategy in the Northeast evolved gradually
in response to changing opportunities and constraints deriving
from the roles of external powers (the United States and the
USSR), the strategy and tactics of the Nationalists, the degree of
popular mobilization achieved at the basic levels and overall developments in the nation-wide conflict. Within the centrally coordinated but flexibly controlled Chinese Communist movement,
political and military leaders in the Northeast apparently had a
major though probably not a decisive voice in devising regional
strategy. Given the rapidly changing structure of opportunities in
1945–46, it is not surprising that alternate solutions to the politico-military strategic questions were offered by different CCP
leaders in the Northeast. By mid-1946, however, as the CCP set
its course on civil war and dismissed the idea of a negotiated
political settlement as a "peaceful illusion," regional strategy for
the Northeast was set in a pattern that persisted until final victory.
    On the eve of Japan's surrender, the CCP had had

merely a determination to contest control of the Northeast rather than a strategy for actually doing so. As noted above, the Seventh Party Congress had approved the active expansion of Communist power into areas controlled by the Japanese so as to secure an advantageous position vis-à-vis the Nationalists in the postwar period. Conscious of the wealth and strategic importance of Manchuria in the impending struggle for power, Communist leaders determined to expand their influence into the region. As noted above, in late August 1945 Mao Tse-tung had stated his party's readiness to make concessions so long as these did not damage "the fundamental interests of the people."[1] The Communists' fundamental strategy was to yield nothing of substance until a transformation of the existing political system had deprived Chiang Kai-shek of the possibility of destroying them by military force. Meanwhile, the CCP moved vigorously to expand the territory under its control. In this connection, the Northeast was seen as the primary objective, possession of which would be equally vital either in a period of peaceful political competition or in outright civil war against the Nationalists. Spurred by Soviet entry into the war and Tokyo's surrender, the Central Committee of the CCP sometime in mid-August 1945 decided to dispatch a large contingent of troops, cadres, and high-ranking leaders to the Northeast.[2] We shall examine below how this decision was implemented. In connection with the international maneuvering over Manchuria, we have already described in a preliminary fashion the CCP's efforts to establish it presence in the region, block the influx of Nationalist troops, alter the regional governing authority, and extract maximum advantage from the complaisant Soviet military occupation. Now let us turn to the question of overall Party strategy in the region.

In abstract terms, two different approaches to the Northeast on the part of CCP leaders may be distinguished. I shall call these the *conventional* and the *situational* approaches. The difference between these approaches turned on the questions of what were the most important bases of power in the Northeast and how the CCP could best gain control of these assets. The *conventional approach* took the Party's wartime growth in North China as the template for postwar expansion into the Northeast. The core idea was to cede the main cities of central and southern Manchuria and the lines of communication to the Nationalists in the early stages of the war and to build up strength in the smaller cities, county seats, and rural areas of the region via policies of mass mobilization with the aim of consolidating secure base areas and promoting military recruitment. It was presumed that a fairly long period of revolutionary development and army-building would be required before Communist military forces would become strong enough to defeat the initially superior Nationalist armies. Eventually, the enemy's urban citadels and garrisons would be conquered in the final stage of a protracted revolutionary struggle.[3] Such a familiar scenario is widely assumed to have been the actual process by which the CCP won the civil war. As I shall seek to demonstrate, this model provides at best only a partial understanding of the CCP's victory in the Northeast.

The *situational approach* was grounded in the hope that the CCP might find a shortcut to power in the Northeast because conditions there differed substantially from those in North China. The presence of friendly Soviet forces, the difficulty Nationalist forces were encountering in extending their control, the fragmentation of local opposition, and the rapid buildup of Communist military and organizational strength raised the possibility that the CCP might gain sole possession of much if not all of the Northeast within a matter of weeks or months. Rather than pursuing a pinchpenny strategy of husbanding military forces and building up strength in the hinterlands, advocates of this alternate strategy apparently favored taking high risks for high stakes. This meant the liberal use of the armed forces in positional battles to retain control of the large cities in southern and central Manchuria that twice came under the CCP's control in 1945–46. This strategy, which dangled the prospect of an early victory in a key area, proved well beyond the military capabilities of the CCP in this period. That certain Communist leaders in the Northeast were drawn to it, however, suggests that there were highly placed individuals within the Party who viewed the Maoist conventional revolutionary strategy as a second-best alternative and saw the cities as a central revolutionary objective and a key power base.

For analytic purposes, it is possible to distinguish between the conventional and the situational approaches as I have done. In reality, however, we have too little reliable information to be able to judge whether a protracted intra-Party conflict over regional strategy actually transpired. Cultural Revolution sources, reflecting the temporary ascendancy of Lin Piao, depicted a struggle in 1945–46 between Lin, the supposed faithful executor of Mao Tse-tung's revolutionary line, and P'eng Chen, cast as Liu Shao-ch'i's faithful lieutenant in the Northeast who opposed Mao.[4] Naturally, this interpretation did not survive Lin Piao's purported treachery and death in 1971. It is possible to suggest an alternate version of intra-Party conflict over Northeast strategy. More plausible than a consistent clash between the aforementioned conventional and situation approaches, I believe, is the possibility that Northeast CCP leaders shifted their positions in response to the changing strategic equation in Manchuria. Rarely did the alternate approaches crystallize into divergent concrete policy choices. For a time, the "situational" approach served as the counterpoint to the dominant "conventional" theme.

When Yenan initially decided to mount a bid for the Northeast, it was in the hope of reproducing the formula for CCP success in North China—a combination of careful organizational work in the base areas and opportune military expansion. Hence Yenan's decision in August 1945 to dispatch large contingents of political cadres and troops to the region. By the time significant numbers of political organizers arrived in Manchuria (October–November 1945), the Communist armies, equipped from Japanese stockpiles and assisted by the Soviets, had already moved with surprising ease into the metropolitan centers of Shenyang, Changchun, and Harbin as well as many smaller cities. For the urban expatriates who constituted the Communist leadership core, the possibility of commanding such cities must have been a dizzying prospect. At the Seventh Party Congress, Mao himself had spoken of the need to conquer the cities.[5] The contrast between poverty-stricken provincial Yenan and the wealthy, urbanized Northeast was not lost on regional leaders like P'eng Chen and Lin Feng who had previously worked in the urban "white areas." Moreover, the occupation and development of urban bases was not necessarily inconsistent with the more familiar North China rural-oriented organizational work that was just getting underway in the Northeast.

This short-lived urban idyll came to an abrupt end

with the Soviet decision of mid-November 1945 to facilitate, however inadequately, the Nationalist takeover and the deployment of powerful National Government forces in Shenyang and the southern districts. Communist forces retreated into the countryside. Ch'en Yün, powerful member of the Northeast Bureau, and his colleagues Kao Kang and Chang Wen-t'ien, in a November 30, 1945, message, said that the Party should disperse its military forces and cadres to northern, eastern, and western Manchuria, to the countryside and medium and small cities such as Mutankiang, Chiamussu, Ilan, Peian, and Naho. Since the Soviet Union was determined to hand over the main cities to the Nationalists, there was no point in concentrating Communist forces around those cities.[6] In the fall of 1945, Kao Kang wrote, "The work in the Northeast should be deep in the countryside, mobilizing the masses, dividing the land, and broadening the resources for soldiers. We must lead the cadres out of the foreign houses, leave the cities, give up automobiles, take off leather shoes and go to the countryside."[7]

Yenan's favorable response to the beginning of Marshall's mediation reenforced the logic of an urban pullback strategy in the Northeast to avoid confrontations while negotiations commenced. It was in this context that Mao issued a directive to the CCP's Northeast Bureau in late December reaffirming his basic line. Addressing those leaders who believed that Northeast conditions were exceptional, Mao argued: "We must thoroughly clear away all ideas among our cadres of winning easy victories through good luck, without hard and bitter struggle, without sweat and blood."[8] Temporarily conceding the major cities and lines of communication to the Nationalists, Mao emphasized the need to build stable base areas in those districts comparatively remote from enemy-controlled territory, a process which he estimated would take several years. Mass mobilization and organizational development were the keys to success.

As noted earlier, Mao and Chou En-lai's shared hope of deriving substantial political benefits from American mediation required the temporary sacrifice of some Communist gains in the Northeast. Marshall had turned a deaf ear to Chou's pleas that restrictions be placed on the number of Nationalist troops permitted into the Northeast. As Chiang Kai-shek's armies moved into

Manchuria, Communist military leaders there had ample reason for concern. They knew much better than Yenan how tenuous was the CCP's position not only in the major cities which were now emptied of all but the CCP's underground apparatus, but even in the smaller towns and the countryside that Mao had targeted. The Northeast was threatening to turn into a strategic cul de sac instead of a promising new base area. The Yenan CCP spokesman who, in mid-February 1946, reasserted the demand that limits be imposed on Nationalist troop movements to the Northeast was very likely articulating a viewpoint pressed strongly in inner Party councils by the Northeast regional leadership.

At the Meihok'ou Conference of the Northeast Bureau in February 1946—the high tide of Marshall's mediation effort—a dispute erupted between First Secretary P'eng Chen and army commander Lin Piao. According to Cultural Revolution sources, Lin accused P'eng of slighting the mass line, fostering the illusion of peaceful accommodation with the Nationalists, and failing to prepare for war. Lin is quoted as having said:

Peace is not possible without a victory for the revolutionary war. We have at present still no base areas in the Northeast, and we are therefore without a home. The cities do not belong to us for the time being, and we can only regard them as hotels and live in them for a while. Unless we build base areas in the countryside, we have no way to overcome the enemy, and might even die of hunger and cold.[9]

P'eng defended himself, saying that conditions in the Northeast were different from elsewhere and justified a policy of defending the cities against the Nationalists. The allegation that P'eng opposed Mao's line on base-building while Lin upheld it is at best a distortion reflecting the likelihood that P'eng did place considerable weight on acquiring and defending the cities. As for the question of peaceful accommodation versus preparations for war, since the CCP was then negotiating with the Nationalists within the Marshall framework, Lin's accusation translates into the charge that P'eng was guilty of faithfully implementing the Mao-Chou policy of the time. In contrast, Lin was expressing the army's irritation with an approach that threatened its power. Let us recall that at the end of February a military reorganization agreement between the CCP and the KMT was signed which, had it been implemented, would have sharply cut the number of Communist divisions and abolished the "party armies." This initial confrontation at Meihok'ou produced no immediate impact on policy which now shifted once more in response to the Soviet military withdrawal commencing in mid-March.

Again the lure of the cities proved too great to resist. While Nationalist troops bivouacked in southern Manchuria awaiting the will-o'-the-wisp of Soviet cooperation, Communist troops reentered the cities of northern and central Manchuria, including Changchun and Harbin, from the surrounding countryside and ousted Nationalist takeover personnel. Whether or not cocky Communist regional leaders forced this decision on Yenan is impossible to say, but it is certain that this bold initiative struck a mortal blow at Marshall's conciliation process. There is no evidence that Lin Piao, whose troops implemented this policy, opposed what was a radical departure from Mao's cautious policy of constructing stable base areas in the Northeast. Nor is it likely that Yenan itself—probably divided in its own counsels as I have suggested—tried to stay this military coup de main.

If P'eng Chen wanted the cities he would have to fight for them. Contrary to their usually cautious tactics of avoiding major enemy forces, the Communists now directly confronted the Nationalist Army in strength in an attempt to stop its drive north along the Shenyang-Harbin rail line. The decision to wage a major positional battle at the key rail juncture of Ssup'ingchieh (April–May 1946) clearly indicates that the regional high command intended to hold on to the cities they had just occupied. This proved to be a nearly fatal mistake. After absorbing thousands of casualties in the course of resisting a prolonged Nationalist siege, the Communist forces at Ssup'ingchieh finally cracked and the rail line north was opened at last to Tu Yu-ming's armies. In short order the NEDUA evacuated Changchun and Kirin. By the time of the June cease-fire, the Nationalists had occupied a score of cities that had been under Communist control, including Anshan, Changchun, K'aiyuan, and Kirin.[10]

The conflict within the Northeast Bureau came to a head as a result of the series of devastating military defeats. Not surprisingly, P'eng Chen was chosen as the scapegoat for the disaster. It was later charged (in the Cultural Revolution) that

May 1946 in Harbin. From the left: First Secretary of the Northeast Bureau Peng Chen; Commander-in-Chief of the Northeast Democratic United Army Lin Piao; and one of his deputies, Lu Cheng-ts'ao.

P'eng had "refused to carry out Chairman Mao's correct policy of shifting positions on our own initiative to avoid losses, thus bringing undue losses to our army at Ssup'ing."[11] In June–July 1946 an enlarged meeting of the Northeast Bureau convened, presided over by Lin Piao, who by this time had apparently gained Mao's backing. P'eng was criticized and demoted from his position as First Secretary of the Northeast Bureau and Chief Political Commissar of the NEDUA and replaced by Lin Piao in both positions.[12] P'eng continued to serve in the Northeast as a member of the Northeast Bureau and as Deputy Political Commissar until late 1947 when he was shifted to North China. From June 1946 until the end of the civil war, Lin Piao was the most powerful Communist leader in the Northeast and accorded honor and attention in the Communist press second only to Mao Tse-tung himself.

P'eng Chen's demotion made very little sense in strictly policy terms because the circumstances that had produced his "deviation" had ceased to exist. Now the line that Mao had decreed in December became the only possible course of action. A Northeast Bureau draft resolution of July 7, 1946, written by

Ch'en Yün reaffirmed the correctness of the Maoist strategy of base-building. Even prior to his victory at the Northeast Bureau plenum, Lin Piao had put an optimistic face on the dim situation, saying that "with our troops withdrawn from Ssup'ing, Chiang Kai-shek will have his men occupy the large cities. That doesn't matter. We can give all the cities south of the Sungari to him . . . When the enemy has many cities to defend, his forces will have to be decentralized and we can then conquer them one by one."[13] Thus, in the wake of military setbacks, making a virtue of necessity, the CCP in the Northeast now under Lin Piao's leadership reverted to the "classic" Maoist pattern of revolutionary warfare.

In the summer of 1946, the CCP indeed renewed its efforts to establish secure base areas in northern Manchuria. In a peculiar sense, as Lin Piao had intimated, the military defeats of 1946 turned out to be a blessing in disguise. They forced the CCP to redirect its energies to the organizational and mobilizational tasks it was best suited for within an area small enough not to overstrain its still limited resources. The severe pruning the transplanted Communist organization received at the hands of the Nationalists proved nearly fatal, but in the longer run it helped promote new and more vigorous growth.

The Renascence of the Northeast Communist Movement

The preceding overview of the evolution of CCP strategy in the Northeast during 1945–46 enables us now to examine in closer detail the actual process of organization-building in the region. In looking toward the Northeast at the end of the anti-Japanese War, the CCP had to start virtually from scratch. The destruction of the Manchurian Provincial Committee and the NEAJUA had left the Communists with no organized political or military presence in Manchuria by the early 1940s. Efforts to reconstruct a military base in the region had begun in 1944, but Japanese and Manchukuo troops stymied the 8th Route Army's attempt to expand into Jehol and southern Liaoning.[14] The Liaoning section of the Hopei-Jehol-Liaoning liberated area was a small patch of thinly populated rough terrain west of Chinchow on the edge of the Liaohsi corridor.[15] The prospects for expanding this base looked dim in early 1945. Nevertheless, at the end of June 1945, Communist troops again fought their way from south of the Great Wall toward Jehol. Lt. General Li Yun-chang, commanding about 10,000 troops in northeastern Hopei, was in charge of the operation. Elements of this force were besieged and surrounded by the Japanese as late as the first week of August 1945. Soviet intervention and the Japanese surrender quickly transformed this unpromising situation.[16]

On or about August 18, Soviet Red Army troops linked up with 8th Route Army forces in the strategic Inner Mongolian town of Kalgan, and a few days later met Communist regular forces at Weichang, almost due north of Chengteh in Jehol, then considered a part of Manchuria.[17] Contact between the Red Army and Communist forces proceeded by land and sea. From the Shantung ports of Lungkow and Yent'ai, which the 8th Route Army entered in late August, it was an easy sea voyage to the Liaotung peninsula. A representative of the Chiaotung District CCP Committee in Shantung, Lo Chu-an, journeyed to the headquarters of the Soviet 39th Army in Lushun (Port Arthur) with a letter inquiring of the Soviets "through what means we can unite with the Red Army and begin our work in Manchuria."[18]

The forces of Tseng K'o-lin and Chang Ts'ai-fang, officers of the Chi-Je-Liao military district, rendezvoused with the Red Army in a small town just south of Suichung on the Peining Railroad and carried out a successful joint attack against Japanese forces in Shanhaikuan who were waiting to surrender to the Chinese Nationalists.[19] These troops continued along the rail line accompanied by Soviet liaison personnel. Their task was as much political as it was military. At every way station they dropped off a platoon or a squad and some cadres from a local work group *(ti-fang kung-tso tui)* to act as the nucleus for establishing local administrations. In this fashion, Tseng's and Chan's forces occupied thirteen counties and two cities, first disarming and then incorporating some 7,000 puppet troops en route to Shenyang.[20] The forces quickly grew to 60,000 men.[21]

Similar Sino-Soviet contacts multiplied during September. According to a Soviet source, Li Yun-chang wrote the commander of the Soviet 17th Army that Chu Teh had ordered his troops "to proceed to Manchuria in order to coordinate efforts with your army, but in view of the fact that we lack modern vehicular transport and because of the rainy weather we did not arrive in time. At once our enemies all capitulated to your troops."[22] On September 14, Chu Teh cabled the Soviet commander of the Zabaikalsk Front seeking permission for 8th Route Army forces operating in Jehol and Liaoning to maintain their positions. These fragmentary reports hint at an initial Soviet reluctance to comply with these calls for cooperation.[23] If this was so, it probably reflected Soviet uncertainty as to the extent of American involvement in restoring Nationalist hegemony in Manchuria. Soon it became clear that overt American support of Chiang would be limited to North China.

The movement of Communist troops from North China to Manchuria continued on a large scale throughout 1945 and into 1946. This military migration consisted of streams with sources in Yenan, Shantung, northern Kiangsu, and elsewhere in North China.[24] Many thousands came across the rough lands of Jehol into Manchuria. Even more came overland from Shantung and Hopei via the Liaohsi corridor or by sea from small ports on the northern Shantung coast. They carried few weapons, expecting to be refitted from arms dumps in the Northeast. Approximately 100,000 Communist troops were redeployed to the Northeast in the first few months after Japan's surrender, approximately one-sixth of the regular forces. Remnants of the NEAJUA led by Chou Pao-chung and Li Chao-lin which had taken refuge in the Soviet Union in 1940–41 returned to Manchuria along with the Red Army in August 1945.[25]

Intensive military recruitment within the region augmented the troops brought in from the outside. Scattered survivors of the anti-Japanese communist resistance began to revive local guerrilla forces following the Japanese capitulation, but this occurred only on a minor scale. Once elements of the 8th Route Army entered the Northeast, they commenced an intensive recruitment campaign, often using rough and ready methods to swell their ranks.[26] There was certainly no shortage of men from among what Katherine Chorley has called "that driftwood set of tough adventurers who are left in any country by the receding tide of a war."[27] The Communists incorporated at least 75,000 soldiers from the former Manchukuo Army, a large reservoir of experienced men whom the Nationalists largely shunned.[28] It was not until many months later, however, that Communist officers were able to shape these disparate materials into a unified fighting force. An American observer noted in late 1945 that the Communist troops in Manchuria "were poorly organized and indoctrinated and the spirit of opportunism makes wholesale defection possible."[29] This evaluation is curiously echoed in another Cultural Revolution charge against P'eng Chen. With respect to building an army, it was charged, P'eng Chen and his associates "resorted to the brigandish policy of 'enlisting followers,' recruited deserters and turncoats to enlarge their forces."[30] Ch'en Yün, complaining of the paucity of old troops in northern Manchuria (there were only 1,500 in November 1946) said that many of the new troops there (25,000) were unreliable and some units revolted when under attack in the field. The Communist forces did grow very quickly, however. By December 1945 there were already about 200,000 men in the Communists' Northeast armies. In January 1946, the various forces were formally merged into the Northeast Democratic United Army *(Tung-pei min-chu lien-chün)*. By July 1946, the Communists had about 300,000 troops in the Northeast of which some 100,000 were main force field army soldiers.[31]

These initial Communist efforts at rapid military recruitment were intended to provide a force which could not only block the Nationalist advance into Manchuria and reap the benefits of covert collaboration with the Soviet Red Army, but could also shield the local administrations which the Communists were feverishly creating from the fall of 1945 on. But this early jerry-built army crumbled under the impact of the crack Nationalist divisions in the late spring 1946 offensives against Communist-held cities. The armies Lin Piao led to victory in 1947 and 1948 were recruited along different lines and were much better trained and indoctrinated than the levies of 1945–46.

These early attempts at army building were paralleled by the initial stages of reconstructing a Communist Party organization in the Northeast. Soon after Japan's surrender, the battered survivors of the Communist prewar party organization emerged from their dispersed underground positions. A provisional provincial committee of the CCP for northern Manchuria was established as early as August 17 in Harbin by underground Party workers, most of whom were probably prisoners liberated by the Red Army or NEAJUA leaders who had returned to Manchuria with the Soviet forces. Over the next several weeks municipal Party committees were established in such other major cities as Shenyang, Talien, Lushun, and Chinchow. Cadres dispatched from the Chi-Je-Liao liberated area established Party committees in various counties in Jehol. These early Party groups were preoccupied with basic organizational work and simple propaganda.[32]

Political workers attached to the Communist armies played a key role in the reestablishment of Party nuclei in the region. As 8th Route Army detachments fanned out across Manchuria, Party cadres helped to organize local civil administrations and Party units in the places occupied by the army. The Party remained dominated by its military component. In northern Manchuria, some 60 percent of new Party members (1,000 in all) were soldiers as of the spring of 1946.[33]

Contemplating the task of reconstructing the Northeast Party organization, Yenan faced two serious problems. The first was the extreme shortage of cadres in Manchuria and the second was the absence of reliable and experienced Party leaders to direct and coordinate the work. No time was wasted in addressing these problems.

Shortly after Japan's surrender, in accordance with a Central Committee decision, the first groups of Northeast-bound cadres were dispatched from Yenan. Most of these were recent graduates of the cadre training schools established in Yenan during the anti-Japanese war. Additional groups were sent throughout the fall on an arduous two-month trek on foot that took them from the wind-swept loess hills of northern Shensi, across the Yellow River, through the mountains of northern Shansi and the rail towns of Kalgan and Ch'engteh before they arrived at Ch'ihfeng where they continued on by train. One trekker's memoir conveys a vivid sense of the trials of this journey.

Setting off with wives and dependents (babies and meager possessions strapped to the backs of mules), the column of cadres marched in semi-military fashion, skirting danger points and slipping past the Nationalists' blockade lines. Reaching the Ch'ihfeng railhead, they discovered that all but one of the engineers had fled. They hooked together some freight cars to a doubtful-looking locomotive. With no coal at hand and the water pump broken, they fired the furnace with wood and soybean cake and filled the boiler by hand from tubs of water. When the train got stuck at one point, the engineer promptly took to his heels and one of the cadres took over the controls. Chugging up the hills and threading through the tunnels, this little engine that could finally arrived in Shenyang.[34] Although an accurate figure is difficult to come by, roughly 10,000 Party workers journeyed to the Northeast in similar fashion. Very likely CCP Organization Department personnel combed their files and their memories for native Northeasterners to join this migration, but there could not have been very many such persons in view of the Party's prewar weakness in the region.[35] In fact, the extremely high proportion of cadres from outside the Northeast posed a recurrent problem with which the leadership struggled throughout the civil war.

Yenan addressed the second problem of regional leadership in a particularly bold and decisive manner. Early Party activities in the Northeast were quite diverse and lacking in centralized coordination. In particular, the scattered Communists who emerged from underground or prison, as well as those who returned with the Red Army, had long since been out of touch with the Party center. During the anti-Japanese war, in fact, the difficulty of communications among the noncontiguous base areas and the demands of guerrilla warfare had favored a devolution of decision making and other leadership functions to intermediate and lower levels of Party and military organizations. With the approach of victory, Yenan felt the need for greater centralization to prepare the organization for the new tasks and tactics that lay ahead. In his report to the Seventh Party Congress, Liu Shao-ch'i condemned mountain-topism—the tendency of local Party groups to encapsulate themselves and display aloofness, indifference, or suspicion to outside comrades—as the main danger to Party solidarity and unity.[36] The specter of local Party groups acting independently at a time when the Party might need to execute rapid changes in policy prompted Yenan to reassert its control over organization and operation.

In the Northeast the problem was particularly acute given the history of the old Manchurian Provincial Committee which had never had more than tenuous links with the Party center and had been unduly influenced by the Soviet Communists. Moreover, the intrinsic importance of the region in the impending struggle for power suggested the need for experienced high-ranking men at the helm. Experienced leaders could manage the problem of administering such cities as Shenyang which at least temporarily had come under Communist control, could deal with the potentially explosive friction between new cadres from outside Manchuria and the remnant underground native cadres, and most effectively secure whatever benefits the Party hoped to obtain from the Soviet presence in the Northeast without being excessively beholden to Moscow.

In early September 1945, Tseng K'o-lin, one of the first Communist military leaders to enter the Northeast, flew from Shenyang to Yenan to report to a meeting of high-ranking Party officials chaired by Liu Shao-ch'i, acting head of the Central Committee during Mao's absence in Chungking. Following Tseng's report, Liu stated that because of its favorable geographical position (its contiguity to the USSR), and its well-developed communications and industry, the Northeast could become an important strategic base for the CCP. He announced that the Central Committee had already decided to dispatch a large number of cadres and main force troops to the region to further the central objective of taking over Japanese and Manchukuo arms, expanding the people's armed forces, setting the masses in motion, and striving to gain control of the Northeast.[37]

When Tseng K'o-lin flew back to Shenyang after several days in Yenan, he was accompanied by the nucleus of the new Northeast Party leadership, including P'eng Chen, Ch'en Yün, Wu Hsiu-ch'üan, and Yeh Chi-chuang. These men were soon joined by Lin Piao, Li Fu-ch'un, Lo Jung-huan, Chang Wen-t'ien, and others.[38] In short order no fewer than nine of the forty-four full members (20.5 percent) and ten of the thirty-three alternate members (30.3 percent) of the Seventh Central Committee were assigned to the Northeast (see table 3.1). There could be no more vivid evidence of the importance Yenan assigned to securing control of the region. In addition to these top-ranking figures, many

TABLE 3.1 Members of the 7th CC Assigned to Manchuria During the Civil War

Name	Native Province
Chang Wen-t'ien	Kiangsu
Ch'en Yü (alt)	Kwangtung
Ch'en Yun	Kiangsu
Ch'eng Tzu-hua (alt)	Shansi
Hsiao Ching-kuang (alt)	Hunan
Huang K'o-ch'eng (alt)	Hunan
Kao Kang	Shensi
Ku Ta-ts'un (alt)	Kwangtung
Li Fu-ch'un	Hunan
Li Li-san	Hunan
Lin Feng	*Heilungkiang*
Lin Piao	Hupeh
Lo Jung-huan	Hunan
Lü Cheng-ts'ao (alt)	*Liaoning*
P'eng Chen	Shansi
T'an Cheng (alt)	Hunan
Wan I (alt)	*Liaoning*
Wang Chia-hsiang (alt)	Anhwei
Wang Shou-tao (alt)	Hunan

(alt) indicates alternate number.

Based on Donald W. Klein and Ann B. Clark, *Biographic Dictionary of Chinese Communism, 1921–1965.*

other important Party leaders joined the swarm of cadres heading for the Northeast.[39] It is worth noting that only three of these men were natives of Manchuria and that they represented all but one of the four Northeastern members of the Seventh Central Committee (the fourth—Kuan Hsiang-ying—was dying of tuberculosis).

Sometime in the early autumn of 1945 the Northeast Bureau of the Central Committee *(Tung-pei chü)* was established as the leading regional Party organization.[40] It functioned throughout the civil war period as the de facto supreme military and political headquarters for the Communist movement in the Northeast. From its establishment until June 1946, as already noted, it was headed by P'eng Chen, who served concurrently as head of its Organization Department and Chief Political Commissar of the NEDUA.[41]

During the civil war period the Northeast Bureau appears to have included at one time or another the persons listed in table 3.2. All but four of these were members or alternates of the Seventh Central Committee. (The exceptions were Hsiao K'o,

TABLE 3.2   Members of the Northeast Bureau of the CC 1945–1948

Chang Wen-t'ien	Li Li-san
Ch'en Yun	Lin Feng
Hsiao Ching-kuang	Lin Piao
Hsiao K'o*	Lo Jung-huan
Kai Feng*	P'eng Chen
Kao Kang	Tsou Ta-p'eng
Ku Ta-ts'un	Wang Chia-hsiang
Li Fu-ch'un	Wang Ho-shou*

* Not a CC member.

K'ai Feng, Tsou Ta-p'eng, and Wang Ho-shou.) The paucity of native Manchurians in the top Party hierarchy is shown by the fact that only two members of the Northeast Bureau (Lin Feng and Tsou Ta-p'eng) were Northeasterners. In striking contrast, the provincial and regional governments that the Communists set up in 1945–46 were headed almost entirely by native Northeasterners at the upper echelons.

Power within the Northeast Bureau was further concentrated within its Standing Committee of five or six top leaders who constituted a kind of regional Politburo. P'eng Chen, Lin Piao, Chang Wen-t'ien, Li Fu-ch'un, Kao Kang, Lin Feng, and Lo Jung-huan appear to have been members of this inner core of the regional leadership.

Functioning under the Northeast Bureau was the West Manchurian Sub-Bureau headed by Li Fu-ch'un, a North Manchurian Sub-Bureau headed by Ch'en Yün, and provincial Party organizations for the nine provinces into which the Northeast had been divided at the end of the war (Nunkiang, Liaoning, Liaopei, Antung, Hsingan, Kirin, Sungkiang, Hokiang, Heilungkiang). The civil war was a time of frequent reorganization in the Northeast at the provincial level as the leadership attempted to achieve an optimum size for effective control and coordination while keeping administrative costs within limits. These administrative changes were reflected within the Party apparatus itself. The Northeast Bureau was divided along functional lines with departments dealing with organization, propaganda, finance, and so forth. Initially located in Shenyang, the Northeast Bureau was transferred to Tunghua in December 1945 and finally came to rest in Harbin in April 1946 for the duration of the revolutionary civil war.

The establishment of the Northeast Bureau facilitated

the integration of the Party's work in the region with the overall policy of the CCP laid down in Yenan. In the 1920s and 1930s the Manchurian Provincial Committee had functioned semi-autonomously and on more than one occasion had strayed from or even resisted central policy directives. Now the danger of such regional particularism was reduced. In true Chinese fashion, the primary means of achieving party integration was through personnel rather than institutional arrangements. The leadership team dispatched to the Northeast in the fall of 1945 comprised men who had held top positions in the central Party apparatus and the Communist base areas. Their loyalty to the center derived from the fact that they themselves were part of the center, and this, more than the formal subordination of the Northeast Bureau to the Central Committee, was to guarantee the implementation of central Party directives in the Northeast. Even so, there were occasional disagreements and differences of emphasis between the center and the regional Party leadership. Yet these never developed into the open conflict and disharmony that marred relations between the Nationalist center and its Northeast apparatus, particularly in the sphere of military operations. In part as a matter of deliberate policy and in part because of inadequate communications and control, Yenan accorded a significant degree of autonomy to its regional politico-military commanders and refrained from specifying operational details or the fine points of policy implementation.

Building a Government Structure

Rebuilding the Party apparatus was one aspect of the CCP's organizational task in postwar Manchuria. No less important, particularly in view of Yenan's national political strategy, was the creation of a network of Communist-led governments at both the local and provincial levels. This represented the other side of the organizational task and required no less urgent attention.

In the political contest for Manchuria, the Communists originally appeared as challengers to the governing arrangements that Chungking had created, albeit largely on paper, in late 1945.

Chiang Kai-shek's strategy in the Northeast took aim at two tar-gets. Hoping to secure Soviet cooperation aimed at keeping the CCP under control, he wished at the same time to reduce if not eliminate that endemic regionalism to which Manchuria had been prone in the prewar era. As described earlier, the rather hastily improvised political arrangements for the Northeast announced by Chungking in late August 1945 comprised a regional authority in the form of the Northeast headquarters and nine provinces carved up from the original three of Liaoning, Kirin, and Heilung-kiang. A parallel but separate Northeast China Command was created in the military sphere. The underlying purpose of these arrangements was to provide Chiang Kai-shek with a strong and loyal regional viceroy overseeing weakened provinces that could no longer give rise to powerful regional leaders like Chang Tso-lin. Designed to check regionalism, the Nationalist political struc-ture also left no room for Communist participation in the gover-nance of the Northeast.

The CCP responded to this situation in two ways. At the provincial level and below, the Communists sought to create supposedly representative governments through "spontaneous" action (actually managed by the CCP) in order to legitimate their control in the areas they occupied militarily and then sought to gain recognition of these governments by Chungking. At the re-gional level the CCP refrained from creating a unified administra-tive structure until August 1946, by which time the Marshall mission's failure to avert civil war had become evident. Until then, the CCP challenged the legitimacy of the Northeast headquarters on the grounds that it represented another example of the Kuom-intang's one-party dictatorship, and they demanded a thorough reorganization of the Northeast headquarters to include Com-munists and nonparty persons. This demand mirrored on a re-gional level the CCP's interim objective of entering a national coalition government.

The form if not the substance of the initial Nationalist-Communist clash over the Northeast was a confrontation between the principle of national sovereignty versus that of provincial/local autonomy. The Soviet occupation of Manchuria provided a con-venient rationale for the National Government's exclusive claim to recovery of the region. Chungking asserted that it had the sole right and responsibility to take possession of the region from the Soviet forces as part of the process of recovering China's national sovereignty. (The corollary of this argument was Chungking's claim that the Soviets were obligated to yield control of Manchuria only to designated National Government officials.) Chungking attempted to divert attention from the internal struggle for political control of the Northeast by defining the issue as an international one. Its possession of international recognition as the legitimate government of China strengthened its claim.

Against this assertion of centralized state power, the CCP championed the principle of provincial and local autonomy which, in the given context, was to their tactical advantage. In actuality, expedience rather than principle dictated their position. A loosely integrated political system in which broad powers were reserved for provincial governments and in which officials were locally elected rather than centrally appointed seemed the best way for the Communists to maintain control in their existing base areas as well as to compete for power in such "new territories" as the Northeast.

The resolutions adopted by the Political Consultative Conference in January 1946 provided support for the Communists' position. Embodying the widespread popular desire to avert civil war, the PCC resolution, entitled "A Program for Peaceful National Construction," endorsed local self-government and popular elections to establish municipal, district, and provincial level governments.[42] Thereafter, the CCP frequently cited this resolution and the underlying principle of "a fair distribution of powers" between the central and local governments as it struggled for power in the Northeast.

In the turmoil of 1945–46 it was impossible for the CCP to construct an orderly hierarchy of governments starting at the local levels and culminating in popular provincial governments. Neither their scant resources nor the pressures of time allowed such an approach. The first stages of Communist political construction in the Northeast occurred in a helter-skelter fashion. Between November 1945 and March 1946 provincial governments were hastily erected throughout the Northeast. Local CCP organizations and the Communist armies played the leading role in this process.[43]

Two patterns may be discerned. In Liaoning and Hsin-gan provinces the Party and the army leadership convoked People's Representative Conferences (jen-min tai-piao hui-i) which then established a provincial government and elected a chairman and other officials. Elsewhere the provincial government was formed directly by the CCP and the army and only subsequently given post-facto "legitimation" through the convocation of a People's Representative Conference. These conferences and the governments themselves were intended as living examples of the coalition government the CCP was still seeking at the national level. The delegates and officials were supposedly a cross-section of the provincial population, including landlords, poor peasants, women, national minorities, and workers. Nonpartisan local notables joined members of the Democratic League, the Kuomintang, trade unions, peasant associations, as well as the CCP in these bodies.[44] CCP propaganda claimed that where the Communists were able to work openly they established neither a class nor a Party dictatorship but a genuine coalition government.[45]

Actually, far from being the spontaneous outgrowth of local democratic initiatives, these governments were formed and controlled throughout by the CCP. Not a few of the purported nonpartisans were really crypto-Communists whose usefulness would have been destroyed had their party membership been revealed at the time. The best known of these was Chang Hsüeh-liang's younger brother, the self-styled New Democrat Chang Hsüeh-ssu, who had joined the CCP in 1933 at the tender age of seventeen. Another was Kao Ch'ung-min, ostensibly a member only of the CDL, who served as provincial governor and then vice-chairman of the Communists' regional government from 1946 to 1949.[46] As long as the CCP retained an interest in American mediation and a national coalition, its control of the Northeast governments was exercised inconspicuously.

Analysis of the men who served as provincial chairmen reveals two interesting points. First, the overwhelming majority of them were natives of the region and, in most cases, of the province in which they served.[47] In these most visible of public positions, the CCP chose to present itself as an organization with supposedly well-established regional roots. Second, the provincial leaders occupied a distinctly subordinate position within the ranks of the CCP regional high command. None of the many Central Committee members or alternates sent to Manchuria in the fall of 1945 was placed in a provincial leadership position. With one or two exceptions the top leaders of the CCP in the region had Party or military rather then government careers. The main criterion for provincial leadership at this stage was regional legitimation conferred by local birth or prior Northeast career.[48] The post-civil war careers of these men were not very significant for the most part. At a particular historical moment they served the function of helping to establish the legitimacy of the Communist movement in Northeast regional terms. Once that moment passed they were shunted aside. Nonetheless, by its astute deployment of its small number of authentic Northeasterners, the CCP showed itself to be more sensitive than the Kuomintang to the regional dimension of Chinese politics even as it sought to substitute new lines of cleavage for the old.

The political programs of these early provincial governments were couched in terms of Mao's New Democracy. The November 1945 Liaoning provincial government program, for example, called for implementing democratic government and local autonomy, liquidating enemy and traitorous elements, restoring industry and commerce, eradicating banditry, and establishing a new democratic educational system and an incorruptible work style in government.[49] A Northeast Bureau resolution of December 1945 confirmed this type of program as official policy for the region as a whole.[50]

The process of political construction was proceeding simultaneously at the county, municipal, town, and village levels throughout the Communist-controlled portions of the Northeast. A closer look at two examples—one municipal and the other county—may convey a better sense of what was going on.[51]

Mutankiang, a city of some 214,000 persons located about 175 miles southeast of Harbin, became an important urban stronghold of the CCP during the civil war. Communist cadres from Yenan arrived there in November 1945 and immediately encountered the chaos and insecurity so widespread in the region at the time. Random shootings, political assassinations, and other indications of public disorder abounded within the city. Bandits roamed the surrounding countryside and made travel hazardous.

Much of the population viewed the Kuomintang rather than the CCP as the legitimate governing party of China.

In this situation, the CCP played the role of a party of revolutionary order. While mobilizing urban workers in factories and neighborhoods, the Communists simultaneously sought out local men of influence and persuaded them to participate in a provisional consultative conference and elections which produced a new municipal government. While the new mayor and a handful of other top officials were Communists, most of the department heads and subordinate personnel were retained cadres from the Manchukuo period. The CCP had too few of its own cadres to go around. Justifiably skeptical concerning the floating loyalties of these permanent bureaucrats, the CCP organized a one-month short-term Administrative Cadres Training class where some sixty persons were hastily prepared to take over the reins of government. These activities were replicated in many other localities.

The metropolis of Harbin served as a dispatch point for the newly arrived Party workers from North China. Small teams of cadres fanned out to the surrounding county seats to establish governments and reorganize local armed forces. These were perilous assignments. Many cadres were assassinated after arrival at their posts or enroute to their destinations. Larger-scale fighting also took place. A 600-man anti-Communist force which assaulted the headquarters of the North Manchurian Sub-Bureau and the Sungkiang Provincial CCP Committee in Pinhsien in early 1946 was fought off with great difficulty. This was followed by an unsuccessful attempt on the life of Ch'en Yün.

Chang Chi-chung, Secretary of the Chaoyuan County CCP Committee from January 1946 until the end of the civil war, provides an intimate look at the difficulties of establishing a Communist presence at this time. His predecessor, the original county Party Secretary Liu Ming-te, arrived in Chaoyuan in mid-November 1945 as head of a six-man work team. They set up a county Party committee and prevailed upon a local Mongol landlord to serve as county magistrate for the county government they organized. (This was a mixed Han-Mongol district.) This new government retained all of the old personnel including a 20–30 man Manchukuo-era police force, except for its chief who was executed as a "bad element." This unstable amalgam soon collapsed, however, when the police mutinied, killing Liu Ming-te and several of his comrades. Communist main forces had to be called in to restore order.

When Chang Chi-chung arrived on the scene he had his work cut out for him. Treading carefully through the minefield of Mongol nationalism by cultivating the local elite while also organizing the lower strata and recruiting new cadres, the county Party committee rebuilt the local government, recruited activists in the course of the movement to settle accounts, and established a county militia or peace preservation force *(pao-an t'uan)* under reliable leadership.[52] In the space of half a year, the county militia grew into a force of 500–600 persons organized in several regiments armed with Japanese-Manchukuo weapons and arms confiscated from defeated bandits. Considerably larger than the armed forces of the old regime, the county militia funneled soldiers into the Communist main line units and provided local security as well.

The county Party committee lacked cadres to serve as heads of the key district (ch'ü) level Party committees within Chao-yang so it drafted some company and platoon leaders from the army to serve concurrently as district Party secretaries and district chiefs. Young, locally recruited cadres were assigned as deputy Party secretaries and deputy district chiefs. New young activists were appointed as village heads.[53] Thus it was precisely because of the shortage of veteran cadres that new recruits enjoyed such broad career opportunities and rapid upward mobility. This capacity for organizational growth by assimilating ambitious young native activists and cadres was a key ingredient in the CCP's success in the region.

Perhaps the most curious and telling feature of this early period of organization building and mass mobilization was that the local Communist Party did not function openly, but operated under the signboard of the All-Circles People's Federation *(ko-chieh jen-min lien-ho hui).*[54] Party Secretary Chang Chi-chung, whose overt position was that of Political Commissar to the Peace Preservation Force, does not tell us when the CCP surfaced from underground. It is clear, however, that not until the winter of 1946–47 at the earliest did the CCP have anything remotely resembling a secure base area in northern Manchuria. The possibility that Communist power might not survive colored the views and actions of cadres and ordinary people alike.

For this reason an important task of the teams of propaganda specialists who labored in town and country was to persuade people that a radical break with the past was really possible. Yet in this sphere as in so many others, the CCP encountered fear and apathy on the part of those whom it sought to mobilize. Later, when the Party stepped up the pace of revolutionary change, it claimed that the old elite had continued to dominate local structures of power in this early period. In Mutankiang and Chaoyuan, as we have seen, and elsewhere in the region, the truth was that the Communists had consciously sought the cooperation of the old elite while the Party struggled to gain a toehold on power. In any case, a beginning had been made. Political activists began to emerge, organizational networks were woven, and local elites, even as they were being wooed, were placed on the defensive.

By the summer of 1946 the CCP had created its own political structures in the Northeast from the village/urban ward up through the provincial level where Communist-controlled governments were functioning in Sungkiang, Heilungkiang, Nunkiang, Hokiang, and Kirin.[55] The next step upward to the creation of a regional government for all of Communist Manchuria in August 1946 was much more than the logical culmination of the preceding political process. By creating an alternate regional adminstration to that of Chiang Kai-shek's Northeast headquarters, the CCP was presenting an integral challenge to Nanking's authority. From that point on, it was clear that the CCP had jettisoned its earlier hope of a negotiated political solution and was preparing for all-out war. A regional administration was considered necessary to impose order and provide direction to the various provincial governments and to enable the Communists to concentrate on the prime task of harnessing the Northeast economy to the war effort. While the Northeast Bureau continued to act as the collective chief of staff for the revolutionary civil war, responsible for policy formulation and decision making, it worked through the regional administration, which provided detailed regulations and instructions to the governments subordinate to it, supervised policy implementation, collected taxes, disbursed agricultural loans, and passed on personnel assignments.

Preparations for establishing a regional government in the Northeast had commenced in the autumn of 1945 with the establishment in Shenyang of a preparatory commission to study the feasibility of convoking a region-wide People's Representative Conference. By August 1946 the time was judged right to proceed with such a meeting and some 177 provincial delegates assembled in Harbin for the Joint Conference of Northeast All-Provinces Representatives *(Tung-pei ko-sheng tai-piao lien-hsi hui-i)*. Adhering to the fiction of a coalition government, fewer than one-third of the delegates were overt Communists; most were said to be non-party democrats.[56] The main order of business was the election of a regional government and the promulgation of a common program. The somewhat tentative nature of the regional organ established is suggested by its cumbersome title of the Northeast All-Provinces and Municipalities Joint Administrative Office *(Tung-pei ko-sheng-shih lien-ho pan-shih ch'ü)*. This soon came to be known simply as the Northeast Administrative Committee *(Tung-pei hsing-cheng wei-yuan-hui)* (hereafter referred to as NEAC) and functioned as the regional government of the Communist Northeast until the summer of 1949 when it was superseded by the Northeast People's Government.

Lin Feng, a native of Wangk'uei county in eastern Heilungkiang, served as chairman of NEAC throughout its existence, and was thus the most visible political leader in the Northeast during the civil war on the Communist side. After joining the CCP in 1931 at the age of twenty-five, Lin distinguished himself in Liu Shao-ch'i's underground Party apparatus in North China, served as a secretary in the Shansi-Suiyuan Liberated Area, and was elected a full member of the Seventh Central Committee.[57] As a member of the Standing Committee of the Northeast Bureau and the head first of the Organization and then of the Propaganda Department, Lin was the direct link between the CCP and the regional government structure.[58] The two deputy chairmen of NEAC were the crypto-Communists Chang Hsüeh-ssu and Kao Ch'ung-min. The former personified the supposed acceptance of the CCP's leadership by the old Manchurian elite, and the latter embodied the revolutionary democratic tradition of the Kuomintang and the Democratic League.

The twenty-seven members of NEAC were a who's

who of native Manchurian Communists and other leaders who were willing to collaborate with the CCP. Only nine were overt Communists, thus preserving the system from the anti-Japanese war period when the CCP had reserved two-thirds of official positions for its non-Communist coalition partners in the united front. The separation between the top-ranking Party officials of the Northeast Bureau who held real power and the lower-ranking communists placed in the government structure was breached only in the persons of Lin Feng and Ch'en Yün, who headed NEAC's Financial Committee. Once more the Party was putting forward its regional profile and keeping its powerful outsiders in positions of supreme but discrete authority.

During its first two years, NEAC consisted of six functional committees plus a Public Security office and a Northeast Branch of the Supreme Court (see table 3.3). In mid-1948 NEAC was reorganized in accordance with a Central Committee directive; the number of its departments increased from six to nine and several additional committees were appended to it. An era of bureaucratic expansion was already underway.

NEAC's program, announced at the end of its nine-day founding conference, was a New Democratic amalgam calling for unity among all classes, nationalities, and parties to establish a democratic Northeast, carry out rent and interest reduction, distribute traitors' and Japanese land, revive industry, reform the educational system, and mobilize human and material resources to support the NEDUA.[59] Most of this program represented little

TABLE 3.3   Northeast Administrative Committee 1946–1948

Chairman: Lin Feng	Vice-Chairmen: Chang Hsueh-ssu
	Kao Ch'ung-min
Committees	*Chairmen*
Civil Administration	Kao Ch'ung-min
Finance	Ch'en Yun
Construction	Ch'en Yun
Education	Ch'e Hsiang-ch'en
Communications	Lu Cheng-ts'ao
Nationalities	Ha (Feng?) A
Northeast Supreme Court	Tsou Ta-p'eng
Public Security Office	Wang Chin-hsiang
Secretariat	Li Yu-wen

more than a statement of intentions at the time it was adopted, for the CCP's ability to survive in the Northeast and work effectively toward these goals was still very much an open question.

Conclusion

A review of the CCP's progress along the road to power in the region just one year after Japan's defeat suggests a mixed picture. Certainly the major accomplishment was the resuscitation of a long moribund political and military organization through a massive transfer of personnel from outside the region. For the first time in the twenty-five year history of their party, the CCP's central leadership had made a significant investment of personnel resources in the Northeast. Underlying this investment was the assumption that the experience accumulated in organization-building, mass mobilization, and revolutionary leadership could be transferred to another region without loss of effectiveness. Thus, after a period of experimentation with an alternate urban-oriented strategy, the cadres and soldiers from North China sought to replicate their successes from the anti-Japanese war period. The creation of a network of local, provincial, and regional governments by the summer of 1946 was part of this effort along with mass mobilization campaigns that will be analyzed below.

Nevertheless, what must be emphasized is that despite the skillful deployment of its small contingent of native Manchurians, as of mid-1946 the CCP had not yet established itself securely in the region. From root to branch, the Communist Party in the Northeast was a transplant from North China whose survival in unfamiliar soil was still uncertain. After a year of intensive efforts marked by wild fluctuations in fortune, the Party still stood a long way from acquiring power. Its recruitment of Northeastern cadres had barely begun; its program of revolutionary change had yet to penetrate beneath the surface of urban and rural life. It still faced the task of demonstrating to a frequently hostile and at best indifferent population that Communist rule represented a legitimate and viable alternative to that of the National Government. Finally, Communist power still rested on shaky military foundations. Despite the rapid buildup of the NEDUA into a sizable force of some 300,000 men by the summer of 1946, the Communists were still militarily inferior to the National Government's army. As the apparently endless game of civil war resumed in China in the summer of 1946 after the time-out called by General Marshall, it was by no means clear yet which side would be able to win the prize of Northeast China.

CHAPTER FOUR
REVOLUTIONARY CIVIL WAR IN THE NORTHEAST

IN the late summer of 1948 while crops ripened on the plains of Manchuria, a Communist victory was waiting to be harvested. As Lin Piao began to unfold his last great campaign in the Northeast, Generals Wei Li-huang and Cheng Tung-kuo in Shenyang and Changchun respectively directed the defense of the two cities which were practically all that remained of Nationalist power in the region. If the position of the encircled garrisons was hopeless, the condition of the people inside was desperate. Food and fuel had long since become virtually unobtainable from the Communist-controlled countryside. In Changchun, according to the British consul's wife, "Crowds of people were always rummaging in refuse dumps for anything that might serve as fuel."[1] An American newsman later recalled the tortured face of Shenyang:

About 300,000 people [one-quarter of the population] were subsisting on barks and leaves, and pressed soybean cakes, ordinarily used as fertilizer or fodder. Thousands were going blind because of vitamin deficiencies, and other thousands, many of them children, were being wasted by noma, pellagra, scurvy, and other diseases of malnutrition. I walked down the desolate streets past the emaciated bodies of the dead in the gutters, pursued by unbearably pitiful child beggars and women crying out for help.[2]

By early October, some 200 persons a day were dying of starvation in Changchun and reports of cannibalism circulated.[3]

On October 17, the Yunnanese 60th Corps of the Changchun garrison rose in rebellion and surrendered to the Communists, who occupied the city over the next two days. Meanwhile, the main drama was taking place to the southwest where some 200,000 Nationalist troops from the Shenyang garrison, trying to recapture the recently lost city of Chinchow, were trapped by Lin Piao's encircling armies and annihilated. On November 2, after a decisive seven-week campaign, the peasant soldiers of the Northeast People's Liberation Army marched into Shenyang. Acting with perfect discipline and proper decorum toward the civilian population, the Communist troops swiftly put an end to looting, restored order and essential municipal services, and began to supply grain at controlled prices to the famished people.[4] The pall of despair and anxiety that had hung over the city for so many months began to dissipate. The civil war in the Northeast had effectively ended.

Revolution and Civil War: The Key Link

Between the resumption of civil war in the summer of 1946 and the Communists' triumphal campaign of the autumn of 1948, Northeast China passed through a great revolutionary transformation. In the villages, towns, and cities of northern and central Manchuria, a new Communist structure of power was erected through a series of often violent campaigns aimed particularly against landlords, rich peasants, and their political agents in the countryside. The Communist Party directed the participation of millions of rural and urban inhabitants in the revolutionary transformation. As the old elite was dispersed and destroyed, Communist party cadres redistributed their land, goods, and chattel. In the strategic rear base of northern Manchuria, bandits and other lawbreakers were hunted down by local and regional forces. Road and rail communications were restored to normal order.

The cities of northern Manchuria, particularly Harbin,

Mutankiang, and Chiamussu, served as the economic and political nerve centers of this revolution. Within them, tens of thousands of administrative cadres and technical specialists were graduated from newly established training institutes. Large- and small- scale industry was encouraged as well as controlled through financial and tax policies. The culture of Chinese communism, strongly influenced by the Soviet Union, spread through newspapers, magazines, radio, and other primarily urban means of communication.

Against this background of rural and urban revolution, and drawing strength from the changes in progress, the Communist armies expanded their manpower, intensified their training, and improved their combat capability. Hundred of thousands of peasant lads were mobilized to serve as soldiers while even larger numbers of people became porters, carters, and stretcher-bearers. The revolution itself became the means by which the Communist Party harnessed the resources of Northeast China to its quest for power. In simplest terms, the Communist Party created and led the revolution in Manchuria; the revolution nourished the Communist armies with manpower and supplies of every kind, and the armies brought the CCP to power. There should be no mistaking the essential direction of the relationship between the revolution and the Communists' armed conquest of power. Without the revolution there could have been no military victory for the Communists, but without the Communists there would have been no revolution.

The attainment of nation-wide power had been the CCP's goal long before the end of the war against Japan, but just how this objective would be pursued did not become clear until midway through 1946. I have already observed that in 1945–46 Mao Tse-tung as well as Liu Shao-ch'i hoped that coalition government and peaceful political competition might be the means by which the CCP could defeat its Nationalist rivals. Had this worked out, the CCP indeed might have followed a different path to power. But the demise of the CCP-KMT agreements for which Marshall had served as midwife made civil war a certainty.

Despite their achievements in the year since Japan's surrender, the Communists in the Northeast were ill-prepared to fight a war in the summer of 1946. Lin Piao himself admitted that his forces were inferior to those of the enemy.[5] His armies had taken a beating at the hands of the Nationalists in May 1946. The territory north of the Sungari to which the NEDUA retreated, far from being a secure base area, was alive with its local enemies. An assault on the entrenched local powerholders had barely begun. In the countryside, most peasants looked suspiciously upon the Communists as outsiders, while in the cities pervasive doubt existed as to the CCP's prospects for survival, let alone victory.

Such was the uncongenial setting in which the CCP turned to revolution in the Northeast as the means of its salvation and the engine of its coming to power. The Communist high command pursued a strategy of revolution primarily in order to advance the party toward military victory. This is clear from the fact that the imperatives of warfare always took precedence over those of revolutionary change when a contradiction surfaced between the two. The CCP leadership was perfectly frank about this point. In its instructions, policy statements and daily propaganda, the Northeast Bureau and NEAC reiterated the need to do everything possible in support of the military effort. This became particularly clear in 1948 when the intensified scale of fighting placed ever heavier burdens on the fragile economy of the Communist Northeast. The Party leadership reponded by stressing the primacy of production in support of the war effort over that of deepening the revolution. Unless directed into the war effort, revolution was an aimless flood that could not turn the turbines producing Communist power, but properly channeled by the CCP, the revolutionary mobilization of workers and peasants could be transformed into military victory. This simple truth guided the CCP to its triumph in the Northeast civil war.

Military Dimensions
of the Civil War

The fragmentation of power in post-Ch'ing China, resulting in an unstable and shifting amalgam of competing regional, provincial, and sub-provincial units, confronted Chinese revolutionaries with a peculiarly difficult task. Unlike their French and Russian revolutionary forebears, the Chinese revolutionaries had to create rather than inherit a modern centralized state. (Later, of course, nationalist leaders of many so-called Third World states frequently confronted this problem in more acute form.) Responding to this reality, by the late 1920s both the Kuomintang and the CCP had developed into thoroughly militarized political movements dedicated to applying military power to the task of national reintegration. These revolutionary parties-cum-armies became the modern version of Machiavelli's armed prophet, brandishing the sword as well as the idea in the service of their causes. The Florentine master had taught that armed prophets conquer while unarmed prophets are doomed to defeat. But what of a contest between two prophets armed?

Chiang Kai-shek's wartime attempt to rebuild his modern military machine, battered and almost destroyed in the first year of the anti-Japanese war, ran up against the reality of factionalized military politics and the fragmentation of power within Nationalist China.[6] But with American help, the hard core of a smaller and tougher new Nationalist Army took shape in the training camps of India and south China. Less well-known is that Communist forces underwent an even more fundamental transformation between 1942 and 1945. Lin Piao and other Yenan-based military leaders concentrated on producing a disciplined regular army capable of fighting large-scale battles and incorporating trained military specialists in artillery, communications, engineering, and machine gunnery. Ch'i Hsi-sheng's observations are worth quoting on this point:

the Communist leaders were able to develop a regular army of high quality out of an irregular military force . . . after 1942, the Communists had at least three uninterrupted years to implement successive waves of massive and intensive military training in the border regions . . . the Communist regulars were far better grounded in the basics of war than any Chinese-trained government forces (American-trained government forces excepted).[7]

During the Northeast revolutionary civil war, the Communists and the Nationalists pitted their best and most modern forces against each other. Lin Piao had taken with him to the Northeast thousands of recent graduates of Yenan's military and technical training institutes along with an impressive corps of seasoned officers including some trained in the USSR.[8] His armies were equipped with modern Japanese weapons and later with U.S. ordnance captured from the Chinese Nationalist Army (CNA). These armies faced the American-trained elite of Chiang Kai-shek's Central Government armies led at the operational level by officers trained by U.S. instructors in India and China. (At the command level, however, the Nationalist generals were outclassed and outperformed by their adversaries.)

The civil war in the Northeast was neither a contest between a Communist David and a Nationalist Goliath nor a guerrilla-style people's war. The Communists and the Nationalists fought what was basically a conventional war deploying large military formations equipped with modern weaponry in mobile warfare. Particularly toward the end of the struggle, when Lin Piao was on the offensive, the Communists made extensive use of the railroad system for logistical purposes.[9] (Soviet military engineers played a crucial though untouted role in the rapid restoration of the transportation system during the latter stages of the war.)[10] Yet the relative underdevelopment of the road and rail network, particularly in northern Manchuria, and critical shortages of motor vehicles, rolling stock, fuel, and technical personnel made the NEPLA highly dependent upon traditional means of transportation, such as horse-drawn carts and peasant carters, to move supplies, ammunition, food and fodder, and the wounded. Similarly, the relative industrial underdevelopment of the Communist north combined with Soviet despoliation, shortages of fuel and spare parts, and the insufficient number of technically skilled persons meant that traditional handicrafts and small-scale rather than modern industry had to supply many essential goods and services for the war effort. For these three crucial inputs—of manpower, labor service, and supplies—the Communists were dependent upon the mobilized people of the Northeast.[11] The conventional war that the Communists fought in Manchuria rested upon a broad popular base and in this sense—and this sense only—the Party fought a people's war in the region.[12] This understanding of people's war excludes the elements of small-scale fighting by peasant guerrillas, a self-supporting army that combines fighting with productive economic activity, and the romantic notion of the revolutionary army as one with the people.

In this restricted sense, the Communists' ability to fight a people's war in the Northeast was of critical importance given the "federal" character of the civil war as a whole which consisted of several large and only loosely integrated theaters of operation. Limited logistical capabilities and simultaneous operations in different military theaters made it difficult for either side to shift substantial military assets from one region to another once the war had begun without incurring great risks. The initial period of 1945–46 when the Communists transferred large numbers of "outside" forces to the Northeast was followed by a take-off period of self-sustaining military growth. The completion of the conquest of the Northeast in November 1948 liberated military resources for investment in North China and greatly accelerated the timetable for final victory on a nation-wide scale. The Nationalists, by contrast, never freed themselves from dependence on extra-regional sources of manpower and materiel. Hoping to redeem their original investment, they faced the necessity of sending ever more assets to Manchuria from a shrinking capital stock in intra-mural China. But by mid-1947 every such transfer weakened the Nationalists' position in the sending areas. The comments of two U.S. diplomats illustrate this dilemma.

From Changchun during the Communists' spring offensive in June 1947, Consul General O. Edmund Clubb wrote: "It is fairly obvious that the Nationalist position in Manchuria cannot be restored without the dispatch of large numbers of reinforcements here from China proper." But Ambassador J. Leighton Stuart noted the difficulty of such transfers: "Any effort to reenforce Manchuria at this time will place Govt in position of robbing Peter to pay Paul . . . it is now apparent that Nationalist campaign in Shantung is completely bogged down and all field commanders in that area are asking for reenforcements and additional air support."[13]

The Nationalist reliance in the Northeast on manpower and supplies shipped in from the outside had two further negative consequences. It placed excessive strain on the CNA's logistical capacity consisting of the Peining rail link through the Liaohsi corridor and air transport. The first of these means was vulnerable to Communist sabotage and the second (given the limited capacity of C-46s) was inadequate. Moreover, in psychological terms, this dependency reenforced the Nationalist preoccupation with passively defending urban points and lines of communication rather than actively seeking out and destroying the enemy's effectives.

No less important was mounting resentment in the Nationalist portions of the Northeast against the often arrogant and condescending behavior of the CNA troops, most of whom were from south China. Fighting far from their native places, in a harsh and unfamiliar climate, amidst an increasingly hostile population, Chiang Kai-shek's forces in the Northeast became increasingly demoralized and less fit for combat. A U.S. observer in Shenyang, sympathetic to the Nationalists, wrote: "Nationalist southern military forces and civil administrators conduct themselves in Manchuria as conquerors, not as fellow countrymen, and have imposed 'carpet-bag' regime of unbridled exploitation on areas under control."[14] But Nanking did virtually nothing throughout the civil war to placate Northeast regional sentiment.

In general terms, the military conflict in the Northeast may be divided into four phases: (1) initial positioning (August 1945–May 1946); (2) Nationalist offensives (May 1946–November 1946); (3) Communist counterattacks (November 1946–December 1947); (4) Communist strategic offensives (January–November 1948).[15]

During the first phase, the Nationalists, with their superior firepower and fresh U.S.-trained troops, by May 1946 had overcome the Communists' early advantage which was based on their massive redeployments from North China and on Soviet assistance. At the time of the June 6 cease-fire (pressed on a reluctant Chiang Kai-shek by General Marshall), the CNA's forward units were within thirty miles of Harbin on the north bank of the Sungari river. That the cease-fire prevented the Nationalists from capturing Harbin is almost certain, but it is hardly likely that Tu Yu-ming's armies could have cornered and destroyed the elusive Communist forces.[16]

In the summer of 1946, Lin Piao began to rebuild his forces in his northern Manchurian redoubt. Meanwhile, the Nationalists attempted to eliminate the Communist military presence along the western and eastern flanks of Manchuria. In the west they captured key towns in the Jehol corridor and in southeastern Manchuria along the border with North Korea they seized Antung and T'unghua by mid-autumn. But while yielding territory, the Communists survived to fight again, inflicted considerable casualties on the enemy, and, by drawing off Nationalist forces, relieved pressure on Lin Piao's center.[17] Around this time Chiang Kai-shek expressed great confidence that his forces could crush the CCP by force of arms in less than a year. In conversation with Marshall and Ambassador Stuart on December 1, 1946, Chiang is reported to have said: " 'Ultimately the problem will narrow down to the situation in Manchuria.' His intention was to control Manchuria south of Changchun, which was the industrially important area and for the present make no attack on Harbin and leave the CCP undisturbed in that area, thus avoiding any possible clashes with Russia."[18]

The Nationalist victories in late 1946 were the high tide of CNA power in the Northeast. Thereafter, even when the Communists were defeated in specific engagements, their overall politico-military position continued to improve. By early 1947, the inherent weakness of the Nationalist position in Manchuria was becoming more evident. Assigned to urban garrison duties under commanders reluctant to hazard offensive operations, Nationalist troops lost their fighting edge. Soldiers were lured to the fleshpots of the cities and many officers and men speculated in commodities, especially soybeans, in an effort to enrich themselves.[19] Meanwhile, highly mobile Communist armed work teams infiltrated Nationalist territory. They distributed propaganda, assassinated local officials, and organized anti-government resistance.

The first half of 1947 was a decisive turning point in the battle for Manchuria. Beginning on a small scale in mid-November 1946 and building toward a major campaign in May-June 1947, Lin Piao launched a series of five offensives across the Sungari designed to alter the strategic situation in the Northeast. Penetrating deeply into Nationalist territory, the Communists seized larger quantities of military equipment and supplies, and disrupted rail communications before retreating northward in the face of superior concentrations of Nationalist forces. The fifth and largest offensive was begun at a time when the Communists' overall military situation in China was still rather weak. William Whitson suggests that "Lin Piao's organization was called upon to produce a sorely needed victory."[20] Amassing some 400,000 troops, Lin sliced down through Kirin province toward Ssup'ing, capturing several dozen district towns en route, and extending a salient toward Shenyang. But Lin's siege of Ssup'ing cost him 40,000 casualties and failed to take the city as Tu Yu-ming rapidly deployed air power and more than a dozen divisions to counter-attack. In late June, the Communists withdrew north across the Sungari once again, but the Government's position in Manchuria was never the same again. Lin Piao's campaigns in the first half of 1947 had demonstrated that the strategic initiative now lay with the NEDUA. Although Lin had failed to capture Ssup'ing which led to his conducting a severe self-criticism, his troops gathered large stores of weapons and other war materiel, shattered Nationalist self-confidence, destroyed large numbers of CNA troops, and assumed permanent control of substantial territories and population in the Northeast. Summing up fifty days of cam-paigning, a *Northeast Daily* report claimed that the NEDUA had liberated forty-two county seats (six of which were recaptured by the Nationalists), wiped out 82,000 enemy troops, and liberated an area of 166,000 square kilometers with a population of ten million persons.[21] This amounted to half of all Nationalist Man-churia. In reaction to these developments, large amounts of capital began flowing out of the remaining Nationalist districts of Man-churia to Hong Kong and Canton.[22]

During the second half of 1947, the Communists re-sumed offensive operations on three fronts—the Liaohsi corridor through which the Nationalists moved reenforcements and sup-plies from North China; in eastern Liaoning; and along the central front—in a successful war of attrition. Gradually they forced the Nationalists into static defensive positions in the large cities such as Kirin, Changchun, and Shenyang, and imperiled the rail link between North China and the Northeast.[23] The isolated garrisons became increasingly dependent upon the aerial exploits of Amer-ican pilots working for General Chennault's Civil Air Transport (CAT) which ferried food into, and Nationalist officials and their families out of, Shenyang under hazardous conditions.[24]

During this time, Chiang Kai-shek replaced Hsiung Shih-hui with Chief-of-Staff General Ch'en Ch'eng, who took over the direction of the Northeast headquarters in September

1947. Exuding confidence, Ch'en shook up the military and political leadership of the Nationalist Northeast and promised to take
the offensive against the Communists. On January 1, 1948, he
declared that the CNA had completed its battle preparations and
that the crisis of the Northeast had already passed.[25] Ch'en
Ch'eng's bluster was ill-timed. On January 5, Lin Piao vigorously
renewed his southward drive, this time in a three-pronged coordinated thrust which once more menaced the Peining rail link,
captured key towns in eastern Liaoning (enabling the NEPLA to
establish a sea link with Shantung), and threatened Ssup'ing and
Shenyang. By mid-March, the Nationalists had withdrawn from
Kirin city, and four Communist columns (120,000 troops) attacked and finally captured Ssup'ing on March 13, 1948.[26] In the
late spring and summer of 1948, Lin Piao refitted his troops with
captured American weapons, and conducted major training ex-
ercises in preparation for the decisive fall campaign.

In mid-January 1948, Chiang Kai-shek had carried
out another change of command in the Northeast. General Wei
Li-huang reluctantly accepted appointment as head of the newly
established Northeast Bandit Suppression Headquarters (NEBSH)
and vice-chairman of the Northeast headquarters. Ch'en Ch'eng,
temporarily disgraced and pleading illness, left Manchuria.[27] A
derisive jingle summed up local feelings about his performance in
the region. "What a marvelous talent is Commander Ch'en! Like
a train that can manage a one-mile run."[28] This reshuffling of
commanders had no positive effect on the course of battle. By the
end of the Communists' winter 1948 offensive, the Nationalists
controlled only 1 percent of the territory of Manchuria.

The head of the U.S. Military Advisory Group in China,
Major General David Barr, had for some time been urging Chiang
Kai-shek to withdraw his forces from their hopeless situation in
Manchuria and use them to consolidate his position in North
China.[29] Chiang was too sensitive to the political costs of "abandoning" Manchuria to accept this advice. However, he was willing
to withdraw the bulk of his forces to Chinchow in the Liaohsi
corridor, leaving only token garrisons in Shenyang and
Changchun. But Wei Li-huang strongly resisted Chiang, insisting
on the possibility of defending Shenyang, provided further reenforcements were sent from North China. Unfortunately, by the

spring of 1948 it was no longer possible to spare any additional troops for the Northeast.[30] Unwilling to withdraw completely from Manchuria and unable to secure compliance from his Northeast commander, Chiang Kai-shek parlayed indecisively with Wei Li-huang's subordinates, Liao Yao-hsiang and Fan Han-ch'ieh, while the military situation worsened. As was often the case, the Nationalist command was at loggerheads with itself.

At the commencement of the Liaoshen campaign in September 1948, Lin Piao disposed of 700,000 main force troops, 53 divisions in all, which faced about 450,000 Nationalists deployed in the isolated strongholds of Chinchow (120,000), Shenyang (230,000) and Changchun (80,000).[31] Cut off from most of its hinterland and with its rail link severed, Shenyang received a thin trickle of supplies by air. Incoming cargo flights by the China National Aviation Corporation, the Central Air Transport Corporation, and CAT increased precipitously in a frantic effort to move in food and other supplies and evacuate many thousands of refugees.[32] Changchun was even worse off. After Communist seizure of its airfield in August, wildly inaccurate airdrops were its only link with the outside, but three days' airdrops were insufficient for one day's supply requirements.[33] Finally, an uprising of the Yunnanese 60th Army and its defection to the Communists precipitated the surrender of the city in mid-October.[34]

Lin Piao's strategy for the Liaoshen campaign contained elements of surprise, rapid movement of large forces, and concentration of firepower. His plan comprised a feint toward Changchun to deceive the enemy and a major thrust to capture Chinchow in order to cut Nationalist links with North China once and for all, and annihilate the relief columns which he correctly surmised would be sent out from Shenyang to Chinchow. Beginning on September 12, and making use of the recently repaired rail lines, Lin repositioned 200,000 troops and 500 pieces of artillery around Chinchow. After a series of bitterly contested preliminary engagements, the Communists launched their all-out attack against Chinchow on October 14 and overwhelmed its defenses in just one day.

Just as the preliminary battles were getting underway, Chiang Kai-shek ordered Wei Li-huang to march west from Shen-

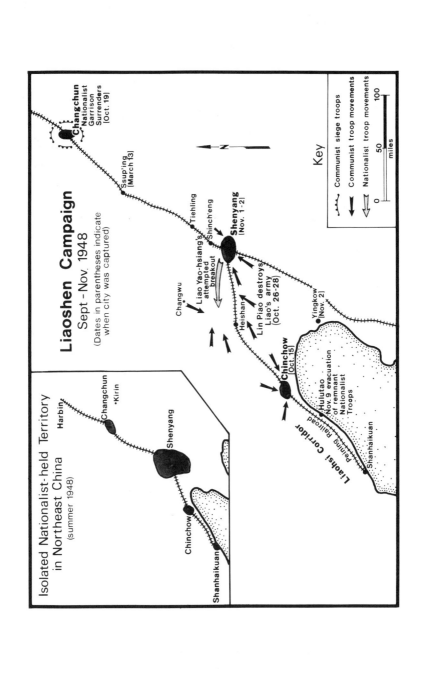

Liaoshen Campaign
Sept - Nov. 1948
(Dates in parentheses indicate
when city was captured)

Isolated Nationalist-held Territory
in Northeast China
(summer 1948)

Harbin

Changchun
•Kirin

Shenyang

Chinchow

Shanhaikuan

Changchun Nationalist
Garrison
Surrenders
[Oct. 19]

Ssup'ing
[March 13]

Tiehling
Shinch'eng

Shenyang
[Nov. 1-2]

Changwu

Liao Yao-hsiang's
attempted breakout

Heishan

Lin Piao destroys
Liao's army
(Oct. 26-28)

Chinchow
[Oct. 15]

Yingkow
[Nov. 2]

Hulutao
Nov. 9 evacuation
of remnant
Nationalist
Troops

Shanhaikuan

Liaohsi Corridor

Peiping Railroad

Key

Communist siege troops

Communist troop movements

Nationalist troop movements

0   50   100
miles

yang and relieve the Chinchow garrison. Wei demurred, while Liao Yao-hsiang favored a breakout from Shenyang to Yingkow from where the Nationalist armies could be sea-lifted to safety in North China. Valuable time was lost while this high-level bickering continued. Finally, after a flying visit to Shenyang on October 1, Chiang again ordered Wei to relieve Chinchow while keeping open the option for an eventual Yingkow evacuation.[35] Making slow progress, Liao Yao-hsiang's relief force had gone less than half-way to Chinchow by the time the city fell. After several days of frantic meetings, Chiang forced his reluctant Northeast commanders to continue their drive westward in coordination with an eastward-bound rescue column from Shanhaikuan in the hope of recapturing Chinchow. But Communist columns held Liao in check at Heishan while Lin Piao redeployed additional forces to encircle the Nationalist troops. In several days of fierce fighting, Liao Yao-hsiang's force was cut to pieces as they futilely strived to retreat to Shenyang. The remnants of the force surrendered on October 28.[36] It took just four more days to complete the capture of Shenyang.[37] Only a few thousand Nationalist troops could be evacuated from Yingkow. The Nationalist position in Manchuria was liquidated completely with the withdrawal of 140,000 troops and equipment from Hulutao on November 9. From Shanhaikuan to the Soviet border, all of Northeast China now lay in Communist hands.

The tally sheet of war revealed the dimensions of the Nationalist catastrophe. In seven weeks of fighting well over 400,000 Nationalist soldiers had been put out of action. The Communists captured over 2,000 trucks and other vehicles, 150 armored vehicles, 76 tanks, 12 U.S. howitzers, thousands of guns, and large stores of weapons, ammunition, and supplies.[38] Perhaps even more important was the psychological shock to the National Government's cause. The loss of this critical region deepened demoralization in Nationalist ranks and gave birth to the perception that it was only a matter of time before the Nationalist collapse assumed nationwide proportions. In military terms, the Nationalist defeat in the Northeast, produced a kind of internal domino effect. The additional weight that the Communist leaders could now bring to bear in North China as Lin Piao's armies moved inside the Great Wall destroyed the equilibrium of forces in that theater and led rapidly to the fall of Peiping and Tientsin. Additional Communist victories accumulated rapidly throughout 1949.

In a perceptive post-mortem of the Nationalist debacle in Manchuria, written in 1950, NEBSH Chief-of-Staff Chao Chia-hsiang suggested that, unlike the Communists, the Nationalists lacked a concept of total war. The CCP, he said, had integrated political, military, and economic tasks, making full use of the population and resources at its disposal while the Nationalists compartmentalized these sectors and had a purely military concept of conflict.[39] By using local sources of manpower and supplies, the Communists built up an indigenous force well-adapted to conditions in the region, and by linking warfare to revolution they assured themselves of adequate numbers of soldiers and service personnel. The Nationalists were constantly short of troops and adopted a defensive posture partly because of this. ·

Chao also pointed to Communist superiority in the areas of leadership, troop management, intelligence, and treatment of POWs. In a rather blunt admission of the military failings of many of his colleagues, Chao observed that in the Communist armies success on the battlefield rather than education, personal background, and connections was the criterion for advancement. At the strategic level, the Nationalists lacked an overall plan for defeating the enemy and unwisely focused on holding lines and points rather then concentrating forces to wipe out Communist effectives. Communist field commanders were accorded greater battlefield authority, assuring tactical flexibility. The Communists stressed intelligence-gathering, and made careful preparations for battle. They were adept at rapid troop movements and excelled in the tactic of surprise. In the psychological sphere, CCP political workers effectively maintained high troop morale and inspired troops in combat. The policy of good treatment for POWs likewise had a great impact on the Nationalist soldiers. In all these areas the Nationalists were deficient.[40] Other observers have pointed to the same catalog of differences between the Communists and the Nationalists with respect to the quality of military leadership, the coordination of military with political and economic activities, the level of morale, and tactical skills.[41]

Chiang Kai-shek himself, in lectures to his civilian and

military leaders delivered during the civil war, castigated his subordinates for military incompetence and indifference to the conditions of the men serving under their command, and accused them of selfishness, corruption, indiscipline, and boastfulness.[42] He expressed admiration for the Communists' individual as well as organizational virtues. One must add that Chiang himself was culpable for appointing unfit officers to command positions, exhibiting indecisive leadership as well as poor judgment at key points in the struggle for the Northeast, and failing to understand the requirements of modern revolutionary warfare.

Securing the Rear Areas

An army can concentrate on its main task—defeating the enemy's armed forces—only if its own rear is secured. Yet securing the rear amidst the turbulence of a revolutionary civil war is not easily achieved. Revolutionary leaders must deal with the array of enemies created by the redistribution of political and economic power. The establishment of a new social order under wartime conditions strains the personnel resources and organizational capacity of the emergent governing authority.

In Manchuria the problem each side faced in securing its rear was foreshadowed by the widespread disorder which had reigned even before the civil war commenced. The Nationalists never really succeeded in bringing their Northeast territories under effective political and security control. Communist-armed work teams roamed the countryside, which was nominally controlled by the CNA, and CCP intelligence agents honeycombed the civil and military apparatus in the Nationalist-held cities. Hundreds of thousands of refugees from the Communist north, fleeing class warfare, conscription, and other tribulations, sought refuge in such cities as Shenyang and Changchun, adding measurably to the burden of feeding, housing, and controlling the urban population. The fluid battle lines of multi-sector mobile warfare made it unusually difficult to cordon off one's own territory from that of the adversary.

The CCP had several advantages when it came to the

problem of securing its rear. First, the core of its territory in northern Manchuria (Heilungkiang) was surrounded by the friendly space of the USSR, so there was no possibility of an enemy force attacking from the rear or taking refuge beyond an international border and conducting raids across it. Second, the Nationalists had virtually no capacity for guerrilla warfare; they possessed a very weak intelligence network and were unable to supply provisions or leadership to the disparate military forces, operating within the Communist core areas, which were holding out against the consolidation of Communist rule. Consequently, the Communist territorial formations—provincial, county, and local security forces—were able to dispose of their divided enemies piecemeal. Third, given the porous character of the boundaries between Communist and Nationalist territories, many of those who opposed Communist rule (particularly in the cities) were able to flee southward rather than having to dig in their heels and resist the CCP. Thus the natural leadership of an anti-communist resistance was in part self-liquidating. Finally, to the extent that anti-Communist armed resistance derived from Manchurian regional particularism and opposition to centralized political authority of any complexion, the Nationalists' animus against recognizing the legitimacy of regional sentiment made it impossible to enlist such resistance on their side.

Nonetheless, the CCP did not have an easy time securing its rear in northern Manchuria. In particular, it faced the problem of suppressing irregular armed forces in the countryside and establishing order in the cities. Although the Communists brought these problems more or less under control by mid-1947, it was not until many months after the end of the civil war in the region in November 1948 that the last organized bandit resistance was eliminated.

Banditry or Irregular Armed Forces

The suppression of banditry *(chiao-fei)* was a high priority for the CCP in 1945–46. Included in the elastic category of bandits *(fei)* were every sort of irregular detachment—tiny bands of traditional highwaymen, landlords' militia, independent village self-defense corps, large, well-equipped remnant forces of the Manchukuo Army, Japanese Kwantung army stragglers, and various private armies. After absorbing the lesson that its fledgling governments in Manchuria were vulnerable as long as military power was widely dispersed, the CCP spared no effort in establishing its own monopoly of armed force.

Banditry, of course, had been endemic in the frontier provinces of the Northeast, battening on the weakness of civil authority and preying on all classes of society. One writer has estimated that there were over 100,000 mounted bandits (ma-fei) in the Northeast in the 1920s.[43] As noted, in the aftermath of Japan's surrender in August 1945, chaos was endemic in Northeast China, and a bewildering variety of local armed forces temporarily filled the vacuum of power. Social disruption and dislocation swelled the ranks of the armed irregular forces as the virtual collapse of industrial and mining enterprises and a slowdown in the agricultural sector set adrift large numbers of men to seek survival by whatever means possible.

Communist leaders had earlier adopted a flexible and pragmatic policy toward bandits, seeing in them a potential source of tested recruits as well as possible rivals for local control. Where Communist forces were strong enough, their preferred method of dealing with bandits was to dissolve the bandit groups and incorporate the individuals and their arms into existing units.[44] In Northeast China during the civil war period, the Communists more often employed force to crush the more powerful of the irregular armed forces, although persuasion was sometimes used to induce surrender. Amidst the welter of competing armed groups, the Communists had to show that they were the strongest by confronting and defeating some of their enemies before they could entertain any hope that those who remained might be overawed into submission.

Not surprising, estimates of the number of bandit forces in postwar Manchuria vary considerably. A well-connected Communist journalist estimated that there were as many as 80,000 local bandits (t'u-fei) in the first half of 1946 distributed as follows: Liaoning-Antung—20,000, North Manchuria—40,000, West Manchuria—20,000.[45] Yet only a few months later a report

CIVIL WAR IN THE NORTHEAST

in the *Northeast Daily* suggested that by August 1946 fewer than 20,000 bandits remained active: in Hokiang—3,400, in Sung-kiang—2,000, West Manchuria—10,000, and South and East Manchuria—1,000.[46] The difference between these estimates is at least partly due to what categories of enemies were to be counted as bandits.

The task of bandit suppression had three components that overlapped in time: (1) defeat of remnant Manchukuo and Japanese troops and of pro-Nationalist independent armies; (2) suppression of armed class enemies; (3) elimination of traditional small-scale banditry. Analytically distinguishable though they were, these several groups frequently merged their forces in reality, although they lacked the organizational capacity or shared interests to aggregate into large military formations on a permanent basis. Beginning in the fall of 1945, the Communists organized village, county, and provincial security forces to do battle with local enemy military detachments ranging in size from a handful of men up to battalion strength. The leaders of these forces were said to be Japanese or Manchukuo officers or police, landlords, rich peasants, and hooligans *(liu mang)*. The cohesive element of most of these forces was more likely small-group solidarity than ideology or any other abstract motive. Where Communist territorial forces (especially village and county militia) were unable to handle their adversaries, main force NEDUA troops from provincial military districts or sub-districts were brought into play. Similarly, cooperation between adjacent provincial forces was sometimes required to deal with so-called border bandits *(pien-fei)*.47

Prolonged fighting was occasionally required before the Communists were able to defeat their local enemies. In Chao-yuan county (Heilungkiang), for example, a 1,000-strong armed rebellion led by a Han Chinese landlord nicknamed #2 Mongol *(Erh meng-ku)*, broke out in June–July 1946 and forces from neighboring Nunkiang were called in to help suppress the rebels.[48] Some of the larger irregular military formations fielded both cavalry and infantry units and boasted artillery, cannon, and other heavy weapons.[49] By the second half of 1946 the number of bandits was certainly dwindling. In the last months of that year concentrated campaigns in northern and western Manchuria resulted in the killing or capture of many thousands of irregular troops including those of such prominent local anti-Communist leaders as Li Hua-t'ang, Hsieh Wen-tung, and Chang Yu-hsing.[50] In time-honored fashion Communist military success stimulated secondary rebel leaders to surrender or seek incorporation in the Communist armies. The CCP occasionally engaged in prolonged negotiations with local leaders, but appears generally to have taken a very hard line against the bandit chieftains. In some cases, public trials pronounced death sentences against bandits by acclamation and summary executions were carried out.[51]

A resurgence of anti-Communist local military activity accompanied the intensification of the CCP's land reform in the spring of 1947. Landlord and rich peasant targets of land reform, their positions threatened by the Party's determination to carry out a thorough purge of the old elite, mobilized their clients, friends, and dependents in last ditch efforts to resist the Communist revolution. In Hokiang province during the spring of 1947, for example, a well-armed 2–3,000 man force calling itself the People's Autonomous Army (jen-min tzu-chih chün), and led by a former battalion commander in the Manchukuo Army, occupied several towns north and west of Hokang before being defeated by superior Communist forces.[52] At the same time, a two-month long bandit suppression campaign in the West Manchurian military sub-district put nearly 400 irregulars out of action including the members of such colorfully styled groups as the Red Universe (t'ien-hsia hung), Twin Mountain (shuang shan), Old Goosefoot Boys (lao lai hao), Ever Victorious (ch'ang sheng), and North Country (pei kuo). In the late spring, county security forces scoured mountainous districts to search out bandit hideouts and collect weapons in order to prevent a recurrence of banditry, which tended to peak in the summertime.[53]

By mid-1947, the Communists had gone far toward ensuring internal security in their rear or base areas by bringing the problem of irregular forces basically under control. However, the problem of banditry was not yet completely solved. Ironically, what turned out to be the most elusive of the Communists' internal enemies (though the smallest real threat) were precisely those small groups of mounted marauders, outlaws, and highwaymen who were most qualified to be called bandits. During the Manchukuo period, the Communist guerrillas had frequently been the object of counterinsurgency operations. Now the hunted became the hunters. One Communist officer later recalled the difficulties of the pursuit:

> It was very hard to find even a trace of the bandits. We pursued them time and again, threaded our way through one dense forest after another, climbed one mountain after another, and yet the enemy left no trace.[54]

Along the Sungari river in Sungkiang province a tradition of frontier hospitality lingered according to which fisherman would take in, feed, and shelter strangers and passersby with no questions asked. The Party had to break this tradition through force and persuasion. A vigorous propaganda campaign was conducted among the families of bandits and directed to the bandits themselves, urging them to surrender without fear of punishment unless they were personally guilty of some heinous crimes.[55]

The political mobilization of the population made it increasingly difficult for bandits or insurgents to obtain support or protection against the troops pursuing them. In addition, land reform eliminated one of the staple sources of banditry—poor men whom the old order could not provide for, and marginal men who found a vocation only in wartime and who reverted to banditry in times of peace. NEAC chairman Lin Feng proclaimed: "The land reform enables former landless men to live without turning bandit."[56] After the end of the civil war, the problem of reintegrating large numbers of demobilized veterans into the civil order was tackled quite successfully.[57] Thus the Communists were able to break the cycle of bandit-soldier-bandit by continuing the mobilization of labor in peacetime. Finally, we may note that the Party pursued a more lenient policy toward minority nationality bandits in the Northeast. For example, one Olunchun bandit chief finally surrendered only in the winter of 1949 after prolonged negotiations with the authorities. He and his men were allowed to keep their hunting rifles in exchange for pledging that they would not attack foresters or set forest fires.[58]

Urban Public Security

The cities played an indispensable role in securing Communist victory in the civil war, but their governance presented a series of challenges that the Party managed only with difficulty. The problem of maintaining public order in the cities, particularly in the metropolis of Harbin with its cosmopolitan, polyglot population, proved especially severe. Quite naturally, most Party cadres, even those with prewar experience in the illegal Party apparatus of North China, had little understanding of how to administer a complex urban system. Their basic tendency, therefore, was to disaggregate the city into a large number of smaller and simpler units in which the arsenal of control and mobilization techniques brought in from the countryside could be applied. Beginning in November 1946, Harbin was divided into six districts *(ch'ü)* below which fifty-eight street offices *(chieh kung-so)* were established. (These were originally called street governments—*chieh cheng-fu*). Each street office, then, embraced an average population of 13,800 persons.[59] In effect, the municipal administration became a sort of holding company for the street offices. Not until mid-1949, amidst a flurry of complaints about too much decentralization, were the district and street offices abolished in favor of a unified and centralized municipal adminstration.[60]

In addition to excessive administrative decentralization, two other generic problems bedeviled urban government. Both had their roots in the rural mystique of the CCP which undervalued, if only in theory, the importance of large cities in the revolutionary process. The first was a tendency to treat the cities as treasure houses of freely expendable resources rather than as the administrative nerve centers and production loci that they in fact were during the civil war. In the spring of 1946, Lin Piao himself had said: "The cities do not belong to us for the time being, and we can only regard them as hotels and live in them for a while."[61] Yet while Shenyang, Changchun, and other cities of southern and central Manchuria slipped from the Communists' grasp at that time, they still retained control of Harbin, Tsitsihar, Chiamussu, Mutankiang, and many smaller cities as well. Even the straitened cities of wartime northern Manchuria presented civilian cadres and soldiers alike with opportunities for misbehavior, illicit dealings, and self-indulgence less frequently encountered in the countryside.

Second, the Party had difficulty in reconciling in practice its policy of rural class warfare with its desire to insulate the cities from prolonged and massive disorder. Despite injunctions to peasants and rural cadres alike that the hot pursuit of landlords and other land reform targets into the cities was inadmissible, the frenzied violence of rural land reform sometimes spilled over into the cities and towns. That the self-same evil landlord could become magically transformed into a legitimate merchant or entrepreneur by merely passing through the city gates was an incomprehensible subtlety of Marxist class analysis, akin perhaps to the fox fairies of Chinese popular tales who disguised themselves as beautiful maidens to deceive the unwary. Yet the Party that stood for revolutionary upheaval in the countrysdide was posing at the same time as the Party of revolutionary order in the cities. The tension resulting from this duality was unavoidable.

Long before the Communists took control, Harbin, the major city of the North, had been renowned for its disorderliness. "By the 1930s," writes one historian, "Harbin was a near lawless city . . . Rampant robbery and kidnapping (sometimes with police connivance) obliged affluent citizens to hire bodyguards."[62] As the transportation, commercial, political, and manufacturing hub of northern Manchuria, Harbin attracted large numbers of persons from the rural hinterlands who made their living as casual laborers, hawkers, porters, carters, and droshky drivers. About 33,000 or 4 percent of the city's population were foreigners from twenty different countries, and this posed an additional problem for the novice CCP personnel.[63] Soon after the Soviet Red Army occupation of the Northeast in August 1945, NKVD agents had arrested many of the leading anti-Communists from among the White Russian emigres who had congregated in Harbin after the end of the Russian civil war. The Soviet consulate in Harbin provided assurances, entry visas, and citizenship papers to thousands of homesick or intimidated Russian emigres who returned home to the fatal embrace of late Stalinism.[64]

Communist municipal authorities in Harbin and other major cities attempted to secure order by superimposing modern mobilization policies on the ancient Chinese Legalist obsession with regulations and decrees. Despite what appears to be a proto-totalitarian penchant for complete control of the population, Communist actions are perhaps better understood as a somewhat desperate attempt by what was still a comparatively weak government to substitute a web of regulations and organization for the legitimacy, personnel, and authority which it lacked or possessed inadequately. Of course, as the government grew stronger, this predisposition to control, an inherent feature of revolutionary civil war situations, blossomed into a full-scale totalitarian organization.

From the first weeks of Communist rule in Harbin, the municipal garrison command concentrated on rounding up criminals, bandits and so-called destructive elements *(p'o-huai fen-tzu)*. By December 1946, the municipal street governments had organized over 17,000 citizens into Night Watchmen Self-Defense Teams *(ta-keng tzu-wei tui)* to patrol the city and interrogate and search suspected wrong-doers. In similar fashion, the residents of one locality in Tsitsihar signed citizens' pledges *(kung-min kung-yüeh)* to conduct surveillance and enhance security by listening for rumors, reporting strangers, checking for weapons, registering household moves, etc.[65]

The threat to order came not only from criminal elements and avowed enemies of the revolution. Harbin Mayor Liu Ch'eng-tung announced in February 1947 that some citizens were commiting robbery and other crimes under the pretext that the revolution had encouraged poor persons to stand up *(fan shen)*, and he warned that any infringement of public or private property would be dealt with according to the law regardless of the class origins of the perpetrator. Military uniforms became another cover for the commission of illegal or unauthorized acts. Harbin Garrison Commander Li T'ien-yu issued an order forbidding unauthorized persons from wearing military garb in order to prevent enemy agents from spreading rumors or ordinary swindlers from extorting money, goods, and services from the population at large. The Garrison Command and the municipal government also repeatedly enjoined soldiers and security personnel from destroying property or bivouacking in buildings without permission, or engaging in offensive behavior on public conveyances and elsewhere, a sign of peasant conscripts' ignorance of basic urban regulations as well as the typical military arrogance toward civilians in China.[66]

After twenty months of Communist rule in Harbin, the city fathers were still dismayed with the state of public order. In an announcement which the founder of Legalist philosophy, Shang Yang himself, might have gladly endorsed, the chief of Harbin's Public Security Headquarters, Ch'en Lung, complained that criminal and bandit activity was still flourishing in the city. Consequently, armed patrols would criss-cross the city from 4:30 p.m. till 6 a.m. daily. Every lane was instructed to organize small guard groups and to coordinate with its neighbors. Those persons failing to report criminal activity immediately to the public security office would be judged equally guilty with the criminals themselves. Everyone was told to be on the lookout for persons without employment, drifters, unregistered persons, and the like. Those sheltering bandits would be punished while those turning in miscreants would be given material rewards.[67] Unfortunately, it is difficult to say just how effective such decrees proved to be in practice.

Population registration and travel controls were two of the vital instruments for enhancing the security of the rear areas. An early attempt to gain an accurate registration of population in 1946 produced widespread evasion and confusion so a re-registration was ordered in the fall of 1947. The explicit purpose was to uncover bad elements, eradicate crime, and strengthen public order, though there may have been tax, conscription, and mobilization aims as well.[68]

Travel restrictions and passport controls served public security and economic warfare objectives. They made it more difficult for enemy agents to move freely through Communist territory and they reduced the volume of illegal economic transactions between the red and the white areas of the Northeast. As such, they complemented the elaborate trade regulations promulgated for the region. In this, as in so many other areas, one can chart a progression toward administrative centralization and control.

Initially, provincial, district, and county governments all issued their own travel documents for travel outside their jurisdictions or to Nationalist territory. In Sungkiang, for example, the Provincial Public Security Office issued passports to travelers fifteen years or older and established a system of checkpoints where travelers had to get their documents inspected and stamped. In June 1947, the Northeast Central Public Security Office established a unified system of travel controls for nonofficial travelers, and invalidated all old passports. (The army and the government had their own separate systems.) All persons ten years old and above who wanted to travel outside of their own county a distance of more than twenty *li* had to apply to their local public security office after obtaining a letter of recommendation from their village or street government. Neither the army nor local governments were authorized to issue travel documents to civilians or commercial travelers. The new system was officially promulgated in a NEAC directive of June 20, 1947.[69] (For travel within the county or distances under twenty *li* into a neighboring county, a local travel document issued by the district sufficed.)

Harbin municipal travel regulations provide additional details. Under the municipal public security department there were established inspection stations and sub-bureaus responsible for vehicular and passenger traffic. Long-distance travelers required a Northeast Liberated Areas Unified Passport, while vehicles (trucks and carts) needed papers from the provincial or other appropriate public security office. Drivers were enjoined not to carry escaping landlords, bandits, bad elements, or military contraband.[70]

A test of the new administrative controls on travel as well as the efficiency of the entire governing system presented itself with the appearance in the autumn of 1947 of that dread camp follower of war and revolution—bubonic plague, no stranger to Manchuria.[71] Several decades earlier, in fact, a major international effort had been mounted in Manchuria to bring under control an epidemic of plague transmitted by flea-infested rats.[72] The Japanese army's 731st Regiment had conducted germ warfare experiments in Harbin during the war and released plague-infested laboratory animals in the summer of 1945, causing a minor outbreak of plague in 1946.[73] The strain of war and revolution contributed to a further deterioration of sanitary conditions in both urban and rural districts of the Northeast.[74] Poor nutrition and inadequate or nonexistent preventive public health care increased the susceptibility to disease of men and animals alike. In the spring of 1947 a serious outbreak of rinderpest (cattle plague) decimated the livestock of northern Manchuria. Then in September an outbreak of plague in eleven counties of Liaopei province quickly felled 1,000 persons and prompted NEAC to issue a directive on means of combating the disease. An urgent call went out for epidemic prevention personnel and high wages were offered to those willing to serve under dangerous, emergency conditions.[75]

Before anything could be done, the disease quickly spread into more than twenty counties, and by the third week of September, 10,000 persons had died in Liaopei and Kirin provinces. One week later an additional 10,000 had succumbed and the death toll eventually reached over 30,000. (A third of the deaths occurred in T'ungliao county alone). At its meeting on September 27, NEAC adopted emergency measures to deal with the plague. It created a regional Northeast Plague Prevention Committee, and decreed that plague prevention should become the focus of all activity in Liaopei, Nunkiang, Sungkiang, Harbin, Tsitsihar, and northern Kirin. The governmental apparatus was ordered to improve quarantine measures, mobilize the population for plague prevention work, and employ the militia in an all-out effort to cope with what had become an extraordinary public health crisis.[76] Travel controls were tightened and strict inspection of road and rail transport enforced. In Harbin, Tsitsihar, and other cities mass inoculations against the plague were carried out by medical personnel drafted by the municipal governments, and all movements into and out of the city were strictly controlled. A key role in the efforts was played by teams of Soviet doctors who brought in vitally needed medical supplies and equipment and helped train Chinese personnel in preventing and combating plague.[77] This aid was dictated as much by self-interest as from internationalist solidarity, because plague could easily have traveled along rail lines to the Soviet Union as it had in earlier times.

Despite the emergency, reports from the most severely affected areas in Liaopei asserted that lack of sufficient concern on the part of the cadres and widespread popular superstitions were hampering plague control efforts. Rather than eradicating rats and fleas and getting inoculated, apparently not a few rural people sought safety in traditional spiritual nostrums and mediums. Since many local governments were helpless because of lack of proper sanitary equipment and supplies, the popular reliance on spirits was perhaps not so deserving of censure as the Communist attitude implied. In any event, by the end of November a combination of administrative measures and the onset of cold winter weather gradually brought the crisis to an end. Quarantine and plague-related inspection measures were lifted except for the epicenter of the plague in T'ungliao. Plague recurred in the Northeast in both 1948 and 1949, but with diminished ferocity. In 1948, just under 6,000 persons died of plague and the next year the figure dropped precipitously to 250.[78]

In the public health crisis engendered by the plague, the administrative machinery and regulations created to enforce public order had generally proved their worth, and demonstrated the increasing ability of NEAC and its subordinate governments to achieve compliance with their directives. At the same time, scattered evidence suggests that shortages of trained personnel and equipment as well as the persistence of traditional responses to crisis continued to limit the ability of the Communist government to enforce its will even though in this case it was clearly acting in the public interest.

Military Recruitment and Mobilization

Men are the oxygen that keep the fires of war burning. The civil war in the Northeast, a conventional war in terms of the scale and type of operations, consumed vast numbers of soldiers and civilian support personnel. The Chinese people are so numerous it would seem that manpower could never become a problem in wartime. Indeed, as a U.S. intelligence report suggested in 1947, it was the availability of materiel and food, not of men, that was the limiting factor controlling the size of the Communist armies.[79] Rebels and revolutionaries in modern China have rarely encountered any difficulty in enlisting large numbers of men willing to fight beneath their banners. Chinese society in the nineteenth and twentieth centuries contained many marginally employed men for whom military service (in whosesoever cause) represented a rational subsistence alternative.[80] However, this was less true of Manchuria because the expanding economy in the twentieth century created a growing demand for labor. Nonetheless, regional militarists like Chang Tso-lin as well as the Manchukuo authorities easily raised large armies from within the region. Even in the Northeast there were substantial numbers of marginally employed persons as well as men who simply preferred military service, with its assurances of food and shelter and the license for occasionally running amuck, to the drudgery of common labor.[81] The venerable tradition of banditry in the Northeast is further evidence of this point.

The revolutionary civil war of the 1940s was qualitatively different from the earlier warlord conflicts with respect to the level of demands it placed on the people and the civilian economy. Rather than the characteristic warlord mode of intermittent warfare alternating with periods of political maneuvering and alliance-building, the civil war was a nearly continuous three-year zero-sum struggle between two antagonists in a fight to the finish.[82] Even the intermittent warfare of the 1920s in support of Chang Tso-lin's ambitions had placed a heavy burden on the Northeast people and, in particular, on the economy of Liaoning (Fengtien), the richest of the Manchurian provinces.[83] How were the Communists able to wage large-scale revolutionary warfare in the Northeast from the much smaller and poorer territory they controlled? In essence, the answer is that Communist organizational capacity applied to the problems of war enabled them to make maximum use of limited resources.

Military Recruitment

The concept of total warfare comes naturally to revolutionaries with their instinct for politicizing all aspects of human activity. Imbedded in the concept of total war is the nationalist axiom that everyone's primary obligation is to serve the state. This is nowhere

better expressed than in the famous levée en masse decreed by
the French Committee of Public Safety in August 1793:

All Frenchmen are in permanent requisition for army service. The young
men will go to fight; the married men will forge arms and carry supplies;
and the women will make tents and uniforms and will serve in the
hospitals; the children will shred the old clothes; the old men be taken
to public squares to excite the courage of the combatants.[84]

This statement of the duties of people's war could be applied with
little change to the civil war in China. What is too often unjusti-
fiably assumed, however, is that those called upon to bear these
burdens do so willingly and even enthusiastically.[85] An analysis
of Communist military recruitment in the Northeast points to a
more complex mixture of voluntarism, persuasion, and coercion
in filling the ranks.

　　　Military recruitment practices in pre-1949 China reflected the absence of a strong centralized state with an effective
administrative machinery. Military service in a wide variety of
armies beckoned many youths who lacked more attractive alter-
natives. An attempt by the National Government to institute a
system of regularized military conscription during the anti-Japanese war was far from successful, and it was not unusual for
officers to dragoon into service whatever unfortunates they could
lay their hands on.[86] As a consequence, desertion was frequent,
army life brutish, morale often very poor, and loyalty precarious.

　　　The Communist armies' methods of recruitment
evolved gradually from the early days of the Kiangsi soviet through
the later stages of the anti-Japanese war. At first, many of the Red
Army soldiers appear to have been pressed into service, and the
Communist commanders had to cope with numerous deserters.[87]
Later, during the Yenan period, the soldiers of the 8th Route Army
and New Fourth Armies were said to be all volunteers, but Tetsuya
Kataoka reminds us that "these 'volunteers' consented to serve
under intense public pressure drummed up by mass organizations
. . . This method was intended to be different from press-ganging,
but in practice it often came close to it."[88]

　　　When the NEDUA began rebuilding its forces during
the summer of 1946, initial emphasis was placed on recruiting
men for local militia and regional security forces. For example,

under the slogan of "Everything in support of victory in the self-defense war," several tens of thousand peasants—from thirty to eighty in each village—were mobilized to join the militia in Chi-an county (eastern Kirin). Acting under instructions from provincial CCP committees, county Party committees prepared recruitment plans for the districts under their jurisdiction, and used methods of individual and collective mobilization to meet the quotas.[89] As the pace of recruitment for local militia and county security forces stepped up in late 1946 and early 1947, increasing numbers of men were "graduated" to the main forces of the NEDUA. As had been the case in nineteenth-century China, the lower level forces served as an important and self-replenishing reservoir of men for the regular army.[90]

In his study of peasant political behavior, Samuel Popkin notes: "it is common for labor demands and military drafts to be pushed onto the poorer villagers."[91] This is usually just another form of their victimization. In Manchuria, for very different reasons, this same group likewise appears to have borne a disproportionate share of the military service burden. Wanting to build a new type of army from those elements which had gained the most from the rural revolution, the Communists introduced class criteria into their recruitment regulations. One typical list contained six so-called "guarantees" concerning recruitment: (1) no use of compulsion; (2) no buying of recruits; (3) good class origins and class status (ch'u-shen and ch'eng-fen); (4) young; (5) healthy; (6) no landlord or rich peasant recruits.[92] Recruitment was often carried out in association with land reform under the slogan of joining the army to protect the land. Presumably, only those who had benefited from the division of land could be trusted to fight in such a struggle.

From the beginning of 1947, as the CCP began to expand its organizational network in rural northern Manchuria, the pace of military recruitment was stepped up. The *Northeast Daily* printed numerous reports of successful recruitment drives in counties throughout the Communist Northeast. Although specific numbers are cited in each of these reports, it is difficult to draw any general conclusions on the basis of what remains only partial statistics. It is clear, however, that up through perhaps the first half of 1947, the NEDUA was drawing most of its manpower from a relatively small population base (Heilungkiang and scattered counties in eastern Kirin and western Liaoning). This led to extremely heavy pressure on the labor supply in the affected areas. For example, 5,000 persons were reported to have joined the main forces in Mingshui county (eastern Heilungkiang) out of a total population of about 60,000. This was 8.3 percent of the people in the county! In six recruitment drives in Harbin over a thirteen-month period, 9,300 people entered the army.[93] Harbin's population was about 800,000.

The pace of recruitment was in direct proportion to the intensity of the fighting. During and immediately after the spring 1947 NEDUA offensives, recruitment was intensified to replace the numerous battlefield casualties. A rare published casualty figure from the Communist side reveals that in nation-wide fighting in the three-month period (March–May 1947), Communist forces lost 116,000 men.[94] Since this was a period of relative quiescence on intramural fronts and intense fighting in the Northeast, it is likely that most of these casualties occurred in Manchuria. In northern and western Manchuria tens of thousands of new recruits poured into the ranks of the NEDUA in July alone. Scattered statistics suggest that somewhat over 100 men per district (ch'ü) was the quota handed down from above. A very high percentage of those examined for service were actually inducted. In Naho county (northern Heilungkiang), for example, 782 of 983 candidates (80 percent) were recruited into the army. As the Communist armies moved south, many new areas for recruitment opened up and most of the new recruits in the last year of the war appear to have come from the newly occupied territory.[95]

The task of military recruitment was carried out by the hierarchy of organizations created by the CCP down to the village level. Recruitment quotas were passed down the chain of authority from NEAC through the provincial governments and the counties and on down to the villages where the actual mobilization of manpower occurred. Cadres accorded this task a very high priority. Within the village or urban ward, those men eligible to serve were easily identified by the local leadership. Mobilization meetings were convened at which these men were encouraged to enlist. The pressure of peers, neighbors, friends, and family was brought to bear insofar as possible to expedite the process.[96] Many peasants were apparently unenthusiastic about leaving the fields and other property which they had just acquired through land reform and marching off to an uncertain fate. Families were often reluctant to send their menfolk into battle.

Party propagandists, faced with the challenge of how to overcome this pressure, tried to transform family anxieties into a positive force. A poem in the *Northeast Daily* described the proper resolution to one familial tug-of-war:

> In Hulan village young Lien-ching
> Deeply yearns to be a soldier.
> His dad says go, his mom says no,
> His wife says don't abandon me.
> She tugs at him and won't let go:
> "If you join up, how long will you be gone?
> How can you leave us young and old alike?"
> The flustered lad says, "Dearest wife,
> Come to your senses please, Hsiao-ching,
> The 8th Route troops and we are one;
> I'll join to smash old bandit Chiang
> For only then will peace be ours."[97]

In village society where family relations were still of utmost importance,[98] the Communists tried to link the family's fortunes to victory in the civil war as another propaganda verse entitled "The Seven Persuasions to Join the Army" suggests:

> If a father gets his son to enlist
> The revolution will take this to heart.
> If a son gets his father to enlist
> He'll be forever revolutionized.
> If an elder brother gets a younger brother to enlist,
> The roots of poverty will soon be excised.
> If a younger sister gets an elder brother to enlist,
> Only then may the roots of wealth reach deep.
> If a younger brother gets an elder brother to enlist
> The Nationalist Army will be smashed to bits.
> If an elder sister gets a younger brother to enlist,
> Victory will soon be ours.
> If a wife persuades her husband to enlist,
> There'll be no worries in the family.[99]

The full resources of the Party's well-developed propaganda apparatus were deployed to encourage enlistment.

More concrete encouragement came in the form of preferential treatment for military dependents, ranging from assistance in tilling newly distributed land to the provision of various free services. Wide variation in the regulations governing the treatment of military dependents led NEAC in February 1948 to enact a uniform code spelling out what was owed to them. This specified preferential treatment for military dependents with respect to the distribution of land, tools, and other equipment, priority access to government agricultural loans, free school tuition and free treatment at local clinics (where available), and provision of substitute labor by local governments to compensate for the person serving in the army.[100] Harbin municipal regulations (approved by NEAC) promised free municipal services (water, electricity, sewerage, housing) for military dependents as well as help in establishing productive enterprises to provide supplemental income. Children below the age of fifteen and adults above the age of fifty-five or disabled could receive a monthly allocation of grain and firewood in addition to medical care and educational benefits.[101] These services would continue in case the serviceman became a casualty of war. The intended effect of these various regulations was not only to stimulate recruitment, but also to improve the morale of those serving in the ranks and lower the rate of desertion. The preferential treatment functioned as a kind of bonus system of material incentives for joining. It is interesting to note that in at least one county, and probably elsewhere too, the wives of military personnel were not allowed to change their marital status and those who sought to entice them into doing so were subject to punishment.[102]

In sum, during the course of the revolutionary civil war in the Northeast, the Communists recruited something on the order of 1 million men into their military forces and swept to victory in the region on the strength of their success in mobilizing local manpower.[103]

Labor Mobilization for Combat Support

No less vital to the Communist war effort were the hundreds of thousands of civilian noncombatant laborers (*min-fu* or *min-kung*) without whose services the only partly mechanized Communist armies could not have functioned. In the Liaoshen campaign, for example, the NEPLA mobilized 96,000 laborers, 13,800 stretcher-bearers, and 36,700 large carts for transport.[104] Most modern Chinese armies filled their need for laborers by simply pressing men into service for however long their work was required, paying little if any heed to the impact upon the laborers themselves or the livelihood of their families.[105] The Communist effort to recruit min-fu was based, at least in theory, on the principle of the equitable distribution of the burden of service while ensuring an adequate supply of manpower. The core idea was to assign manpower quotas to the local levels and to see that these were filled without resort to outright coercion or mechanisms which could easily be manipulated by the wealthier rural inhabitants.

Early in the war, one Communist newspaper pointed out that the central task of every war zone was war mobilization.[106] Each county, district, and village was responsible for organizing a stretcher-bearer corps ranging from a large brigade at the county level down to a small team (8 persons) at the village level. What was initially an ad hoc system of min-fu mobilization was given a more regular form by a NEAC decision of April 1, 1947. This decree specified that males between 17 and 50 years old and women between 18 and 45 as well as persons with draft animals, carts, and boats were liable to service obligations. These included transport of such things as military supplies, ammunition, and grain, provision of stretcher service, and field station attendance and nursing. Each eligible person was liable to five days of service per month up to a cumulative annual total of sixty days of labor which could, if necessary, be bunched in one block of time.[107] It is important to note that the family rather than the individual was the unit for assessment of this obligation. Parallel provisions applied to draft animals, carts, and boats. In rear areas away from the fighting the obligation was thirty rather than sixty days. Exempt from labor service were Party, government, military, and mass organization cadres at or above the ch'ü (district) level as well as workers in public enterprises. Not quite one year later, NEAC reissued these regulations which suggests that there may have been some difficulty in securing compliance with the limitations contained therein.[108]

Recruitment of min-fu was often done through the labor exchange groups that began to be organized in many areas in 1947, but those who were not thus organized were also subject to service. The actual registration of the quota of "volunteers" was done at village meetings where the *min-fu* were organized into functional units, and then assembled into district and county brigades for the trip to the front, accompanied by cadres from their localities. "Alien class elements" such as struggled landlords or refractory persons like the *erh-liu- tzu* (vagrants or idlers) were used as mobile labor to replace peasants recruited as *min-fu*. The desire to ensure that *min-fu* were politically reliable, however, had to be balanced against the overwhelming need for manpower, and cadres were advised to be less finicky about the class status of *min-fu* than they were about military inductees. Even landlords' sons could be used as stretcher-bearers if properly supervised.[109]

Cadres and activists strived to achieve a high degree of voluntarism in the mobilization of *min-fu* through propaganda appealing to both patriotism and self-interest. One article in the *Northeast Daily* touted the use of such catchy slogans as "Good men should join up or they're not heroes," and "If everyone would shake a leg, we'll put an end to Chiang bad egg." Inevitably, the stress on voluntarism was often jettisoned as harried cadres pressed unwilling peasants into service in order to meet the quotas set from above. The other side of the coin was that families sometimes offered their less able-bodied members as *min-fu* in the hope of minimizing the economic impact of labor service. One analysis of war mobilization work adjured cadres to inspect the members of stretcher-bearer teams carefully (there were 8 *min-fu* to a team) in order to weed out the undersized, the aged, the sick, and the hired substitutes.[110]

Once recruited, attention was paid to organizing the *min-fu* into appropriate units, giving them adequate supplies, making provision for their dependents, and installing them with an esprit de corps so that they would not desert en route or break under attack. *Min-fu* were often made to swear a collective oath that they would not desert—a probable indication of the persistence of this problem. In Liaopei (and presumably elsewhere as well) poor families which performed *min-fu* service were treated as military dependents for the period of their family member's service. *Min-fu* injured in the line of service were treated like soldiers and the government provided compensation for draft animals and carts injured or destroyed in service.[111]

Understandably, many peasants were reluctant to serve as *min-fu* because of the grave risks entailed. To counter this fear, Party propagandists were instructed to spread news of Communist victories in order to bolster *min-fu* morale, to hold appropriate send-offs for the volunteers, and also to welcome back those returning from the field as a way of refuting rumors about the devastation wreaked by Nationalist bombers.[112] *Min-fu* were rewarded or punished for outstanding or deficient service.

In the areas where the Communists had had time to initiate the agrarian revolution, the peasants who were called upon to serve in the army or as *min-fu* could perceive a stake in the outcome of the revolutionary civil war because many of them had already benefited from the distribution of land and movable property. Yet as the war moved southward at an accelerating pace, the Party was increasingly compelled to recruit soldiers, mobilize labor, and requisition supplies in areas just behind the front lines, where it had not yet had the time to carry out the revolutionary transformation.[113] It imposed heavy burdens on the local population before it conveyed any advantage by its presence. Nor did it have time to organize and properly motivate the men who were pressed into service as the military machine ground forward. Under the strain of campaign conditions, it is questionable whether peasants experienced such mobilization as very much different from the burdens imposed by the militarists, the Japanese, and the Nationalists in their turn. Yet from the Party's viewpoint, there was no feasible alternative to this politically premature mobilization.

In addition to this structural problem, the Communists' mobilization efforts, while impressive in scope and results, were not without flaws. Reporting to a ten-day conference of the General Rear Services Department of the NEPLA (December 1947–January 1948), General Huang K'o-ch'eng pointed out many defects in the work of his department. In particular, there was much waste of manpower. In the trans-Sungari operations, for example, four *min-fu* had been needed for each combat soldier. Despite the system of field stations and stretcher-bearers, an unsatisfactory percentage of the tens of thousands of wounded were treated well enough to be able to return to battle duty. (Huang omitted the percentage for security reasons.) In addition, much of the material supplied to frontline troops (e.g., shoes) was of poor quality or simply unusable. Finally, he pointed to costly corruption and bureaucratism in the department. Another report refers to the insufficiency of food supplies for the *min-fu*.[114] However, the Party press rarely spoke of these shortcomings, preferring to dwell on the steady stream of men, carts, horses, fodder, and supplies that flowed to the front in support of the war.

Despite shortcomings in the implementation of the mobilization policies caused by the pressure of ongoing military campaigns, inadequately trained cadres, and the general atmosphere of revolutionary fervor, the Communist Party's approach to the problem of manpower recruitment probably went far to neutralize peasant suspicions of the Party and even to win over a substantial number of supporters in the villages, particularly once it became evident that Communist power was there to stay. Yet it would be a mistake to minimize the burden which the Party placed on the peasantry in the Northeast China or to suggest that most peasants were enthusiastic about CCP power.

Army-Civilian Relations

In the days of the Northern Expedition, the National Revolutionary Army of the Kuomintang behaved in an exemplary fashion and enjoyed excellent relations with the people in the areas through which it passed.[115] However, the Nationalist armies in Manchuria during the civil war had a far different reputation. Feared for their arrogant behavior and despised as outsiders by the Northeast people, the CNA got very little cooperation or support in the areas it controlled. The Communists, however, paid considerable attention to the problem of civil-military relations. They could not afford to engender popular hostility since, as we have just seen, they were dependent upon the people in many ways. Yet it was not easy to achieve the ideal rapport between soldiers and civilians depicted in this lesson from a civil war era peasant literature reader:

The PLA is resolute and brave,
They love the nation and the people
And are as one with the workers and peasants.
The NEDUA's commander General Lin Piao is most famous,
At the battle of Ssup'ing the enemy lost heart,
Thrice the NEDUA counterattacked south of the Sungari.
The army loves the people, the people support the army.
They support Commander-in-Chief Chu Teh.
The army kills the enemy, protects the land
And quickly drives bandit Chiang south to Nanking.[116]

In the first months of the civil war, the Communist armies, harried and on the defensive, could spare little effort to cultivate good relations with the people. Many of the early recruits were of low caliber and quite unused to the strict discipline of a revolutionary army. The result was that the relations between the army and the people were poor. An important directive from the Political Department of the NEDUA (January 1, 1947) bemoaned the fact that relations between the army and the people were not as good in the Northeast as in the old liberated areas. It blamed arrogant attitudes within the army including the notion that Northeasterners were accustomed to enemy rule and therefore could be abused with impunity. Even when army discipline within the Communist rear areas was said to be good, the army behaved improperly toward civilians when conducting operations in Nationalist areas.[117]

Local governments and mass organizations were instructed to promote activities designed to improve civilian-army-relations. From the army side this took the form of the movement to Support the Government and Cherish the People (yung-cheng ai-min yün-tung) and from the civilian side the movement to Support the Army and Give Preferential Treatment to Army Dependents (yung-chün yu-shu yün-tung) in accordance with a NEAC directive of January 1, 1947. Residents in urban areas collected large sums of money and sent thousands of comfort parcels to the soldiers containing articles for daily use and personal letters. Local governments organized visits to army dependents' households, bringing gifts of food and clothing during the Lunar New Year.[118]

At the same time, soldiers were instructed to establish contact with the local people and ask for their frank criticisms of behavioral shortcomings. Army mess units *(huo-shih tan-wei)* were told to send representatives to help the poor and comfort army dependents' family members. The West Manchurian Sub-Bureau of the CCP publicized a typical Support the Government and Cherish the People compact which soldiers were supposed to sign containing a long list of do's and don'ts.[119]

Relations between the army and the people were said to have improved as a result of efforts on both sides, but it was not possible, of course, to eliminate all friction. A directive from the Political Department of the Kirin Military District (August 16, 1947) asserted that many violations of military discipline had occurred during the recent NEDUA offensive and had been too lightly dismissed as caused by the exigencies of the situation. It called for further rectification and education. Harsher measures were sometimes imposed, including the death penalty.[120] Despite the continuing friction, lapses, and transgressions, what is most worthy of note is the generally good character of the relations between the Communist armies and the people of the Northeast based upon the overall restraint of the troops. Viewed against the background of the often troubled and exploitative relations between other modern Chinese armies and the people, this was no mean accomplishment.

Cadres—Recruitment and Behavior

The French Marxist Regis Debray observed: "Revolutionaries make revolutionary civil wars, but to an even greater extent it is revolutionary civil wars that make revolutionaries."[121] Revolution—a kind of secular salvation—can be realized only through the imperfect instrument of those who enter into its service for diverse motives. If a revolutionary party is to succeed in taking power, it must possess an adequate supply of cadres with training appropriate to the multiple functions they must perform and whose standards of behavior do not alienate those people whom the party hopes to lead in making revolution. By its own account, the CCP fought the revolutionary civil war in Northeast China under the double handicap of inadequate numbers of well-trained cadres whose behavior, moreover, often fell considerably short of the norms the Party had established. Nevertheless, as the Catholic Church has long held, even a wayward priest can be a vehicle for salvation. The men and women whom the Communist Party recruited to its standard during the civil war in Manchuria were often too few in number, inadequately indoctrinated and indifferently motivated, but they proved capable nonetheless of making the revolution that brought the Party to power.

Just one week after the NEPLA occupied Shenyang, the *Northeast Daily* took note of the critical need for experienced cadres whose numbers were still far from adequate.[122] In fact, the occupation of the Northeast's largest cities in 1948 simply exacerbated the long-standing problem of the supply of cadres. From the very first stages of its postwar activity in the Northeast, the Party had to cope with formidable personnel problems. In his report "On the Party" to the Seventh Party Congress, Liu Shao-ch'i pointed out that "the theoretical and cultural level of our Party members is not high," and he complained of continuing tendencies toward subjectivism, commandism, bureaucratism, and warlordism in cadre work style. Liu paid particular attention to the problem of outside cadres, noting that while it was necessary to use outside cadres in new areas, they should turn over the work to local cadres as soon as possible. He concluded by suggesting: "The main yardstick for measuring our Party work in a given place is whether or not we have developed a sufficient number of good cadres and leaders from among the people in a given place."[123]

The Communist Party attacked the problem of regional legitimation at the basic cadre level just as it did with respect to that of the upper echelon leadership. Provincial particularism or regionalism was not as deeply rooted in the Northeast as it was in the old historic provinces of intramural China, but it was by no means negligible. Within Manchuria itself there were differences in the self and mutual perceptions of persons from Liaoning, Kirin, and Heilungkiang; however, vis-à-vis intra-mural China one may speak of a Manchurian regional identity.[124] In addition, because of the large number of recent migrants to the region, there still existed a complex of provincial and sub-provincial identifications which these migrants brought with them.[125] The CCP took considerable pains to identify itself with these particularistic sentiments without sacrificing the substance of centralized control over the regional Communist movement.

Especially during the first postwar year, but even thereafter, the regional Party apparatus was heavily dependent upon outside cadres. According to Communist estimates, some 50,000 political cadres were transferred to the Northeast beginning in 1945 from base areas in North and East China.[126] Outside cadres could play a vital role in "starting up" the machinery of revolution, but a continuing preponderance of such cadres, particularly in the rural areas, would make it extremely difficult for the Party's revolutionary work to proceed. In order to penetrate the xenophobic suspicions frequently encountered in Chinese villages, particularly during periods of political instability, and to establish the bonds of trust and mutual advantage upon which organization could be built, local cadres were indispensable.

As the Party rapidly expanded into new territories after the Japanese surrender, the problems involved in the relationship between outside and local cadres were exacerbated. In an inner-Party directive dated December 15, 1945, Mao Tse-tung noted that outside cadres were playing the leading role at all levels in many areas, including the Northeast. He ordered outside cadres to make "the selection, training and promotion of local cadres an important task for themselves," and to avoid condescending toward local people.[127]

The problem of a condescending work style was at the center of the tension between outside and local cadres. Many Chinese from intramural China tended to view Northeasterners as *t'u-pao tzu* (country bumpkins), and Manchurian sentiment toward outsiders, particularly from southern China, returned the compliment. Added to this was a widespread feeling in China that Northeasterners (like Taiwanese but to a lesser degree) had been ideologically contaminated by fourteen years of Japanese education and propaganda and needed to be re-inoculated with national values. The CCP was not immune to these sentiments.[128] Both attitudes represented obstacles to the indigenization of the Communist Party in the Northeast.

The natural tension between outsiders and locals was

extremely difficult to address under the conditions that prevailed during the initial stages of Communist activity in the Northeast. Starting with only a handful of local supporters, the outside cadres of the Communist Party had to throw together an army and a political organization under severe pressure of time. The impending withdrawal of the Soviet Red Army (November 1945–May 1946) and the proximity of hostile Chinese Nationalist forces poised to strike into Manchuria allowed no margin for careful and cautious recruitment of local personnel. At this stage, either outside cadres ran the show or there would be no show to run. Small-scale efforts to recruit and train local cadres began even prior to the summer of 1946, but it was not until the Communists secured more or less stable base areas in northern Manchuria toward the end of 1946 that local persons could be recruited and trained for political leadership on a large scale. In addition to the outside cadres, the Party still depended very much upon retained personnel from the Manchukuo period to supplement its own meager resources. Much of the early Party work was performed by active-duty soldiers on temporary assignment. In a report to the West Manchurian Sub-Bureau of the Central Committee, Ch'en Yün said that military units should detach one-third of their officers and men for service in the countryside in order to mobilize the masses.[129] According to another source, in the summer of 1946, each brigade of the NEDUA contributed five men to rural work, and by the end of July 1946 some 12,000 soldiers were on assignment in the countryside.[130] Thus, even the initial stage of the agrarian revolution was an army operation in this respect.

The *ch'ing-suan movement* (to settle accounts) was the Party's first serious attempt at entering into the political life of the region at the local level, and the Party recruited thousands of persons during its course. In Sungkiang province, for example, under the leadership of 285 old cadres, over 7,000 new cadres were recruited and trained during a three-month period in late 1946, and the Party aimed at absorbing an equal number in the first months of 1947.[131] During the course of land reform, the Party took into its ranks a very large number of peasant cadres who thereupon played a key role in establishing Communist power within the villages.

The Party organization had a difficult time absorbing,

training, and indoctrinating this flood of new recruits, most of whom had a very low cultural level and at best a rudimentary understanding of CCP policy. Although the focus of Party activity was the countryside, the direction and coordination of the complex tasks of waging a revolutionary civil war was an urban task that required administrative and technical skills which very few of the peasant cadres could offer. Thus, while continuing its efforts in the countryside, the CCP simultaneously attacked the problem of attracting and training urban recruits as well.

The Communists set up both long- and short-term training institutes where they aimed at producing administrative cadres as well as a wide variety of technical specialists. In September 1946, NEAC established a Northeast Administrative Institute (Tung-pei hsing-cheng hsüeh-yuan) which recruited several hundred students between the ages of 18 and 25 for a one-year all-expenses paid course in civil administration, finance, and education. (Lin Feng was the titular head of the institute; the dean was Wei Chen-wu.) The only thing a student had to provide was his own quilt. Upon completion of the course, graduates were assigned jobs in the government apparatus.[132] A similar institution, apparently with a somewhat broader mission, was the Northeast Military-Civilian University (Tung-pei chün-cheng ta-hsüeh), modeled on Yenan's famous K'ang-Ta.[133] Originally located in Peian (northern Heilungkiang), it moved to Tsitsihar in December 1947. It provided six-month training courses to prepare young people for work in political, economic, and military affairs. (Lin Piao was the titular principal, P'eng Chen the titular political commissar. The school was actually administered by Ho Ch'ang-kung as Vice-Principal, Wu Kai-chih as Deputy Political Commissar, and Ch'en Po-chün as Dean of Education.) An April 1947 notice of recruitment for the university's tenth matriculation stipulated that applicants must be healthy males between 18 and 25 years old, from a good class background, and must be either college graduates or have two years of high school or high school equivalency. Admission was by oral and written exams in Chinese language, math, history, and current events; tests were administered in Tsitsihar, Harbin, and Peian. Graduates were promised civilian or military employment.[134]

In addition to these major regional institutions, there

were a number of other cadre training schools run by municipal or other authorities, such as the Harbin Young Cadres School and the Military-Civilian School in Poli (eastern Heilungkiang). Although direct information on the curricula of these schools is unavailable, some idea of the subjects studied is suggested by the following list of titles recommended for cadre reading in an advertisement by the Northeast Bookstore in Harbin: *Leadership Style, Handbook for Newspaper Work, Northeast Rural Investigation, Military-Civilian Relations, Army Culture Study and Correspondence Work, A Portrait of Mao Tse-tung, Handbook for Mass Work, The Victorious Self-Defense War*, many Marxist-Leninist classics, and titles in history, social science, and natural science.[135]

Naturally, the revolution could not mark time until the graduates of these long-term training institutes were ready to commence work. Therefore, a large number and variety of short-term, practical training courses were established to deal with the immediate shortage of cadres. A short-term training course for new cadres in Chiamussu, sponsored by the municipal CCP committee, was probably typical with respect to the students it enrolled and its pedagogical objectives. Most of the new cadres enrolled had been activists in the *ch'ing-suan* or land reform movements and had only rudimentary education. The in-service training sessions focused on current problems from a practical rather than a theoretical perspective. Included were such issues as the transformation of political power, development of industry and commerce, anti-traitor activity, land reform and the establishment of peasant associations, and the mass line. Veteran cadres with experience in these areas served as instructors. Rural cadre training sessions appear to have been crash courses in class consciousness-raising. Their particular objective was to get village cadres to think in class categories about the familiar people in their midst rather than viewing them as individuals embedded in local networks.[136] Through such a process of abstraction and dehumanization, the revolutionary transformation of village power relations could be more effectively promoted.

As the fighting intensified in 1947, the Communist armies occupied many medium-sized cities and increased their stocks of motorized transport, machinery, and other equipment. Both the army and the government urgently required the services of technical specialists who were in critically short supply. To meet this need, technical training institutes were set up in Harbin, Chiamussu, Mutankiang, and elsewhere to train thousands of auto mechanics and drivers, railroad technicians, veterinarians, doctors, and other health service workers.[137] These institutions typically recruited young men and women of "good" class background and provided free tuition, room, and board in courses ranging from six months to four years depending upon the specialty. The Communist armies operated their own schools across a wide spectrum of military specialties including aviation, antiaircraft, logistics, vehicle maintenance, rear services, army medicine, and artillery.[138]

In the Northeast, as elsewhere, the Communists faced the question of whether class background criteria should be applied to candidates for admission to their cadre training schools. Children from so-called bad class backgrounds (landlords, rich peasants, the urban middle class) were generally better educated than worker and peasant offspring, and thus were more suitable candidates for specialized training from a purely pedagogic point of view. The Party's instinct then as later was to mistrust the motivation of such well-educated youth. In a speech to the Hokiang Young Cadres School on October 11, 1947, Northeast Bureau member Chang Wen-t'ien (Lo Fu) denied that the CCP rejected these young intellectuals, but he maintained that only students from poor families could attend cadre training schools because their class interests predisposed them to favor Party policies of revolutionary change. Intellectual youth from landlord and rich peasant families would have to prove that their ideology had been transformed before they might be admitted to training institutes. Meanwhile, they could be used only in relatively innocuous cultural work.[139] Chang's speech reflected the extreme leftist mood prevailing within the Party during this season of land equalization. However, in the face of the urgent demand for intellectuals and technical specialists of every kind, the Party could not afford to indulge its penchant for class and ideological purity.[140]

In intramural China, a significant minority of young urban intellectuals had already shown their receptivity to Communist appeals for nationalism and social reform. During the civil war years, these youth were quite solidly anti-Kuomintang and a small but steady stream of leftist youths flowed out of the KMT-held cities to the rural Communist areas.[141] In the Northeast the wave of student discontent was somewhat attenuated, and the student protests which occurred failed to assume the scope or significance of similar demonstrations elsewhere in China.[142] The Communists had been disappointed by the lack of responsiveness of young Northeast intellectuals to revolutionary appeals. A pamphlet from 1946, for example, criticized those youths who wavered and did not join the revolutionary struggle. Many Northeasterners were politically backward, it was alleged, and even among the youth who joined the revolutionary ranks, the intellectuals and especially the young women were reluctant to devote themselves wholeheartedly to the struggle.[143] However, given the Party's suspicions of and condescension toward these young intellectuals, it is not surprising that so few of the Northeast young people were willing to cast their lot with the CCP.

On January 15, 1948, the Northeast Bureau sounded a new note in a directive concerning intellectuals. It criticized as a deviation the wide-spread practice of automatically discriminating against the older intellectuals and their children solely on the basis of class. In particular, it was deemed wrong to apply the criteria of rural class struggle to the setting of urban schools, factories, and organizations. Enunciating a policy of absorbing and reeducating intellectuals, the Northeast Bureau decreed that individual attitude and performance should be used in evaluating intellectuals of landlord-rich peasant background. Only those who opposed the revolution and aided the Kuomintang should be excluded from cadre schools and other training institutions. In practical terms, this meant that technicians and other specialists of suspect background were to be employed under supervision, and that intellectual youth would be permitted to work in government offices at the county level and above as well as in factories, mines, transport, finance, and trade.[144] The Party's long-term solution, of course, was to free itself from the unfortunate necessity of relying on those it despised by training a new generation of politically orthodox specialists and technicians.

As if the Party did not have enough problems simply in recruiting adequate numbers of cadres, it faced no less difficulty in enforcing standards of cadre behavior consistent with the Party's self-image as an upright, just and incorruptible proletarian political authority. To the degree that the Party was successful in mobilization and recruitment, it contributed to the emergence of serious behavioral problems among cadres. In periods of rapid expansion such as civil war, the Party inevitably recruited large numbers of persons whose understanding of and dedication to the Communist cause lagged far behind their enthusiasm for improving their own and their families' positions. During the Yenan period, Party leaders had developed techniques of rectification to deal with the frailties and imperfections of low-ranking cadres, and these were applied in due course in the Northeast.

Two categories of behavioral problems may be distinguished—errors of personal deportment or workstyle, and errors of class standpoint. The first including such traditional forms of corrupt behavior as bribe-taking, gambling, opium-smoking, conspicuous consumption, womanizing, and abuse of public office for private profit. In a report that emphasized the urgency of peasant mobilization, Ch'en Yün complained that many cadres were irresolute, pleasure-loving, corrupt, and disinclined to abandon the relative comfort of urban life for the rigors of the countryside.[145] Not a few of the new cadres, particularly at the local levels, apparently assumed that their new-found authority was a license to behave like the worst of the recently overthrown old elite.[146] It was not always easy for higher-level authorities to learn of such abuse, but, when they did, such erring cadres were warned, demoted, or dismissed depending upon the severity of their transgressions. Of course, higher-level officials themselves were not immune from corrupt behavior, and several cases involving fairly important provincial officials were exposed in the press. For example, the auditor of the Hokiang provincial government's General Affairs Department, Kao Kuo-tung was summarily executed after a public trial for embezzling substantial sums.[147] Not long after this case, NEAC issued to all provinces, counties, banners, and special districts a set of Temporary Regulations for Punishing Corruption. Offenses covered were: 1) diverting supplies and gain for personal use or profit; 2) illegally selling or stealing public property; 3) accepting bribes or kickbacks; 4) extorting goods from people in the guise of public contributions; 5) abusing one's position of authority to receive bribes. Punishments ranged from three months in prison up through the death penalty depending upon the severity of the infraction.[148]

The other category of errors—those reflecting mistakes in class standpoint—basically involved deviations from the Party's punitive policy toward its targeted enemies, particularly during periods of extreme leftism such as the autumn of 1947. Many cadres were accused of protecting landlords and rich peasants, restraining the masses from fear of excess, and helping to conceal property that should have been confiscated.[149] During the high tide of the land equalization movement, many regional Party leaders encouraged a species of vigilante justice vis-à-vis the class enemy, believing that the righteous anger of the poor peasants and hired laborers would sweep away the remnants of the old village power structure. Ironically, many of the new cadres—the organized instrument of class warfare—proved to be impediments to acting out this scenario. Finally, we should note that to the catalog of cadre shortcomings were added the usual charges of bureaucratism, commandism, and subjectivism.

In the fall and winter of 1947–48, the Party conducted a rectification movement to combat these problems. Under the supervision of the Northeast Bureau, provincial Party committees set the pace by initiating a series of activities including nightly meetings for criticisms and self-criticism, ideological study, and careful scrutiny of the conduct of ranking officials at both the provincial and sub-provincial levels.[150] Several provincial and county-level officials were dismissed from their posts and expelled from the Party while others were suspended and given serious warnings. In a report to a 1,000 cadre conference in Harbin in late January 1948, Li Fu-ch'un gave a mixed assessment of the results of the three-month rectification drive. Claiming some success in the effort to combat bureaucratism and corruption and improve Party work style, Li asserted that serious problems of class standpoint and work style still persisted within party ranks. He singled out old cadres as chiefly responsible because too many of them provided poor examples of leadership to the newer Party workers. Preoccupations with one's own small unit (departmentalism), lack of concern with planning, waste of public resources, and poor reporting were some of the continuing defects he pointed out. An important result of the rectification campaign was a 12 percent

personnel reduction (1,805 of some 15,000) in the central organs
of the Northeast Bureau and the Sungkiang Provincial Government. Considerable savings in administrative costs (electricity,
fuel, telephones, motor vehicles) were also claimed. Redundant
personnel were reassigned to the army and the work of land
reform or production.

The rectification campaign was conducted within the
confines of the Party rather than involving mass criticism from the
outside, and the whole movement was a relatively mild affair.
Saying that intra-Party problems were ones of ideology, not of
traitors in the ranks, Li Fu-ch'un mandated that administrative
cadres engage in collective study and spend one or two weeks in
the countryside or in urban factories on a rotating basis to engage
in practical labor, the penitent cadres' equivalent of the mortifi-
cation of the flesh.[151] The rectification campaign appears to have
been limited for the most part to cadres at the regional and provincial levels. Lower down the hierarchy, so thinly spread were
Party cadres and so urgent the need for their services that the
leadership could ill afford to indulge in a full-scale housecleaning.
Moreover, the central leadership's repudiation of the extreme
leftist line on rural revolution in early 1948 undermined the rationale for condemning rural cadres whose moderation was no
longer viewed as a vice.

In 1948, the year of victory in the Northeast, the uninterrupted successes of the NEPLA in occupying new territory
outstripped the Party's organizational capacity with respect to
urban administration and rural revolution. Just as Yenan had
exported cadres to the Northeast in 1945 to seed the ground for
revolution, so the northern region of Manchuria itself dispatched
cadres to the central and southern districts of the region in late
1947 and 1948.[152] These cadres laid the groundwork for setting
up mass organizations and establishing the framework for revolutionary changes in the newly occupied areas. The NEPLA itself,
however, provided military administration for the newly occupied
cities during the initial takeover period.

One of the keys to the CCP's success in the Northeast
during the revolutionary civil war was its ability to absorb large
numbers of new recruits into the ranks and to assimilate and train
both rural and urban cadres. During the civil war years, the Party

trained hundreds of thousands of new cadres and activitists within Manchuria. Undoubtedly, some of these men and women were motivated by idealism and fidelity to the revolutionary ideology and objectives of the CCP. Many others, however, may well have viewed joining the Communist revolution as the best way to advance their own interests by becoming part of the new governing authority in the region. As long as the outcome of the civil war was in doubt, of course, joining the ranks of local leaders was risky. Had the old order been restored in the countryside, the white terror against the Communists would probably have been every bit as bloody as the red terror against the landlords was in reality. Once the Communists appeared to be winning, however, the mix of motives of those joining its ranks almost certainly changed. The revolution created an unprecented and unparalleled opportunity for status advancement and social mobility for tens if not hundreds of thousands of persons at both the local and higher levels. The revolution needed people to fill the positions of leadership in villages, counties, provinces, and region, in Party, government, army, and mass organizations. Those who flocked into the Party during the civil war lacked the prestige or power of the hard-bitten veterans of earlier Party struggles, but coming in on the ground floor of a rapidly expanding organization presented marvelous career opportunities for ambitious as well as talented persons. To be sure, the civil war cohort of Party cadres in the Northeast as elsewhere before long found its upward mobility blocked by the presence of earlier leadership generations in a Party that found its arteries increasingly clogged with the heroes and hangers-on of bygone days.

Given the organic link between the revolution and the war effort, the Party urgently required the services even of those cadres who failed to measure up completely to ideal standards. That many of the cadres—new and old—exhibited the behavioral shortcomings of Chinese bureaucrats from ages past is not surprising. It is much easier to change one's ideology than to alter one's behavior. In any case, revolutionary idealism is an often corrosive concentrate which unless diluted with some concern for basic human values and even some ordinary careerism can destroy the foundations of social and political community. What can be considered noteworthy is the Party leadership's attention to the deficiencies among its organizational staff as well as the basic-level cadres. The attempts to control abuses and to instill an ethic of disinterested service to the revolutionary cause were not always successful, but they bespoke the central leadership's determination to exercise coordination and control over the entire network of revolutionary workers and at least to keep in check the most flagrant abuses of revolutionary discipline.

CHAPTER FIVE

THE POLITICAL ECONOMY
OF CIVIL WAR

WAR mobilization extended beyond
conscription of soldiers and laborers to the economy of the Communist Northeast as a whole. For only by putting their territories
on a total war footing were the leaders of the CCP able to wage a
successful revolutionary civil war. However, the requirements of
war often conflicted with those of revolution and no permanent
resolution of the resulting tension was possible during the civil
war period itself. Since the war effort rested in large measure on
a peasantry mobilized through revolution, it was not possible
simply to suspend the revolution until military victory in the civil
war was assured. Yet such byproducts of the revolution as disorder, destruction of property, excessive consumption, and, above
all, a decline in agricultural and industrial production could not
be permitted to go unchecked because of their negative impact on
the war effort. Party leaders as well as propagandists attempted to
portray the two objectives of fighting the civil war and carrying
out the revolution not only as compatible but as mutually reenforcing, but this was true only in the abstract. During the course
of the war, one can trace an increasing preoccupation on the part
of the regional party high command with economic problems and
policy issues. A history of the civil war in the Communist areas of

the Northeast is in part a study of the problems of running a wartime economy under the enormously complicating condition of a highly disruptive revolution. This chapter examines the problems of grain production, taxation, and urban grain supply as well as labor supply, labor mobilization, and urban resettlement schemes. A more detailed and complete examination of the economic history of the civil war in the Northeast is a task for an economic historian.

Although Manchuria was the wealthiest region of China with the most advanced industry, a highly developed transportation and communications network, and an exportable agricultural surplus, the Communist government in the north was hard-pressed to manage the economic efforts needed to sustain the war. This may appear strange in view of the fact that all but the most destitute of economies contains sufficient surplus to fight a war. By increasing production and reducing civilian consumption, the managers of a wartime economy can usually squeeze out the goods and services they require.[1] The Communist-ruled northern districts of Manchuria lacked major industry with the exception of such agricultural-processing industries as flour-milling, brewing, soybean processing, and lumbering.[2] It also lacked self-sufficiency in such a basic sector as textile production. The normal flow of intra-regional trade was disrupted by the war itself, of course, and Communist authorities clamped their own additional restrictions on trade, fearing a hemorrhaging of capital, equipment, raw materials, and livestock to the Nationalist-held southern districts. To compensate for the cutoff of northern Manchuria's natural economic intercourse, the Communist authorities promoted the development of a high degree of economic autarky and depended upon trade with the USSR for crucial supplies of key industrial commodities they could not attain elsewhere.

Grain and the Urban Food Supply

An adequate supply of grain was essential to feed the armies in the field and the urban population as well as to help pay for the import of industrial goods from the USSR. Ensuring an adequate supply was difficult for several related reasons. First and foremost was the massive disruption that rural revolution inflicted on the sensitive cycle of agricultural production. The redistribution of land, livestock, and agricultural implements in the name of revolutionary equity rarely took account of the impact on production. The beneficiaries of land reform all too often lacked one or more of the crucial inputs needed to maintain production. A peasant who received a plow might lack a draft animal to pull it; another who received a horse might lack fodder to keep the animal healthy. Many peasant families that received land lacked sufficient labor power to exploit it fully. Similarly, supplies of fertilizer and seed and traditional sources of rural financing were also disrupted. In addition, many of the most enterprising and skillful of the agricultural producers—rich peasants and middle peasants—either had their lands confiscated outright during land reform or were afraid to work too hard lest their comparative prosperity mark them for attack. This was especially true during periods of leftist excesses such as those during the fall of 1947.

Second, a severe shortage of rural labor power developed during the course of the war as the army and its support services drained manpower from the countryside. The calendar of war naturally took precedence over the calendar of agricultural production for the most part, and much of the fighting—in the spring of 1947 and the autumn of 1948, for example—occurred during busy agricultural seasons. Those who were called to military service generally were the strongest and the healthiest while many of those who were left behind were less fit for labor in the fields.

Third, various obstacles impeded the collection and transfer of grain and other agricultural commodities from the countryside to the city. Many peasants were inclined to increase their own very modest standards of living by keeping what they raised for their own consumption rather than selling on the market. Party leaders, conscious of the needs of the cities and of the front, severely condemned but could not entirely check the tendency to celebrate the victory of land reform by feasting on the stores of distributed landlord-rich peasant grain, poultry, and small livestock. Finally, the scarcity and high price of industrial goods reduced peasants' incentive to sell their grain on the market.

The autarky of Communist northern Manchuria as a whole was mimicked by the micro-level autarky of the villages in a period when market forces failed to function effectively.

During the Japanese colonial period, Manchuria had shipped considerable amounts of better-quality grain to Japan.[3] The coarse grains, particularly kaoliang (sorghum), were consumed locally. During the civil war period, it was estimated that the Northeast produced a grain surplus (millet, corn, kaoliang, and soybeans) of approximately 1.1 million tons in 1947, most of which was shipped to the Soviet Union.[4] It is not clear what criteria were used to judge that this grain was surplus, because, in fact, the Communists managed to export grain to the USSR only through considerable belt-tightening and by keeping urban grain consumption at low levels. Grain shipped to the Soviet Union in 1947 represented roughly 8 percent of the total grain grown in the Communist portions of the Northeast.[5] The 1948 Economic Plan for the Northeast Liberated Areas, unveiled by NEAC in late 1947, envisaged a 1 million ton increase in grain production—an amount equal to that exported. This was to be accomplished by increasing the amount of cultivated land by 680,000 *shang* (8.2 percent), and improving methods of cultivation on the 8,320,000 *shang* already in production. NEAC encouraged rural entrepreneurs to open up uncultivated land by a tax policy that promised to remit the grain tax entirely in the first year and assess only one-third and two-thirds of the normal taxes in the succeeding two years. Similarly, the goal of expanding acreage devoted to cotton, flax, sugar beets, and tobacco was adopted and agricultural loans were disbursed through provincial and lower-level governments.[6]

Given a new and untried administrative structure, inexperienced personnel, and inadequate statistical information concerning both the amount of land under cultivation and the actual harvests, it is is not surprising that wide disparities existed in the percentage of the harvest collected as grain tax. In 1947 the range was from a low of 13 percent to a high of 40 percent. To rectify this disparity, NEAC ordered population enumeration and land registration in the rural areas. Local governments were directed to estimate the productivity of the land so that the grain tax could be collected more equitably.[7] These measures apparently had some effect in leveling out the unevenness in public grain tax and purchases. In 1948, NEAC obtained 23 percent of Northeast agricultural output through tax and compulsory purchase (requisition).[8] A *Northeast Daily* editorial from early 1948 termed the task of grain purchase and requisition "the key link in the effort to support the war, and the central element in the government's economic plan which can play a decisive role in victory." Cadres were admonished that their performance would be judged, in the first instance, on whether or not they succeeded in achieving the plan for grain purchase and requisition. Implicitly acknowledging peasant reluctance to turn over a substantial part of their harvests to the state, the editorial condemned the "mistaken idea" that grain purchase/requisition would interfere with land reform. Peasants, it was claimed, properly understood the importance of supporting the war effort by delivering their grain. At the same time, cadres were given the rather superfluous advice that peasants could more easily be induced to cooperate with the grain purchase/requisition program if they were provided capital and agricultural tools in return. Finally, the editorial also alluded to the additional problems of getting the peasants to send grain confiscated from landlords and rich peasants to the state rather than retaining it for their own use, getting peasants to provide *good quality* grain rather than the dregs of the harvest, and the transport bottleneck which could best be dealt with in the cold season when frozen waterways and roads provided superior transportation.[9]

An examination of the problem of supplying grain to Harbin reveals several important dimensions of the CCP's wartime economic policy. The fundamental objective, of course, was to provide a secure grain supply at steady prices. In pursuing this goal, the municipal government found itself forced to employ an ever-widening array of administrative controls. Although it proved impossible to control inflation completely or to eliminate a black market in grain, illicit grain transfers, and speculative hoarding, the relative success of the government in exerting its will stands in marked contrast to the dismal record of the Nationalists both in Manchuria and in intramural China.

Because of fighting, widespread disorder, and shortages of agricultural implements, the harvest of 1946 was below normal. Consequently, both city and countryside faced the specter of shortages and rising prices.[10] In Harbin, grain prices, which had apparently held steady through 1946, suddenly became very "confused" and "chaotic" soon after New Year's 1947 as the grain supply into the city was curtailed. Stating that the grain trade would remain in private hands, Harbin Mayor Liu Ch'eng-tung promised municipal action to stabilize prices including prosecution of hoarders and speculators. At this time, the per catty price of kaoliang (the staple grain for most persons) had risen to between 40 and 50 yuan, of rice to 90 yuan, and of bean oil to 180 yuan. The city secured a short-term drop in commodity prices by having the official Northeast Trading Corporation dump large quantities of goods on the market with the result that by mid-February the per catty price of kaoliang had fallen to 30, of rice to 70, and of bean oil to 160.[11] This was a temporary expedient, however, which could not easily be repeated because of the tightness of supply.

In mid-February 1947, the municipality established a Grain Regulation Committee which quickly moved toward abolishing the free market in grain and instituting a rationing system in order to achieve long-term price stability. Charging that some private grain merchants (of whom there were roughly 200 in Harbin) had evaded government regulations on grain sales and connived with grain millers to squeeze the public, the municipal government closed all retail grain outlets on March 7, 1947, and turned over their function to local cooperatives whose numbers quickly doubled. Shortly thereafter, a grain rationing system was introduced to guarantee low-priced grain to the urban poor. The system was administered through small groups of five to fifteen households, which designated eligible persons on lists cross-checked by the street office and then the district government. The core idea was to limit the amount of grain anyone could buy within a given period in order to stretch out supplies and avoid hoarding. However, the original rationing system proved unworkable and considerable tinkering was done to try to iron out its defects.[12]

Among the many problems of the system was the difficulty in securing compliance with the regulations by the over 100 grain co-ops in the city. In addition, the army through its purchasing agents sometimes competed directly with civilian consumers of grain. In May 1947, for example, a rise in grain prices was blamed on illegal storage and selling of grain by certain military units which were ordered to desist at once.[13] Throughout the civil war, there continued to be inflationary pressure on grain as well as on other basic commodity prices. The government worked to control inflation through both market and administrative mechanisms. Additional supplies of grain were brought into Harbin whenever prices began to soar, and strict measures were taken to prevent profiteering by wholesale grain dealers.[14] An important administrative lever which NEAC employed was control over inter-provincial grain transfers as well as supervision of intra-provincial grain trade. As the Communist noose tightened around the few remaining Nationalist urban strongholds in late 1947, grain wholesalers in Communist territories were tempted to take advantage of the soaring grain prices. However, NEAC strictly forbade grain sales to KMT-held territory and controlled all large-scale grain transfers through its Central Trade Administration. A NEAC order of December 26, 1947, reiterated the long-standing ban on grain shipment to Nationalist cities and decreed that all inter-provincial grain transfers must be effected through the Central Trade Administration. Intra-provincial grain transfers required only the permission of the provincial trade bureau, but had to conform with central regulations and appropriate (but unspecified) grain transfer taxes had to be paid. These restrictions did not apply to transfers of grain below the amounts of 50 kilograms for unhulled grain, 25 kilograms for processed grain, and 5 kilograms for bean oil. The obvious purpose once again was to reduce hoarding and control speculation while not interfering with ordinary, small-scale commodity movements. Another measure taken to conserve grain was to cut back sharply on the production of alcohol for consumption. At least one province banned the production of drinking alcohol in state-owned or joint state-private factories and ordered a 50 percent reduction in production at private factories while raising the tax on alcohol by 100 percent.[15]

The attempts to control the constant inflationary pressures were never very successful during the civil war years, but they did involve the creation of a large administrative apparatus which in Harbin alone employed 1,300 grain supply and distribution workers by early 1948 and controlled thousands of freight cars and innumerable carts. Naturally, such a large-scale system was not immune from corruption and other illegal practices which continued to be exposed and criticized throughout the civil war.[16]

Grain was not the only commodity in short supply and subject to the vicissitudes of the market as well as manipulation. In the case of coal, the primary form of energy in Manchuria, a Northeast Fuel Corporation *(Tung-pei jan-liao kung-ssu)* was set up to monopolize the sale of coal and charcoal to all military, industrial, domestic, and other consumers. This unified supply and distribution system succeeded in stabilizing or even somewhat reducing coal prices between July 1947 and January 1948.[17]

Industrial Policy

Most branches of industry were considerably less developed in northern Manchuria than in the Nationalist-held central and southern districts. For example, in the machine-building industry, only 13 percent of the enterprises and 2 percent of the regional labor force of 38,000 were located in Harbin in 1938. Less than 10 percent of Northeast coal was mined in the north, and the bulk of the cotton textile industry was likewise located in the south.[18] However, the concentration of industry in the south conveyed little if any advantage to the Nationalists because it proved impossible under wartime conditions to restore the equipment and facilities ravaged by the Soviets in 1945–46. Industrial production virtually collapsed in southern Manchuria during the civil war. Thus, the Nationalists' hope of using Manchuria's industrial base as the core of the postwar reconstruction of China's economy could not be realized.

Under revolutionary civil war conditions, the Communists were unable to transform the relative underdevelopment of north Manchurian industry. However, within the limits of time, finances, and available resources, they vigorously promoted small-scale and handicrafts industry, especially those that directly supported the war effort. The impetus to develop industrial production was seriously hampered, however, by the attitude of many cadres who promoted the interests of labor over those of management. The spillover of rural class warfare onto urban entrepreneurs and specialists also had a negative effect.

In Shen-Kan-Ning and other North China base areas, the Party had considerable experience in promoting rural handicrafts and other small-scale, low-technology, labor-intensive industry using locally available sources of raw material.[19] In the spirit of the wartime united front, the Party had also encouraged landlords and local capitalists to invest in small-scale industry and engage their entrepreneurial, managerial and technical skills in production. Tax holidays and interest-free government loans had also been used to stimulate development. Among the industries promoted in North China were cotton textiles, paper-making, agricultural implements, soap, matches, earthenware, oil-pressing, and mining.[20]

In northern Manchuria, the Communist regime likewise used tax incentives and government loans to encourage industrial production. Particular attention was paid to the textile industry because of its importance to both the army and the civilian population. In May 1947, for example, NEAC distributed 100,000 catties of cotton to the provinces and instructed subordinate units to mobilize the labor of women, the urban poor, and the unemployed for textile production. To overcome the critical materials shortage, it was suggested that flax, wool, and camel hair be developed as cotton substitutes according to local conditions. A Northeast Textile Administration had been established in April 1947 to coordinate development of small-scale textile enterprises, workshops,and cooperatives and provide loans of material as well as financial and technical assistance.[21] Other industries that the government assisted in the equivalent of a policy of "import substitution" included bean-oil pressing, shoes, cigarettes, matches, and other daily use commodities.[22] As in the case of grain, the Northeast Central Trade Corporation responded to the inflationary pressures by releasing commodities to the market at reduced prices in order to keep a lid on prices and provide light industrial goods for the countryside in exchange for grain.[23]

As the civil war progressed, the Communist leadership reiterated time and again that increased production was the key to victory and the main responsibility of the rear areas. This emphasis on productivity clashed, however, with the primary concern of many rank and file cadres as well as ordinary workers which was to improve wages and labor conditions. Encountering more or less genuine proletarians for the first time in their Party careers, the initial impulse of many Communists was to appeal to the workers by raising wages, shortening hours, and otherwise improving labor conditions. Worker participation in management was another early goal of the labor unions which the CCP helped organize in the cities. By the spring of 1947, it was claimed that all public enterprises in Harbin were under worker management, although this was not precisely defined.[24] Unfortunately, this preoccupation with the workers' benefits (later condemned as a leftist error) had a negative impact on production.[25] Higher wages, poor labor discipline, and waste threatened the war effort. In 1947, profit-sharing schemes pegged to workers' output and skill levels were widely introduced into industry. But by this time a counter-vailing trend also appeared as the Party became increasingly conscious of the economic costs of tampering with the existing industrial enterprises by favoring the workers. The press began to publicize cases of workers who "voluntarily" accepted lower wages (the usual cuts were 10–20 percent), or who sacrificed their days-off in order to increase production.[26] Although the Party continued to pay lip-service to the goal of raising workers' living standards, its primary concern clearly shifted to wresting the maximum output from the labor force, particularly in war-related industries.

Central to this effort was an attempt to create a stable and secure atmosphere for entrepreneurs in keeping with the policies of Mao's New Democracy. This was not easy. On countless occasions rural dwellers ignored the Party's policy of protecting urban merchants and industrialists by pursuing landlords into the cities where these same persons owned commercial or industrial property. Urban property was often confiscated and divided and merchants and factory owners struggled against because of their previous dealings with the Japanese or Nationalists. This resulted in the shutting down of their enterprises and a loss of production.[27] As the Communists conquered cities and towns in central and southern Manchuria, many individuals as well as military and civilian administrative units swarmed over factories, stripping machines and other equipment for their own or their unit's use, and staked out claims to buildings, factories, hospitals, and schools without order or discipline.[28] In fact, the behavior of the Communists in "liberated" southern Manchuria was very reminiscent of the Nationalist carpetbaggers who devastated East China cities and Taiwan in 1945–46.[29]

The restoration of industrial order took several forms. First, the Party reaffirmed its policy of protecting and encouraging private commercial and industrial enterprise which, at that point, was indeed vital to the wartime economy. Second, the rights of management were recognized and trade unions were directed not to interfere with legitimate management functions. At the same time, however, private enterprises were enjoined from stopping production or shutting down without permission from appropriate government agencies. These latter were also empowered to pass judgment on proposals for opening new enterprises. Transfer of capital or other assets to Nationalist territory was strictly forbidden under severe penalty of law.[30] Third, an effort was made to improve the intra-enterprise relations between ordinary workers and the technical managerial staff, many of whom had tainted political backgrounds. The Party decreed that technical specialists of all kinds should be given appropriate work, pay, and honor irrespective of their political attitude as long as they did not actually engage in disruption or industrial sabotage.[31] Labor unions, which had earlier sanctioned the transformation of power relations within industry, were now enlisted in the effort to convince workers that production was of paramount importance.[32] Material incentives were offered to workers who contributed to increasing production by outstanding work, inventions, and labor and material saving innovations.[33] Although firm evidence is difficult to come by, it seems that these exhortations, policy pronouncements, and proclamations at best may have arrested the slide in production, but failed to produce any spectacular results. The economy of the Communist Northeast limped through the civil war under its enormous burden of supporting the front, but only peace and a massive dose of Soviet economic assistance completely restored and then further developed the Northeast economy.

Wartime belt-tightening supplemented the efforts to increase production. In the winter of 1946–47, NEAC and the Northeast Bureau launched an economy and production campaign to reduce the cost of running the bureaucracy. Cadres in government and Party offices demonstratively pledged to skip their noon meal in order to save on food and to economize on clothing. Between January and March 1947, NEAC reportedly cut its staff by 48 percent (no specific numbers were given), and cut its bill for fuel, food, and supplies by 75 percent.[34] A *Northeast Daily* editorial warned that "an extremely small number of cadres" had become corrupted by landlord-bourgeois ways since entering Manchuria and it advised a return to the tradition of simple living and spare-time production lest this colossal error *(t'ien-ta ti tso-wu)* further infect the ranks.[35] The Northeast Bureau directly operated both industrial enterprises and farms whose earnings reportedly covered about one-quarter of the Bureau's total expenditures in 1947, and funneled grain and goods into the economy, but these were mainly of symbolic importance. An atmosphere of frugality was promoted by decree as well as by example. NEAC forbade elaborate celebrations of the New Year's holidays and directed soldiers not to accept gifts from the people on that occasion. Public entertainment was similarly circumscribed. In Harbin the municipal Public Security Department decreed a dark and silent Chinese Lunar New Year by banning fireworks and firecrackers, ostensibly to reduce the danger of fire.[36]

Economic Planning
and Labor Mobilization

As economic problems increasingly commanded the attention of Communist leaders in the Northeast, NEAC convened a lengthy regional meeting on finance and the economy in August-September 1947. Before the assembled provincial chairmen and financial-economic specialists, Li Fu-ch'un, speaking on behalf of the Northeast Bureau asserted that the demands of the war had far outstripped the performance of the economy and of the financial system. Li called for the implementation of planned economic development in order to bring order out of chaos and meet the urgent requirements of the war effort. He condemned a number of mistaken views: (1) reliance on guerilla warfare and neglect of the main-line forces; (2) belief in the primacy of peaceful construction; (3) egalitarianism; (4) separation of the task of economic construction from that of supporting the front; (5) overlooking the long-term nature of the war; and (6) paying excessive attention to the immediate interest of the masses. Above all, he stressed the need for unity and coordination of economic efforts.[37] Li's central message, in other words, was that in order to ensure victory even greater contributions from rural and urban dwellers alike were necessary.

The 1948 economic outline prepared by NEAC's Financial-Economic Committee was endorsed by the Northeast Bureau on 10 October 1947. It listed the following as the Party's principal tasks for 1948:

- Development of agriculture, particularly grain.
- Restoration and further expansion of war-related industries.
- Protection of legitimate private enterprise.
- Control of external trade.

Cadres engaged in mass work were instructed to make production the pivot of their activity. The outline set a target of a 12 percent increase in grain production (or an additional million tons), along with expanded production of cotton, flax, sugar beet, tobacco, and livestock. In industry, the outline emphasized increasing coal production and developing the machine tool, textile, shoe, electric power, and chemical industries to serve the war effort.[38]

The outline pointed to the mobilization of additional supplies of labor as the key to achieving the agricultural targets. Such labor mobilization is a typical feature of revolutionary civil wars and, as Wilkinson notes, involves the creation of new workers as well as the reassignment of existing ones through such means as the rationalization of wasteful practices, the elimination of strikes, and the employment of those persons hitherto unemployed, underemployed, or misemployed.[39] The economic outline claimed that the labor force could be increased by 1.2 million persons in northern Manchuria alone, by organizing labor exchange groups in the villages to embrace at least 60 percent of the labor force and by mobilizing 40 percent of village women. In addition 3–5 percent of the urban population were to be mobilized for agricultural production.[40] After publication of the outline, individual provinces drew up concrete plans of implementation.

Increasing the labor supply was far from easy. Com-

pared to other regions of China, the Northeast had relatively few
unemployed or underemployed rural or urban workers. In fact,
first as an expanding frontier economy and later as an industrial-
izing region, the Northeast's constant need for additional labor
had been met from migration from North China to supplement
natural intra-regional increase.[41] During the civil war, military
recruitment, by draining able-bodied labor from the countryside,
exacerbated an already serious agricultural situation. The rural
revolution had disrupted the intricate pattern of agricultural production relations and the government was as yet unable to restore
production by allocating sufficient resources to production. Only
an increased labor supply might provide a short-term solution to
agricultural production problems. Let us look at three expedients
for achieving that increase: (a) the campaign to mobilize *erh-liu-
tzu;* (b) the transfer of urban labor to the countryside; and (c) the
establishment of labor exchange and mutual aid teams.

In the spring of 1947, NEAC initiated a campaign to
compel *erh-liu-tzu* (vagrants or idlers, i.e., nonproductive elements
of the rural population) to join the agricultural work force.[42] The
erh-liu-tzu were exemplars of what one sociologist has termed a
"culture of shiftlessness"—persons lacking a work ethic who survive by sponging on the labor of family, friends, and acquaint-
ances.[43] Local peasant associations mobilized the wives and children of vagrants to persuade their delinquent husbands and fathers
to work. Meetings, remonstrances by model workers and cadres,
and compulsory assigned labor were used to reform the village
idlers. In one village, for example, a certain Wang Yung-chiang
was labeled a Special Class Vagrant and ordered to chop 700 catties
of wood in two weeks and to gather one load of manure every
morning. Vagrants were forced to confess their errors and given
two weeks in which to mend their ways or face additional struggle
meetings, confiscation of their land, and even banishment from
the village.[44] Various articles in the press estimated that perhaps
1–3 percent of the rural population were vagrants whose disin-
clination to work could no longer be tolerated in a period of
revolutionary warfare.

A potentially more important source of labor power
was the 3–5 percent of the urban population deemed surplus by
the Communist authorities. This may be very roughly estimated

at perhaps 150,000 persons. As early as the first months of 1947, the Harbin municipal government began resettling several thousand households *(hu)* into the countryside. By imposing licensing procedures on carters, droshky drivers, hawkers, peddlers, and those in similar occupations, the municipal Public Security and Social Departments sought to limit the number engaged in what were perceived as unproductive callings. Despite the provision of some limited assistance for these unwilling migrants, the policy of resettlement met considerable resistance.[45] Nevertheless, the economic advantages of relocating "surplus" persons to the countryside ensured the continuation of the policy. In the autumn of 1947, a population census and registration was conducted in the cities. On this basis, NEAC decided to shift substantial numbers of persons to the countryside. Although this policy served the important secondary purpose of easing the strain on the urban food supply, unlike the *hsia hsiang* campaigns of the 1960s and 1970s, the primary objective was to provide additional labor power for agriculture rather than to alleviate urban problems.

Those targeted for rural resettlement included not only redundant urban petty tradesmen and transport workers, but also refugees from the countryside and revolutionary struggle targets such as landlords, ex-Manchukuo officials, vagrants, and bandits. Many if not most of these persons were reluctant migrants, so NEAC stipulated that where persuasion failed to evoke compliance compulsion should be applied.[46] The urban governments dispatching the migrants were generally responsible for transportation of the settlers and the receiving points were supposed to provide land (mostly virgin land), and assistance with temporary shelter, fuel, and agricultural tools, but most of the expense of relocating was to be borne by the migrants themselves. Upon relocation, local governments organized settlers in such winter activities as timber-felling and charcoal-making.[47]

Apparently, much of the resettlement work was carried out hastily and inadequately. Urban cadres packed parties of settlers off to unknown destinations under conditions amounting to coercive exile, while reception points grudged committing scarce resources to these unwelcome charges. Settlers, many of whom lacked farming experience, were sometimes dumped on the fields like so much night soil and left to fend for themselves.

Tools, seed, and agricultural implements were in very short supply. Critical reports in the Communist press suggested the need to organize resettlement more carefully, ease the fears of the migrants, see that they had tools and other materials to engage in production, and ensure that local officials in the receiving points discharged their responsibilities fully.[48]

During the winter of 1947-48, several tens of thousands of persons were resettled from Harbin, Mutankiang, Antung, and other cities. It was estimated that each able-bodied person could plant 3.5–4 *shang* of land and thereby increase grain production. The Hokiang provincial government allocated 55 million yuan in loans to the migrants to buy cattle, tools, and seeds, while in Antung local committees provided hot water, food, and clothing to migrants en route to the countryside, and local receiving points furnished land, housing, and 100 catties of grain to the settlers.[49] Scattered evidence suggests that the resettlement program was not developed to its full potential, presumably because of the aforementioned problems. One wonders how much the unfortunate settlers were ever really able to contribute to solving agricultural problems. They may have been doing very well if they harvested enough to keep themselves alive.

It is worth mentioning that draft animals were as urgently needed as human labor in the rural areas. Many horses and other draft animals had been requisitioned for military service and the toll on the beasts was heavy. The rural revolution had redistributed livestock, but many peasants lacked the fodder to maintain the animals they had received through land reform. Substantial numbers of livestock died or were too weakened to work. Therefore, county and urban public security and tax offices registered urban livestock (particularly horses) and shipped surplus animals to the countryside. Horses and oxen were needed more urgently to plow fields than to service Harbin's taxi industry!

Still more important as a source of additional manpower was the exchange of labor and the formation of mutual aid teams. Traditionally, the exchange of labor was more prevalent in Manchuria than elsewhere in China because of the shorter growing season. The greater use of draft animals also predisposed peasants to develop labor exchange relationships.[50] The many types of labor exchanges can be traced back to farming practices in Shantung whence many of the peasants in the Northeast had originally come. Ramon Myers notes that most traditional cooperation involved friends and neighbors who "pooled their tools, livestock and labor during the busy farming season in an arrangement called *ho-chü.*" Other expedients included joint purchase of draft animals by two or more families *(huo-mai)* and simple exchange of labor *(huo chung).*[51] In the Northeast perhaps a third or more of the peasants—mostly the poor and middle peasants—were involved in labor exchanges. These tended to be among family friends and were limited in duration and scope.[52]

The Party believed that by broadening the scope and prolonging the duration of these traditional exchanges, it could squeeze out the additional labor power needed for agriculture as well as lay the foundation for an eventual socialist agriculture. The transition from old- to new-style exchanges was not without its problems, however. Even though traditional exchanges were contracted between people with good *kan-ch'ing* (feeling, emotion) the persons who were involved very carefully calculated their mutual obligations.[53] Since a fine balance existed between the need for cooperation and the suspicion that one might be taken advantage of even by one's friends and neighbors, the traditional form of labor exchange was not an ideal stepping-stone to a more universal form of labor exchange. Nevertheless, the Party encouraged the spread of traditional forms of labor exchange. It simultaneously sought to expand the circle of those who participated in this type of agricultural cooperation and to transform the small-scale, seasonal arrangements into permanent mutual aid teams.[54]

In pursuing the objective of universalizing labor exchange, local cadres frequently violated the principle of voluntary participation and pressured unwilling peasants into mutual aid teams.[55] No less important, when poor and rich households were thrown together in labor exchange groups, it was frequently the better educated and shrewder rich peasants, particularly those with draft animals, who controlled the organization and gained unequal benefit from the exchanges.[56] This suggests an important point. Whenever the Party allowed poor and rich peasants to compete or cooperate on an equal footing without exercising leadership in support of the former, the poor peasants lost out. So the Party, looking toward the objective of transforming power relations in the countryside, provided a compensatory balance on the side of the poor in what might be called a program of revolutionary affirmative action. But this had to be done very carefully lest the primary objective of increasing production be injured. In advertising the advantages to be gained through cooperation among agricultural laborers, poor peasants, middle peasants, rich peasants, and even small landlords, the Party was unwittingly demonstrating yet again that the imperative of agricultural production contradicted its own revolutionary class policy in the countryside.[57] Whenever leftist enthusiasm for overthrowing the old social order instantaneously attained temporary ascendancy, the insistent need for grain, fodder and other agricultural commodities helped pull the Party leadership back toward a more moderate policy.

The rationale for establishing labor exchange groups is well illustrated by the example of Kaoshan, a village with 1,446 *shang* of land but shortages of draft animals, seed, fodder, carts, and tools, and little experience in intra-village cooperation. The initiative for labor exchange was taken by cadres and activists of the land reform work team who convened a village-wide meeting and secured the consent of the people to establish thirty-three mutual aid teams. A system of awarding work points for both human and animal labor was devised, and the participation of all classes except landlords was solicited.[58] To cope with the problems that had arisen during the movement to promote labor exchange in the spring of 1947, other localities also emphasized the utility of establishing systems for recording work accurately and ensuring equity in benefits received from participation in the labor exchanges. A typical report from Hulan county likewise underlined the need for thorough discussion of the work with all members of the group and the importance of upholding the principles both of voluntarism and of leadership. It also condemned a practice which sheds an interesting sidelight on the assimilation of Communist-inspired changes in the countryside.

In many areas competition between individuals, labor exchange groups, and even entire villages had been fostered as a means of increasing output. But peasants had assimilated this "revolutionary competition" into their traditional village culture which included elements of inter-village rivalry, gambling, and shaming. In labor competitions, the loser would have to pay a penalty, such as parading about in woman's clothing or having paper cutouts indicating cuckoldry pasted on their doors while winners were given such things as a pig or liquor. This practice was censured as damaging unity and causing humiliation.[59] Party leaders were loath to sanction anything that might reenforce existing social cleavages in the countryside which were proving difficult to eradicate in any case.

Despite the problems that arose in implementation, labor exchange groups and mutual aid teams continued to be promoted vigorously throughout the Communist Northeast. It is difficult to assess just how much additional labor power was made available through the several means just described, but the fact is, however shakily, the economy was barely able to meet the expanding needs of the war as well as to supply agricultural exports to the USSR. The Party's experience in organizing and promoting rural labor exchange, even in the face of peasant reluctance or opposition, proved useful in the post-civil war period as well.

Taxation and Contributions

A complete examination of the financial situation and the taxation system of the Northeast Communist areas is beyond the purview of this study. Here I shall simply sketch a few dimensions of the issue. NEAC had to finance the revolutionary civil war from current income, but the problems of collecting taxes in wartime were immense, especially given an inexperienced adminstration. Major contributors to NEAC's income were proceeds from a tax-in-kind on grain, a wide assortment of levies on commercial transactions of various sorts, profits from public enterprises, and proceeds from property confiscated from the old rural elite. In addition, the Communists constantly solicited financial "contributions" from the urban population in support of the war effort, an inexpensive alternative to issuing war bonds. An improvisational or "guerilla-style" tax system was a general feature of the revolutionary civil war period and its immediate aftermath as reports from other parts of the country attest.[60]

Collection of the grain tax was very uneven. In September 1946, NEAC canceled the existing land tax and imposed a flat 10 percent tax on agricultural food production (main crop) per persons producing more than 200 kilograms.[61] In practice, it proved impossible to assess agricultural output accurately at this time, with the result that actual rates of collection (varying from roughly 13 to 40 percent of the harvest in 1947) depended upon the zeal or ruthlessness of local cadres and the skill of peasants in concealing harvests or evading collection. Livestock slaughter and transfer taxes (5 percent and 4 percent respectively of the animal's value) were assessed too, but the main purpose of the complex regulations applied to these activities was to prevent disaffected landlords and rich peasants from slaughtering their livestock in anger rather than let them be confiscated.[62] With appropriate documentation from their local government, hired laborers and poor peasants were exempted from paying the livestock transfer tax when they purchased an animal for draft purposes.[63]

Commercial and sumptuary taxes were used to curb consumer spending on luxury items, soak up spare income, and supplement regulations on trading with enemy areas as well as to raise revenue. The percentage of sales tax collected varied from just a few percent for essential commodities like grain, coal, matches, and cooking oil to 40 percent on tobacco products and 70 percent on cosmetics.[64] Under a grant of authority from NEAC, the Harbin municipal government (and presumably other cities) collected a twice yearly enterprise tax which varied according to the type of business.[65] Regulations governing trade with the Nationalist-held areas of Manchuria prohibited the importation of nonessential commodities or the export of essential goods to those areas, but permitted traders to sell nonessential goods to the Nationalists and levied a tax of from 5 to 35 percent on such goods.[66]

Ordinary sources of revenue were rarely adequate in wartime and governments in China had long resorted to the expedient of levying special assessments (t'an-kuan) on the population.[67] These took the form of payments in cash, goods, and services. The Communist variant of this time-tested method was to solicit "voluntary" contributions for the war effort from the people—in particular the urban population—through Support the Army campaigns. In Harbin a municipal Support the Army Committee (later renamed the Wartime Mobilization Committee) was established, and it worked through district and street govern- ments, labor unions, and other mass organizations. The first month of the lunar calendar was designated Support-the-Army month and large meetings, propaganda posters, banners, news- papers, and magazines were used to spread the message.[68] Al- though precise details are lacking, one may assume that mer- chants, tradesmen, factory owners, and other bourgeois strata were put under considerable pressure to contribute. In Harbin over one nine-month period, 200 million yuan in cash and goods was contributed to the army.[69] These actively solicited contribu- tions were a not subtle form of disguised taxation in effect, al- though it is unlikely that they constituted much of an additional burden. (The scattered statistics given in the Communist press do not relate contributions to the number of persons contributing nor to frequency of contribution.) A final source of government in- come worth mentioning was the confiscated property of landlords, rich peasants, ex-Manchukuo officials, bandits, and other targets of the revolution. Considerable sums of precious metals, jewelry, stores of grain, and other movable property were seized during the course of land reform in violent and often humiliating searches of the houses, property, and persons of the Communists' foes. Although many of these goods were distributed to the villagers as the fruits of the rural revolution, Party cadres were instructed to siphon off a portion of this property for the war effort and villagers were frequently reminded that the needs of the front were para- mount. Excessive consumption of the fruits of land reform might imperil the ultimate victory of the revolution itself. The need to reiterate this message at frequent intervals suggests that many villagers were reluctant to subordinate their particular wills to the general will of the Party.

Conclusion

Notwithstanding the numerous problems it encountered in the realm of economic work the Communist leadership succeeded in the difficult task of supplying grain, industrial goods, and services to the armies in the field and providing for the needs of the urban population without engendering the economic chaos that plagued the Nationalist territories. Inflation, although substantial, was not runaway, economic disparities were reduced, industrial production in factories and workshops sufficed to provide for minimum needs, and the population was fed. From an organizational point of view, the Party had mustered the personnel to run an increasingly complicated economic bureaucracy while keeping the damper on corruption within its ranks. The Northeast during the civil war functioned as a kind of preparatory school for many officials who assumed high-ranking positions in the economic policy arena after 1949. The most prominent of such men, of course, was Ch'en Yün, chairman of NEAC's Finance Committee. Others included Yeh Chi-chuang, later the PRC Minister of Foreign Trade, and Li Fu-ch'un, chairman of the State Planning Commission. Emerging from the civil war with its economy poised for a rapid recovery, Northeast China soon became the focus of the First Five Year Plan's Stalinist model economic development and the engine of China's further industrialization in the 1950s.

CHAPTER SIX
REVOLUTION IN THE NORTHEAST COUNTRYSIDE

IN Northeast China the CCP victory in the revolutionary civil war was facilitated by a massive rural revolution which destroyed the old rural elite, established new structures of power dominated by the Party and its village-level supporters, and redistributed land to millions of landless and land-poor peasants. Most scholars agree that a significant degree of peasant support was a key factor in the CCP's coming to power. Yet how this support was gained and what was the precise character of the relationship between the Communists and the peasantry is a subject of considerable controversy in the literature on the Chinese Communist revolution.[1] Much of the controversy derives from the fact that the CCP-peasant relationship between 1921 and 1949 comprised a wide range of experiences varying from time to time and place to place. Scholars face a great temptation to generalize their findings, based on the study of a single region or subregion of China during a specific time period, and to apply them to the Chinese Communist revolutionary process as a whole.[2] Yet surely the enormous disparities in the political ecology of China and the wide variations in the history of the CCP from region to region should caution us against any simplified view of the universe of revolutionary experience.

This chapter analyzes the rural revolution in Northeast China within the context of the civil war. Others may judge whether and to what extent the processes and sequences described below are relevant to an understanding of the rural revolution in other regions of China.

How are we to understand the relationship between the rural revolution in Manchuria and the Communist victory? Mao Tse-tung's famous report on the Hunan peasant movement of 1927 is permeated by the image of the peasantry as an elemental force whose struggle for land and social justice is the very essence of revolution.[3] In a similar vein, a recent study of the Taihang mountain region of North China interprets the Communist victory as a self-generated "folk revolution" in which the autonomous "Little Tradition" of the oppressed and politically self-aware peasantry was supposedly actualized through the triumph of the CCP. The Party is said to have gained legitimacy and come to power by adapting itself to its rural environment.[4] Whatever else one may say about them these revolutionary-romantic ideas bear little resemblance to the actual processes through which peasants became involved in revolutionary activity in Manchuria.

Many students of peasant politics have noted that the transition from traditional familist, clan, or village identification and orientation to the intense social activism of the mobilized participant in rural revolution entails a basic change in perception and individual and group identity. A transformation in the calculus of trust and commitment is required as well as the development of a new sense of what kind of links are possible between the village and the larger world.[5] To effect such a transformation ordinarily requires a great deal of time and patience. Yet in Manchuria the rural revolution began and climaxed within the space of only eighteen months. For the Communists in the Northeast time was the commodity in the shortest supply. They had to make the revolution in a hurry or face defeat. The exigencies of the civil war did not provide the CCP the opportunity to gather peasant support after a lengthy season of cultivation. Instead the rural revolution in Manchuria was wrenched from the soil of the region by hard-pressed and often inexperienced cadres using double-quick methods. The result was an uneven harvest of change.[6]

Abrupt shifts in policy toward the rural areas during the civil war bespoke frantic, even desperate attempts by Party leaders to reconcile the pressures generated in the countryside with the relentless demands of the war. The fledgling local Party organizations and mass organizations, often burdened with confusing and contradictory orders from above, struggled not only against opposition from the "class enemies," but also against fear, apathy, suspicion, and disbelief on the part of many of the intended beneficiaries of land reform. Thus the process of revolutionary change in the countryside was anything but smooth. The revolution, like a backfiring jalopy steered by a novice driver, careened along the road from right to left, lurching toward victory.

Settling Accounts:
The Early Phase of Land Reform

The agricultural system of Manchuria, a region with a frontier economy developed under the auspices of foreign imperialism, differed from that of intramural China in certain important respects. The unusual combination of large numbers of agricultural laborers and tenant farmers on the one hand and substantial quantities of expropriated land on the other provided the CCP with a unique opportunity to bid for support in the rural areas by pursuing redistributionist policies. It should be stressed at this point that there was almost no self-generated impulse for revolutionary change in the Northeast countryside in the early postwar period. Land reform and the transformation of power relationships in the rural areas came about through the persistent and determined efforts of the CCP, often operating in local environments where the initial mood was hostile or at best indifferent to the Party's radical program. This was so not because of massive elite repression of a restive peasant underclass but because the expanding pre-1945 agricultural economy of Manchuria contained sufficient opportunities for economic advancement. Hard-working poor agriculturalists could hold out hope for a better future through their own individual efforts rather than through the collective instrumentality of revolution.

In comparison to intramural China, the Northeast had

TABLE 6.1 Landholding in Manchuria in 1930

Size of Holdings	Number of Households Within Each Province					
	Liaoning		Kirin		Heilungkiang	
	1,736,309	100%	584,551	100%	336,896	100%
Smallholders						
1 shang	345,899	19.9	43,431	7.4	19,910	5.9
1–3 shang	371,038	21.4	96,977	16.6	32,740	9.7
Middleholders						
3–5 shang	412,744	23.8	161,046	27.6	36,653	16.5
5–10 shang	348,367	20.1	132,261	22.6	76,968	22.9
Large landholders						
10 shang and up	238,264	14.9	150,836	25.8	151,617	45.0
Cultivated area	8,613,330 shang		5,823,072 shang		4,925,392 shang	
Average number of shang per household	4.96		9.89		14.68	

an abundance of land. The dramatic growth of population within the region from the 1870s to 1940 (from approximately 4.5 million to 38.4 million) was paralleled by an equally dramatic expansion in cultivated land (from 1.8 million hectares to 15.3 million hectares). The pressure of population on the land was considerably less than elsewhere in China with approximately one acre (.4 hectares) of cultivated land per capita in the Northeast, more than twice that in intramural China.[7]

Information on patterns of landholding and the distribution of social classes in the Northeast countryside is spotty and somewhat inconsistent, but the main outlines are reasonably clear. Generally speaking, there was considerably greater inequality in the pattern of landholding than in North China, with large numbers of landless laborers and tenant farmers, a substantial class of owner-cultivators, and a small but disproportionately wealthy class of landlords and rentier-farmers.[8] For political purposes the CCP used a simplified rural sociology whose objective was to dramatize the difference between rural oppressors and the rural oppressed. In reality, as Party documents admitted from time to time, the actual pattern of land tenure and distribution of wealth was far more complex than the schematic division of the rural population into landlords, rich peasants, middle peasants, poor peasants, and hired laborers.[9] Tenancy and poverty were by no means always equatable. Some poorer families with very little labor power might rent out a portion of the land. Did this make them landlords? There was much overlapping of categories and multiple status.

Let us look at some of the available data. A report on landholding from 1930 (which omits landless laborers, however) reveals several interesting points (see table 6.1). In the southernmost province of Liaoning 41.3 percent of the agricultural households were small owner-cultivators farming up to 3 *shang* of land. (A standard *shang* is 10 mou or 1.7 acres.) In Kirin 24 percent and in Heilungkiang only 15.6 percent of agricultural households were in this category. At the other end of the scale, the percentage of landlords with 10 or more *shang* of land was three times as great in Heilungkiang as in Liaoning. Unfortunately, the categories used in this table are nowhere clearly defined with respect to tenure relationships. Nevertheless, it appears clear that in Liaoning, where Chinese settlement was of longest duration and greatest density, the pattern of land tenure most closely approached that of North China, with widespread small-scale individual owner-cultivators and a comparatively low percentage of landlords, although the latter owned a disproportionate share of the cultivated land. Kirin was a transitional zone toward the pattern of tenure in Heilungkiang where land ownership was concentrated to a fairly high degree and much of the agricultural population was tenant farmers or laborers on holdings which were large by the standards of intramural China.[10]

In two Japanese-conducted surveys in the mid-1930s based on samplings of villages in different sub-regions of Manchuria, the percentage of landless laborer households was 65 percent and 41 percent. Households owning from 1 to 50 acres of land (0.4 to 20 hectares) were 25 percent in one survey and 45 percent in the other, while holders of over 50 acres (20 hectares) were 10 percent in one survey and 3 percent in the other.[11] Communist sources estimated that on the eve of land reform in the Northeast, landlords, who comprised only 3–4 percent of the population, controlled 40–50 percent of the land. Landless laborers were estimated at between 30 and 40 percent of the population. The percentage of poor peasants was said to be roughly equal to that of landless laborers.[12]

All these figures, which give us only an approximation of the landholding system in Manchuria, should be looked at in a dynamic rather than a static frame of reference. In his work on Manchurian social structure in the Republican period, Ramon Myers suggests that considerable opportunities for social and economic mobility existed in the Northeast.[13] Over a period of years, large numbers of landless laborers were able to move up into the ranks of owner-cultivators and the status of other groups was equally fluid over time.[14] Of course, the ranks of the landless were constantly replenished by the influx of impoverished rural workers from North China. In sum, the expanding frontier economy, while certainly no promised land for the dispossessed, promoted a relatively rapid turnover of fortunes and illustrated the aptness of the old Chinese saying, "Nobody stays rich for three generations; nobody stays poor for three generations."[15]

REVOLUTION IN NORTHEAST COUNTRYSIDE   203

In addition, the class cleavages that the CCP portrayed as the primary rural fault lines initially proved less salient in most villages than the countervailing cohesive forces which bound individual villages together against the outside world. Thus, Party cadres, whose outlook on rural society had been shaped by the very different milieu of North China, often encountered unanticipated resistance when they attempted to mobilize laborers and poor tenant farmers to make revolution in Manchurian villages.

A further distinctive feature of Northeast agriculture in 1945 was that some 10–15 percent of the cultivated land was owned by Japanese settlers and land companies or by the Manchukuo government.[16] Official efforts to establish settlements of Japanese colonies in the Northeast countryside had not been very successful, but large tracts of land had been purchased for the project.[17] It is worth noting in this connection that there were still large tracts of arable but as yet uncultivated land in Manchuria, particularly in Heilungkiang and northern Kirin—the areas where the Communist revolution first took root in the region. One contemporary analyst estimated that such land could support an additional agricultural population of some 18–20 million persons. Thus the critical weakness in Manchurian agriculture at the end of the Sino-Japanese War was not a shortage of land; rather, there was an acute shortage of labor and draft animals, and a worn-out stock of agricultural implements.[18]

In sum, the availability of large amounts of landlord- and Japanese/Manchukuo-held land presented the CCP with a broad vista for the radical redistribution of land in order to establish a base of support in the countryside. In retrospect one can see that the dislocating short-term effects of a radical restructuring of land-tenure relationships were likely to produce a negative impact on agricultural productivity, in particular on the marketed portion of major food and industrial crops.

As part of its united front policy during the anti-Japanese war, the CCP pursued an outwardly moderate agrarian policy of rent and interest deduction rather than the radical redistributionist land policy of the Kiangsi period.[19] In November 1945, Mao confirmed the policy of rent and interest reduction as an effective means to mobilize mass support in areas newly occupied by the Communist armies.[20] This policy remained in effect throughout the CCP-KMT negotiations and political maneuvering of the winter and early spring of 1946.

The first phase of the CCP's agrarian policy in the Northeast from the fall of 1945 through the summer of 1946 combined two complementary elements. The first was a reduction of rents and interest rates within the existing framework of land tenure. By the spring of 1946, for example, Chang Hsüeh-ssu, chairman of the Liaoning provincial government, could claim that 70 percent of peasants in the province had benefited from rent reduction.[21] The second element was the redistribution of land belonging to Japanese settlers, Japanese land companies, the Manchukuo government, and Chinese landlords who had collaborated with the Japanese-Manchukuo regime. As noted, this was 10–15 percent of the arable land. A Northeast Bureau directive of April 17, 1946, affirmed the right of all citizens, with the exception of enemies, puppets, Japanese, and traitors, to own land. It ordered the confiscation of all land within the Northeast formerly held by the Japanese and Manchukuo authorities and its redistribution to the families of Communist soldiers who had died in service, landless laborers, and poor peasants.[22] Provincial Party committees issued detailed directives for distributing the lands of the Japanese land companies. This was done bureaucratically rather than via the mechanism of mass struggle.[23] Thus, within the existing framework of a moderate land policy, the CCP in the Northeast was able to begin implementing a redistributionist program thanks to the windfall of confiscated enemy properties. For the time being, the criterion for confiscating and distributing land was a patriotic rather than a class one.

The CCP's first attempt to mobilize popular support in the Northeast in 1945–46 took advantage of the natural postwar desire for vengeance against enemies and collaborators in the form of the ch'ing-suan campaign (the movement to settle accounts). Directed against landlords, officials, entrepreneurs, police, and others who had collaborated with the Manchukuo regime, it was carried out in both rural and urban areas. In many occupied countries there had developed a large reservoir of popular enmity toward the alien rulers and their native collaborators. Untold thousands of collaborators and informers were dispatched via a swift but irregular justice at the hands of former partisans and resistance fighters in the chaotic aftermath of the war.[24] In postwar Manchuria the CCP tried to channel popular rage into its own efforts to gain a foothold in the region. By so doing it hoped to intimidate where it did not directly destroy large numbers of the old official class who naturally gravitated toward the Nationalist side of the civil conflict.

Following the pattern established during the Kiangsi period, the most important of those accused of collaboration with the Japanese were brought before mass trials where, in a highly charged atmosphere whipped up by Party cadres, they were accused, condemned, and often summarily executed.[25] The land, livestock, houses, and other property of the condemned were distributed to the poorer elements in the villages for, as a *Northeast Daily* report on the *ch'ing-suan* movement pointedly noted, "first of all, we have to give swift and substantial benefit to the people.[26] At this time workers' and peasants' self-defense groups, peasant associations, and women's and youth groups were established by CCP organizers.

The Party press made no bones about the vital role of cadres in adequately preparing for and orchestrating these struggles. Where work teams conscientiously investigated local circumstances and cultivated local activists to assist them, things went reasonably well. Where they did not, struggle meetings were poorly attended and sometimes were entirely without result.[27] The effects of the long years of repressive Japanese-Manchukuo rule and the weak tradition of organized peasant protest activity in most of the Northeast were manifested in a generally weak response to these initial Communist mobilization efforts. Civilian and military cadres assigned to the villages often assumed the burden of *ch'ing-suan* activities while a cautious peasantry passively accepted the gifts of land and other goods from their new rulers. Later, these cadres came under sharp attack for having carried out rural transformation without first effecting revolutionary mobilization.

The limited distribution of land carried out in the *ch'ing-suan* movement was meaningful only within areas under effective Communist military control, for the most part in northern Manchuria. Elsewhere in the region CCP cadres also hastily distributed Japanese and Manchukuo land during the high tide of Communist military power in the spring of 1946, but once the NEDUA had retreated northward these lands were reclaimed by landlords and Kuomintang officials.[28]

As the prospects for peace in China faded, overall Communist land policy took a modest step to the left. A Central Committee directive of May 4, 1946, decreed the takeover of "surplus" landlord holdings to be compensated for with government bonds. Rich peasants' property was not to be affected by this order. In the Northeast, however, a considerably more thoroughgoing and radical line was prescribed in a Northeast Bureau directive of July 7, which ordered the confiscation of rich peasants' surplus lands as well as the lands of all remaining landlords. Livestock, agricultural equipment, and other property were also subject to expropriation and redistribution.[29] The changeover to this straight class line was justified on the grounds that landlords and rich peasants had opposed the moderate measures of agrarian reform and other democratic changes that had already been introduced by the CCP.[30]

The July 7th directive signaled the beginning of a year and a half of bitter conflict in the Northeast countryside, pitting the Communist Party, its fledgling mass organizations, and a portion of the rural poor against the rural leaders and their networks of kin, local retainers, clients, and other village elements. In this struggle between revolution and counter-revolution in the countryside, the Communists possessed the decisive advantage of an effective regional political organization and a mobile armed force in control of the territories within which the rural revolution was carried out.

The rural revolution commenced in earnest in the summer of 1946 at a time when the CCP was still in an extremely precarious position within Manchuria. Communist military fortunes were at a low ebb. Lin Piao had just replaced Peng Chen as the top leader of the Northeast Bureau after a bruising intra-Party conflict. Above all, the Party was still not very far along the path to acquiring the secure base areas in the rural hinterlands and district towns that Mao Tse-tung had urged upon it more than six months earlier. Ch'en Yün, head of the West Manchurian Sub-Bureau of the Central Committee, noting the weakness of the CCP organization in the countryside, said, "We are still 'renting a house,' we haven't yet built our own." He further stated, "Rural work must occupy eighty percent of our entire work."[31] This weakness was reflected in the character of the revolution itself. The first stage of the Communist-initiated land reform, beginning in the summer of 1946, was like a quick sweep through a broad field with a dull scythe. More than anything else, it was an act of desperation by a Party leadership concerned that the Northeast might rapidly fall to the Nationalists unless rural bases of support were quickly acquired.

Lin Piao, once again speaking as an apostle of Maoist-style revolutionary warfare, is quoted at this same time as saying, "Several tens of thousands of cadres should be sent to the countryside to carry out land reform . . ." Under the slogans of "Remove your leather shoes and lay down your suitcases" and "Wear peasant clothes and eat sorghum," some 15,000 cadres—over three-quarters of them seconded from their military units—were sent down to the countryside to make revolution.[32] Special short-term land reform classes were organized to train these cadres.[33]

After several months of feverish efforts by these thousands of sent-down cadres and the village activists whom they recruited, Lin Piao was able to proclaim in his New Year's message of January 1, 1947, that the face and the spirit of the Northeast countryside had significantly changed.[34] In cases which came closest to the Party's model, the involved process of determining class status, measuring and evaluating the land, and finally distributing it in accordance with complex criteria, was an intense education in political participation for the peasants concerned. The day when peasants took title to their new holdings was turned into a festive occasion marking the consummation of a revolutionary transformation, a collective *fanshen* (literally "turning over one's body").[35]

However, a very different picture of the actual state of rural revolution emerges from detailed reports in the Communist press at this time. After evaluating the progress of land reform during the second half of 1946, CCP leaders concluded that in only a minority of villages had the land reform work been properly conducted. In the large majority of villages land reform had been carried out in an unsatisfactory manner or not at all. The Communists called these villages "half-cooked" or "raw" rice. For

Celebrating *fan-shen*. Woodcut. *Tung-pei jih-pao*.

example, a report based on a sampling of several districts in Sung-kiang said that between 10 and 20 percent were satisfactory, about 60 percent half-cooked, 5 to 10 percent fouled up *(kao-luan)*, and the rest were raw.[36]

Responsibility for this unfortunate state of affairs was placed on local cadres who had not done their jobs properly and on landlords who were seeking to retain economic and political power in their own hands. The main charge against cadres was that for the most part they had failed to mobilize the masses to carry out land reform through class struggle in the countryside. Instead they themselves had performed the work the masses were supposed to shoulder *(pao pan t'ai-t'i)*. Therefore, the poor peasants and laborers had remained passive, and the local elites had been able to retain their real power. Cadres were admonished to rid themselves of the condescending attitude toward the peasants: "We are Chu-ko Liang and they are blockheads." When poor agriculturalists received land and other property from Communist cadres who were behaving like new village patrons, they felt (according to a report from Heilungkiang) that "this country is

much better than Manchukuo." Yet they remained passive observers rather than active participants, and were still uncommitted
to the emerging revolutionary order.[37]

The acute shortage of qualified personnel underlay the
problem of poor cadre performance. For example, in Mingshui
county, with an estimated population of 160,000 in 1947, there
were only 111 cadres in land reform work teams, or one cadre for
every 1,441 persons. With so few cadres available, work teams
could not afford the luxury of "squatting on one point" for very
long in order to make sure their work was carried out properly,
but rather shuttled rapidly back and forth from one village to
another. Typically, a work team had *just one week* in which to carry
out an investigation of the village, identify activists, target enemies,
organize struggle meetings, lay the groundwork for mass organizations, and initiate land reform. In such circumstances it is hardly
surprising that most cadres chose the short-cut to rural transformation, bypassing the uncommitted peasantry, and taking matters
into their own hands. An article in the *Northeast Daily* noted the
consequences of such haste—the quicker the reforms were put
into practice the more fouled up things became.[38]

An opposite practice, which derived from the same
source, was for cadres to distribute peacefully and without a process of mass struggle gifts of land donated by landlords who hoped
to preserve much if not all of their properties by adapting themselves to the revolutionary regime. The CCP had encouraged such
donations of land during the summer of 1946 (as it had earlier
during the Yenan period), but by the winter of 1946–47 this
practice was condemned as a landlord trick.[39]

As previously noted, the *ch'ing-suan* movement and
the first stage of land reform was the time when the CCP in
Manchuria first acquired a significant number of local cadres to
supplement its original contingent of outside personnel. However,
now the Party leadership discovered that many of these new basic-
level cadres were supposedly opportunists, scoundrels, landlord
agents, and the like who had infiltrated the local organizations to
take them over from the inside. In Peian Special District, for
example, 70 percent of the villages were said to be infested with
hooligan cadres *(liu-mang kan-pu)*.[40]

One must be cautious about accepting these accusations at face value, given the organic tendency of Communists of this era to blame their own shortcomings on spies and infiltrators. However, in this case there is reason to believe that the accusations, although grossly distorted, were grounded in reality. (See below on the dynamics of revolution at the local level.) One can hardly suppose that rural leaders would graciously yield their power without a struggle. In their eyes the revolutionaries must have appeared as a ragtag and bobtail collection of local upstarts set into motion by outside Communist agitators who, through some fluke of fate, temporarily enjoyed military predominance. As for those rural leaders who bowed to the Communist presence, their natural desire to adapt and survive by joining the new organizations established in their villages was interpreted by the leaders of the CCP as evidence of malevolent intent. What Party leaders condemned as the crafty efforts of inveterate feudal elements to resist historical progress can equally well be seen, then, as understandable efforts of local leaders to defend their prerogatives as best they could under the changed circumstances.[41]

Perhaps the most striking feature of the revolution in the Northeast countryside was precisely the capacity of rural leaders to maintain their positions in the face of mounting Communist efforts to oust them, and the concomitant reluctance of much if not most of the rural population to support Communist attacks on these local leaders. I shall explore this issue from a theoretical perspective in a later section. Here let us examine briefly some of the techniques of evasion and resistance which led the Party leadership in early 1947 to conclude that most of the Northeast was still half-cooked or raw rice.

In northern Manchuria, as elsewhere in China during the land reform, many landlords tried to conceal the true extent of their landholdings either by failing to report lands that had not been registered for tax purposes or by putting ownership of the land in the names of dependent kin or clients while retaining de facto control of their properties. Given the weakness of the Communist administrative organs, it was quite difficult to detect the so-called black land *(hei-ti)* which, at the end of 1947 was still estimated at one-sixth to one-fifth of the total cultivated land.[42] Second, some landlords donated poorer quality land for distribution while retaining their better quality properties. Perhaps the most common tactic employed by the rural leaders was to cultivate the good graces of work team cadres. This took many forms—feigning enthusiasm for the new reforms, giving food and other daily necessities to cadres, bribing them with cash, providing male cadres with women.[43] Using their networks of personal relations, rural leaders joined the peasant associations, local governments, and mass organizations that were set up in the countryside during land reform. They tried to persuade rentier-farmers and owner-cultivators to join them in blunting the force of revolutionary changes. When all else failed, some rural leaders organized their own anti-Communist military forces, assisted bandits or irregular military detachments, or assassinated local cadres.[44]

From the Party's point of view overt opposition was easier to deal with than the forms of adaptive behavior which the CCP perceived as more subtle forms of resistance. An integral part of rural revolution is the creation of new networks of economic and political institutions to replace the existing ones.[45] Yet, rural leaders were adept at entering and taking over control of precisely those peasant associations, local governments, and other institutions that the Party had established in the countryside. Thus, many of the rural folk who responded to the revolutionary call were apparently members of the old rural leadership or, more frequently, their clients, who sought to preserve as much as they could of the old distribution of power by controlling the very organizations the Party had established to wrest power from their hands.[46] Organized into itinerant work teams, veteran Party cadres, most of whom were unfamiliar with the local environment, often finished up work in one village and hurried on to the next one with no inkling that many of the newly recruited activists and local cadres were far from being disadvantaged and exploited class elements engaged in seizing power. Thus many villages had to be struggled and organized over and over again.

In the first months of 1947, prior to the spring planting season, the Party leadership in the Northeast launched a campaign to cook the "half-cooked" rice and to uproot bad roots—the latter a reference to the landlords and their clients who were holding on to power.[47] Work teams returned to villages where they had already been before to remeasure the land, organize poor peasants and hired laborers to attack landlords in struggle meetings, distribute grain, livestock, and other goods, and revamp the local governments and mass organizations.[48] The active participation of the poorer village elements was deemed crucial to the success of this second round of land reform. And once more the Party attempted to gain a foothold in the countryside by conferring material advantage on its supporters. An integral part of this phase of land reform was a "dig out the cellars" movement designed to uncover hidden sources of landlord wealth that had previously been concealed.[49] Confiscated grain helped to ease the chronic spring hunger of the rural poor while the distribution of landlord houses, furniture, livestock, clothing, and other movable property gave the recipients a tangible interest in the new order.[50]

The "dig out the cellars movement" involved local activists and other peasants in direct confrontations with landlords and their families; the targets of attack were frequently subjected to humiliation, rough handling, and worse. Undoubtedly these confrontations between the new and the old orders rectified some long-standing abuses and injustices and may have promoted the "psychic liberation" of the poor from their habitual deference to the more powerful and wealthy members of their communities. One may be equally certain, however, that the public license freely provided by the new authorities for the commission of violent acts against the local elites resulted in much random violence in which anti-social elements indulged their worst passions under the banner of revolutionary justice. Such violence, which, as Philip Kuhn reminds us, was long an integral feature of Chinese rural life, reached a crescendo in the late fall of 1947 during the land equalization movement.[51]

Within the areas under effective Communist military control, the resort to violence against the old rural leaders was not a defense against the armed attacks of the "class enemy." The local elites were fragmented and their armed opposition was largely ineffectual. The Communist Party itself promoted violence because it was the medium in which the new forms of revolutionary organization and governance grew most effectively. Given the Party's initial weakness in the rural areas and the shortage of time to effect a rural transformation, violence became the essential catalyst of change. It was the sharp-pointed spade with which the Party dug up the "bad roots," the sharp-edged axe with which it cut down the "big trees"—metaphors for the landlords and other prosperous rural people. In Northeast China, the evidence suggests that for the most part violence did not flow from the liberated anger of the village poor turned against their erstwhile oppressors. It was nothing so spontaneous or elemental. Rather, violence was a form of destructive energy generated and employed by Party cadres to prevent the emergence of a state of equilibrium in the village that might leave the old rural leaders in retention of a substantial portion of their former economic and social power.

The apparent necessity of conducting a never-ending struggle in the rural areas, broken only by the cyclical tasks of the agricultural calendar, points to an important truth. The Party realized that in the absence of continuing pressure from outside forces, the natural tendency in the rural areas was to revert to a slightly modified version of the pre-revolutionary status quo. But the Party leadership obviously could not allow this to occur without placing at risk the entire revolutionary project. Therefore, through a series of campaigns directed against the old local leaders over a period of a year and a half, the balance of power in the villages shifted to the Communist side, materially aided by the instrument of violence.

In the late winter and early spring of 1947, the Communist press in the Northeast reported innumerable victories in the intensified land reform campaign. Hundreds of thousands of *shang* of concealed landlord holdings were discovered and land and other properties were distributed in the course of struggle meetings—this time involving wider circles of the rural poor. Party branches—fortresses as they were called in a revealing metaphor—were established in more and more villages. Slowly, improvements in the land reform were registered, although wide variations remained from county to county and district to district. At a Joint Conference of County Party Secretaries in Sungkiang province in June 1947, Kao Kang, a member of the Northeast Bureau, called for completing the process of cooking the half-cooked rice by the end of the year. He proposed two standards for judging whether the work had been accomplished: 1) feudal power was smashed and the fruits of struggle had been divided; 2) the basic masses were in power and cadres from good class backgrounds were working alongside them. He reminded his audience not to worry about excesses because, as Mao taught, it was natural that excesses be committed in the course of revolutionary struggle.[52] This soon became a constant refrain in Party propaganda during the second half of the year.

Some of the core problems in the area of rural transformation may be seen by looking at an individual case—Fushu district of Yenchi county.[53] In this district, 10,000 landless and land poor peasants—55 percent of the total population of 18,000—received 4,405 *shang* of land or 4.4 mou per person. In addition to the land, 99 head of cattle, 15 horses, 120 pigs, 382 units of housing *(chien)*, and 712 piculs of grain were distributed to the same number of poor folk. On the average each person received 9.5 pounds of grain. The other figures attest to the paucity of livestock even in the hands of the wealthiest rural strata. Obviously, while the distribution of property might help the CCP gain village supporters, it would do nothing to address the poverty of the district as a whole.

In fact, at least in the short run, land reform caused serious disruption to the cycle of agriculture and had a negative impact on production. There were several major factors involved. In many areas, rural work teams, and the villagers whom they mobilized, attacked and confiscated the property of rentier-farmers and owner-cultivators as well as of landlords.[54] If, as one slogan put it, "There are two families under Heaven—one is named Poor, the other is named Rich," what was the point of observing or even trying to understand the complicated criteria for differentiating one class from another that the Party set forth?[55] Quite naturally, even those better-off owner-cultivators who had not been attacked were leery of provoking the wrath of the new authorities. Many of them sharply reduced their efforts in the fields to the minimum required to sustain their own families. They were also extremely reluctant to join the labor exchange schemes that the Party promoted in the countryside to alleviate the labor shortage.

A second problem was the dependent attitude of the beneficiaries of land reform. Having received land, grain, and other commodities from the hands of work team cadres, some of the village poor came to believe that their new Communist patrons would provide for their needs from then on. "Now that there are *fanshen-hui* [as the peasant associations were sometimes called]

there's no need to worry about starving" was one such expression
of dependency. Poor villagers sometimes sold off livestock, tools,
and other instruments of production they had received from the
distribution of confiscated property, and splurged on food, drink,
and festivities.[56] In the universe of the village the revolution was
a good thing if it brought some concrete improvement to the lives
of the local people, but the Party leadership in the region, with its
eyes on the abstract goal of victory, saw such indulgence as a
threat to production and, ultimately, to the very concept of the
revolution.

   This gap between elite and mass goals was a major
source of the radicalizing dynamic of land reform in the Northeast.
The Communist Party gained local support by distributing the so-
called fruits of struggle—property confiscated from the more prosperous rural classes. But at the same time, the Party began to make
a series of demands on the peasantry for grain, fodder, livestock,
carts, and, above all, military and civilian labor power. In the short
term, not only did the revolution fail to improve conditions in the
countryside, the disruptions and demands of the war actually
produced a negative impact on the lives of many if not all villagers.
To be sure, the landless and the land-poor had been given land,
but land by itself was of limited value.

   In this context, the repeated campaigns against landlords and other relatively prosperous villagers served two objectives in addition to the goal of "overthrowing" their power. First,
the campaigns squeezed every last bit of property from their victims in order to provide a little more to the village supporters of
revolution who had come to expect some reward for their commitment. Second, the campaigns deflected dissatisfaction in the
countryside from the new authorities to the old rural leaders. The
message conveyed was that only repeated and ever harsher
searches and confrontations would force the landlords to surrender their hidden property.[57] Moreover, the need to distribute additional goods to the supporters of the revolution provided the
rationale for widening the target of confiscations to include owner-
cultivators—both rich and middle peasants. In sum, for the dis-
locations and hardships brought about by the turmoil of the revolution the revolutionaries prescribed larger and stiffer doses of
revolution as the remedy. The result was a self-generating cycle

of radicalization that was not brought under control until the spring of 1948.

A third factor in the agricultural crisis generated by the land reform was the impact of the revolution on the complicated pattern of production relations associated with the old land tenure system. This involved such things as the provision of agricultural credits, the supply, distribution, and provisioning of draft animals, the supply of human labor power, the availability of seeds and agricultural tools, and decisions concerning the type of crops to be planted. The division of the land and the distribution of live-stock and tools set into motion an intricate chain reaction in the agricultural system that threatened production. Most of the agri-cultural commodities produced for the market—including the grain that fed the cities, provisioned the armies, and was sold for export—had been produced by the more prosperous strata of the rural economy, in particular by the rentier-farmers and the owner-cultivators.[58] Yet these were among the prime targets during the radical phases of land reform. Land alone would not produce soybeans, millet, sorghum, corn, flax, or anything else. The attacks against landlords and rich peasants seriously disrupted the supply of agricultural credit.[59] Seeds, draft animals, and fodder were in desperately short supply. Finally, the beneficiaries of land reform for the most part lacked the skills, experience, and sufficient labor power to make the most effective use of the available inputs.[60] In sum, the revolution threatened to produce a significant decline in the amount of crops grown for the market.

In these circumstances, on the eve of the spring 1947 planting season, the Party resorted to a number of temporary expedients in order to promote an adequate harvest. In the first place, cadres were instructed to protect middle peasants from attack and to promote unity among middle peasants, poor peas-ants, and laborers. Owner-cultivators were assured that they too would benefit from land reform, and that the wealth they earned through their own labor was not subject to confiscation. In a speech to the Ning-an Labor Model Assembly, NEAC Chairman Lin Feng asserted that prosperity was the CCP's goal, and that Northeasterners should rely on their own efforts to become pros-perous. Rich and middle peasants were even assured that it was permissible to rent out land and to hire labor as long as the rates were fair.[61]

Second, attempting to make up for the now shattered system of agricultural credit that landlords and rich peasants had provided, NEAC authorized 500 million yuan of agricultural loans to be distributed through the provincial, prefectural, and county governments for the purchase of tools, draft animals, seeds, fertilizers, and other productive purposes. These interest-free loans, to be repaid after the autumn harvest where possible, were to be for the use of the poorest agriculturalists whose eligibility and specific needs would be determined by village meetings. On February 25, 1947, a NEAC directive on preparations for spring planting stressed, inter alia, the need to stimulate sideline production, hunting, fishing, wild herb gathering as well as promote industrial crops such as cotton and flax and to open up new lands for cultivation. On May 1, NEAC established a 100 million yuan production incentive fund which county governments were told to distribute in the form of horses, tools, and other material rewards to diligent and hard-working labor models. The NEAC order unambiguously encouraged peasants to get rich *(fa ts'ai chih-fu)*.[62]

Third, cadres encouraged the spread of traditional forms of labor exchange in the countryside as well as the organization of newer forms of cooperation in order to alleviate the acute shortage of labor. At this time, Party and government leaders tightened their own belts a notch, conserving grain wherever possible and pressing efforts to become partially self-sufficient in vegetable and grain supply. To cope with the acute shortage of draft animals, NEAC issued a decree on January 2, 1947, prohibiting the slaughter of healthy domestic livestock, and banning the transfer of draft animals to Nationalist-held territory. Finally, the Party geared up its propaganda organs to promote production education among the masses, emphasizing that only through hard work could there be prosperity.[63] Hard-working owner-cultivators whose wealth had been expropriated during periods of excessive revolutionary enthusiasm must have greeted this lesson in Marxist economics with a certain degree of skepticism.

In sum, the campaign to promote production in the spring of 1947 (and a similar campaign just one year later) was a response to the disequilibrium that land reform had brought about, a condition fraught with danger in view of the expanding demands of the front as the civil war grew in scope and intensity. However, by no means had the radical redistributionist impulse of land reform been exhausted. The CCP was still far from satisfied with the results of the first two waves of land reform. Consequently, from the summer of 1947 through the winter of 1947–48, a new and even more radical wave of rural revolution engulfed the region. The revolutionary violence which scourged the Northeast countryside in these months was accompanied by a whirlwind of terror which extinguished the lives of untold numbers of persons condemned as enemies of the revolution. When the terror finally abated, the surviving members of the old rural leadership who had held on to their power tenaciously during the earlier phases of the rural revolution were thoroughly defeated. In early 1948, after eighteen months of struggle, Party leaders proclaimed a cease-fire in the rural class warfare, secure in the knowledge that local Party organizations and the local governments they had established were now in control of a pacified countryside.

Throughout the civil war period (and thereafter as well), CCP leaders were hard-pressed to reconcile the goal of revolutionary change with that of production or development. Officially, of course, Party leaders proclaimed that by transferring the means of production from the hands of the landlord class into those of the working peasantry, land reform would liberate the full production potential of the countryside. Things rarely worked out this way in practice, so Party leaders had to choose. Since they all shared Lenin's view that "the question at the root of any revolution is the question of governmental power," the choice was not really very difficult.[64] Only by eliminating its opponents in the countryside through an intensified process of revolutionary change could the CCP firmly establish itself as the governing power at the local level.

The organizational interests of the Party as defined by its top leadership coincided with the personal interests of the cadres charged with implementing policy. Almost from the beginning of land reform in the Northeast, cadres had been criticized for failing to arouse poor peasants and hired laborers to take part in the rural revolution. When, pressed to accomplish miracles of instantaneous revolutionary transformation, cadres took matters into their own hands, they were rebuked for substituting their own action for that of the masses. Yet if they stood aside and waited for spontaneous revolutionary action to occur in the villages, they were criticized for inaction and "tailism" *(wei-pa chu-i)*. It was very difficult to strike the proper balance between "letting go" *(fang-shou)* or "setting the masses in motion" *(fa-tung ch'ün-chung)* on the one hand and maintaining effective leadership on the other.

The Leninist norm of leadership, which the Party established for cadres engaged in rural revolution, was to achieve the appearance of spontaneous action on the part of the peasantry while carefully avoiding any actual spontaneity that might result in a conflict with Communist goals. Therefore, work team cadres, in conjunction with local activists, were enjoined to plan every stage of village class struggle very carefully. This included collecting information, selecting targets for struggle, setting up meetings, arranging for speakers, selecting charges against the accused, recording the wealth of the class enemy, and finally prearranging the method of dealing with the object of "revolutionary justice" in order to avoid on the spot disagreement between the leaders and the masses.[65] Like skillful theatrical directors, work team cadres were supposed to guide the production of revolution authoritatively but inconspicuously and without taking the spotlight away from the dramatis personae visible on stage. Of course, this was a difficult role to perform successfully. When local cadres fell short of this high standard, it was usually safer for them to commit the "leftist" error of sanctioning revolutionary excesses than the "rightist" error of seeking to curb the masses. By the summer of 1947, then, the Party's determination to firmly establish its power in the countryside meshed with the cadres' need to demonstrate their mettle by "unleashing" the masses.

The agricultural calendar regulated the timing and content of political campaigns. During the spring it was important to focus the attention of all agriculturalists, irrespective of class status, on the tasks of the planting season. At this time, the CCP appeared in the guise of a party of production—mobilizing capital and labor inputs, extending agricultural loans, and exhorting everyone to maximize their efforts. Once the crops were in the ground and a lull in the agricultural cycle was at hand, the season of planting gave way to a season of politics.[66] Moreover, there was no need to suspend politics during the harvest season. Quite the contrary. Expropriating the harvest of the better-off peasants (as

well as the remaining landlords) provided new fruits of struggle
to distribute to the Party's rural supporters as well as to supply
the front.

In the summer of 1947 attacks on the persistent power
of the landlords were renewed in the Communist press. In many
areas, it was said, landlords still dominated local politics through
their influence and connections, aided by the leniency and lack
of vigilance of village-level cadres. The army, too, was accused of
interfering with land reform in order to protect landlords. A Northeast Bureau directive of August 25, 1947, initiated a three-month
program of agrarian reform education in rear area army organs to
rectify incorrect thinking, uproot bad elements within the ranks,
and expose landlord machinations. Furthermore, landlords were
said to be taking advantage of loopholes in Party policy by dis-
guising themselves as rich or middle peasants. Rich and middle
peasants themselves were exerting undue influence in their villages by becoming labor models and activists.[67]

Despite some progress registered during the movement
to cook the half-cooked rice, the Party claimed that in too many
villages the revolution had not yet taken hold and in others, after
initial progress, there had been reversion to the status quo ante.
An editorial in the *Northeast Daily* estimated that by the end of
November 1947 land reform had been properly conducted in no
more than 30 to 40 percent of the rural districts. In a dialectical
counterpoint to the recent emphasis on production, a report from
Hunch'un county said that too many villages treated production
as a task that was divorced from class struggle.[68] The burden of
the numerous bulletins from the countryside was that ultimate
control over the villages was still in dispute and the class struggle
was growing more acute. Scarcely concealed in these messages
was the warning that the Party would have to alter its supposedly
lenient policy toward rich and upper middle peasants because this
policy provided a haven for landlords and other opponents of
Communist power in the countryside.

In August and September the attacks against landlords
became more strident and insistent. Sensational stories of landlords colluding with underground agents to assassinate local officials and oppose Communist power filled the press. The Ch'ang-
p'ai County Party Committee catalogued landlord tricks to oppose

Seizing the landlord and transporting his movable property. *Tung-pei jih-pao,* October 9, 1947.

the people: 1) pretend to be enlightened to lull the masses; 2) stir up trouble, cause splits; 3) bribe backward persons with money; 4) use beautiful women to corrupt cadres and activists; 5) infiltrate dog's legs [agents] into peasant associations; 6) feign poverty to avoid being struggled; 7) act impudently and engage in effrontery; 8) encourage factionalism; 9) collude with agents and bandits to carry out assassinations. Speaking on behalf of the Party leadership, the *Northeast Daily* summoned the Party and the peasantry to wage an unrelenting struggle to eradicate the landlords once and for all.[69]

The third wave of revolution that now engulfed the Northeast countryside was much more violent and all-embracing than the preceding two. The Party encouraged revolutionary violence by repeatedly emphasizing the cunning malevolence of the landlords who allegedly stopped at nothing in their counter-revolutionary machinations. By presenting the landlords as monsters in human form, the Party sought to negate any inhibitions against violent actions. Moreover, since landlords were said to be masquerading as rich and middle peasants, they too became the targets of mass violence. Bloody retributions against landlords and others condemned as enemies of the revolution soon became commonplace.[70]

It is clear that initiation of this Red Terror in the Northeast preceded promulgation of the CCP's Draft Land Reform Law on October 10, 1947 (the actual draft had been adopted on September 13). Yet there is no doubt that the draft law not only sanctioned but stimulated the extreme leftist mood that gripped all levels of the CCP in the region over the next several months. In essence, the Draft Land Reform Law called for the equalization of landholdings throughout liberated China (i.e., the territories occupied by the CCP). In order to achieve this goal the land either had to be redivided anew even in those areas which had already undergone land reform or, where this was not desired by the peasants, existing landholdings had to be adjusted to achieve parity.[71]

By the time the Draft Land Reform Law was circulated, the Communist areas of the Northeast had already passed through more than a year of protracted revolutionary struggles. Yet in one of the periodic moods of self-flagellation which alternated with excessive self-congratulations in a kind of collective manic depressive syndrome, the CCP now bewailed the superficiality and incompleteness of the rural revolution in Manchuria up to this point. In a December 1, 1947, open letter addressed to the peasants, the Northeast Bureau asserted that earlier efforts at rural revolution had failed to uproot the feudal land system thoroughly or to distribute the land fairly. Because of inadequate methods of struggle, landlords and rich peasants had retained too much land, and the just demands of the poor peasants and hired laborers had not been met. In order to remedy these defects, the current movement to implement the land equalization provision of the Draft Land Reform Law would be spearheaded by the poor peasants and hired laborers. In each village a local congress or representative conference of these two groups would choose a Committee to Divide the Land and the Fruits (fen-p'ei t'u-ti fen-p'ei kuo-shih ti wei-yuan-hui). Only after ensuring that power was firmly in the hands of these classes would it be proper to bring middle peasants into the revolutionary alliance.[72]

In a report to land reform work team leaders on October 18, Ch'en Yün stressed the need to untie the hands of the poor peasants and hired laborers who were the main force in the revolution. The establishment of separate Poor Peasant and Hired

Laborer Associations, distinct from the existing peasant associations which had supposedly become dominated by the old rural leaders, would enable the revolutionary transformation to succeed. Ch'en condoned violence against landlords and other enemies of the revolution as justified retribution for their crimes against the people, and he abjured cadres to learn from the rural underclasses.[73]

The hallmarks of the land equalization movement were attempts to mobilize hitherto quiescent elements of the rural population on the one hand and the adoption of new forms of struggle on the other. In previous struggles only an active minority of villagers had cast their lot with the CCP by participating in struggle meetings against local elite members and joining mass associations. Some fragmentary sociological data on nonparticipants in the earlier phases of the land reform emerged during the land equalization movement. A report on one supposedly typical village revealed that only 33 percent of the potentially mobilizable inhabitants (217 of 650 in a total population of 941) had participated in the movement. Old folks and women participated at the lowest rates. Only 33 of the 217 active villagers (15 percent) were women, and most of these were young and single. Evidently it was not considered fitting and proper for married housewives to join in revolutionary activities. Another interesting point is that rates of participation in satellite or dependent villages (fu-shu ts'un) were much lower than in administrative villages (hsing-cheng ts'un). Presumably the Party's meager strength in the countryside was concentrated in the larger administrative villages in which participation could more easily be elicited by cadres and local activists.[74] Since nonparticipants were seen as backward elements who functioned frequently as the landlords' "air-raid shelters"—helping them to conceal their wealth—it was deemed essential to bring these laggards into the revolutionary process. Although there is little available data on the subject, one may suppose that the Party had only limited success in boosting the rates of participation among old people and women.

Several points are worth noting with respect to the methods of struggle used during the land equalization movement. The most important was the Party's injunction to cadres not to restrain in any way the revolutionary activity of the village poor once they had been aroused to action. If in the earlier phases of land reform, cadres acted very much like theatrical directors, now they were supposed to be more like spectators at the Colosseum, cheering on the underclass gladiators who were doing battle with the counter-revolutionary lions. Once more, Party propagandists intoned that so-called excesses were not only normal but even necessary in the course of pursuing the class foe, and that those who doubted this were hypocrites and enemies. In this connection, a report from Pei-an county describing the important role that public security departments played in the campaign against landlords is particularly interesting.[75] Although there is scant information on the public security departments during the Northeast civil war, one should recall that these organs of the embryonic Party dictatorship had already acquired considerable experience in violence and repression during the *cheng-feng* (rectification) campaign in Yenan (1942–1944).

The attempts to break down persistent local resistance to the new Communist order involved more than mobilizing hitherto passive elements of the village population. In the course of the earlier struggles, Party leaders had learned that village particularism—expressed in the defense of the village as a corporate community in times of danger—was itself a major obstacle to revolutionary change. The Communist work teams were frequently perceived as unwelcome outsiders threatening community values that the village shared across class lines. Yet between villages there was often a tradition of rivalry and distrust based on a variety of factors. Knowledge of these circumstances inspired a new method of revolutionary attack designed to counteract local particularism and village solidarity and make use of inter-village competition.

In the so-called Sweep the Courtyard movement of the fall and winter of 1947–48, the masses in one village were mobilized to attack targets in neighboring villages while their own traditional leaders (bound to them by ties of kinship and neighborhood) were attacked by mobs from the neighboring villages for whom such particularistic ties were far less vital. The Party's attempt to control and manipulate inter-village conflict was not always successful, however. Apparently, in no small number of instances, Party directed inter-village class conflict blossomed into full-scale battles between neighboring villages in which class lines were all but forgotten. Because of this danger, in some areas provincial and local Party leaders successfully opposed applying the draconian methods of the Sweep the Courtyard movement.[76]

A related method also in vogue at this time was to attack enemies of the revolution at the district (ch'ü) rather than the village level. In order to ensure that targets in a given village did not escape to the safety of a neighboring village or town, peasants in at least several adjacent villages were mobilized simultaneously. In raids that typically commenced at dawn—that favorite time for hunters when the quarry sleeps—multi-village detachments of activist peasants, like beaters in an expedition, would converge on the homestead of a given target or, if the intended victim had been alerted in advance and made his escape, they would track down, flush out, and destroy their quarry on the spot. (During the Cultural Revolution, incidentally, Red Guard raids against landlords and bad class elements were also conducted at night.)[77] In Hulan county, a countywide meeting of 6,000 poor peasants and hired laborers cooperated in tracking down landlords, and villages competed with each other to see which could bag the most landlords.[78]

This was the peak period of violence in the Northeast rural revolution. Although the Party press occasionally suggested that beating to death was not a good method for dealing with landlords, the general atmosphere of unrestricted revolutionary terror overrode such counsels of moderation.[79] As in the Cultural Revolution just twenty years later, the exhortations to seize power and destroy the old forces were inscribed in the blood of uncounted victims of revolutionary violence, by no means all of them "class enemies." It is impossible to provide overall statistics on this point. One revolutionary memoir refers to the beating to death of five persons in a single hamlet in one evening. The author laconically remarks that "during the high tide of the movement there were not a few persons beaten to death."[80] In a speech from April 1948, Ch'en Yün said that "a wave of beating was rampant. There were too many deaths."[81] In Changling district of Hulan county, some 800 households (roughly 20 percent of the total or 8 per natural village) were targeted during the land equalization movement, although how many victims there were is not specified in the account that has come down to us. In Chian county 1,800 "oppressors and exploiters of the peasants" were struggled and punished without forgiveness according to the severity of their crimes. How many of these were executed it is impossible to say. In Suihua-Chinhua district poor peasant-hired laborer meetings were convoked at the township (hsiang) level. In one night's work members of 136 "feudal households" were arrested.[82]

On January 1, 1948, in a belated effort to establish Party control over a process that had deliberately been intended to get out of hand, NEAC established temporary people's courts at the local level, which in turn were supposed to institute judgment committees (shen-p'an hui) to deal with violators of the land reform law. These judgment committees could mete out punishment, but their sentences had to be confirmed at the higher administrative level. Death sentences required approval from both the county and provincial authorities, for example. Punishments involving mutilation were forbidden, suggesting strongly that they had been utilized, but how widely one cannot say.[83] Thus, revolutionary class justice was to be filtered through quasi-judicial procedures even if it was not to be tempered by mercy. However, since December 1947 was the high point of the land equalization movement in the Northeast, this decree was promulgated too late to mitigate the worst fury of the revolutionary pogroms.

The end of the extreme leftist phase of land reform was signaled in a mid-January 1948 speech by Politburo member Jen Pi-shih who systematically criticized many of the essential features of the Party's rural policy during the preceding four months. Castigating left-wing adventurist attitudes which were responsible for unwarranted attacks on middle peasants, excessive violence including numerous executions and random beatings to death, and violations of the Party's policy of protecting urban commerce and industry, Jen called for a significant narrowing of the target of attack in the countryside and said the death penalty should be applied only in exceptional cases.[84] After sanctioning an unprecedented orgy of violence in the Northeast countryside in order to promote its own power objectives, the Party now assumed a stance of statesmanlike moderation. The consolidation phase of the land reform movement in the region had begun.

In response to this signal from the center, the Northeast

Bureau applied the brakes to the runaway locomotive of rural revolution. An authoritative editorial in the *Northeast Daily* on February 15, 1948, said that because of its unprecedented scope many mistakes had been committed in the land equalization movement. The main defect was in the area of leadership, where cadres, striving to avoid the sin of *pao-pan tai-t'i*, had followed a policy of drift and tailism and failed to provide proper leadership to the aroused masses. As usual, the Party chiefs were blaming the rank-and-file for "errors" that were inherent in and virtually demanded by the policies that had been set from above. Echoing Jen Pi-shih's emphasis on the need to narrow the target, the editorial stressed that the criteria for defining class status were neither political attitudes nor personal history but the percentage of one's income derived from exploitation, ownership of the means of production (particularly land), and living standards.[85] In words that suggested the fluidity of class relations in Manchuria, it was said that in defining the class status of an individual, one should examine his circumstances for no more than three years prior to August 1945.

During the land equalization movement, the interests of owner-cultivators had been seriously infringed. Now the Party strictly defined middle peasants as those whose income derived from exploitation (i.e., hiring labor) amounted to no more than 25 percent (or in special cases 30 percent) of their total income. Furthermore, in calculating the income of rich tenant farmers and middle tenant farmers, one should deduct that part of their income which they paid out in rent before defining their class status. Subsequently, on May 25, 1948, the Central Committee of the CCP reissued and gave wide circulation to the documents for defining class status that had originally been drawn up in Kiangsi in 1933.[86] These complex documents are filled with complicated criteria for defining percentages of exploitation and contain numerous exceptions and qualifications. One wonders how the mostly poorly educated local cadres were expected to make sense of them.

Finally, the February 15 editorial proclaimed that in most areas of northern Manchuria (i.e., the Communist districts) "feudalism" had been basically destroyed. There would be no further division of the land because to do so would damage productivity by decreasing peasant incentive to care for and improve their land—a rather interesting statement in view of the post-liberation collectivization campaigns. Henceforth, the main effort in the countryside would be to organize production in order to strengthen the liberated areas and support the long-term war effort. Toward this end, struggled landlords and rich peasants were told—not for the first time—that as long as they worked hard and refrained from engaging in counter-revolutionary activity, they would no longer be targeted.[87] One may judge the worth of this assurance by noting that in 1980, the CCP finally removed the "labels" of pre-liberation class status from landlords and their families as well as other civil war era opponents who had borne these festering stigmata through numerous post-1949 political campaigns.

On June 1, 1948, NEAC proclaimed that land reform had been completed throughout all but a very small part of North-east China. Land certificates would soon be distributed to individual peasant heads of households confirming their ownership.[88] With this proclamation, the Party signaled the successful conclusion of land reform in the Northeast—a process that proved to be only the first phase in a continuing effort by the CCP to transform both power and production relations in the countryside. In this first phase, it had proved difficult for the embryonic state to impose its authority on a still vibrant rural society. As the CCP strengthened its organizational presence in China's rural districts after 1949 and systematically eliminated the vestiges of the old order, it became easier for the state to impose its will on society, but the price of this success rose proportionately and, as usual, ordinary villagers bore the cost.

Given the turmoil of revolution and the low level of education of most land reform work team cadres, one must view the statistics of land reform in the Northeast as order of magnitude figures rather than as precise indicators of change. In mid-1947 the *Northeast Daily* reported that by the end of 1946 some 4.2 million peasants in northern Manchuria had acquired 33 million mou (5.5 million acres or 2.2 million hectares) of land, or an average of 7.9 mou per person.[89] According to incomplete statistics, by the end of the rural transformation in the north 37.1 million mou of land had been distributed with an average of 7 mou per person, indicating that 5.3 million peasants in the northern districts received land.[90] For all of Manchuria 6.3 million peasants were said to have benefited from the distribution of land, although in the south the number of mou each person received on the average was only 3.[91] However inaccurate these figures may be, they tend to confirm two points suggested earlier in this chapter: 1) that tenancy and landlessness were much more serious problems in northern Manchuria than elsewhere in the region, and 2) that owner-cultivators were the predominant social group in most of the Northeast countryside.

Toward a Theoretical Understanding of Communist Power in the Northeast Countryside

As has been frequently noted in this study, the large-scale conventional war fought in Manchuria in 1946–48 imposed its own requirements upon the participants. Unlike the guerrilla-style anti-Japanese war of the North China base areas, which was fought on a shoestring, the fighting in Northeast China devoured huge supplies of men, weapons, war materiel, provisions, horses, and transport equipment. An endless supply of military recruits and hundreds of thousands of civilian noncombatant support personnel had to be raised for the most part from among the Manchurian rural population. Grain, fodder, cooking oil, fuel, shoes, clothing, and numerous other items had to be supplied to a large army which lacked the leisure to produce its own supplies on the model of Nanniwan.[92] In addition, the several tens of thousands of officials, cadres, local organizers, and others administering the revolution were also consumers dependent upon requisitioned supplies. In sum, the Communists, lacking foreign benefactors or well-established mechanisms for taxing the rural population, were compelled by force of circumstances to procure what they needed from a population which at least initially viewed them with suspicion and no little hostility.

Manchurian peasants were inured to being squeezed to support military and administrative machines. Chang Tso-lin in the 1920s and the Manchukuo government in the 1930s and the early 1940s had imposed heavy burdens on the Northeast countryside.[93] How is it, then, that these earlier regimes had alienated the peasantry and were widely perceived to be exploitative while the Communists were able to achieve decisive support from among the rural population? The key distinction between the Communists and these earlier powerholders was not that Communist levies were less severe or even that different strata of the rural population bore the chief burden. Although part of the property confiscated from landlords, rich peasants, collaborators, and other enemies was funneled directly into the war effort, most of it was first distributed to the peasants, who were expected thereafter to contribute to defraying the costs of the war. The costs of the war were far too great to be borne by confiscated wealth alone and the middle peasants, poor peasants, and laborers who were the beneficiaries of Communist rule also bore a very substantial part of the total economic burden as well as most of the manpower burden.

The essential Communist innovation in the course of the Chinese rural revolution consisted of instituting an exchange relationship with the peasantry marked by reciprocity and a measure of justice. Taxation, military and labor service, provisioning and other obligations were not unilaterally extracted by the Communist Party from the peasantry in exchange for nothing, but were rather one side of the equation of revolutionary transformation. Without an understanding of how this exchange was instituted and functioned, it is impossible to grasp the process which led the Communist Party to victory in Manchuria.

In recent years a growing number of scholars have addressed the question of how and why peasants become participants in revolutionary activity. A few basic points in the literature may serve as the starting point for analysis of the Manchurian case.[94] Modern rural revolution (as distinct from sporadic, traditional jacqueries) typically originates in an effort by an urban-centered revolutionary movement to develop contacts with rural dwellers. In this process, ideologically based appeals for political action stand little chance of success for, as Migdal notes, "The revolutionary looks no different from all the other city folk who have taken advantage of the peasants' weaknesses. The most successful approach is likely to be one that speaks directly to needs perceived by rural dwellers and offers them something tangible in return for their political participation.[95] Revolutionary action, then, begins as an exchange relationship in which both elements in the exchange pool their resources or values to their mutual advantage. Cooperation yields an increase in available power.[96]

However, the peasant's decision whether or not to enter into exchange relations is contingent upon a calculation of risk. Popkin notes that such calculation involves weighing the resources expended against the possibility of punishment in case of failure, estimating the anticipated rewards, gauging the probability of success, and judging the quality of the leadership of the joint enterprise.[97] The probability of a positive decision to participate is increased to the extent that the scope of the project is narrow enough to provide for a short-term payoff. If the initial commitment turns out to have been justified and trust in the revolutionary leadership increases, it becomes progressively possible to substitute longer-term and more abstract goals requiring successful collective action for the short-term individual goals that first elicited participation.[98]

Exchange theory (as presented by Race, Migdal, and Popkin) explicitly addresses the question of how revolutionary organizations get started in rural areas previously lacking a tradition of collective peasant activity. In its emphasis on the problem of "starting up" the revolutionary machine and on individual decision making as the proper focus of analysis, exchange theory is to peasant revolution as liberal social contract theory is to the origins of the state: provocative but somewhat abstract and excessively individualistic. Nevertheless, a modified version of exchange theory will help us to understand the connection between the Communist Party and rural dwellers in civil war Manchuria.

As applied to the development of peasant revolution, exchange theory asserts the need for a prolonged investment of effort passing through several stages before peasant participation in revolutionary organization becomes institutionalized. As Migdal says, "Revolutionaries create power through a painstaking, step-by-step process of social exchange, a process which routinizes behavior, rather than trying to foment unpredictable and uninstitutionalized action."[99] Such efforts take a great deal of time.

Among the major empirical evidence for this notion of accumulative revolutionary participation is the development of the Chinese Communist movement, particularly in North China. The logical corollary of this proposition is that political movements which for one reason or another try to accelerate the pace of recruiting rural dwellers into the ranks of the revolution will run afoul of peasant conservatism, suspicion of outsiders, and low political consciousness. How does exchange theory help us understand the particularities of the rural revolution in Northeast China?

In Manchuria Communist rural organizing began in earnest only in 1946, under the intense pressure of the burgeoning civil war. The Party lacked the time necessary to cultivate relations with peasants step by step. It could not wait. The civil war, then, greatly accelerated the process of forging links between the Communist cadres and the peasants, but it did so at a price.

The growth of the Communist Party in rural Manchuria is unlike the problem of initially emerging organizations analyzed by exchange theorists. The CCP came to the Northeast as an existing organization with a large number of trained cadres, a well articulated program of social change, and extensive experience in rural organizing. The problems it faced differed substantially from those of a fledgling revolutionary organization attempting to start up operations for the first time. Here, the major problem was that of organizational growth in a new territory under wartime conditions. Its major difficulties were in recruiting enough reliable local leaders to supplement the core of outsider veterans who had been shifted into the region, and in overcoming the reluctance of many rural inhabitants to become involved in revolutionary activity.

The Party's handling of these problems entailed less innovation than marginal adjustment to the standard operating procedures which had stood the test of time and circumstances in the North China base areas during the Resistance War. It already had three existing assets. First, its established organizational structure provided an internal system of command and coordination whose smooth functioning ensured both centralized direction and local flexibility. Second, precisely because it was an already established organization, the Party had rewards to distribute to those

willing to join its ranks and work for its goals. Since the Party and
its auxiliary organizations expanded at a particularly rapid rate in
the civil war years, it could offer inducements of prestige, power,
upward mobility, and status to recruits willing to assume local
leadership positions. Third, as the possessors of a large, well-
organized and well-equipped military force, the Communists
could offer protection and security to those willing to join them
(both individuals and villages) and could also impose sanctions
on those who demurred or resisted. This system of rewards and
sanctions structured the environment in which individuals and
entire communities responded to Communist revolutionary
organizing.

The establishment of exchange relationships between
villagers and revolutionary organizers is a complex phenomenon
even though the essential notion of exchange is a simple one. If
decisions whether or not to join the Communist revolutionary
enterprise or participate in local activities such as land reform and
struggle meetings represent a calculated weighing of costs and
benefits, it must be stressed that rural inhabitants do not make
such decisions in a value-neutral atmosphere. The choice is perhaps typically made in a highly charged atmosphere of cross-
cutting pressures generated by the local elite which is trying to
preserve its power and the outside organization which is trying to
oust them. The decision, obviously not a trivial one, may entail
enormous action consequences not all of which can be anticipated.
Yet the villager does not confront the gestalt of revolution but a
concrete choice, such as whether or not to attend a meeting called
by revolutionary organizers, to provide or conceal goods wanted
by the revolutionary army, to serve or to seek to evade labor
service or conscription.

The cost of participating must be weighed not only
against the potential or actual benefits derived therefrom, but also
against the possible sanctions for refraining from participation. In
sum, the local coercive balance may be decisive in structuring the
participatory choice. Finally, it may be observed that choice may
be the prerogative not of the individual but of a group such as the
family or the village leadership. For example, local elites faced
with a demand to provide men and materiel by a Communist (or
other) military detachment operating in their vicinity may decide

to comply without consulting more than a small number of those individuals who will bear the burden of conscription, labor service, or provisioning.

In northern and central Manchuria, where rural revolution occurred in 1946–47, the Communist military presence provided a more or less secure environment in which the political transactions between villagers and Party organizers could take place. Even if peasants and village leaders doubted the longer term viability of the Communist cause (rumors about the imminent return of the Nationalists were disseminated by the CCP's opponents), it was difficult to say no in the short term to Communist commanders and organizers who physically controlled a particular territory. This makes it difficult if not impossible to assess the mixture of voluntary response versus grudging compliance with demands in any given locality on the basis of available information.[100]

If Communist success in northern and central Manchuria originated in the local military superiority enjoyed by the Communist armies, it was certainly consolidated and expanded as a result of the reciprocal benefits exchanged in the course of developing the Communist-villager ties. Through the rural revolution, many peasants received land, a portion of the wealth confiscated from the old elite (landlords, rich peasants, moneylenders), and the right to participate in the new institutions established in the countryside to exercise power. Those who made an active commitment to the revolutionary side were also provided with opportunities for mobility outside of the village as well as increased status and power within their own localities. Peasants who had often before borne the burden of conflict without getting anything in return were now being rewarded for their efforts. This was a profound change which undoubtedly generated significant popular support for the CCP in the Northeast countryside.

Perhaps no less important in shaping villagers' attitudes toward the revolution was the principle of equity incorporated in the Communist system of taxation and corvee labor (the latter, to be sure, disguised as voluntary contributions). Instead of the arbitrary and capricious methods of the past used to recruit soldiers and civilian support personnel, levy taxes, and secure carts, livestock, food, and fodder, the CCP initiated an equitable and fairly predictable system which spread the burden quite evenly across the rural population and protected villagers from repeated labor service or overly onerous contributions to the military effort.

In sum, Communist success derived from a number of interlocking factors—organizational support, a program that elicited a substantial degree of popular support through a genuine exchange relationship, and an equitable system for distributing the burden of conflict.

CHAPTER SEVEN
CONCLUSIONS

AS the Nationalist house of cards col-
lapsed in the last days of October 1948, Chiang Kai-shek invoked
the memory of the Manchurian Incident of 1931, the symbolic
beginning of World War II. "History is now repeating itself," he
said, ". . . should the Communists rule over the nine Northeastern
provinces, it would mean the virtual beginning of another world
catastrophe. . . . I can firmly say the ominous and treacherous
clouds will gather with the trouble in the Northeast as their starting
point."[1] Chiang's analogy was flawed, and the implicit plea for a
large-scale American intervention to rescue his doomed regime
fell on unsympathetic ears. The victory of the Chinese Communists
in the Northeast, while it owed not a little to the Soviet Union,
was hardly the equivalent of Japan's creation of Manchukuo. The
revolutionary civil war waged by the Chinese Communist Party
transformed the bases of political and economic power in the
Northeast and throughout China, spelling the end of the traditional elitist oligarchy and initiating an era of mass revolutionary
authoritarianism. The new Communist elite that emerged in town
and country after 1949 exhibited many of the same behavioral
characteristics of the elites that they replaced, but the bases of
legitimacy and the methods as well as many of the goals of the

new Communist rulers differed considerably from their predecessors.

The Communist revolutionary victory in Northeast China was the result of a complex set of interacting factors and circumstances. Given the complexity and variety of politico-military situations throughout China in this period, an attempt at understanding the process of Communist victory must begin with modest objectives. This study has examined the Communist side of a regional struggle for power that was itself nested in national and international contexts. Until many more scholarly studies of this period have been completed, it is premature to present an overall explanation of the Chinese Communist revolution that pretends to be anything but tentative.

The international politics of the early Cold War era created a relatively hospitable environment for revolutionary activity in China. Japan's defeat had removed the one foreign power that was unalterably opposed to revolution in Manchuria. The United States, a new hegemonic power, found itself with a surfeit of obligations and responsibilities, facing a challenge from the Soviet Union whose revolutionary ideology and ambitions as a great power clashed with postwar American concepts of stability and security. The restoration of order and prosperity in war-devastated Europe, challenged from within by powerful Communist movements, commanded the attention of American statesmen. By comparison, the chaotic politics of China was a distant sideshow.

Nevertheless, fear that the Russians might grab Manchuria—the one region in China presumed to have strategic significance—triggered the mission to China of General Marshall. Although his mediation effort failed to avert civil war, China did not become an arena of direct Soviet-American competition in this early period of the Cold War.[2] The dearth of convincing evidence of Soviet aid to the CCP, the perception that the Nationalist regime was beyond saving, and, above all, the low weight assigned to China in the strategic balance of power, combined to restrict American assistance to Chiang Kai-shek. Nanking's ambassador to Washington, Wellington Koo, was quick to point out the discrepancy between Truman's globalist anti-Communist rhetoric in 1947 and his failure to aid effectively an anti-Communist regime engaged in a desperate struggle for survival.[3] After the battle for Manchuria was over, however, President Truman told Ambassador Koo that "the loss of Manchuria was a great blow not only to China but also to the United States."[4] But this meant nothing more than that even plain-talking Missouri politicians can engage in *k'o-ch'i hua* (polite talk) on occasion.

The security and power interests of the USSR were more directly engaged in Manchuria than were those of the United States, but the attainment of Soviet objectives did not necessitate a prolonged Soviet military intervention in the region. Through the Sino-Soviet Treaty of August 1945, the USSR secured a naval base at Port Arthur (Lushun), recognition of its preeminent interests in Talien, condominium over the main Northeast railroad system, and Chinese recognition of the Soviet client state, the Mongolian People's Republic. Stalin failed to turn the Northeast into an economic appanage of the Soviet Union, but the civil war in any case rendered this objective unattainable.

From a Soviet perspective, America's unwillingness to commit itself fully to the Nationalist side so as to ensure Chiang's victory in the civil war guaranteed that China would not become an integral part of the American Cold War coalition of anti-Soviet states. Thus, there was no need for Moscow to become *overtly* engaged on the Communist side in the conflict. In effect, then, a tacit understanding emerged between Washington and Moscow not to make of China yet another arena of competition. The consequence of this unspoken agreement was that domestic factors—the ability of the Chinese antagonists to mobilize and effectively use internal resources—became the decisive element in the outcome of the civil war.

Nevertheless, Moscow's contribution to the Chinese Communist victory—generally ignored by the CCP and denied by most Western scholars—was substantial in two major respects. As Lloyd Eastman observes, the Soviet intervention and Red Army occupation of Manchuria at the end of World War II effectively blocked the Nationalists from establishing their control over the region and provided the Chinese Communists with a "springboard for the conquest of China proper."[5] Had the Nationalists succeeded in controlling the Northeast (a moot point even in the absence of Soviet intervention), the resources of the region might have enabled them to do a better job of managing the economy, promoting reconstruction and development, and satisfying popular aspirations.

More valuable even than the Japanese weapons transferred to the CCP by the Red Army was the gift of time, a head start in the competition for power. For, as David Wilkinson notes, in a revolutionary civil war "time must be understood as a resource . . . [it] becomes a factor in determining victory and defeat."[6] By the time the Red Army completed its withdrawal from Manchuria in May 1946, the Chinese Communists, while still inferior to the Nationalists in strength of arms, had dispatched tens of thousands of troops and cadres from North China and had begun the arduous task of organizing the countryside for revolutionary warfare. Without Soviet assistance, it would have been far more difficult for the CCP to mount a challenge to the Nationalists in Manchuria—an area where the Party lacked support, experience, and local cadres. Moreover, the proximity of Soviet territory to the Chinese Communist bastion of northern Manchuria reportedly caused the Nationalists to refrain from attacking Harbin in the fall of 1946 when their military power peaked so as not to provoke Moscow's wrath.[7] Although Lin Piao's forces would very likely have survived in the rural districts of the Northeast, the loss of Harbin, particularly in conjunction with the loss of Tsitsihar and Chiamussu, would have been a heavy blow to the CCP for, as we have seen, these cities played an important role in the revolution.

Second, Soviet trade with northern Manchuria and the technical, medical, and other assistance rendered to the Communist authorities there made it easier for the weak and struggling revolutionary government to cope with the numerous problems of revolutionary civil war. In particular, Soviet assistance in restoring the rail network to operating condition facilitated the final stages of Lin Piao's military campaigns, and the anti-plague work of Soviet medical personnel helped contain what could have been a far more disastrous outbreak of the disease. Finally, there is an intangible element that should not be ignored. The Chinese Communist leaders of the 1940s may have followed their own path to power, but they were, and for the most part felt themselves to be, a part of an international Communist movement whose center was in Moscow and whose leader was Stalin. For tactical reasons they may have wanted a relationship with the United States, but they were not neutral with respect to the contest between American imperialism and Soviet Communism. As Marxists-Leninists, they felt themselves to be a part of a wave of postwar revolutionary change that was bringing closer the epochal transformation that the fathers of the faith had prophesied. These feelings of solidarity and self-assurance were bolstered by the tangible if discreet evidence of Soviet support for their cause in northern Manchuria and the influx of Soviet culture into the region.

   Repeated reference has been made in this study to both American and Soviet intervention in the Chinese civil war. Such usage is appropriate in general terms, but at this point a more precise and restrictive understanding of interventionary behavior is desirable. Richard Little proposes a stimulus-response model of intervention that I find analytically useful:

An interventionary situation exists when an actor responds to an intervention stimulus. The stimulus emerges when conflict develops between the units in a bifurcated actor, creating a potential for system transformation. Maintaining a relationship with one side of a bifurcated actor constitutes an intervention response; maintaining a relationship with both sides of a bifurcated actor constitutes a nonintervention response.[8]

According to this definition, it is obvious that the United States, which eschewed a relationship of any sort with the CCP once the Marshall mission had terminated, exhibited an interventionary response, whereas the Soviet Union, which did in fact maintain a relationship with both sides to the conflict, exhibited a noninterventionary response. As Little further suggests, from the viewpoint of external actors, nonintervention is:

a policy which is designed to minimize potential costs and reduce uncertainty. It can be defined as a "rational" response to civil war . . . there is a clear rationale for [nonintervention[. . . it is intervention, not nonintervention, which requires explanation.[9]

   As previously noted, had the Nationalists, not the Communists, won the civil war, the Soviet Union, which maintained diplomatic and commercial relations with the Nationalists throughout the civil war, could have continued those relations without prejudice to Soviet interests just as Moscow was able to formalize and expand relations with the CCP after the Communist triumph. America's one-sided relationship with the Nationalists can be explained by reference to Washington's view of legitimacy, the lingering attachment to Chiang Kai-shek (itself a complex phenomenon), and above all the ideology of anti-Communism which made it extremely difficult for American statesmen to view the Chinese Communists as basically autonomous political actors. The Sino-American confrontation in Korea and the ensuing twenty years of hostility was the consequence of this inability to practice realpolitik during and immediately after the Chinese civil war.

Is there a contradiction between the assertion that Moscow made an important contribution to the CCP victory in Manchuria and the claim that Soviet behavior in the Chinese civil war was noninterventionary? I think not. To assert that the Soviets maintained relations with both sides in the conflict is not to say that these relations were equal. Moscow was certainly not neutral in the civil war. Its policy, while designed to keep all options open, clearly favored the Chinese Communists in important ways. Soviet nonintervention (as defined in Little's terms), aimed at maximizing Soviet influence within the Chinese political arena while minimizing the risk of confrontation with the United States. Moscow did not pretend to be an impartial arbiter of Chinese political conflict, and actually rejected out of hand such an opportunity when offered it.[10] In practice, Soviet "nonintervention" was fully compatible with Soviet assistance to the CCP.

Turning to the internal dimension of the Communist revolution in Manchuria, two related points need to be made. The first concerns the involvement of the peasantry in the revolution; the second the relation between local elites and the hierarchy of power in the countryside.

Our analysis of the process of revolutionary change in the Northeast countryside suggested the virtual absence of any self-acting impulses toward revolution. The radical transformation in the countryside effected between 1946 and 1948 was the direct result of a strategic political decision by CCP leaders to base their quest for power in the rural areas. The agrarian revolution—land reform, the destruction of the old elites, the creation of new organs of power—was a crude but effective instrument fashioned by the CCP to advance the Party along the path to power. (Much of the

violence attendant upon the agrarian revolution was instigated by
the Party in order to break the continuing hold of customary power
relations at the local level.) The revolution in the Northeast countryside, then, was not a peasant jacquerie. It was not the triumph
of the revolutionary countryside over the counterrevolutionary
city. It did not represent the resurgence of traditional agrarian
ideas of social justice over the cash nexus of commercialized agriculture and capitalist industry. It was, rather, the triumph of
revolutionary organization advancing a program of radical reform
that *within the context of civil war* successfully mobilized a significant
portion of the rural *and* urban population in support of the Communist war effort. This mobilization was made possible by the
local superiority of the Communist armed forces, which provided
a structured environment in which country and city folk "chose"
to support the revolution. The fragmentation of the forces opposing the Chinese Communists enabled their initially weak politico-
military organization to survive and expand.

In sum, it is misleading and inaccurate to term the
Communist revolution a peasant revolution if by that term one
means a radical rural transformation carried out by a movement
led by authentic peasant leaders in order to achieve the reordering
of political, economic, and social power relations in the countryside. The leadership role of the CCP, an organization whose ideology, structure, and objectives derived not from rural China but
from the larger political stage of Chinese and international politics,
was crucial to the genesis, development, and success of rural
revolution in China.[11] The land reform which generated considerable support for the CCP in the Northeast countryside was an
instrument of political warfare, not an end in itself. The divergence
between the aspirations of rural folk and the ideological and power
objectives of the central Party leadership—a central theme of post-
1949 Chinese history—thus does not represent a break with the
revolutionary civil war tradition at all. To be sure, the partial and
intermittent congruence of peasant and Party interests enabled
the Party to promote its goals in the countryside with a minimum
of overt violence once the bloodletting of land reform was past,
but the price for China's industrialization, for Mao's revolutionary
megalomania, and for China's international pretensions was ultimately paid by the peasants.

Organization as the key to victory emerges as a central

conclusion of this study when one reflects upon the way in which the CCP attacked and overcame the initial superiority of locally entrenched rural elites in the Northeast. In seeking to transform the countryside into reliable bases for their revolutionary civil war, the Party had to eliminate the power of local elites and to establish new organs of revolutionary power. That, as we have seen, was no easy task. Although in normal times, Northeast villages were not closed corporate communities—they were linked to the wider world through a network of commercial and cultural relations— they were capable of exhibiting a closed defensive response at certain times. Such political encapsulation occurred when local elites organized their dependents and clients into local defense forces to preserve order and minimize the depradations that outside forces inflicted upon the villages in times of turmoil. Strengthening intra-village solidarity across class lines, this defensive encapsulation was perceived as a collective goal and a collective good because the exactions of outside forces fell upon all sectors of the village community, even if not equally. It is with such collective "organized survival strategies," to borrow Elizabeth Perry's term, that so many villages in the Northeast initially reacted to the CCP and its armed forces, seeing in the Communists not liberators but predators.[12] Of course, intra-village solidarity was not absolute. Eventually Party work teams overcame the superior political resources of the local elites.

How, then, were the Communists able to displace the local elites in the countryside? The answer to this critical question lies in the relationship between regional, provincial, and local elites on the one hand and the Communist counterelites on the other. In the prerevolutionary society, the forces of order and stability had possessed one decisive advantage over the assorted rebels, bandits, and revolutionaries who periodically challenged their authority. The disparate rebels of the late nineteenth century or the anti-Japanese guerrillas of the 1930s lacked well-integrated and coordinated organizations which interlocked at the regional, provincial, county, and local levels. Lacking such vertical and horizontal ties, rebels or guerrilla patriots were isolated and vulnerable to attack.

Local elites by contrast were embedded in a hierarchical network of power relationships which stretched outward and upward from the villages through the market towns and county seats to the urban centers of economic and political power in Manchuria. The authority and security enjoyed by local elites derived in large measure from their position within this hierarchy of power and status. Their ability to maintain order in their own communities depended not only upon the resources and support they could mobilize within their localities, but also on the coercive power they could call in from the outside.[13] If local security forces were insufficient to cope with challenges from either bandits or revolutionaries, mobile military power could be dispatched from higher-order administrative units. The prestige and aura of legitimacy that local elites derived from their membership in the nested hierarchy of power no doubt also enhanced their position within their local communities.

 The fourteen-year Japanese colonial interlude had a shattering effect on the hierarchy of power. The Japanese conquest of Manchuria in 1931–32 failed to produce a Communist-led "peasant nationalism" or widespread networks of resistance organizations as in North China, and during the Manchukuo period centrally dispatched and coordinated military units amply demonstrated their efficacy in suppressing local Communist resistance forces.[14] However, Japanese rule was no less significant in preparing the ground for the postwar revolutionary movement. The Japanese occupation of Manchuria splintered the regional and provincial elite, some of whom fled southward into exile in Nationalist territory while others remained in Manchuria as collaborators with the puppet regime. Following Japan's surrender, the collaborators became targets for attack during the movement to settle accounts *(ch'ing-suan yün-tung)*. The exiled pre-1931 elite was unable to recover its lost authority. Chiang Kai-shek, fearing Northeast regionalism almost as much as he did the CCP, systematically excluded Northeasterners from the administration he established in the region. In sum, the old elite at the upper levels lost its cohesion, its legitimacy, and its ability to rule. This in turn profoundly affected the position of the local elite.

 Although local elites retained much of their economic power and political influence into the postwar period, they became fatally isolated. The normal networks of power were disrupted. The local elite which had normally been connected to higher-level administrative centers now found themselves cut off and vulnerable.[15] In north and north-central Manchuria, where the CCP attacked local elites, carried out land reform, and established the institutions of revolutionary power in 1946–47, the Nationalists had neither the political organization nor the mobile military power to come to the rescue of their potential adherents. Thrown back upon their own resources, local elites ultimately proved unable to resist the repeated assaults directed by the CCP.

In this context, the scope and intensity of the Communist organizational and military challenge became decisive. In post-1945 Manchuria, the CCP was the only organization that operated successfully on a regional basis, coordinating and controlling political and military campaigns across a broad territory. The local rebels, those traditionally disadvantaged in organizational terms, were now the ones connected to outside organizations and able to enjoy the advantage of superior coercive power and growing ideological legitimacy. The CCP and the NEDUA functioned as the critical agencies bridging the gap between the villages and the larger world. Party cadres and soldiers became the political brokers who entered the villages to identify and then link up with villagers who were willing to make or support revolutionary changes.

In the struggle between revolution and counterrevolution, the Communists thus had a decisive advantage. They were able to overcome the initially superior position of the local elites because the CCP could choose the time and place for its revolutionary attack and could mobilize organizational and coercive power from outside the village to bring down its targets.

The revolutionary civil war period cannot be viewed in isolation from the continuum of modern Chinese history. The history and political ecology of Manchuria, the experiences of the CCP in the Northeast and elsewhere in China prior to 1945, the character and resources of competing politico-military actors, and the international environment are all vital elements in setting the Northeast civil war in context. It is equally obvious that the revolutionary civil war experience itself became a part of the historical legacy that helped to shape the policies and practices of the CCP after victory. This is too rich a theme to explore here, but two consequences of the Communist path to victory in the Northeast must be noted.

First, let us recall our initial observation that time was the taskmaster of revolution in the Northeast. Operating under severe time pressures, the CCP managed to mobilize large numbers of rural and urban dwellers to contribute to and support revolutionary objectives in the civil war. This pattern of induced mobilization—setting the masses in motion *(fa-tung ch'ün-chung)*—became the habitual method of Maoist revolutionary change after 1949. It should by now be abundantly clear that such mobilization has nothing in common with the participatory democracy of open political systems. Giovanni Sartori makes this point very well:

participation means self-motion. . . . the idea of a free citizen who acts and intervenes—if he so wishes—according to *his* best judgment. So conceived, participation is the very opposite, or very reverse of mobilization. Mobilization does not convey the idea of individual self-motion, but the idea of a malleable, passive, collectivity which is being *put into motion* at the whim of persuasive—and more than persuasive—authorities.[16]

The seemingly endless series of changes carried out in the Chinese countryside after 1949 were the work of a CCP leadership which had learned how to *mobilize* peasants beginning in the 1920s and continuing through the civil war, but which had no inclination to consult the peasants as to their own preferences on important issues or to provide for their authentic *participation* in the political process.

Similarly, as a result of experiences confirmed during the civil war, the Maoist leadership of the Party pushed the pace of change recklessly, eschewing adequate planning, ignoring possible adverse consequences, and rushing helter-skelter toward arbitrarily determined objectives. Such leaders preferred to correct the "errors" and "excesses" committed in the first flush of change rather than to risk a slower rate of march.[17] To be sure, in the post-1949 leadership of the CCP there were also quite a few men who counseled moderation along the road to social and economic transformation. But Mao Tse-tung and his supporters were inclined to presume that the peasants would eventually support whatever policies the Party prescribed. This dominant leadership group became increasingly out of touch with the realities of rural life and heedless of the consequences of their erroneous policies, which would, in any case, be borne by the peasants, not by themselves. In short, for Mao and his followers the overriding lesson of the civil war was that whatever the adverse odds and no matter what the obstacles, revolutionary objectives could be reached by mobilizing the masses and mustering up sufficient will and determination. This proved to be a costly and fatal delusion.

The Chinese civil war of the late 1940s remains barely studied by students of modern Chinese history. Vast areas remain to be researched. Regional variation alone provides fertile ground for many future studies. The regional history of Manchuria in a tumultuous era is itself too large a subject to be encompassed within a single scholarly monograph. This study has simply explored selected aspects of the subject. Detailed studies of the civil war years will likely reveal many variations in the pattern of Communist victory. Our general understanding of the Communist revolution in China must constantly be refined or altered as new findings are published. I have made no assumption that the explanation of the Communist victory in the Northeast that I have presented is a model for understanding events elsewhere in China. At this still tender stage of our understanding of the Chinese revolution let us at least entertain the possibility that the victory of the CCP may have involved very diverse paths to power in different regions, provinces, and even localities on the complex gameboard of Chinese politics.

NOTES

INTRODUCTION

1. U.S. Dept. of State, *FRUS 1948*, 7:543.

2. For a perceptive historiographical review of interpretations of the Chinese Communist revolution, see Steven M. Goldstein and Kathleen J. Hartford, "Introduction: Perspectives on the Chinese Communist Revolution," in Steven M. Goldstein and Kathleen J. Hartford, eds. *Single Sparks: China's Rural Revolutions.*

3. Chi Hsi-sheng, *Nationalist China at War: Military Defeats and Political Collapse, 1937–1945.*

4. Mao Tse-tung, "The Situation and Our Policy after the Victory in the War of Resistance against Japan," *Selected Works of Mao Tse-tung,* 4:11–22.

5. David Wilkinson, *Revolutionary Civil War: the Elements of Victory and Defeat,* p. 1.

6. In his study of the Northeast under Chang Tso-lin, Gavan McCormack eschews use of the term Manchuria as connoting foreign control over an inherently Chinese territory. *Chang Tso-lin in Northeast China, 1911–1928: China, Japan and the Manchurian Idea,* p. 4. He has a valid point. But because Manchuria is still a commonly used term for Northeast China, and one whose association with imperialism has faded with time, I use it interchangeably with the Northeast and Northeast China for variety's sake.

7. A paper by Edwin A. Winckler, "Military Outcomes in the Chinese Civil War: Organizational and Spatial Models," provides an extremely stimulating schema for tackling this problem.

8. See Harry Eckstein, ed. *Internal War: Problems and Approaches.*

9. See Nancy B. Tucker, *Patterns in the Dust: Chinese-American Relations and the Recognition Controversy, 1949–1950;* Dorothy Borg and Waldo Heinrichs, eds. *Uncertain Years: Chinese-American Relations, 1947–1950.*

10. U.S. Dept. of State, *FRUS 1949*, p. xvi.

11. Tsou Tang, *America's Failure in China, 1941–1950.*

12. See Steven M. Goldstein and Kathleen J. Hartford, "Introduction: Per-

spectives." The third view is represented, inter alia, in Ralph Thaxton, *China Turned Rightside Up: Revolutionary Legitimacy in the Peasant World*.

13. James Reardon-Anderson, *Yenan and the Great Powers: The Origins of Chinese Communist Foreign Policy, 1944–1946*, pp. 148–159.

14. Tetsuya Kataoka, *Resistance and Revolution in China: The Communists and the Second United Front*, p. 47.

15. *Ibid.*, p. 9.

16. "Mao Tse-tung's Oral Report to the Seventh Party Congress: Summary Notes (April 24, 1945)," *Chinese Law and Government*, p. 20.

17. Suzanne Pepper, *Civil War in China: The Political Struggle, 1945–1949*; Lloyd Eastman, *Seeds of Destruction: Nationalist China in War and Revolution*.

1. POLITICAL CONFLICT IN CHINA

1. S. M. Shtemenko, *General'nyi shtab v gody voiny* (The General Staff During the War Years), p. 370. The garrison quickly grew to 1,000 men.

2. A. I. Kovtun-Stankevich, "Komendant Mukdena" (Mukden Commander), in *Na Kitaiskoi zemle: vospominaniia sovetskikh dobrovol'stev, 1925–1945* (On Chinese Soil: Memoirs of Soviet Volunteers, 1925–1945), pp. 423–425.

3. *Ibid.*, p. 357.

4. The 1891 figure is from V. A. Anuchin, *Geograficheskie ocherki Manchzhurii* (Geographical Features of Manchuria), p. 42; the other figures are from Wang I-shou, "Chinese Migration and Population Change in Manchuria, 1900–1940," pp. 46, 54.

5. Wang I-shou, pp. 100–101. Before the advent of railroads much of the grain from northern Manchuria was distilled into liquor. H. E. M. James, *The Long White Mountain or A Journey in Manchuria*, p. 321.

6. Wang I-shou, "Chinese Migration," pp. 55–60. Gavan McCormack notes that the rapacity of Chang Ts'ung-chang's rule in Shantung in the 1920s spurred higher emigration to the Northeast. *Chang Tso-lin in Northeast China, 1911–1928: China, Japan and the Manchurian Idea*, p. 155.

7. Ramon Myers, "Socio-Economic Change in Villages of Manchuria During the Ch'ing and Republican Periods: Some Preliminary Findings."

8. McCormack, *Chang Tso-lin*, p. 86.

9. The most forceful statement of this thesis is provided by Tetsuya Kataoka in *Resistance and Revolution in China: The Communists and the Second United Front*. In an earlier book, Chalmers Johnson provided a somewhat similar explanation. *Peasant Nationalism and Communist Power*.

10. Yen Ying, *Tung-pei i-yung-chun chan-shih* (A Battle History of the Northeast Volunteer Army), passim; Lo Ta-yu, ed. *Wu-erh-san meng-nan erh-shih chou-nien chi-nien wen-chi* (A Collection of Reminiscences of the Twentieth Anniversary of the Great Disaster of May 23), passim.

11. For a superb history of the early years of Communism in Manchuria see Chong-Sik Lee, *Revolutionary Struggle in Manchuria: Chinese Communism and Soviet Interest, 1922–1945*.

12. Chong-Sik Lee, "Witch Hunt Among the Guerrillas: The Min-Sheng-T'uan Incident."

13. Among a large literature on the subject see Chi Yun-lung, *Yang Ching-yu ho k'ang-lien ti-i lu-chün* (Yang Ching-yu and the First Route Army of the United Army); Feng Chung-yun, *Tung-pei k'ang-jih lien-chun shih-ssu nien k'u-tou chien-shih* (A Brief History of the Bitter Fourteen Year Struggle of the Northeast Anti-Japanese United Army).

14. This hypothesis should be tested through further research into Manchurian social structure.

15. Edward Friedman develops the notion of rural religious patterns of solidarity as a key element in peasant-based revolution. *Backward Toward Revolution: The Chinese Revolutionary Party.*

16. James Pinckney Harrison, *The Long March to Power: A History of the Chinese Communist Party, 1921–1972,* pp. 271–308.

17. Kataoka, *Resistance and Revolution,* passim; Carl E. Dorris, "Peasant Mobilization in North China and the Origins of Yenan Communism," 702ff.

18. James Reardon-Anderson, *Yenan and the Great Powers: The Origins of Chinese Communist Foreign Policy, 1944–1946,* pp. 34–35, 57–61.

19. See, among many works on this subject, Herbert Feis, *The China Tangle: The American Effort in China from Pearl Harbor to the Marshall Mission;* Warren I. Cohen, *America's Response to China* (New York: John Wiley, 1971).

20. Russell Buhite, *Patrick J. Hurley and American Relations with China;* Liang Ching-tung, "Hsia Erh-li t'iao-t'ing kuo-kung chih ching-kuo," (Hurley's Mediation Between the Nationalists and the Communists), *Chung-mei kuan-hsi lun-wen chi* (Collection of Essays on Sino-American Relations), pp. 57–106.

21. On this point see, Hung-mao Tien, *Government and Politics in Kuomintang China, 1927–1937* (Stanford: Stanford University Press, 1972).

22. James C. Thomson, *While China Faced West: American Reformers in Nationalist China, 1928–1937* (Cambridge: Harvard University Press, 1969), p. 8.

23. Yet the Central Government faced continuing problems with regional militarists such as Lung Yün in Yunnan. See Lloyd Eastman, *Seeds of Destruction: Nationalist China in War and Revolution,* pp. 10–44.

24. See Charles F. Romanus and Riley Sunderland, *Time Runs Out in CBI,* p. 382, for the Chinese order of battle as of August 31, 1945. See also Chang Ch'i-yun, ed., *K'ang-jih chan-shih* (A Battle History of the Anti-Japanese War of Resistance), p. 406.

25. James Harrison, *The Long March to Power,* p. 366–367; *Mao Tse-tung's Oral Report to the Seventh Party Congress: Summary Notes,* "Chinese Law and Government 10(4):20. A U.S. intelligence report of July 1945 provided significantly lower estimates of Chinese Communist strength. See Lyman P. Van Slyke, ed. *The Chinese Communist Movement: A Report of the U.S. War Department, July 1945,* p. 168.

26. See, inter alia, Mark Selden, *The Yenan Way in Revolutionary China;* Peter Schran, *Guerrilla Economy: The Development of the Shensi-Kansu-Ninghsia Border Region, 1937–1945.* Carl Dorris emphasizes the importance of the North China base areas behind Japanese lines in contrast to Yenan and the Shen-kan-ning area which, he says, "remained a small, isolated district." "Peasant Mobilization in North China," p. 700.

27. Mao Tse-tung, "The Situation and Our Policy After the Victory in the War of Resistance Against Japan," *Selected Works of Mao Tse-tung,* 4:11–22.

28. During the Cultural Revolution, one of the charges against Liu Shao-ch'i was his alleged advocacy of a "capitulationist" line in opposition to Mao's supposed insistence on armed struggle. See "I-ko t'ou-hsiang chu-i fan-tung kang-ling" (A Reactionary Capitulationist Outline), *Jen Min Jih Pao,* September 19, 1967, reprinted in Chung-kung yen-chiu tsa-chih, ed., *Liu Shao-ch'i wen-t'i tzu-liao chuan-chi* (Special Collection of Materials on the Liu Shao-ch'i Case) (Taipei, 1970), pp. 562–569.

29. Michael Lindsay, who advised Mao to negotiate with Chiang Kai-shek in Chungking, says that Mao was criticized later for making real concessions in exchange for vague promises, but that Mao defended himself by saying that the avoidance of civil war necessitated taking considerable risks. Michael Lindsay, *The Unknown War: North China 1937–1945,* unpaginated but equivalent to pp. 98–99.

30. For Liu see "Tui ch'u-fa tung-pei kung-tso t'ung-chih pao-kao" (Report to Comrades Departing to Work in the Northeast), *Liu Shao-ch'i wen-t'i,* pp. 564 ff. This is a speech of August 28, 1945.

31. Tsou Tang, *America's Failure in China, 1941–1950,* p. 319.

32. Takeuchi Minoru, ed., *Mao Tse-tung chi* (The Works of Mao Tse-tung), 9:329, 333–334; *Chung-ch'ing t'an-p'an tzu-liao* (Materials on the Chungking Negotiations), pp. 9–16.

33. Schran, *Guerrilla Economy,* makes this very clear.

34. "Mao Tse-tung's Oral Report to the Seventh Party Congress," p. 20.

35. John Lewis Gaddis, *The United States and the Origins of the Cold War, 1941–1947,* ch. 7; also Martin Sherwin, *A World Destroyed: The Atomic Bomb and the Grand Alliance,* pp. 179–185.

36. Myron Rush, ed., *The International Situation and Soviet Foreign Policy,* pp. 117–123; Joseph Starobin, "Origins of the Cold War," p. 285.

37. Bruce Russett, "Toward a Model of Competitive International Politics," pp. 121–122.

38. In fact, Western strategic superiority, despite the U.S. nuclear monopoly, in the period 1945–1949 may have been as much of a myth as that of the overwhelming strength of Stalin's conventional forces. George Quester, *Nuclear Diplomacy: The First Twenty-Five Years,* pp. 1–9.

39. Adam Ulam, *The Rivals: America and Russia since World War II,* p. 35.

40. For an instructive account of the political emasculation of the Communist-led European resistance movements, see Gabriel Kolko, *The Politics of War,* pp. 79–98, 172–193, 435–456.

41. Joseph Starobin traces the Soviet contribution to the origins of the Cold War to Stalin's attempt "to stifle the nascent polycentrism" within the international Communist movement and ensure Soviet control. "Origins of the Cold War," pp. 284–287.

42. Compare Akira Iriye, *The Cold War in Asia,* p. 103, and "Was There a Cold War in Asia," pp. 14–16.

43. Allen S. Whiting and Sheng Shih-ts'ai, *Sinkiang: Pawn or Pivot,* pp. 104–110.

44. For details see George A. Lensen, *The Damned Inheritance: The Soviet Union and the Manchurian Crises, 1924–1935,* and *The Strange Neutrality: Soviet-Japanese Relations During the Second World War, 1941–1945.*

45. For an early discussion of the Yalta Agreement on the Far East see, George A. Lensen, "Yalta and the Far East." A recent scholar demonstrates that Chiang Kai-shek was privy all along to the "deal" with Stalin that Roosevelt arranged at Yalta. Peter M. Kuhfus, "Die Risiken der Freundschaft: China und der Jalta-Mythos."

46. U.S. Dept. of State, *FRUS 1955, The Conferences at Malta and Yalta 1945,* p. 984. Note that this Soviet pledge concerned only military cooperation in wartime and not Soviet postwar policy in China.

47. Liang Ching-tung, "The Sino-Soviet Treaty of Friendship and Alliance of 1945: The Inside Story," in *Nationalist China During the Sino-Japanese War, 1937–1945,* pp. 373–397; also Steven I. Levine, "Comments," on pp. 398–404; and Liang Chin-tung, "Further Observations," on pp. 405–408.

48. W. Averill Harriman and Elie Abel, *Special Envoy to Churchill and Stalin, 1941–1946,* pp. 483, 495; U.S. Dept. of State, *FRUS 1945,* 7:955–956.

49. Brian Crozier, *The Man Who Lost China,* p. 273.

50. *China Handbook, 1937–1945* (New York, 1947), pp. 168–169. This source contains all of the agreements between China and the USSR. The tendentious and unreliable character of Soviet historical writing on this period is revealed by the fact that no Soviet source mentions the Soviet commitment to extend aid only to the Central Govern-

ment, i.e., the Nationalists. See, for example, Genadii V. Astaf'ev, *Interventsiia SShA v Kitae i ee porazheniie* (U.S. Intervention in China and Its Defeat), pp. 122–123.

51. Department of State, Interim Research and Intelligence Service, "Manchurian Prognosis, Fall 1945" (R & A Branch R7A 3292, November 9, 1945), National Archives, p. 7.

52. John P. Davies wrote that "his [Stalin's] objective was initially preventative—to prevent the emergence out of the chaos in China of an independent, unified strong government . . ." *Dragon by the Tail*, p. 424.

53. This was of a piece with the instructions given to West European Communist parties at the same time. Martin F. Herz, *Beginnings of the Cold War*, pp. 136, 151, n. 166.

54. Ulam, *The Rivals*, p. 91.

55. *FRUS, 1944*, 6:253–256; Harriman and Abel, *Special Envoy*, p. 472. At Postsdam, Stalin allegedly called the Chinese Communists "a bunch of fascists" and said that only Chiang Kai-shek and the KMT presented China with a chance for stability. John M. Blum, ed., *The Price of Vision: The Diary of Henry A. Wallace, 1942–1946*, p. 506.

56. For the genesis and early development of this duality, see Allen S. Whiting, *Soviet Policies in China, 1917–1924;* Leong Sow-theng, *Sino-Soviet Diplomatic Relations, 1917–1926.*

57. Joseph Grew, *Turbulent Era*, 2:1445–1446. At almost the same time, Secretary of Commerce Henry Wallace more presciently noted in his diary that "at present it looks like the United States was getting ready to embark on an era of power politics and imperialism in international affairs." Blum, *The Price of Vision*, p. 446. (diary entry of May 10, 1945).

58. John Gaddis, *Origins of the Cold War*, p. 206; Sherwin, *A World Destroyed*, pp. 146–153.

59. Cf. John S. Service, *The Amerasia Papers: Some Problems in the History of U.S.-China Relations*, pp. 75–135.

60. Walter Millis, ed. *The Forrestal Diaries*, passim.

61. Warren Cohen, *America's Response to China: An Interpretive History of Sino-American Relations* (New York: Wiley, 1971), pp. 173 ff.

62. U.S. Dept. of State, *The Conference of Berlin* (Potsdam) (Washington, D.C.: PO, 1960), 2:1225–1227, 1241.

63. For details of Manchuria's industrial and resource potential as perceived at this time, see H. Foster Bain, Manchuria: A Key Area."

64. For a particularly striking expression of this view see the State-War-Navy Coordinating Committee (SWNCC) memorandum to the Secretary of State, June 1, 1946, *FRUS 1946*, 9:934–945.

65. *FRUS 1944*, 6:671.

66. Davies, *Dragon by the Tail*, pp. 352, 371, 394; *FRUS 1944*, 6:695–697.

67. Davies, *Dragon by the Tail*, p. 371.

68. For a contrary view that stresses the Leninist orthodoxy of the CCP, see Steven M. Goldstein, "Chinese Communist Policy Toward the United States: Opportunities and Constraints, 1944–1950," pp. 235–278.

69. Buhite, *Patrick J. Hurley*, pp. 188–209; Service, *The Amerasia Papers*, pp. 115–116.

70. For a definition of "ideological thinking," see Morton H. Halperin et al. *Bureaucratic Politics and Foreign Policy*, pp. 22–23.

71. *FRUS 1945*, 7:520.

72. Kolko, *Politics of War*, pp. 600–601; Tsou, *America's Failure*, p. 308; Feis,

China Tangle, pp. 340–341. For Chiang Kai-shek's first order to General Okamura, see Chang Chi-yun, *K'ang-jih chan-shih*, p. 402.

73. Benis Frank and Henry Shaw, *History of U.S. Marine Corps Operations in World War II, Victory and Occupation*, 5:532. This official history is an extremely valuable account of American policy in action and provides much concrete evidence of the significance of the U.S. intervention in North China. See also Tsou, *America's Failure*, pp. 308–309.

74. Frank and Shaw, p. 544; Daniel A. Barbey, *MacArthur's Amphibious Navy*, p. 332.

75. *FRUS 1945*, 7:528.

76. *Ibid.*, p. 527.

77. *Ibid.*, p. 532.

78. Frank and Shaw, *Victory and Occupation*, pp. 542–543. Compare Romanus and Sunderland, *Time Runs Out*, p. 382, where it is claimed that there were 50,000 Nationalist troops in Shantung as of the end of August. This seems too high but is plausible if the puppet troops which the Nationalists enrolled in their ranks right after the war are included. See also Alan I. Shilin, "Occupation at Tsingtao," *Marine Corps Gazette*, 30: 32.

79. Lt. Col. James D. Hittle, "On the Peiping-Mukden Line," *Marine Corps Gazette*, 30:19. Frank and Shaw, *Victory and Occupation*, pp. 561–590.

80. Frank and Shaw, *Victory and Occupation*, p. 580; Edward Klein, "Situation in North China," *Marine Corps Gazette*, 30:14; Barbey, *MacArthur's Amphibious Navy*, p. 337.

81. Frank and Shaw, *Victory and Occupation*, pp. 578–579.

82. P. P. Vladimirov, *Osobyi raion Kitaiia* (Special District of China), pp. 443, 616.

83. *FRUS 1945*, 7:282–283.

84. Mao Tse-tung, *Selected Works*, 3:339–340.

85. Wang Chin-mu, *Chung-kuo K'ang-chan shih yen-i* (A popular History of the Chinese War of Resistance), p. 215.

86. E. Iu. Bogush, *Mif ob 'eksporte revoliutsii' i Sovetskaia vneshniaia politika* (The Myth about the "Export of Revolution" and Soviet Foreign Policy) p. 99; Cohen, *America's Response*, p. 182. A U.S. intelligence report at the time suggested that "the chief and most obvious result of the treaty is to deprive the Communists of bargaining strength they might otherwise have if their opponents continued to fear the possibility of Soviet military or other aid to the Communists." OSS Research and Analysis Branch, R and A No. 3248, September 7, 1945, "Implications of the Sino-Soviet Agreement for the Internal Politics of China," p. 1, National Archives.

87. *Chieh-fang jih-pao*, August 27, 1945, cited in O. Borisov [pseud.]*Sovetskii Soiuz i Man'chzhurskaia revoliutsionnaia baza* (The Soviet Union and the Manchurian Revolutionary Base), p. 87; also see Reardon-Anderson, *Yenan and the Great Powers*, pp. 102–104.

88. Bogush, *Mif ob 'eksporte,'* p. 108.

89. O. Borisov and B. T. Koloskov, *Sino-Soviet Relations, 1945–1973: A Brief History*.

90. Vladimir Dedijer, *Tito Speaks*, p. 331. In his speech to the 10th Plenum of the 8th Central Committee on September 24, 1962, Mao Tse-tung said, "In 1945, Stalin obstructed China from making revolution. He said we could not fight a civil war, and that we should cooperate with Chiang Kai-shek. Otherwise, the Chinese race would be destroyed." *Mao Tse-tung ssu-hsiang wan-sui* 1:432.

91. It would not have been out of character for Stalin to attend to such details.

Harriman testifies that unlike many persons at the pinnacle of power, Stalin was a master of detail who realized that such grasp was necessary to ensure proper policy implementation. Harriman and Abel, *Special Envoy,* passim.
92. *Pravda,* August 31, 1945, p. 4.

2. SOVIET-AMERICAN RIVALRY IN MANCHURIA AND THE COLD WAR

1. A. I. Kovtun-Stankevich, "Komendant Mukdena" (Mukden Commander), in *Na Kitaiskoi zemle: vospominaniia sovetskikh dobrovol'tsev, 1925–1945* (On Chinese Soil: Memoirs of Soviet Volunteers, 1925–1945), p. 432.

2. Tung Yen-p'ing, *Su O chü tung-pei* (Soviet Russia's Invasion of the Northeast), p. 145; Hsiung Shih-hui papers, "Report of the Military Mission of the Republic of China on Negotiations with the Soviet Military Authorities for the Withdrawal of Soviet Troops from the Northeast Provinces" (in Chinese), p. 121. Cited hereafter as Hsiung Shih-hui report.

3. Paul Frillman and Graham Peck, *China: The Remembered Life,* p. 264.

4. Austin Fulton, *Through Earthquake, Wind and Fire: Church and Mission in Manchuria, 1867–1950,* pp. 188–189.

5. Paul Frillman, interview in New York city, January 17, 1969.

6. Frillman and Peck, *China,* pp. 263–264.

7. Chung-yang she-chi chu tung-pei tiao-ch'a wei-yuan-hui, *Wei-man hsien-chuang* (Contemporary Manchukuo).

8. Wu Huan-chang, "Jih-pen t'ou-hsiang hou tung-pei chieh-shou ti hui-ku" (Reminiscence of the Northeast Takeover After Japan's Surrender), in Wang Ta-jen, ed., *Tung-pei yen-chiu lun-chi* (Essays on Northeast China), pp. 4–5.

9. Tong Te-Kong and Li Tsung-jen, *The Memoirs of Li Tsung-jen,* pp. 434–435.

10. *Ibid.*

11. Howard L. Boorman and Richard Howard, eds. *Biographical Dictionary of Republican China,* 2:115.

12. Boorman and Howard, eds., *Biographical Dictionary,* 1:29. Chang Kia-ngau's appointment was announced without his ever having been consulted or informed in advance. Yao Sung-ling, ed., "Chang Kung-ch'üan jih-chi chung yu-kuan tung-pei chieh-shou chiao-she ching-kuo" (Extracts from the Diary of Chang Kia-ngau Relating to the Negotiations Over the Takeover of the Northeast), *Chuan-chi wen-hsüeh* (Biographical Literature) (February 1, 1980), 37(1):30. Cited hereafter as Chang Kia-ngau diary.

13. For information on the structure of the National Government's administration in the Northeast, see T'ang Yün, *Tung-pei wen-t'i chih chen hsiang* (The True Face of the Northeast Question), p. 68. On Chiang Ching-kuo, see Boorman and Howard, *Biographical Dictionary of Republican China,* 1:307–308.

14. U.S. Dept. of State, *United States Relations with China: with Special Reference to the Period 1944–1949,* p. 247.

15. United States Consulate in Mukden, *Chinese Press Review,* 70/47, August 29, 1947, p. 5.

16. On September 18, 1945, the Joint Chiefs of Staff cabled General Wedemyer: "It is U.S. policy to assist the Chinese Government on the establishment of essential Chinese troops in liberated areas, particularly Manchuria, as rapidly as possible." U.S. Dept. of State, *FRUS 1945,* 7:565; also Herbert L. Feis, *The China Tangle: The American Effort in China from Pearl Harbor to the Marshall Mission,* pp. 382–383.

17. Chiang Kai-shek, *Soviet Russia in China: A Summing Up at Seventy,* p. 143;

Chinese Delegation to the United Nations, *China Presents Her Case to the United Nations*, p. 12. For the central importance of Dairen as a military port, see United States Armed Forces, Far East Headquarters, Military History Section, Japanese Special Studies on Manchuria, *Strategic Study of Manchuria's Topography and Geography*, 3:46–47, and *Logistics in Manchuria*, 8:99.

18. Cheng Tien-fong, *A History of Sino-Russian Relations*, pp. 275–276. Cheng, then a high official in the National Government, cites his notes of a report to the Supreme National Defense Council on October 8, 1945.

19. Tung Yen-p'ing, *Su O chü tung-pei*, p. 7. Housed in a compound guarded by foreign troops, Chang Kia-ngau noted that it was "like being in a foreign country." Chang Kia-ngau diary, February 1, 1980, p. 32.

20. For detailed treatments see Tung Yen-p'ing, *Su O chü tung-pei*; Hsiung Shih-hui report; Chang Kia-ngau diary.

21. Tung Yen-p'ing, *Su O chü tung-pei*, p. 18; Hsiung Shih-hui report, pp. 16–20; Daniel E. Barbey, *MacArthur's Amphibious Navy*, p. 340.

22. Tung Yen-p'ing, *Su O chü tung-pei*, pp. 15–25; Hsiung Shih-hui report, pp. 17–21.

23. Hsiung Shih-hui report, p. 22; Chang Kia-ngau diary, June 1, 1980, p. 91. For Sladkovsky's account of these talks see his partial autobiography, M. I. Sladkovsky, *Znakomstvo s Kitaem i kitaitsami* (My Acquaintance with China and the Chinese), pp. 305–313.

24. *FRUS 1945, China*, 7:798.

25. Chiang Kai-shek, *Soviet Russia in China*, p. 146; Hsiung Shih-hui report, p. 21.

26. Tung Yen-p'ing, *Su O chü tung-pei*, pp. 28–29; Chang Kia-ngau diary, June 1, 1980, p. 90.

27. Tung Yen-p'ing *Su O chü tung-pei*, p. 26; Chang Kia-ngau diary, June 1, 1980, p. 92.

28. Tung Yen-p'ing, *Su O chü tung-pei*, pp. 47–50; Hsiung Shih-hui report, pp. 24–29. Ch'en Yün, a top Communist leader in the Northeast, noted the duality of Soviet policy in the region, saying that Soviet policy was to hand over the big cities and the railroads to the Nationalists, *and* to help the CCP in the Northeast. Ch'en Yün, *Wen-hsüan* (Selected Works of Ch'en Yün), p. 221.

29. Tung Yen-p'ing, *Su O chü tung-pei*, pp. 52–55; Hsiung Shih-hui report, pp. 30–34.

30. Tung Yen-p'ing, *Su O chü tung-pei*, pp. 63–65; Hsiung Shih-hui report, pp. 42–44, 53.

31. Hsiung Shih-hui report, pp. 34–35; Chang Kia-ngau diary, June 1, 1980, pp. 91–94; September, 1980, pp. 94–98; October 1980, pp. 119–124; January 1981, pp. 111–114. Sladkovsky claims in his memoirs that the proposals for extensive joint Soviet-Chinese co-ownership of Northeast industry originated from the circumstance that most enterprises were shut down due to a shortage of competent Chinese technical and managerial personnel. His account makes the Soviet proposal appear as a form of technical-developmental assistance rather than a species of economic imperialism. *Znakomstvo s Kitaem i kitaitsami*, pp. 305–306.

32. *FRUS 1945*, 7:628, 613, 665, and 600.

33. *FRUS 1945*, 7:633. See also John Paton Davies' comments on this policy in *Dragon by the Tail*, pp. 417–418.

34. Secretary of State Byrnes, for example, asserted that a strong, unified China was needed in order to avert Soviet control of Manchuria and paramount influence in

north China. *FRUS 1945*, 7:762. Secretary Forrestal said that "he did not like to see us withdraw as a result of Russian pressure." *Ibid.*, p. 646.

35. John M. Blum, ed., *The Price of Vision: The Diary of Henry A. Wallace, 1942–1946*, p. 520. Wallace viewed Marshall as strongly anti-Russian. p. 522.

36. Feis, *China Tangle*, pp. 418–420.

37. *United States Relations with China*, p. 607.

38. *FRUS 1945*, 7:770. See also James F. Byrnes, *All in One Lifetime*, p. 330.

39. D. C. Gupta, *United States Attitude Toward China*, p. 138.

40. *FRUS 1945*, 7:748.

41. *United States Relations with China*, p. 608.

42. *FRUS 1946*, 10:559–560.

43. *Ibid.*, pp. 27–28. Colonel Marshall S. Carter to General Marshall, August 14, 1946.

44. Typically, this was expressed by means of reporting U.S. public and Congressional discontent with American intervention in China. *Pravda*, November 21, 1945, p. 4; November 28, 1945, p. 2; November 30, 1945, p. 4.

45. N. Sokolovskii, "O polozhenii v Kitae posle kapitulatsii Iaponii" (The Situation in China After Japan's Surrender), *Pravda*, December 19, 1945, p. 4.

46. Feis, *China Tangle*, pp. 424–426; *FRUS 1945, China*, 7:845–847.

47. *FRUS 1945*, 7:848–849; James F. Byrnes, *Speaking Frankly*, p. 228.

48. Byrnes, *Speaking Frankly*, p. 228; for the Russian text see *Vneshniaia politika Sovetskogo Soiuza 1945* (Foreign Policy of the Soviet Union 1945), pp. 161–162.

49. Byrnes, *Speaking Frankly*, p. 122; Byrnes, *All in One Lifetime*, p. 335. Stalin was pursuing his long established ploy of reassurance with respect to U.S.-China policy. Molotov more nearly expressed the actual Soviet view of the Marshall mission. But a week later, in conversation with Ambassador Averell Harriman, Molotov had adopted his master's voice in stating that the USSR looked with favor on the Marshall mission. *FRUS 1946*, 6:680–681.

50. Chiang Ching-kuo, *Wo-ti fu-ch'in* (My Father), unpaged. Stalin gave Harriman a very different version of these talks. The Soviet leader said that he had refused Chiang's request for Soviet mediation between the CCP and the Kuomintang because he had the impression that "the Communists would not agree with the Soviet position on China." Averell Harriman and Elie Abel, *Special Envoy to Churchill and Stalin, 1941–1946*, p. 532. This is quite implausible since Marshall had only just begun his mediation effort, and the Soviets preferred to let him take fire from both sides while standing clear themselves.

51. Chao Chia-hsiang, *Chiang-chün shih wen chi* (Historical Works of the General), 1:8b.

52. *Ibid.; The New York Times*, November 17–December 4, 1945.

53. *New York Times*, December 4, 1945, p. 3.

54. Chou En-lai and Wang Jo-fei in talks with the Kuomintang leaders wanted "the Chinese Communist Party to participate in the government of the Northeast Provinces." *FRUS 1945*, 7:458.

55. Chu Teh et al., *Chung-kuo kung-ch'an-tang tui tung-pei ti t'ai-tu* (The Attitude of the Chinese Communist Party Toward the Northeast), pp. 1–2.

56. *Chieh-chüeh tung-pei wen-t'i ti t'u-ching* (The Path to Solving the Northeast Question), p. 19.

57. *Hsin-hua jih-pao*, November 30, 1945; *Chieh-fang jih-pao*, November 30, 1945, cited in James Reardon-Anderson, *Yenan and the Great Powers: The Origins of Chinese Communist Foreign Policy, 1944–1946*, p. 127.

58. Reardon-Anderson, pp. 128–130.

59. *FRUS 1946*, 9:12.

60. Reardon-Anderson, pp. 125–126.

61. Mao Tse-tung, *Selected Works of Mao Tse-tung*, 4:81–86.

62. See the perceptive comments by Tang Tsou on CCP strategy in *America's Failure in China, 1941–1950*, p. 403.

63. *United States Relations with China*, pp. 617, 613.

64. Takeuchi Minoru ed. *Mao Tse-tung chi* (The Works of Mao Tse-tung), 10:27.

65. Chung-kung yen-chiu tsa-chih she, ed., *Liu Shao-ch'i wen-t'i tzu-liao chuan-chi* (Special Collection of Materials on the Liu Shao-ch'i Case) (Taipei, 1970), pp. 182–185.

66. The CCP's problem was not unique but was duplicated by many of the European communist parties after World War II which found themselves torn between insurrection and parliamentarianism. See William O. McCagg, *Stalin Embattled, 1943–1948*, pp. 31–71. The same question confronted the Portuguese Communist Party in 1974 after forty years of battling the Salazar-Caetano dictatorship.

67. *Liu Shao-ch'i wen-t'i*, p. 184.

68. *FRUS 1946*, 9:151–152.

69. *Wei tung-pei ti ho-p'ing min-chu erh tou-cheng* (Struggle for Peace and Democracy in the Northeast), pp. 6–7.

70. *FRUS 1946*, 9:513–516.

71. Chou, of course, may have been ordered to employ stalling tactics while Communist military victories were strengthening his bargaining position.

72. This was a period when the Communists were frantically entrenching themselves in the countryside.

73. Lyman P. Van Slyke, ed., *Marshall's Mission to China, December 1945–January 1947: The Report and Appended Documents*, 1:53.

74. *FRUS 1946*, 9:387.

75. Full details are available in Hsiung Shih-hui report and in Tung Yen-p'ing, *Su O chü tung-pei*.

76. Tung Yen-p'ing, *Su O chü tung-pei*, pp. 91, 97, 107–108.

77. From the beginning of the renewed negotiations the Chinese had sought to have Soviet liaison officers attached to their takeover teams in order to provide a measure of security en route to the localities from the provincial capitals where Nationalist authority already functioned. At first the Russians suggested that local Red Army commands could turn over authority but the Nationalists refused to dispense with liaison officers appointed by the Red Army headquarters and the Russians finally acquiesced. Tung Yen-p'ing, *Su O chü tung-pei*, pp. 56, 59–62, 110; Hsiung Shih-hui report, pp. 61–63, 85–87.

78. Tung Yen-p'ing, pp. 52, 84, 102–104, 113.

79. Chang Kia-ngau diary, March 1, 1980, p. 76; Hsiung Shih-hui report, pp. 70, 76–77; Tung Yen-p'ing, *Su O chü tung-pei*, pp. 84, 92, 117; B. G. Sapozhnikov and V. V. Vorontsov, "Osvoboditel'naia missiia SSSR na Dal'nem Vostoke v gody vtoroi mirovoi voiny" (The Liberating Mission of the USSR in the Far East During the Second World War), *Istoriia SSSR* (History of the USSR), p. 45.

80. Sapozhnikov and Vorontsov, p. 17.

81. Hsiung Shih-hui report, pp. 70–115 passim.

82. *Pravda*, February 24, 1946, p. 4; *Tung-pei wen-t'i* (The Northeast Question), p. 34, citing Soviet radio broadcasts.

83. Tung Yen-p'ing, *Su O chü tung-pei*, pp. 73, 76, 107; *New York Times*, January 30, 1946, p. 4.

84. U.S. Dept. of State, *The Conference of Berlin (Potsdam)* (Washington, D.C.: GPO, 1960), 2:846–847, 888 for the two Soviet definitions presented at the conference. This source is hereafter cited as *Potsdam Papers*.

85. *Ibid.*, p. 834. The United States consistently used the term "war booty" while the Soviets used the term "war trophies" (voennye trofei). That the American definition was consistent with that contained in existing international law is demonstrated by Daniel Lew, "Manchurian Booty and International Law," *American Journal of International Law*.

86. *Potsdam Papers*, 2:854, 857, 1485–1487, 1505–1506; see also the illuminating discussions in Robert Slusser, ed., *Soviet Economic Policy in Postwar Germany*.

87. The most complete account of the Soviet actions and their impact on the Manchurian economy is in Edwin A. Pauley, *Report on Japanese Assets in Manchuria to the President of the United States, July 1946*. Pauley was the Ambassador for Reparations. See also George Moorad, "The Rape of Manchuria," a first-hand account. A vivid pictorial report is in *Life*, (March 25, 1946), 15:27–33.

88. E. Zhukov in *Izvestia*, January 29, 1947. The Soviet figure, unlike the careful work done by the Pauley commission, is unsupported by any published documentation whatsoever. However, Pauley once estimated that industrial plants had a value of only 10 cents to 20 cents on the dollar once they were moved. *New York Times*, November 16, 1945, p. 2. Taking the lower figure and applying it to the estimate of direct damages one arrives at $89.5 million, a figure close to the Soviet estimate. Transported to Siberia, the property may indeed have been worth no more than the Russians claimed. See also Slusser, *Soviet Economic Policy*, pp. 14, 41, for the German comparison.

89. It has been suggested that industrial removals were one aspect of a recovery program associated with a Soviet leadership group headed by Georgi Malenkov, head of the Special Committee under the Council of People's Commissars, who favored the "economic disarmament" of Germany. See Slusser, *Soviet Economic Policy*, p. xii; see also Roy F. Grow, "Soviet Politics and Chinese Communist Strategies: The Struggle for Manchuria, 1945–1946."

90. The competition among different Soviet ministries for the spoils of Germany is vividly described in an essay by Vladimir Rudolph, "The Agencies of Control: Their Organization and Policies." Rudolph comments that "during the period from May to October 1945 the Soviet zone of Germany was transformed into something like the Klondike during the Gold Rush" (p. 20).

91. Hsiung Shih-hui report, pp. 22, 33. Chang Kia-ngau diary, October, 1980, pp. 119–120. Sladkovsky himself estimated that the proposed jointly operated industry would cover 18 percent of the coal mining, 33 percent of machine-building, 81 percent of the metalurgical industry, 89 percent of electric power, 37 percent of cement, and 94 percent of ferrous metal industry. *Znakomstvo s Kitaem i Kitaitsami*, p. 312. In Germany joint corporations were established in the summer of 1946. Slusser, *Soviet Economic Policy*, pp. 52–59.

92. Rudolph, "The Agencies of Control," pp. 41–42. He notes that from the fall of 1945, "Mikoyan's concept of dominating the Soviet zone for the economic benefit of the Soviet Union began to gain the upper hand. This did not mean the sharp and decisive abandonment of the policy of 'economic disarmament,' the two policies existed side by side for some time supplementing one another." (p. 42).

93. In fact, in his talks with presidential envoy Harry Hopkins in May 1945, Stalin, pursuing his policy of reassurance to the United States, had said that he expected America to shoulder the burden of postwar economic assistance to China. *FRUS 1945*, 7:890.

94. Chang Kia-ngau diary, September 1980, p. 94; Carsun Chang, *Third Force in China*, p. 167. Carsun Chang was Chang Kia-ngau's younger brother.

95. *FRUS 1946*, 10:1103–1104; Chang Kia-ngau, June 1980, pp. 108–109.

96. *FRUS 1946*, 9:427; Chang Kia-ngau diary, June 1980, p. 109. Chang is very critical of T. V. Soong and Wang Shih-chieh for their rigid diplomacy of principles that failed to take account of political realities (p. 111). This is also suggested by Sladkovsky's account, *Znakomstvo s Kitaem i kitaitsami*, pp. 311–312.

97. Hsiung Shih-hui report, p. 88; Tung Yen-p'ing, *Su O chü tung-pei*, p. 112.

98. Chang Kia-ngau diary, June 1, 1980, pp. 109–110; October 1980, pp. 119–124; January 1981, pp. 111–114; *FRUS 1946*, 10:460–461; Chang, *Third Force*, pp. 167–168.

99. Hsiung Shih-hui report, pp. 88–90; Tung Yen-p'ing, *Su O chü tung-pei*, p. 55. For another version of the Soviet demands, see the U.S. War Department Strategic Services report, "Manchuria: Soviet Demands."

100. See General Marshall's Washington press conference statement of March 16, 1946, in *New York Times*, March 17, 1946, p. 27.

101. Lloyd Eastman, *Seeds of Destruction: Nationalist China in War and Revolution*, pp. 109–113.

102. These papers represented the remains of the wartime united front policy.

103. A Kuomintang official of that time confirms that the CC clique used the Chungking demonstrations to strike at the Political Study clique and at Chiang Kai-shek and his son. Tsai Hsing-san, *Chiang Ching-kuo yü Su-lien* (Chiang Ching-kuo and the Soviet Union), pp. 48–50. Tsai was head of the San Min Chu I Youth Corps in Chungking at this time and came into conflict with Chiang Ching-kuo over the issue of student participation in the demonstrations which Chiang opposed.

104. *FRUS 1946*, 9:440–441. Dissatisfaction with the government's policy in the Northeast was not limited to Kuomintang intraparty critics. Much of the Chinese press criticized the secrecy of the diplomatic negotiations between China and the USSR and demanded a public accounting. Northeast natives were in the forefront of criticism, urging the government to hold firm against Soviet demands and asking that the top officials in Manchuria—Hsiung Shih-hui and Chang Kia-ngau—be dismissed.

105. *New York Times*, March 7, 1946, p. 3; March 16, 1946, p. 6; March 17, 1946, p. 27; *FRUS 1946*, 9:538–539; Eastman, *Seeds of Destruction*, pp. 116–117.

106. *Pravda*, February 24, 1946, p. 4; February 25, 1946, p. 4; Hsiung Shih-hui report, pp. 96–101.

107. *Vneshniaia politika Sovetskogo Soiuza 1946* god (Foreign Policy of the Soviet Union 1946), pp. 98–99, reprinting General Trotsynko's statement from *Izvestia*, February 27, 1946.

108. Kovtun-Stankevich, "Komendant Mukdena," p. 366.

109. *FRUS 1946*, 10:1104–1105, 1112–1113. A second U.S. note on March 5 was similarly rebuffed (pp. 1114, 1122–1123).

110. *Ibid.*, 9:428.

111. *Ibid.*, 9:143, 427–428.

112. *Ibid.*, 10:164.

113. See, for example, Joseph Keeley, *The China Lobby Man: The Story of Alfred Kohlberg*, pp. 155, 183.

114. John Robinson Beal, *Marshall in China*, p. 51.

115. *FRUS 1946*, 9:528–529.

116. Chiang Kai-shek, *Soviet Russia in China: A Summing Up at Seventy*, p. 148.

117. *FRUS 1946*, 9:295–300.

118. *FRUS 1946*, 9:376, 206, 259, 387, 428, 502.

119. *FRUS 1946*, 9:590–591, 737.

120. Hsiung Shih-hui report, pp. 121, 123.

121. *New York Times*, March 9, 1946, p. 1; March 10, 1946, p. 4; March 19, 1946, p. 14.

122. A possible ambivalence may be suggested, however. Insofar as Executive Headquarters, by bringing the fighting under control, promoted the chances for a peaceful settlement, i.e., a coalition solution, the Russians may have favored it despite its American sponsorship. For his part, Marshall in speaking of the need for truce teams in Manchuria, stated that no other power (meaning the USSR) "can find justification for suspicion as to our motives in China." *New York Times*, March 17, 1946, p. 27.

123. *FRUS 1946*, 9:428–429.

124. Walter LaFeber, *America, Russia and the Cold War, 1945–1966*, pp. 30ff; Myron Rush, ed., *The International Situation and Soviet Foreign Policy*, pp. 117–123.

125. See, for example, Joseph P. Kennedy, "The U.S. and the World," *Life*, March 18, 1946, p. 107. For the Iranian case, Gary Hess, "The Iranian Crisis of 1945–46 and the Cold War."

126. This point is made with respect to Iran by Adam Ulam, *The Rivals*, pp. 118–119. The same argument applies to Manchuria.

127. *FRUS 1946*, 9:530–538, 549–550, 556. Chou may simply have been stalling or he may have differed from the Northeast commanders as to the proper strategy for the region. On March 13, Chou was urging the Committee of Three to arrange the terms of reference for the truce teams on the spot, pleading that: "If we publish the stipulations here right now without explaining to our people in the Northeast, trouble is bound to occur and at that time I shall be held responsible." If indeed Chou still supported the option of cooperating with Marshall's peace efforts, it is quite unlikely he could have prevailed over Peng Chen and the other Northeast leaders who scented a great victory on the battlefield.

128. *FRUS 1946*, 9:603. Marshall was very sensitive to the possibility that the USSR might ask to participate in the Northeast truce effort. He instructed General Gillem to notify the Soviets of truce team operations but not to grant them a responsible role (p. 599).

129. *FRUS 1946*, 9:603.

130. For the difficulties truce teams encountered in the Northeast, see *FRUS 1946*, 9:714, 726, 738–739, 767–776.

131. Tung Yen-p'ing, *Su O chü tung-pei*, pp. 121–122, 138.

132. Hsiung Shih-hui report, p. 145.

133. A U.S. intelligence report of mid-February 1946 alleged complicity between the Soviet garrison commander in Chilin city and local Communist leaders to facilitate Communist takeover of the city during the Red Army withdrawal. War Department, Strategic Services Unit YV 1087, "Communists at Chilin, Kirin Province," February 28, 1946, National Archives, Modern Military Records Branch, RG 226, Box 353.

134. Tung Yen-p'ing, *Su O chü tung-pei*, pp. 102, 106, 108, 157, 160–163.

135. Chang Kia-ngau diary, April 1980, p. 90; O. B. Borisov and B. T. Koloskov, *Sovetskie-Kitaiskie otnosheniia, 1945–1970* (Soviet-Chinese Relations, 1945–1970), p. 32.

136. Robert Rigg, "Campaign for the Northeast China Railway System," pp. 27–28.

137. Tung Yen-p'ing, *Su O chü tung-pei*, pp. 165–183.

138. The Soviet evacuation schedule had been presented to the Nationalists on April 3, at Changchun. *Ibid.*, p. 179.

139. See T'ang Yün, *Tung-pei wen-t'i*, pp. 15–18; Chinese Ministry of Information, *China Handbook, 1937–1945* (New York: MacMillan, 1947), p. 762.

140. Tung Yen-p'ing, *Su O chü tung-pei*, p. 154.

141. "Po Chiang Chieh-shih" (Refuting Chiang Kai-shek), *Mao Tse-tung chi*, 10:31-39.
142. *FRUS 1946, The Far East: China*, 9:727.
143. *FRUS 1946*, 9:788–790, 752–753, 818, 832.
144. *FRUS 1946*, 9:828, 906, 912, 978.
145. *FRUS 1946*, 9:1010.
146. *United States Relations with China*, pp. 162, 644–645.
147. In chapter 7 I shall argue that in formal terms the USSR did pursue a policy of nonintervention, but a brazenly opportunistic rather than a principled one.

3. BUILDING A STRUCTURE OF COMMUNIST POWER IN MANCHURIA

1. Mao Tse-tung, "On Peace Negotiations with the Kuomintang," *Selected Works of Mao Tse-tung*, 4:49.
2. Tseng K'o-lin, "Ta -ti ch'ung kuang" (Fighting for the North), in *Hsing-huo liao-yuan* (A Single Spark Can Set a Prairie Fire), 7:453–456.
3. Mao Tse-tung, "Build Stable Base Areas in the Northeast," *Selected Works*, 4:81–86.
4. See "Chairman Mao's Successor—Deputy Supreme Commander Lin Piao," *Current Background* October 27, 1969, no. 894, pp. 16–18.
5. "Mao Tse-tung's Oral Report to the Seventh Party Congress: Summary Notes (April 24, 1945)," p. 20.
6. Ch'en Yün, "Tui Manchou kung-tso ti chi-ko i-tien" (Some Thoughts on Work in Manchuria), *Wen-hsüan* (Selected Works), pp. 221–223.
7. Quoted in Carroll R. Wetzel, Jr., "From the Jaws of Defeat: Lin Piao and the 4th Field Army in Manchuria," p. 129.
8. Mao, "Build Stable Base Areas in the Northeast." In context, "good luck" may well have meant the kind of assistance which the Soviet Union had been providing until the new Nationalist-Soviet agreements of early December.
9. Yen Chung-ch'üan, "Follow the Splendid Example of Vice-Chairman Lin, Be Boundlessly Loyal to Chairman Mao's Revolutionary Line," *Current Background*, (November 20, 1969), no. 896, p. 24.
10. Interview with Lin Piao, October 21, 1946, *Chung-kuo chü-ta pien-hua ti i-nien* (A Year of Great Changes in China), p. 106.
11. "Chairman Mao's Successor," p. 17.
12. Thomas W. Robinson, *A Politico-Military Biography of Lin Piao, Part 1, 1907–1949*, p. 51; Wetzel, "From the Jaws of Defeat," p. 157.
13. Ch'en Yün, *Wen-hsüan*, pp. 230–235; Chou Chih-p'ing, "Comrade Lin Piao in the Period of Liberation War in the Northeast," *Chung-kuo ch'ing-nien* (Chinese youth) April 16, 1960, p. 26.
14. Lyman P. Van Slyke, ed., *The Chinese Communist Movement*, p. 123.
15. P. N. Pospelov, ed., *Istoriia velikoi otechestvennoi voiny Sovetskogo Soiuza, 1941–1945* (History of the Great Fatherland War of the Soviet Union, 1941–1945), 5:504–505, map 17; Gunther Stein, *The Challenge of Red China*, map facing p. 458. Compare Chang Chi-yün, *K'ang-jih chan-shih* (A Battle History of the anti-Japanese War of Resistance), map following p. 414.
16. *FRUS 1945*, 7:214; Wang Wen et al., "Yung-heng ti yu-i" (Eternal Friendship), in *Hsing-huo liao-yuan*, 7:464; A. M. Dubinsky, *Osvoboditel'naia missiia Sovetskogo Soiuza na Dal'nem Vostoke* (The Soviet Union's Liberating Mission in the Far East) p. 558, citing a Soviet Defense Ministry document.

17. Pospelov, *Istoriia*, 5:577. There is evidence to suggest that the Communists did not receive the degree of cooperation which they expected or at least desired from the Soviets. See George Moorad, *Lost Peace in China*, pp. 123–124. It may be that in the initial period there was a fairly wide degree of local variation in the amount of Red Army cooperation in the absence of unified directives on the matter from Moscow. For the link-up at Weichang, see Wang Wen et al., "Yung-heng ti yu-i," pp. 464–466.

18. A. M. Dubinsky, "Osvoboditel'naia missiia Sovetskogo Soiuza na Dal'nem Vostoke" (The Soviet Union's Liberating Mission in the Far East), *Voprosy Istorii* (Historical Problems), p. 59.

19. Tseng K'o-lin, "Ta-ti ch'ung kuang," pp. 446–448; William Whitson, *The Chinese High Command*, p. 301.

20. Tseng K'o-lin, p. 450.

21. Whitson, *The Chinese High Command*, p. 301.

22. Dubinsky, *Osvoboditel'naia missiia*, p. 559.

23. An American diplomat noted the bitterness of members of the CCP delegation in Chungking over Soviet actions in Manchuria. "The Communists had quite obviously expected to be welcome in Manchuria, and they were dismayed when the Russians not only denied them military help, but excluded them as far as possible." John Melby, *The Mandate of Heaven: Record of a Civil War, China 1945–49*, pp. 25, 30–31.

24. Wetzel, "From the Jaws of Defeat," pp. 56–63.

25. Fan Shou-yeh, "Tsai pei-man chiao-fei ti jih-tzu" (Bandit Suppression Days in Northern Manchuria), p. 161. The Fourth Regiment of the NEAJUA was flown on Red Army transports to Chiamussu from the vicinity of Vladivostok.

26. Tseng K'o-lin, "Tai-ti ch'ung kuang," pp. 452–453; Robert Rigg, *Red China's Fighting Hordes*, pp. 248–251. In North China, the CCP had considerable experience in recruiting *yu min*—rootless ex-peasants and non-peasant rural riffraff as a major source of their soldiers. See Ralph Thaxton, *China Turned Rightside Up*, pp. 169–173.

27. Katherine Chorley, *Armies and the Art of Revolution*, p. 58.

28. Rigg, *Red China's Fighting Hordes*, pp. 248–251; Wetzel, "From the Jaws of Defeat," p. 219.

29. *FRUS 1945*, 7:700.

30. Yen Chung-ch'üan, "Follow the Splendid Example of Vice-Chairman Lin Piao," pp. 24–25. Unlike many Cultural Revolution allegations, this one is consistent with available evidence.

31. Ch'en Yün, *Wen-hsüan*, pp. 223 and 237; T'u Chien et al., *Chung-kuo jen-min chieh-fang chün chien-shih* (A Short History of the Chinese People's Liberation Army), p. 59; Whitson, *The Chinese High Command*, p. 301.

32. Dubinsky, *Osvoboditel'naia missiia*, p. 561.

33. Ch'en Yün, *Wen-hsüan*, p. 227.

34. Chin T'ieh-ch'un, "Chuang-chien pei-man ken-chü-ti ti i-tuan hui-i" (Reminiscences of Founding the North Manchurian Base Area), pp. 101–103.

35. Chu Chih-yuan, "Cheng-ch'uan ch'u-ch'ien ti nien-tai" (The Initial Period of Establishing Political Power), pp. 89–90.

36. Liu Shao-ch'i, "On the Party," *Collected Works, 1945–1957*, pp. 15, 76.

37. Tseng K'o-lin, "Tai-ti ch'ung kuang," pp. 453–454.

38. *Ibid.*, pp. 454–456.

39. Donald W. Klein and Ann Clark, *Biographic Dictionary of Chinese Communism, 1921–1965* (Cambridge: Harvard University Press, 1971), 2:1069. Klein and Clark list sixty such persons in Appendix 38.

40. *Wei tung-pei ti ho-p'ing min-chu erh tou-cheng* (Struggle for Peace and Democracy in the Northeast), p. 4.

41. Klein and Clark, *Biographic Dictionary*, 2:715.

42. *Cheng-chih hsieh-shang hui-i tzu-liao* (Materials on the Political Consultative Conference), pp. 273–275.

43. Chou Erh-fu, *Tung-pei heng-tuan mien* (Cross-Section of the Northeast), p. 59.

44. *Tung-pei hua-pao* (Northeast Pictorial) (May 1946), 1:2; Liu Pai-yü, *Shih-tai ti yin-hsiang* (Contemporary Impressions), p. 164; Liu Yun-an, *Demokraticheskoe i sotsialisticheskoe stroitel'stvo v severo-vostochnom Kitae* (Democratic and Socialist Construction in Northeast China), p. 21.

45. *Tung-pei jen-min ying-kai tsou shen-mo tao-lu* (What Road Should the People of the Northeast take), p. 16.

46. For Chang see Fan Chao-fu, "Chang Hsüeh-ssu ts'an-chia kung-ch'an-tang chi ts'an-ssu ti ching-kuo" (Chang Hsüeh-ssu's Experience in Joining the Communist Party and his Tragic Death); Richard Lauterbach, *Danger from the East*, p. 298. For Kao Ch'ung-min, see his obituary in Foreign Broadcast Information Service, *Daily Report, China* (April 23, 1979), L6. Kao joined the CCP in 1946.

47. I have been unable to trace the background of several of these figures.

48. One of the most prominent of the CCP figures in the Northeast was Yunnan-born Chou Pao-chung who had been a top leader in the anti-Japanese guerrilla struggle.

49. Chou Erh-fu, *Tung-pei heng-tuan mien*, p. 51.

50. Liu Yun-an, *Demokraticheskoe i sotsialisticheskoe stroitel'stvo*, pp. 36–37.

51. The following paragraphs are based on Chu Chih-yuan, "Cheng-ch'üan ch'u-nien ti nien-tai."

52. Chang Chi-chung, "Wo tsai Chaoyuan ssu-nien" (My Four Years in Chaoyuan).

53. *Ibid.*, p. 117.

54. *Ibid.*, p. 118.

55. Liu Yun-an, *Demokraticheskoe i sotsialisticheskoe stroitel'stvo*, p. 51.

56. *Ibid.*

57. Klein and Clark, *Biographic Dictionary*, 1:554; John Israel and Donald W. Klein, *Rebels and Bureaucrats: China's December 9ers*, p. 38.

58. See Lin Feng's obituary in *Jen-min jih-pao* (People's Daily), October 9, 1977, p. 2.

59. *Tung-pei wen-t'i* (The Northeast Question), pp. 158–160; *Tung-pei jih-pao* (Northeast Daily), August 13, 1946, p. 1.

4. REVOLUTIONARY CIVIL WAR IN THE NORTHEAST

1. Dorothy Jacobs-Larkcom, *As China Fell: The Experiences of a British Consul's Wife, 1946–1953*, p. 64.

2. Seymour Topping, *Journey Between Two Chinas*, p. 312.

3. Jacobs-Larkcom, *As China Fell*, p. 153.

4. U.S. Dept. of State, *FRUS 1948*, 7:571–572.

5. Chou Chih-p'ing, "Tung-pei chieh-fang chan-cheng shih-ch'i ti Lin Piao t'ung-chih" (Comrade Lin Piao During the Period of the Northeast Liberation war), pp. 133–147.

6. See, inter alia, Hsi-sheng Ch'i, *Nationalist China at War: Military Defeats and Political Collapse, 1937–1945*; Aleksandr Ya. Kalyagin, *Along Alien Roads*; Dick Wilson, *When Tigers Fight: The Story of the Sino-Japanese War, 1937–1945*.

7. Ch'i, *Nationalist China at War*, pp. 124–125, and 129.

8. William Whitson, *The Chinese High Command: A History of Communist Military Politics, 1927–1971*, p. 83.

9. Earlier in the war, the Communists had successfully interfered with Nationalist use of the railroads by inflicting extensive damage to the tracks. Robert Rigg, "Campaign for the Northeast China Railway System," pp. 27–28.

10. O. Borisov, *Sovetskii Soiuz i Man'chzhurskaia revoliutsionnaia baza, 1945–1949* pp. 189–196.

11. Ralph Thaxton claims that the Communists in North China during the Resistance War for the most part made minimal claims upon the civilian population. When circumstances compelled the CCP to increase its demands on the peasantry, he suggests, the Party jeopardized its popular support. *China Turned Rightside Up: Revolutionary Legitimacy in the Peasant World*, pp. 174, 184.

12. Whitson comments: "To the extent that 'people's war' means mobilization of primitive and dispersed resources of war, this was 'peoples's war.' " *The Chinese High Command*, p. 86.

13. *FRUS 1947*, 7:180 and 171.

14. *FRUS 1947*, 7:210.

15. For fuller treatments, see Whitson, *The Chinese High Command*, passim; Lionel Max Chassin, *The Communist Conquest of China: A History of the Civil War, 1945–1949*; Dept. of the Army, Office of the Chief of Military History, *The Civil War in China, 1945–1950* (a translation of a Chinese Nationalist work); Colonel Trevor N. Dupuy, *The Military History of the Chinese Civil War*, pp. 75–86; O. Edmund Clubb, "Manchuria in the Balance," and "Military Debacle in Manchuria."

16. Whitson, *The Chinese High Command*, p. 304; cf. Carroll R. Wetzel Jr., "From the Jaws of Defeat: Lin Piao and the Fourth Field Army in Manchuria," p. 159.

17. Chassin, *The Communist Conquest*, p. 90; Whitson, *The Chinese High Command*, pp. 305–306; Chao Chia-hsiang, *Chiang-chün shih wen chi* (Historical Works of the General), p. 10-A.

18. *FRUS 1946*, 10:581.

19. Interview with former staff member of Sun Li-jen's New 1st Army, Tainan, Taiwan (ROC), June 1968.

20. Whitson, *The Chinese High Command*, pp. 87, 307.

21. *Tung-pei jih-pao* (Northeast Daily), July 9, 1947, p. 1; see also Chu Chi-fu, "Nothing to Mobilize"; C. T. Lin, "Mukden-Yangtze."

22. *Ho-p'ing jih-pao* (Peace Daily), July 1, 1947, in *Chinese Press Review*.

23. Chassin, *The Communist Conquest*, pp. 131–136.

24. William M. Leary, *Perilous Missions: Civil Air Transport and CIA Covert Operations in Asia*, pp. 38–39.

25. Ch'en Shao-hsiao (Major Ch'en), *Kuan-nei liao-tung i chü ch'i* (The Chessboard from Inside the Pass to Liaotung), p. 21.

26. Whitson, *The Chinese High Command*, pp. 310–311; Chassin, *The Communist Conquest*, pp. 165–166.

27. Ch'en Shao-hsiao, *Kuan-nei liao-tung*, pp. 24–26.

28. Hung Huang, *Tsui-hou ti ch'a-tzu* (The Last Dregs), p. 1. Ch'en tsung-chang chen neng-kan, huo-ch'e nan-chan t'ung pei-chan.

29. U.S. Dept. of State, *United States Relations with China: with Special Reference to the Period 1944–1949*, p. 325.

30. Ch'en Shao-hsiao, *Kuan-nei liao-tung*, pp. 49–55.

31. Whitson, *The Chinese High Command*, p. 312; Fan Kun-yuan, "Chin-chou

chan-i ti sheng-li ch'ien tsou" (The Victorious Prelude to the Battle of Chinchou), in *Hsing Huo: Ko-ming hui-i lu* (Sparks: Revolutionary Reminiscences) 1:127; Yeh Chien-ying, "The Great Decisive Battle of Strategy," *Hong Ch'i* (Red Flag).

32. Leary, *Perilous Missions*, p. 49; and *The Dragon's Wings: The China National Aviation Corporation and the Development of Commercial Aviation in China*, p. 212.

33. Chao Chia-hsiang, *Chiang-chün shih wen chi*, p. 7-A.

34. Lloyd Eastman, *Seeds of Destruction: Nationalist China in War and Revolution*, p. 41.

35. Ch'en Shao-hsiao, *Kuan-nei liao-tung*, pp. 76–79 and 90–94; Chao Chia-hsiang, *Chiang-chün shih wen chi*, pp. 7-B–8-A.

36. Whitson, *The Chinese High Command*, pp. 315–318; Chassin, *The Communist Conquest*, pp. 188–191; Ch'en Shao-hsiao, *Kuan-nei liao-tung*, pp. 140–209.

37. For details on CCP takeover policy for cities see Ch'en Yun, "Chieh-shou shen-yang ti ching-yen" (The Experience of Taking Over Shenyang), a report to the Northeast Bureau, November 28, 1948, *Wen-hsuan* (Selected Works), pp. 269–274. Ch'en was a member of the Shenyang Military Administrative Committee.

38. Whitson, *The Chinese High Command*, p. 319; Ch'en Shao-hsiao, *Kuan-nei liao-tung*, p. 223.

39. Chao Chia-hsiang, *Chiang-chün shih wen chi*, pp. 33-A–33-B.

40. *Ibid.*, pp. 33-A–37-B.

41. Ch'en Shao-hsiao, *Kuan-nei liao-tung*, pp. 228–231; F. F. Liu, *A Military History of Modern China*, p. 256.

42. Lloyd Eastman, "Who Lost China? Chiang Kai-shek Testifies," pp. 659–661.

43. Ho Hsi-ya, *Tao-fei wen-t'i chih yen-chiu* (A Study of the Bandit Question), p. 15.

44. Tetsuya Kataoka, *Resistance and Revolution in China: The Communists and the Second United Front*, pp. 106–107.

45. Chou Erh-fu, *Sung-hua chiang-shang ti feng-yün* (Events Along the Sungari River), p. 85. Anna Louise Strong reports that Lin Feng claimed 10–20,000 bandits had been active in Manchuria. *The Chinese Conquer China*, p. 241. This is a low estimate.

46. *Tung-pei jih-pao*, February 9, 1947, p. 1.

47. Chang Chi-chung, "Wo tsai chao-yuan ssu-nien," pp. 118–119; *Tung-pei jih-pao*, February 9, 1947, p. 1.

48. Chang Chi-chung, pp. 120–121.

49. Fan Shou-yeh, "Tsai pei-man chiao-fei ti jih-tzu," (Bandit Suppression Days in Northern Manchuria), pp. 162–163.

50. *Tung-pei jih-pao*, February 9, 1947, p. 1; Liu Pai-yü, *Shih-tai ti yin-hsiang* (Contemporary Impressions), p. 125.

51. For example, *Tung-pei jih-pao*, January 18, 1947, p. 1; see also Patricia Griffin, *The Chinese Communist Treatment of Counterrevolutionaries, 1924–1949*, p. 104.

52. Fan Shou-yeh, "Tsai pei-man chiao-fei," pp. 163–164.

53. *Tung-pei jih-pao*, March 29, 1947, p. 2; May 31, 1947, p. 2.

54. Fan Shou-yeh, "Tsai pei-man chiao-fei," p. 168.

55. Chang Chi-chung, "Wo tsai chao-yuan ssu-nien," pp. 121 and 122.

56. Strong, *The Chinese Conquer China*, p. 242.

57. John Gittings, *The Role of the Chinese Army*, p. 98.

58. Fan Shou-yeh, "Tsai pei-man chiao-fei," p. 172.

59. *Tung-pei jih-pao*, April 12, 1947, p. 2; April 28, 1947, p. 2.

60. Suzanne Pepper, *Civil War in China: The Political Struggle, 1945–1949*, p. 382.

61. Yen Chung-ch'uan, "Follow the Splendid Example of Vice-Chairman Lin, Be Boundlessly Loyal to Chairman Mao's Revolutionary Line," *Current Background* (Nov. 20, 1969), no. 896, p. 24.

62. John Stephan, *The Russian Fascists: Tragedy and Farce in Exile, 1925–1945* (New York: Harper & Row, 1978), p. 46.

63. *China Digest* (June 15, 1948), 4(3):16.

64. John Stephan, *The Russian Fascists*, pp. 320–334. Ironically, thousands of these homesick White Russians had greeted the Red Army tumultuously upon its arrival in Harbin in August 1945.

65. *Tung-pei jih-pao*, July 18, 1946, p. 1; January 7, 1947, p. 2. Hereafter *Tpjp*.

66. *Tpjp*, February 9, 1947, p. 4; January 7, 1947, p. 4; June 1, 1947, p. 4; November 14, 1947, p. 4.

67. *Tpjp*, December 11, 1947, p. 1.

68. *Tpjp*, September 14, 1947, p. 2; November 13, 1947, p. 4.

69. *Tpjp*, May 6, 1947, p. 4; June 10, 1947, p. 4; June 20, 1947, p. 2.

70. *Tpjp*, February 6, 1948, p. 4.

71. William H. McNeill, *Plagues and Peoples*, pp. 61 ff.

72. Carl F. Nathan, *Plague Prevention and Politics in Manchuria*.

73. *New York Times*, March 22, 1983, p. 4; John W. Powell, "Japan's Germ Warfare: The U.S. Cover-up of a War Crime."

74. For a graphic sketch of the plague epidemic in a Northeast village see Hsiao Hung, *The Field of Life and Death and Tales of Hulan River*, pp. 69–72.

75. *Tpjp*, March 7, 1947, p. 2; September 5, 1947, p. 1.

76. *Tpjp*, September 9, 1947, p. 1; September 24, 1947, p. 1; October 2, 1947, p. 1; September 29, 1947, p. 1.

77. Borisov, *Sovetskii Soiuz i Man'chzhurskaia revoliutsionnaia baza*, pp. 197–198; Oleg E. Vladimirov, *Nezabyvaemye stranitsy istorii i maoistskie fal'sifikatory* pp. 33–34. (Unforgettable Pages of History and the Maoist Falsifiers).

78. *Tpjp*, October 18, 1947, p. 1; November 27, 1947, p. 1; December 22, 1947, p. 1; Vladimirov, *Nezabyvaemye stranitsy*, p. 34.

79. Department of State, Office of Intelligence and Research, "Major Factors Controlling the Size of the Chinese Communist Armies."

80. A student of the Republican period suggests that "the abject economic conditions caused the Chinese peasants in this period to view a military career not as a curse but as a welcome opportunity to escape from starvation and to lift themselves from an otherwise hopeless situation." Ch'i Hsi-sheng, *Warlord Politics in China*, p. 82.

81. Ch'i notes that "looting, burning, raping, and killing were regular features of the conduct of most Chinese soldiers. When a town was taken, the commander of the victorious army would sometimes deliberately stay out until the soldiers had a chance to loot systematically. Or he might simply declare a three-day period when the soldiers were allowed to act freely." *Ibid.*, p. 94.

82. David Wilkinson notes that in a revolutionary civil war "the success of one party demands the destruction of the other." *Revolutionary Civil War: The Elements of Victory and Defeat*, p. 86.

83. Gavan McCormack, *Chang Tso-lin in Northeast China*, p. 91.

84. Cited in Theda Skocpol, *States and Social Revolution*, p. 189.

85. Roy Hofheinz aptly comments: "The myth that because people's wars are

fought in the name of the people they are willingly supported by young men of fighting age would nevertheless not be easily dispelled." *The Broken Wave: The Chinese Peasant Movement, 1922–1928*, p. 260.

86. Ch'i Hsi-sheng, *Nationalist China at War*, pp. 161–164. Charles F. Romanus and Riley Sunderland, *Time Runs Out in CBI*, pp. 370–71.

87. Ilpyong Kim, *The Politics of Chinese Communism: Kiangsi under the Soviets*, p. 18; Griffin, *Chinese Communist Treatment of Counterrevolutionaries*, pp. 59–60.

88. Kataoka, *Resistance and Revolution*, p. 283. Writing about the civil war period, Jack Belden, a writer very sympathetic to the CCP, observed, "It should not be thought, however, that it was easy for a villager to avoid joining the army. The pressures were terrific." *China Shakes the World*, p. 342.

89. *Tpjp*, July 10, 1946, p. 1; December 18, 1946, p. 1.

90. Philip Kuhn, *Rebellion and Its Enemies in Late Imperial China: Militarization and Social Structure, 1796–1864*, p. 151.

91. Samuel Popkin, *The Rational Peasant: The Political Economy of Rural Society in Vietnam*, p. 42.

92. *Tpjp*, January 6, 1947, p. 1.

93. *Tpjp*, March 9, 1947, p. 2; January 14, 1948, p. 1.

94. *Tpjp*, August 11, 1947, p. 1.

95. *Tpjp*, July 20, 1947, p. 1; July 25, 1947, p. 1; June 18, 1947, p. 1; July 9, 1947, p. 1; January 4, 1948, p. 1, February 18, 1948, p. 1.

96. *Tpjp*, December 18, 1947, p. 1.

97. *Tpjp*, May 24, 1947, p. 4. See also Huang Tsao, *T'u-ti ho ch'iang* (Land and a Gun), pp. 1–27. This is a fictional account of a similar intra-family struggle over joining the army.

98. For the importance of family relations, see Judith Stacey, *Patriarchy and Socialist Revolution in China* (Berkeley: University of California Press, 1983), passim.

99. *Tpjp*, March 27, 1947, p. 4.

100. *Tpjp*, February 19, 1948, p. 2. Passed at the 38th regular meeting of NEAC Standing Committee, February 13, 1948.

101. *Tpjp*, February 2, 1948, p. 2. Harbin municipal regulations of January 28, 1948.

102. *Tpjp*, July 14, 1947, p. 2. Article on Hailun county.

103. *Tpjp*, August 11, 1949, cited in Genadii Astaf'ev, *Interventsiia SShA v Kitae i ee porazheniie* (U.S. Intervention in China and Its Defeat), p. 499, n. 3. Compare Gittings, *The Role of the Chinese Army*, p. 63.

104. Yeh Chien-ying, "Wei-ta ti chan-lüeh chieh-chan," (A Great Strategic Decisive Battle) *Hsing-huo liao-yuan* (A Single Spark Can Set a Prairie Fire), 10:20.

105. Donald Jordan writes: "Warlord recruiting meant sending patrols into the countryside to seize sturdy males wherever encountered. Shackled together in a line, the carriers were prodded along and handled like cattle. For a shelter, the coolies could count on little more than cattle cars, the dank holds of riverboats, or overcrowded unsanitary bamboo sheds. After a long day's haul, they had no blankets to cover their overheated bodies. For food, they could expect little more than a large communal pot of rice once a day." Donald A. Jordan, *The Northern Expedition: China's National Revolution of 1926–1928*, p. 191.

106. *Shengli pao*, December 1, 1946, reprinted in *Tpjp*, January 1, 1947, p. 1.

107. In contrast, in the T'aihang mountain region of North China during the resistance war, the CCP required only three days of labor service per month, and supposedly suspended these demands during the planting and harvest seasons. Thaxton, *China Turned Rightside Up*, p. 184.

108. *Tpjp*, April 6, 1947, p. 1; NEAC decision of February 13, 1948, *Tpjp*, February 19, 1948, p. 2.

109. *Tpjp*, April 3, 1948, p. 1; June 13, 1947, p. 2; July 5, 1947, p. 2.

110. *Tpjp*, February 1, 1947, p. 1; April 4, 1947, p. 2.

111. *Tpjp*, May 21, 1947, p. 1; July 5, 1947, p. 2.

112. *Tpjp*, April 4, 1947, p. 2; June 13, 1947, p. 2.

113. *Tpjp*, March 12, 1948, p. 1; March 30, 1948, p. 1.

114. *Tpjp*, January 30, 1948, p. 1; April 3, 1948, p. 1.

115. Jordan, *The Northern Expedition*, pp. 239–250.

116. *Tpjp*, December 11, 1947, p. 4.

117 *Tpjp*, January 16, 1947, p. 1; January 4, 1947, p. 2; January 16, 1947, p. 1.

118. *Tpjp*, January 4, 1947, p. 1; September 9, 1946, p. 2. One letter said, "Towels in the bag are for your sweat. Tiger balm is for stimulating your spirit. As we are unable to repair your broken clothes personally, we are sending you specially some needles and thread. Wishing you will soon smash Chiang Kai-shek's offensive." *Tpjp*, January 20, 1947, p. 1.

119. *Tpjp*, January 4, 1947, p. 1. The list follows: 1) respect government and local work personnel; 2) do not disobey government laws; 3) do not strike or curse the people; 4) do not strike or curse village heads and personnel; 5) don't take people's property; 6) borrow things only with permission; 7) don't interfere with production, assist in plowing and production; 8) respect people's customs and don't blame them for backwardness; 9) show care for the poor and help them improve their livelihood; 10) don't waste anything, help lighten the people's burden.

120. *Tpjp*, September 3, 1947, p. 1; April 15, 1947, p. 4.

121. Regis Debray, *Revolution Within the Revolution*, p. 111.

122. Suzanne Pepper, *Civil War in China*, p. 365.

123. Liu Shao-ch'i, *Collected Works of Liu Shao-ch'i, 1945–1957*, pp. 15 and 81–82.

124. Owen Lattimore wrote (in 1931) that the pejorative term *man-tzu*, an old North Chinese term for the southern barbarians, was used in Manchuria to refer to people from China proper. *Manchuria: Cradle of Conflict*, p. 62, n. 2.

125. Thus a pro-Communist propagandist writing in 1946 appealed to the provincial solidarity of Shantung-born residents as a basis of support for the Communists, citing the many Shantung men who served with distinction in the Communist movement. Mou Yuan, *Hsin-yen: hsien-chi tung-pei t'ung-pao* (Words from the Heart for My Northeast Compatriots), pp. 15–17.

126. Chou Chih-p'ing, "Tung-pei chieh-fang chan-cheng shih-ch'i ti Lin Piao t'ung-chih," p. 26.

127. Mao, *Selected Works*, 4:78. Mao returned to this theme in his December 28, 1945, directive to the Northeast Bureau (4:83).

128. Chang Yeh-chou, *Chieh-fang ti tung-pei* (The Liberated Northeast), p. 77.

129. Ch'en Yün, *Wen-hsüan*, p. 238.

130. Wetzel, "From the Jaws of Defeat," p. 189.

131. *Tpjp*, January 7, 1947, p. 1; *Ch'ün-chung kung-tso shou-ts'e* (Handbook of Mass Work), pp. 2–3.

132. *Tpjp*, September 27, 1946, p. 4; September 15, 1946, p. 4.

133. T'u Chien, *Chung-kuo jen-min chieh-fang chün chien-shih* (A Short History of the Chinese People's Liberation Army), p. 68.

134. *Tpjp*, April 29, 1947, p. 4.

135. *Tpjp*, July 2, 1947, p. 4.

136. *Tpjp*, January 10, 1947, p. 2; March 13, 1947, p. 2.

137. A partial list of these schools includes: Northeast Railroad Academy, the Chiamussu Motor Vehicle School, Northeast Pharmaceutical Academy, the Sungkiang Medical School, Chinese Medical Sciences University (Advanced Nurses School), the Suihua Health School. *Tpjp*, February 25, 1947, May 1, 1947, June 30, 1947, August 9, 1947, September 3, 1947, September 4, 1947, January 1, 1948, p. 4 in all cases.

138. *Tpjp*, February 5, 1947, February 26, 1947, May 20, 1947, July 18, 1947, July 21, 1947, p. 4 in all cases. Wetzel notes that many of these schools were located in Chiamussu, earning that city the sobriquet of "the new Yenan." "From the Jaws of Defeat," p. 225. See also Hsinhua, September 13, 1977, in Foreign Broadcast Information Service, *Daily Report, PRC* (September 14, 1977), E4, regarding the first PLA aviation academy.

139. *Tpjp*, October 25, 1947, p. 4.

140. Despite its mass character, the CCP periodically exhibited the sectarian attitude expressed in the Calvinist hymn, "We are the pure selected few / And all the rest are damned! / There's room enough in hell for you / We don't want Heaven crammed!" Cited in Raymond Challinor, *The Origins of British Bolshevism*, p. 35.

141. A. Doak Barnett, *China on the Eve of Communist Takeover*, pp. 40–51; Suzanne Pepper, "The Student Movement and the Chinese Civil War."

142. Not a few of the students in KMT-held south Manchurian cities were refugees from the Communist-held north.

143. Mou Yuan, *Hsin-yen*, pp. 28–29.

144. Northeast Bureau decree of January 15, 1948, *Tpjp*, January 24, 1948, p. 1.

145. Ch'en Yün, *Wen-hsüan*, p. 240.

146. See reports in *Tpjp*, June 1, 1947, p. 2; July 5, 1947, p. 2.

147. *Tpjp*, March 2, 1947, p. 2.

148. *Tpjp*, May 11, 1947, p. 1. The penalties were:
a) up to 10,000 yuan—up to three months in prison;
b) 10–100,000 yuan—three months to one year in prison;
c) 1000–200,000 yuan—one to three years in prison;
d) 200–400,000 yuan—three to five years in prison;
e) 400–600,000 yuan—five to ten years or an indeterminate period;
f) over 600,000 yuan—ten years or more up to and including the death penalty. These sums were figured at a price of 30 yuan per catty of kaoliang.

149. See, for example, a speech by Hokiang Province Party Committee Secretary Chang P'ing-chih, *Tpjp*, December 27, 1947, p. 1; also Edwin E. Moise, *Land Reform in China and North Vietnam: Consolidating the Revolution at the Village Level*, p. 52.

150. *Tpjp*, December 27, 1947, p. 1, for Hokiang; January 15, 1948, p. 2, for Sungkiang.

151. *Ibid.*

152. See, for example, *Tpjp*, November 12, 1947, p. 2.

5. THE POLITICAL ECONOMY OF CIVIL WAR

1. David Wilkinson, *Revolutionary Civil War: The Elements of Victory and Defeat*, p. 164, n. 167. As Wilkinson notes: "Even a semi-developed society will have income, capital and waste enough to reward quite substantially a determined elite bent on squeezing out as much as it can spend on the quest for power. The means of appropriation come readily to hand once wealth is located and a decision to have it is taken."

2. Ann Rasmussen Kinney, *Japanese Investment in Manchurian Manufacturing, Mining, Transportation and Communications, 1931–1945*, passim.

3. Even North China, a grain deficit area, had shipped grain to Japan during the war years. Lincoln Li, *The Japanese Army in North China 1937–1941: Problems of Political and Economic Control*, p. 179.

4. U.S. Dept. of State, Office of Intelligence and Research, OIR Report No. 4579, January 27, 1948, pp. 6–7, National Archives.

5. *Tung-pei jih-pao* (Northeast Daily—hereafter *Tpjp,*) October 27, 1947, p. 1, indicates a harvest of about 12 million tons.

6. *Tpjp*, October 27, 1947, p. 1. The target for increase in production was distributed by province as follows:

Heilungkiang	240,000	Nunkiang	185,000
Sungkiang	140,000	Kirin	100,000
Liaopei	70,000	Hokiang	60,000
Mutankiang	55,000	South Manchuria	50,000

7. *T'u-ti cheng-ts'e fa-ling hui-pien* (Compilation of Laws and Regulations Concerning Agrarian Policy), pp. 137–138.

8. Suzanne Pepper, *Civil War in China: The Political Struggle, 1945–1949*, p. 384.

9. *Tpjp*, February 3, 1948, p. 1.

10. See, for example, a report from Pinhsien, *Tpjp*, June 20, 1947, p. 1.

11. *Tpjp*, January 29, 1947, p. 1; February 13, 1947, p. 1.

12. *Tpjp*, February 20, 1947, p. 3; March 4, 1947, p. 2; March 12, 1947, p. 2; March 22, 1947, p. 2; April 13, 1947, p. 2; June 18, 1947, p. 2.

13. *Tpjp*, May 9, 1947, p. 1. This was a joint announcement by Harbin Garrison Commander Nieh Hua-t'ing, Political Commissar Chung Tzu-yün, and Mayor Liu Ch'eng-tung.

14. *Tpjp*, June 18, 1947, p. 2; June 20, 1947, p. 4; May 7, 1947, p. 2.

15. *Tpjp*, January 25, 1948, p. 4; March 25, 1947, p. 2.

16. *Tpjp*, April 6, 1948, p. 1, editorial reprint from *Harbin Jih-pao*, undated. See also Ch'en Yün, "Pa ts'ai-ching kung-tso t'i-tao chung-yao wei-chih shang lai" (Elevate Finance Policy to a Top Priority), *Wen-hsüan* (Selected Works), pp. 265–268. This is a very useful report.

17. *Tpjp*, July 14, 1947, p. 1; December 29, 1947, p. 1; January 8, 1948, p. 4.

18. Wang I-shou, "Chinese Migration and Population Change in Manchuria, 1900–1940," pp. 128, 113, 124.

19. Peter Schran, *Guerrilla Economy: The Development of the Shensi-Kansu-Ninghsia Border Region, 1937–1945*, passim; Mark Selden, *The Yenan Way in Revolutionary China*, passim.

20. Schran, *Guerrilla Economy*, pp. 92–93; Tetsuya Kataoka, *Resistance and Revolution in China: The Communists and the Second United Front*, pp. 252–253.

21. *Tpjp*, May 20, 1947, p. 2; April 23, 1947, p. 2.

22. Cigarettes sported such glamorous names as "Communication," "Production," and "Movement." Advertisement in *Tpjp*, June 2, 1947, p. 1.

23. *Tpjp*, January 13, 1947, p. 1.

24. *Tpjp*, April 28, 1947, p. 2.

25. Pepper, *Civil War in China*, p. 352.

26. *Tpjp*, February 21, 1947, p. 2; April 28, 1947, p. 2; June 1, 1947; p. 1; June 11, 1947, p. 1.

27. See, for example, Hokiang Province Directive on Preserving Urban Commerce and Industry during the Land Equalization Movement, *Tpjp*, February 7, 1948, p. 2. The directive is dated January 26, 1948.

28. Pepper, *Civil War in China*, pp. 370–371; *T'u-ti cheng-ts'e*, pp. 182–185 (Northeast Bureau and NEAC Directive Concerning Unified Administration of Public

Housing Property, August 8, 1949; "Pao-hu kuo-chia ts'ai-ch'an" (Protect State Property), *Tpjp*, editiorial in *Kuan-yu ch'eng-shih cheng-ts'e ti chi-ko wen-hsien* (Some Documents on Urban Policy), pp. 27–28.

    29. Pepper, *Civil War in China*, pp. 20–28; George Kerr, *Formosa Betrayed* (Boston: Houghton-Mifflin, 1965).

    30. *Tpjp*, February 2, 1948, p. 2. Harbin municipal regulations approved by NEAC.

    31. "Tung-pei-chü kuan-yü kung-ying ch'i-yeh chung chih-yuan wen-t'i ti chueh-ting" (Northeast Bureau Decision on Personnel in Publicly Operated Enterprises), August 1, 1948, *Kuan-yü ch'eng-shih cheng-ts'e*, pp. 30–36.

    32. Pepper, *Civil War in China*, pp. 354–357.

    33. NEAC directive of May 6, 1947, *Tpjp*, May 12, 1947, p. 1.

    34. *Tpjp*, February 7, 1947, p. 1; February 11, 1947, p. 1; February 12, 1947, p. 2; April 11, 1947, p. 1.

    35. *Tpjp*, February 21, 1947, p. 1; Samuel Popkin, *The Rational Peasant: The Political Economy of Rural Society in Vietnam*, p. 241.

    36. *Tpjp*, December 19, 1947, p. 1; December 17, 1949, p. 1; February 10, 1948, p. 1.

    37. *Tpjp*, October 26, 1947, p. l.

    38. *Ibid.*

    39. Wilkinson, *Revolutionary Civil War*, p. 66.

    40. *Tpjp*, October 26, 1947, p. 1.

    41. Wang I-shou, "Chinese Migration and Population Change," passim.

    42. I am indebted to Peter Schran for suggesting the term "vagrant" as an appropriate translation of *erh-liu-tzu*.

    43. Chandler Davidson, "On the 'Culture of Shiftlessness.' " The novelist Lao She had written: "The shiftlessness of the poor is the natural result of having their bitter toil amount to nothing." *Rickshaw*, p. 213. Now the Communist Party was saying that with the advent of revolutionary power, any social justification for idleness was removed.

    44. *Tpjp*, March 9, 1947, p. 2.

    45. *Tpjp*, February 1, 1947, p. 2; March 23, 1947, p. 4; April 22, 1947, p. 4.

    46. *Tpjp*, November 11, 1947, p. 2, referring to Hokiang province.

    47. *Tpjp*, November 25, 1947, p. 1.

    48. *Tpjp*, December 4, 1947, p. 2; December 12, 1947, p. 2.

    49. *Tpjp*, February 25, 1948, p. 2; April 3, 1948, p. 2.

    50. For some observations on traditional labor exchange and cooperation see, Ramon Myers, "Cooperation in Traditional Agriculture and Its Implications for Team Farming in the People's Republic of China."

    51. Ramon Myers, *The Chinese Peasant Economy: Agricultural Development in Hopei and Shantung, 1890–1949*, p. 92.

    52. *Tpjp*, March 20, 1947, p. 2, for traditional labor exchange in Mulan county. See also Popkin, *The Rational Peasant*, p. 97.

    53. As Samuel Popkin observes for the very similar situation in Vietnam, "Caution and distrust structures the forms of cooperation but does not prevent cooperative behavior . . . all the groups and associations that existed were specific and entailed precise and 'well-defined' obligations limited to small groups where maximum vigilance could be exercised without need for skilled leadership." *The Rational Peasant*, p. 97.

    54. *Tpjp*, February 23, 1947, p. 2.

    55. *Tpjp*, May 28, 1947, p. 2. The newspaper carried numerous such reports at this time (right after spring planting).

56. *Tpjp*, June 28, 1947, p. 2.

57. *Tpjp*, February 20, 1947, p. 3.

58. *Tpjp*, March 23, 1947, p. 1.

59. *Tpjp*, June 7, 1947, p. 2.

60. See the observations by Vivienne Shue, *Peasant China in Transition: The Dynamics of Development toward Socialism, 1949–1956*, p. 103; see also Jack Belden, *China Shakes the World*, p. 102. Belden reports that in one North China Communist area, government income tax in 1947 derived as follows: land tax, 70%; commodity taxes, 5%; corporation taxes, 10%; and miscellaneous levies, 15%. For Nationalist China's tax system, see Lloyd Eastman, *Seeds of Destruction: Nationalist China in War and Revolution*, pp. 71–82.

61. *Tpjp*, September 26, 1946, p. 1.

62. NEAC Regulations, January 23, 1948, *Tpjp*, February 1, 1948, p. 4. Anyone wishing to slaughter allegedly weak or useless draught animals needed to secure permission of the local government. A hide tax was also collected.

63. Northeast General Tax Administration Order, December 15, 1947, *Tpjp*, December 17, 1947, p. 4.

64. *Tpjp*, December 28, 1947, p. 4. Some other tax rates were: matches, 3 percent; soap, 4 percent; coal, 3 percent; cooking oil and coarse grains, 5 percent; fine grains, 10 percent.

65. Tax rates varied from 2 to 10 percent of sales. Certain enterprises including co-ops, publishers, transport companies, and the professions were exempted. *Tpjp*, April 19, 1947, p. 4.

66. *Tpjp*, January 29, 1948, p. 4; February 10, 1948, p. 4.

67. Myers, *The Chinese Peasant Economy*, p. 264; Hsi-sheng Ch'i, *Warlord Politics in China, 1916–1928*, p. 167.

68. *Tpjp*, January 11, 1947, p. 1.

69. *Tpjp*, August 8, 1947, p. 1. This was in addition to the mobilization of volunteer soldiers, *min-fu*, medical personnel, and carts.

6. REVOLUTION IN THE NORTHEAST COUNTRYSIDE

1. Among many books on this subject, the following present the range of issues and views: Roy M. Hofheinz, *The Broken Wave: The Chinese Peasant Movement, 1922–1928*; Suzanne Pepper, *Civil War in China: The Political Struggle, 1945–1949*; Elizabeth J. Perry, *Rebels and Revolutionaries in North China 1845–1945*; Ralph Thaxton, *China Turned Rightside Up: Revolutionary Legitimacy in the Peasant World*; Chalmers Johnson, *Peasant Nationalism and Communist Power*; Lucien Bianco, *Origins of the Chinese Revolution, 1915–1949*; William Hinton, *Fanshen: A Documentary of Revolution in a Chinese Village*; Eric R. Wolf, *Peasant Wars of the Twentieth Century*.

2. Thaxton, *China Turned Rightside Up*, is an unfortunate example of this tendency.

3. Mao Tse-tung, "Report on an Investigation of the Peasant Movement in Hunan," *Selected Works* (Peking: Foreign Languages Press, 1967) 1:23–59.

4. Thaxton, *China Turned Rightside Up*, pp. 18, 93, 100, 129.

5. This is a theme in the following works, among many others: Joel Migdal, *Peasants, Politics, and Revolution: Pressures toward Political and Social Change in the Third World*; James C. Scott, *The Moral Economy of the Peasant: Rebellion and Subsistence in Southeast Asia*; Samuel L. Popkin, *The Rational Peasant: The Political Economy of Rural Society in Vietnam*.

6. Edwin Moise is one of the very few scholars who explicitly recognizes the importance of time as a factor in the Communist revolution. He writes: "CCP experience

both before 1937 and after 1945 indicates that the peasants would have accepted and supported a radical land reform; the problem was that they would have done so rather slowly. The CCP would have had first to arouse the peasants to want to overthrow the traditional elite and then to organize them and give them the self-confidence actually to do so. Only after this would they have become a political force, a major asset in the expansion of Communist power." *Land Reform in China and North Vietnam: Consolidating the Revolution at the Village Level*, p. 40.

    7. Kang Chao, *The Economic Development of Manchuria: The Rise of a Frontier Economy*, p. 9.

    8. These are the more precise and restrictive equivalents of the CCP's terminology which will be used on occasion in the discussion below for the sake of convenience, viz, landless laborers, poor peasants, middle peasants, rich peasants, and landlords.

    9. For example, in Liaoning from one-half to two-thirds of those households classified as rich peasants were tenant farmers rather than rentier-farmers or owner-cultivators. *Tung-pei jih-pao*, November 15, 1947, p. 2.

    10. A Japanese estimate from 1931 was that in North Manchuria fewer than 3 percent of the population held 51 percent of the cultivated land whereas 63 percent of all the peasant households were landless. (These figures were provided to me by Herbert P. Bix.) The Communist chairman of the Hei-lungkiang provincial government in 1945 claimed that 60-80 percent of the peasants were landless with 60 percent of these being tenants. Chou Erh-fu. *Tung-pei heng-tuan mien* (Cross-Section of the Northeast), p. 134.

    11. Calculated from Ramon Myers, "Farm Production and Marketing in a Rural Economy of Surplus Land: Northeast China during the Republican Period," pp. 231–232.

    12. *Tpjp*, August 15, 1947, p. 2.

    13. Ramon Myers, "Socioeconomic Changes in Villages of Manchuria during the Ch'ing and Republican Periods: Some Preliminary Findings."

    14. Myers, "Farm Production and Marketing," pp. 276–278.

    15. Cited in Migdal, *Peasants, Politics, and Revolution*, p. 74.

    16. *Tpjp*, August 15, 1947, p. 2; *Ch'ün-Chung Weekly* (Hong Kong), (January 1948), 50:12–13, cited in John Wong, *Land Reform in the People's Republic of China: Institutional Transformation in Agriculture*, p. 57, n. 14.

    17. For Japanese land purchases in Manchuria see *Tung-pei t'ung-chi chien pien* (Concise Edition of Northeast Statistics), table 27, p. 17-B.

    18. Andrew J. Grajdanzev, "Manchuria as a Region of Colonization," pp. 14 and 7–8. Stavis suggests that perhaps 30 percent of agricultural tool stock was lost during the anti-Japanese war, and that it took until 1954 to restore these losses. However, this percentage may have been lower for Manchuria where relatively little fighting occurred between 1937 and 1945. Benedict Stavis, *The Politics of Agricultural Mechanization in China*, p. 38.

    19. As Kataoka shows, this "moderate" policy was actually more radical in practice than it appeared to be at first blush. Tetsuya Kataoka, *Resistance and Revolution in China: The Communists and the Second United Front*, pp. 116–135.

    20. Mao, *Selected Works*, 4:71–72. Rent reduction, Mao said, was to come as a result of mass struggles in which excesses were unavoidable (and could be corrected later) rather than as a favor from the government.

    21. Chou Erh-fu, *Tung-pei heng-tuan mien*, p. 52. This is unquestionably an exaggeration as the percentage of tenants did not approach the figure given.

    22. Chou Erh-fu, *Sung-hua-chiang shang ti feng-yün* (Events Along the Sungari River), pp. 93–94. In order to prevent reconcentration of land and non-use it was stipulated

that the land had to be tilled, could not be rented out (with the exception of households without labor power), and could not be sold without permission of the local government and then only for a special reason (p. 95).

23. *Tpjp,* January 12, 1947, p. 1.

24. In various colonial countries—e.g., Burma, the Philippines, Indonesia—collaboration did not have the same stigma which attached to it elsewhere, of course.

25. For reports of such trials see *Tpjp,* June 30, 1946, p. 1; for the Kiangsi precedent see Patricia E. Griffin, *The Chinese Communist Treatment of Counterrevolutionaries,* p. 57.

26. *Tpjp,* July 16, 1946, p. 2.

27. For a successful example, see *Tpjp,* July 16, 1946, p. 1; for an unsuccessful example see *Tpjp,* August 5, 1946, p. 1.

28. *Tpjp,* October 4, 1947, p. 2.

29. Liu Yun-an, *Demokraticheskoe i sotsialisticheskoe stroitel'stvo v Severo-Vosto-chnom Kitae* (Democratic and Socialist Construction in Northeast China), p. 54.

30. It was also plausibly argued that those landlords and rich peasants who had prospered under the Japanese were ipso facto collaborators. *Chung-kuo chü-ta pien-hua ti i-nien* (A Year of Great Changes in China), p. 33.

31. Ch'en Yün, *Wen-hsüan* (Selected Works), pp. 237–238.

32. Chou Chih-p'ing, "Comrade Lin Piao in the Period of Liberation War in the Northeast," *Survey of China Mainland Magazines,* pp. 27 and 28. There is an obvious suggestion in these slogans of a reluctance among some cadres to leave the urban amenities of a city such as Harbin for the difficult and spartan task of leading the land reform. Other sources mention the figure of 12,000 as the number of cadres sent to the countryside to carry out land reform in 1946. Liu Yun-an, *Demokraticheskoe i sotsialisticheskoe stroitel'stvo,* pp. 54–55.

33. *Tpjp,* September 28, 1946, p. 1.

34. Lin Piao, "I-chiu-ssu-ch'i nien ti jen-wu" (The Tasks for 1947), *Chung-kuo chü-ta pien-hua ti i nien,* pp. 197–198.

35. Liu Pai-yu, *Shih-tai ti yin-hsiang* (Contemporary Impressions), pp. 79–81.

36. *Tpjp,* October 5, 1947, p. 1.

37. *Tpjp,* January 14, 1947, p. 2; February 9, 1947, p. 2. Moise comments: "the land reform cadres did not know how to teach the peasants about government policies, did not have the time to do so, or simply did not trust the peasants, and therefore they did everything themselves. The peasants became essentially passive, and sometimes even disapproving spectators." *Land Reform in China and North Vietnam,* p. 16. See also his perceptive comments on p. 55.

38. *Tpjp,* March 9, 1947, p. 1; January 25, 1947, p. 2; January 12, 1947, p. 1.

39. See, for example, *Tpjp,* August 10, 1946, p. 1.

40. *Tpjp,* February 15, 1947, p. 2. Writing about North China at around the same time, Jack Belden commented in a similar vein: "By elevating those who were most active in the land reform campaigns, they (the CCP) also gave ambitious hooligans the chance to take power." *China Shakes the World,* p. 88.

41. Angus McDonald notes a similar phenomenon among local elites in the 1920s during the establishment of peasant associations in Hunan. Angus W. McDonald Jr., *The Urban Origins of Rural Revolution: Elites and the Masses in Hunan Province, China, 1911–1927,* p. 272.

42. Editorial in *Tpjp,* December 8, 1947, p. 1.

43. Isabel and David Crook suggest that the first cohort of revolutionary cadres was rather easily corrupted. *Ten Mile Inn: Mass Movement in a Chinese Village,* p. 133.

44. See, for example, report by the Ch'angpai County Party Committee, *Tpjp*, August 21, 1947, p. 2; Sungkiang Provincial Party Committee, *Tpjp*, January 6, 1947, p. 1. For similar reports from South China during the land reform in 1950, see Geoffrey Shillinglaw, "Land Reform and Peasant Mobilization in Southern China, 1947–1950," pp. 132–133.

45. Migdal, *Peasants, Politics, and Revolution*, p. 233.

46. In the fury of the land reform campaign, Party propaganda undoubtedly exaggerated the extent of this phenomenon in order to heighten cadre vigilance, but there is no reason to doubt it was widespread.

47. So-called bad roots were further divided into: a) old roots—big landlords and big "bad eggs"; b) little roots—small landlords and small "bad eggs"; c) parasitical roots—agents of the landlords and the "bad eggs." *Tpjp*, February 8, 1947, p. 2.

48. See, for example, the report from Lanhsi county, *Tpjp*, March 9, 1947, p. 2.

49. For example, *Tpjp*, February 20, 1947, p. 3, a report on Chih-ta village in Payen county.

50. *Tpjp*, July 14, 1947, p. 2.

51. Philip A. Kuhn, *Rebellion and Its Enemies in Late Imperial China: Militarization and Social Structure, 1796–1864*, p. 32.

52. *Tpjp*, July 2, 1947, p. 1; see also *Tpjp*, March 8, 1947, p. 2.

53. *Tpjp*, January 17, 1947, p. 1; January 31, 1947, p. 2.

54. See the report from Lunkiang county in *Tpjp*, April 27, 1947, p. 2.

55. *Tpjp*, February 15, 1948, p. 1.

56. *Tpjp*, January 9, 1947, p. 2.

57. By the summer of 1947 in the campaign to "cut the feudal tail" *(ko feng-chien wei-pa)* body searches were used extensively to discover gold, jewelry, etc., that "feudal elements" were hiding on their persons. *Tpjp*, July 6, 1947, p. 2.

58. Myers, "Farm Production and Marketing," p. 270.

59. Shillinglaw notes that rich peasants gave out almost 50 percent of cash loans in Kiangsi between 1941 and 1947. "Land Reform and Peasant Mobilization in Southern China," p. 131.

60. Landless and land-poor households had less labor power on the average than households with substantial land holdings. Myers, "Farm Production and Marketing," pp. 264–265.

61. *Tpjp*, March 21, 1947, p. 2; June 11, 1947, p. 1; March 30, 1947, p. 1.

62. *Tpjp*, February 17, 1947, p. 2; March 1, 1947, p. 1; May 3, 1947, p. 1.

63. *Tpjp*, February 28, 1947, p. 2; January 20, 1947, p. 1; January 9, 1947, p. 2; February 21, 1947, p. 1.

64. Cited in Robert V. Daniels, *The Conscience of the Revolution: Communist Opposition in Soviet Russia*, p. 37.

65. For a frank and vivid description of the preparations for village-level struggles see *Tpjp*, February 22, 1947, p. 2. For a similar report of how work teams choreographed struggle meetings during the Four Cleanups campaign of the early 1960s, see Anita Chan et al., *Chen Village*, pp. 57–59.

66. *Tpjp*, June 27, 1947, p. 2.

67. *Tpjp*, September 1, 1947, p. 2; September 2, 1947, p. 1; July 13, 1947, p. 2; June 20, 1947, p. 2.

68. *Tpjp*, December 8, 1947, p. 1; June 20, 1947, p. 2.

69. *Tpjp*, August 21, 1947, p. 2; September 22, 1947, pp. 1–2 (editorial).

70. *Tpjp*, September 12, 1947, pp. 1–2; December 15, 1947, p. 1. Moise

accurately observes: "The reform that the CCP was trying to bring to the villages during the winter of 1947–48 was so egalitarian as to appear profoundly unnatural not only to village elites but to the poor. When ordinary peasants were told that they should take not only wealth but also political power into their own hands, the initial reaction of many was that this was impossible and that if they tried they would incur the enmity of the elite by their presumptuous effort; they would do themselves more harm than good." Moise, *Land Reform in China and North Vietnam*, pp. 59–60.

71. For the draft law, see *T'u-ti cheng-ts'e fa-ling hui-pien* (Compilation of Laws and Regulations Concerning Agrarian Policy), pp. 1–5; see also Jane L. Price, "Chinese Communist Land Reform and Peasant Mobilization, 1946–1948."

72. *Tpjp*, December 6, 1947, p. 1.

73. *Tpjp*, November 1, 1947, p. 1.

74. *Tpjp*, January 8, 1948, p. 1.

75. *Tpjp*, November 3, 1947, p. 4; November 27, 1947, p. 2 (reprint of undated Liaotung jih-pao editorial); and October 16, 1947, p. 2.

76. See Chang Chi-chung, "Wo tsai Chao-yuan ssu-nien" (My Four Years in Chaoyuan), *Hsing-huo: ko-ming hui-i lu* (Sparks: Revolutionary Reminiscences), 1:123.

77. Anita Chan, et al., *Chen Village*, p. 118.

78. *Tpjp*, December 27, 1947, p. 1.

79. *Tpjp*, September 1, 1947, p. 2. Moise notes: "The mass struggle, once started, often went to extremes. This extremism was encouraged by the cadres to some extent, especially in the years 1945–1947. Some felt that the best way for the peasants to show that they had really escaped the psychological bonds of the old order was for them to beat or kill the landlords." *Land Reform in China and North Vietnam*, p. 50.

80. Chang Chi-chung, "Wo tsai Chao-yuan ssu-nien," p. 123.

81. Ch'en Yün, *Wen-hsüan*, p. 244.

82. *Tpjp*, January 25, 1948, p. 1; December 18, 1947, p. 1; February 8, 1948, p. 2.

83. *Tpjp*, January 4, 1948, p. 1.

84. *T'u-ti cheng-ts'e fa-ling hui-pien*, pp. 10–31.

85. *Tpjp*, February 15, 1948, p. 1.

86. *T'u-ti cheng-ts'e fa-ling hui-pien*, pp. 40–59.

87. *Tpjp*, February 15, 1948, p. 1.

88. *T'u-ti cheng-ts'e fa-ling hui-pien*, pp. 131–136.

89. *Tpjp*, June 2, 1947, p. 1; *Chung-kuo chü-ta pien-hua ti i nien*, p. 314.

90. Lin Feng, "Kuan-yü san-nien lai ti cheng-fu kung-tso pao-kao" (Report Concerning Government Work During the Past Three Years), *Tung-pei jen-min tai-piao hui-i chung-yao wen-hsien* (Important Documents of the Northeast People's Representative Conference), p. 30.

91. Lin Feng, "Tung-pei chieh-fang ch'ü ti cheng-ch'üan chien-she" (Political Construction in the Northeast Liberated Area), *Ch'ün Chung* (The Masses), (September 18, 1947), 34:7–8.

92. Nanniwan was the district near Yenan famous for its economically self-sufficient troops.

93. Gavan McCormack, *Chang Tso-lin in Northeast China*; Ronald Suleski, "Manchuria under Chang Tso-lin;" Chong-sik Lee, *Counterinsurgency in Manchuria: The Japanese Experience, 1931–1940*.

94. I have found the following to be among the more stimulating recent works on peasant politics: James C. Scott, *The Moral Economy of the Peasant: Rebellion and Subsistence in Southeast Asia*; Migdal, *Peasants, Politics, and Revolution*; Samuel L. Popkin, *The Rational*

Peasant: The Political Economy of Rural Society in Vietnam; Jeffrey Race, "Toward an Exchange Theory of Revolution."
95. Migdal, *Peasants, Politics, and Revolution*, pp. 232–233 and 211; Popkin, *The Rational Peasant*, p. 262.
96. Race, "Toward an Exchange Theory of Revolution," passim.
97. Popkin, *The Rational Peasant*, p. 24.
98. Race, "Toward an Exchange Theory of Revolution," pp. 182–183; Popkin, *The Rational Peasant*, p. 262.
99. Migdal, *Peasants, Politics, and Revolution*, pp. 263–264.
100. For evidence on this point based on interviews with Chinese POWs from the Korean War, see Allen S. Whiting, "The New Chinese Communist," pp. 597–600.

7. CONCLUSIONS

1. U.S. Dept. of State, *United States Relations with China: with Special Reference to the Period 1944–1949*, p. 893. This was said during an interview with A. T. Steele of the *New York Herald Tribune*, October 31, 1948.
2. Akira Iriye writes: "The United States chose not to engage the Soviet Union in a cold war in this region [China] during these years. *There was a cold war perception but no cold war.*" Akira Iriye, "Was There a Cold War in Asia?" p. 14.
3. "Notes of a Conversation with Mr. Dean Acheson, Acting Secretary of State, 5:15 P.M. March 11 [1947[at the State Department," pp. 5–6. Wellington Koo papers.
4. "Notes of an Audience with President Harry S. Truman, November 24, 1948, at the White House," Wellington Koo papers.
5. Lloyd Eastman, *Seeds of Destruction: Nationalist China in War and Revolution*, pp. 223–224.
6. David Wilkinson, *Revolutionary Civil War: The Elements of Victory and Defeat*, p. 27.
7. U.S. Dept. of State, *FRUS 1946*, 10:569.
8. Richard Little, *Intervention: External Involvement in Civil Wars*, p. 8.
9. *Ibid.*, p. 32.
10. Tong Te-kong and Li Tsung-jen, *The Memoirs of Li Tsung-jen*, pp. 500–501.
11. This point is made very well by Lloyd Eastman, *Seeds of Destruction*, p. 85. See also Theda Skocpol, *States and Social Revolution: A Comparative Analysis of France, Russia and China*, p. 262. However, Skocpol suggests that with CCP assistance the peasants acquired "an organizational autonomy and solidarity" they had not previously possessed, and were therefore able "to become (within the villages) a class for themselves," and to proceed to attack landlords. This is an unfounded Marxist gloss. The evidence from Northeast China (as well as civil war era studies of North China villages such as those by the Crooks and by William Hinton) convincingly demonstrates that peasant organization at the village level was an artifact of CCP policy, possessing solidarity to be sure, but lacking in autonomy, and harnessed to higher level objectives. See also Moise, *Land Reform in China and North Vietnam*, p. 9.
12. Elizabeth J. Perry, *Rebels and Revolutionaries in North China, 1845–1945*, p. 253.
13. Migdal notes: "The key to the power of lords on every level lay in their degree of monopoly over essential rural resources and the external forces they could call in to protect that monopoly." Joel S. Migdal, *Peasants, Politics, and Revolution: Pressures toward Political and Social Change in the Third World*, p. 41.
14. Chong-Sik Lee, *Counterinsurgency in Manchuria: The Japanese Experience, 1931–1940.*

15. Skocpol writes that "within the local rural communities, the gentry land-lords and other economically dominant elements became at once more entrenched and more vulnerable. They were vulnerable especially to attacks from an extra-locally organized force that might be determined to ally with the restive peasantry rather than with the local dominant classes." *States and Social Revolution,* p. 241.

16. Giovanni Sartori, "Concept Misinformation in Comparative Politics," p. 1,050.

17. See the comments along these lines by Vivienne Shue, *Peasant China in Transition: The Dynamics of the Development toward Socialism, 1949–1956,* p. 6.

BIBLIOGRAPHY

Unpublished Sources

Grow, Roy F. "Soviet Politics and Chinese Communist Strategies: The Struggle for Manchuria, 1945–1946." A paper presented to the Workshop on Chinese Foreign Policy, University of Michigan, August, 1976.

Hsiung Shih-hui Papers. Butler Library, Special Collections, Columbia University.

Lacy, Creighton. "Protestant Missionaries in Communist China." Ph.D. dissertation, Yale University, 1953.

Min-chu lien-chün cheng-kung-tui. *Kao ch'ang-ch'un shih ch'ing-nien shu* (Letter to Changchun Youth). Bureau of Investigation, Taipei, Taiwan.

Min-chu lien-chün cheng-kung-tui. *Kao kuo-min-tang-yuan shu* (Letter to Kuomintang Members). Bureau of Investigation, Taipei, Taiwan.

Stauffer, Robert Burton Jr. "Manchuria as a Political Entity: Government and Politics of a Major Region of China." Ph.D. dissertation, University of Minnesota, 1955.

Suleski, Ronald S. "Manchuria under Chang Tso-lin." Ph.D. dissertation, University of Michigan, 1974.

Tung-pei chü. "Kuan-yu ch'ien tung-pei ti-hsia tang tsu-chih chih tang-yuan yu k'ang-jih lien kan-pu ti chueh-ting" (Decision [of the Northeast Bureau] Concerning Party Members and Anti-Japanese Cadres of the Former Underground Party Organizations). January 1, 1948. Bureau of Investigation, Taipei, Taiwan.

United States Department of State, Office of Intelligence and Research, Division of Research for Far East. "Interrogation Reports on Soviet Removals of Japanese Industrial Facilities from Manchuria." OIR No. 4727, October 8, 1948. Diplomatic Branch, National Archives, Washington, D. C.

United States Department of State, Office of Intelligence and Research, Division of Research for Far East. "Major Factors Controlling the Size of the Chinese Communist Armies." OIR No. 4387, June 25, 1947. Diplomatic Branch, National Archives, Washington, D.C.

Urken, Arnold B. "Coalitions in the Chinese Civil War." Ph.D. dissertation, New York University, 1973.

Wang I-shou. "Chinese Migration and Population Change in Manchuria, 1900–1940." Ph.D. dissertation, University of Minnesota, 1971.

War Department, Strategic Services Unit YV 1201. "Manchuria: Soviet Demands." March 12, 1946. Diplomatic Branch, National Archives, RG 226, Box 362.

Wellington Koo Papers. Butler Library, Special Collections, Columbia University.

Wetzel, Carroll R., Jr. "From the Jaws of Defeat: Lin Piao and the 4th Field Army in Manchuria." Ph.D. dissertation, George Washington University, 1972.

Winckler, Edwin A. "Military Outcomes in the Chinese Civil War: Organizational and Spatial Models." A paper prepared for delivery at the 1976 Annual Meeting of the American Political Science Association, September 2–5, 1976.

Published Sources

Anuchin, V. A. *Geograficheskie ocherki Manchzhurii* (Geographic features of Manchuria). Moscow: Gosudarstvennoe izdatel'stvo geograficheskoi literatury, 1948.

Astaf'ev, Genadii V. *Interventsiia SShA v Kitae i ee porazheniie* (U.S. Intervention in China and Its Defeat). Moscow: Gosudarstvennoe isdatel'stvo politicheskoi literatury, 1958.

Bain, H. Foster. "Manchuria: A Key Area." *Foreign Affairs* (October 1946), 25 (1):910: 106–117.

Barbey, Daniel E. *MacArthur's Amphibious Navy.* Annapolis, Md.: U.S. Naval Institute Press, 1969.

Barnett, A. Doak. *China on the Eve of Communist Takeover.* New York: Praeger, 1963.

Beal, John Robinson. *Marshall in China.* Garden City, N.Y.: Doubleday, 1970.

Belden, Jack. *China Shakes the World.* New York: Monthly Review Press, 1970.

Beloff, Max. *Soviet Policy in the Far East, 1944–1951.* London: Oxford University Press, 1953.

Bianco, Lucien. *Origins of the Chinese Revolution, 1915–1949.* Stanford: Stanford University Press, 1971.

Blum, John M., ed. *The Price of Vision: The Diary of Henry A. Wallace, 1942–1946.* Boston: Houghton-Mifflin, 1973.

Bogush, E. Iu. *Mif ob 'eksporte revoliutsii' i Sovetskaia vneshniaia politika* (The Myth About the Export of Revolution and Soviet Foreign Policy). Moscow: Izdatel'stvo mezhdunarodnye otnosheniia, 1965.

Bohlen, Charles E. with the editorial assistance of Robert H. Phelps. *Witness to History 1929–1969.* New York: Norton, 1973.

Boorman, Howard L. and Richard Howard, eds. *Biographical Dictionary of Republican China.* New York: Columbia University Press, vol. 1, 1967, vol. 2, 1968.

Borg, Dorothy and Waldo Heinrichs, eds. *Uncertain Years: Chinese-American Relations, 1947–1950.* New York: Columbia University Press, 1980.

Borisov, O. *Sovetskii Soiuz i Man'chzhurskaia revoliutsionnaia baza, 1945–1949* (The Soviet Union and the Manchurian Revolutionary Base). Moscow: Mysl, 1975.

Borisov, O. and B. T. Koloskov. *Sovetskie-Kitaiskie otnosheniia, 1945–1970* (Soviet-Chinese Relations, 1945–1970). Moscow: Nauka, 1971.

Borodin, B. A. *Pomoshch' SSSR Kitaiskomu narodu v antiiaponskoi voine 1937–1941 (Aid from the USSR to the Chinese people during the anti-Japanese war 1937–1941). Moscow: Mysl, 1965.*

Brugger, William. Democracy and Organisation in the Chinese Industrial Enterprise (1948–1953). Cambridge: Cambridge University Press, 1976.

Buhite, Russel D. " 'Major Interests': American policy Toward China, Taiwan, and Korea, 1945–1950." *Pacific Historical Review* (August 1978), 3:425–451.

Buhite, Russel D. *Patrick J. Hurley and American Relations with China.* Ithaca, N.Y.: Cornell University Press, 1973.

Byrnes, James F. *All in One Lifetime.* New York: Harper, 1958.

Byrnes, James F. *Speaking Frankly.* New York: Harper, 1947.

Challinor, Raymond. *The Origins of British Bolshevism.* London: Croom Helm, 1977.

Chan, Anita et al. *Chen Village.* Berkeley: University of California Press, 1984.

Chang, Carsun. *Third Force in China.* New York: Bookman, 1952.

Chang, Chan. *Tung-pei san-yueh chi* (Three Months in the Northeast). N.p., 1946.

Chang Chi-chung, "Wo tsai Chao-yuan ssu-nien." (My Four Years In Chao-yuan) In *Hsing-huo: ko-ming hui-i lu* (Sparks: Revolutionary Reminiscences), pp. 113–125. Shenyang: Liaoning jen-min ch'u-pan she, 1981.

Chang Ch'i-yun, ed. *K'ang-jih chan-shih* (A Battle History of the Anti-Japanese War of Resistance). Taipei: Kuo-fang yen-chiu yuan, 1966.

Chang Yeh-chou. *Chieh-fang ti tung-pei* (The Liberated Northeast). N.p.: T'ieh-liu shu-tien, 1946.

Chao Chia-hsiang. *Chiang-chün shih wen chi* (Historical Works of the General). Taipei, 1960.

Chao Kuo-chun. *Agrarian Policy of the Chinese Communist Party 1921–1959.* Bombay: Asia Publishing House, 1960.

Chao Kuo-chun. *A Historical Survey of the Land Policy of the Chinese Communists, 1921–1950.* Cambridge, Mass.: East Asian Research Center, 1954.

Chassin, Lionel Max. *The Communist Conquest of China: A History of the Civil War, 1945–1949.* Cambridge: Harvard University Press, 1965.

Ch'en Shao-hsiao. *Kuan-nei liao-tung i chü ch'i* (The Chessboard from Inside the Pass to Liaotung). Hong Kong: Chih-ch'eng ch'u-pan she, 1964.

Ch'en Yün. *Wen-hsüan* (Selected Works). Peking: Jen-min ch'u-pan she, 1984.

Cheng-chih hsieh-shang hui-i tzu-liao (Materials on the Political Consultative Conference). Chengtu: Ssu-ch'uan jen-min ch'u-pan she, 1981.

Cheng Tien-fong. *A History of Sino-Russian Relations.* Washington, D.C.: Public Affairs Press, 1957.

Chern, Kenneth S. *Dilemma in China: America's Policy Debate, 1945.* Hamden: Archon Books, 1980.

Ch'i Hsi-sheng. *Nationalist China at War: Military Defeats and Political Collapse, 1937–1945.* Ann Arbor: University of Michigan Press, 1982.

Ch'i Hsi-sheng. *Warlord Politics in China, 1916–1928.* Stanford: Stanford University Press, 1976.

Chi Yun-lung. *Yang Ching-yu ho k'ang-lien ti-i lu-chün* (Yang Ching-yu and the First Route Army of the United Army). N.p., 1946.

Chiang Ching-kuo, "My Encounter with Stalin." In Dun J. Li, ed. *Modern China: From Mandarin to Commissar,* pp. 296–307. New York : Scribners, 1978.

Chiang Ching-kuo. *Wo ti fu-ch'in* (My Father). Taipei, 1956.

Chiang Chün-chang, "Sung Tzu-wen mo-ssu-k'o t'an-p'an chuei chi" (Recollections of Sung Tzu-wen's Negotiations in Moscow). In *Chung-kuo i chou* (March 24, 1952 100:14–16.

Chiang Kai-shek. *Soviet Russia in China: A Summing Up at Seventy.* New York: Farrar, Straus and Cudahy, 1957.

Chieh-chüeh tung-pei wen-t'i ti t'u-ching (The Path to Solving the Northeast Question). N.p.: Liaotung chien-kuo shu she, n.d.

Chieh-fang le ti tung-pei (The Liberated Northeast). N.p.: Lu-chung hsin-hau shu-tien, 1945.

Ch'ien Tuan-sheng. *The Government and Politics of China.* Cambridge: Harvard University Press, 1961.

Chin T'ieh-ch'un, "Chuang-chien pei-man ken-chu-ti ti i-tuan hui i" (Reminiscences of Founding the North Manchurian Base Area). In *Hsing-huo: ko-ming hui-i lu, pp. 101–112.* Shenyang: Liaoning jen-min ch'u-pan she, 1981.

China Handbook Editorial Committee. China Handbook 1950 New York: Rockport Press, 1950.

Chinese Delegation to the United Nations. *China Presents Her Case to the United Nations.* New York, 1949.

Chinese Ministry of Information. *China Handbook 1937–1945.* New York: MacMillan, 1947.

Chinese Press Review. Mukden: U.S. Consulate General, 1947–1948.

Chorley, Katherine. *Armies and the Art of Revolution.* 1943; rpt., Boston: Beacon Press, 1973.

Chou Chih-p'ing, "Tung-pei chieh-fang chan-cheng shih-ch'i ti Lin Piao t'ung-chih" (Comrade Lin Piao in the Period of Liberation War in the Northeast). In *Hung-ch'i p'iao–p'iao* (The Red Flag Waves). vol. 14. Translated in *Survey of China Mainland Magazines* (July 11, 1960).

Chou Erh-fu. *Sung-hua chiang-shang ti feng-yün* (Events Along the Sungari River), Hong Kong, 1947.

Chou Erh-fu. *Tung-pei heng-tuan-mien* (Cross-Section of the Northeast). Harbin, 1946.

Chou Li-po. *The Hurricane.* Peking: Foreign Languages Press, 1955.

Chou Pao-chung, "Chi tung-pei k'ang-jih yu-chi chan-chang" (Remembering Northeast Anti-Japanese Guerrilla Warfare). In *Hsing-hou liao-yuan*, 4:368–377. Peking: Jen-min wen-hsueh ch'u-pan she, 1961.

Chu Chi-fu. "Nothing to Mobilize." *China Digest* (July 15, 1947), pp. 4–5.

Chu Ch'i-p'ing. *Cheng Tung-kuo fang-wen chi* (Notes on Visiting Cheng Tung-kuo). Hong Kong: Ta Kung pao, n.d.

Chu Chih-yuan, "Cheng-ch'üan ch'u-ch'ien ti nien'tai" (The Initial Period of Establishing Political Power). In *Hsing-huo: ko-ming hui-i lu*, pp. 89–100. Shenyang: Liaoning jen-min ch'u-pan she, n.d.

Chu Teh et al. *Chung-kuo kung-ch'an tang tui tung-pei ti t'ai-tu* (The CCP's Attitude Toward the Northeast Question). N.p.: Hsin-hua shu-tien, 1946?

Ch'ün-Chung (The Masses). Hong Kong, 1947.

Ch'ün-Chung kung-tso shou-ts'e (Handbook of Mass Work). N.p.: April 1947.

Ch'ung-ch'ing t'an-p'an tzu-liao (Materials on the Chungking Negotiations). Chengtu: Ssu-ch'uan jen-min ch'u-pan she, 1980.

Chung-kung tung-pei chung-yang chü. *Pao-hu hsin shou-fu ch'ü ti chih-shih* (Directive on Protecting Newly Recovered Areas). N.p., June 10, 1948.

Chung-kung tung-pei chung-yang chü, *Tung-pei chih-shih fentzu ti chueh-ting* (Resolution Concerning Northeast Intellectuals). N.p., 1948.

Chung-kuo chü-ta pien-hua ti i-nien (A Year of Great Changes in China). N.p., 1947.

Chung-yang she-chi chü tung-pei tiao-ch'a wei-yuan-hui, *Wei-man hsien-chuang* (Contemporary Manchukuo). N.p., March 1945.

Clubb, O. Edmund. "Manchuria in the Balance, 1945–1946." *Pacific Historical Review* (November 1957), 26:(4):377–389.

Clubb, O. Edmund. "Military Debacle in Manchuria." *Army Quarterly and Defence Journal* (January 1958), 75(2):221–232.

Crook, Isabel and David Crook. *Ten Mile Inn: Mass Movement in a Chinese Village*. New York: Pantheon, 1979.

Crozier, Brian. *The Man Who Lost China*. New York: Scribner's, 1976.

Current Background. Hong Kong: United States Consulate General.

Dallin, David J. *Soviet Russia and the Far East*. New Haven: Yale University Press, 1948.

Daniels, Robert V. *The Conscience of the Revolution: Communist Opposition in Soviet Russia*. Cambridge: Harvard University Press, 1960.

Davidson, Chandler. "On the 'Culture of Shiftlessness.' " *Dissent* (Fall 1976), 23:349–356.

Davies, John Paton. *Dragon by the Tail*. New York: Norton, 1972.

Debray, Regis. *Revolution Within the Revolution*. New York: Grove Press, 1967.

Dedijer, Vladimir. *Tito Speaks*. London: Weidenfeld and Nicolson, 1953.

Dorris, Carl E. "Peasant Mobilization in North China and the Origins of Yenan Communism." *The China Quarterly* (December 1976), 68:697–719.

Dubinsky, A. M. "Osvoboditel'naiia missiia Sovetskogo Soiuza na Dal'nem Vostoke (1945)" (The Soviet Union's Liberating Mission in the Far East, 1945). *Voprosy Istorii* (August 1965), pp. 49–61.

Dubinsky, A. M. *Osvoboditel'naiia missiia Sovetskogo Soiuza na Dal'nem Vostoke* (The Soviet Union's Liberating Mission in the Far East). Moscow: Mysl', 1966.

Dupuy, Trevor N. *The Military History of the Chinese Civil War.* New York: Franklin Watts, 1969.

Eastman, Lloyd. *Seeds of Destruction: Nationalist China in War and Revolution.* Stanford: Stanford University Press, 1984.

Eastman, Lloyd. "Who Lost China? Chiang Kai-shek Testifies." *China Quarterly* (December 1981), 88:658–668.

Eckstein, Harry. *Internal War: Problems and Approaches.* New York: Free Press of Glencoe, 1964.

Epstein, Israel. *The Unfinished Revolution in China.* Boston: Little, Brown, 1947.

Fan Chao-fu. "Chang Hsüeh-ssu ts'an-chia kung-ch'an-tang chi ts'an-ssu ti ching-kuo" (Chang Hsüeh-ssu Experience in Joining the Communist Party and His Tragic Death). *Chuan-chi wen-hsüeh* (July 1981), 232:43–48.

Fan Kun-yuan. "Chin-chou chan-i ti sheng-li ch'ien tsou." (The Victorious Prelude to the Battle of Chinchow). In *Hsing-huo: ko-ming hui-i lu,* pp. 126–141. Shenyang: Liaoning jen-min ch'upan she, 1981.

Fan Shou-yeh. "Tsai pei-man chiao-fei ti jih-tzu." (Bandit Suppression Days in Northern Manchuria). In *Hsing-huo: ko-ming hui-i lu,* pp. 161–172. Shenyang: Liaoning jen-min ch'u-pan she, 1981.

Fang Ching-wen. *Wo-men ti tung-pei* (Our Northeast). Shanghai: Lao-tung ch'upan she, 1951.

Fang Chun-kuei, ed. *Liu Shao-ch'i tzu-liao chuan-chi* (Special Compilation of Materials on the Liu Shao-chi'i Question). Taipei: Chung-kung yen-chiu tsa-chih she, 1970.

Feis, Herbert. *The China Tangle: The American Effort in China from Pearl Harbor to the Marshall Mission.* New York: Atheneum, 1965.

Feis, Herbert. *Contest Over Japan.* New York: Norton, 1968.

Feng Chung-yun. *Tung-pei k'ang-jih lien-chün shih-ssu nien k'u-tou chien-shih* (A Brief History of the Bitter Fourteen Year Struggle of the Northeast Anti-Japanese United Army). Harbin, 1946.

Feng-huo tung-pei (Stormy Northeast). Hong Kong, 1947.

Feng Shu-yen. "Nu-ch'ao ch'ung-chuan ch'üan-yen-ho" (The Raging Tide Again Rolls through Ch'üan-yen-ho.) In *Hsing-huo liao-yuan,* 7:441–445. Peking: Jen-min wen-hsüeh ch'u-an she, 1958.

Fleron, Fredric and Erik Hoffman, eds. *The Conduct of Soviet Foreign Policy.* Chicago: Aldine, 1971.

Fochler-Hauke, Gustav. *Die Mandschurei: Eine Geographishch-Geopolitische Landeskunde.* Heidelberg: Kurt Vowinckel, 1941.

Frank, Benis M. and Henry I. Shaw Jr. *History of U.S. Marine Corps Operations in World War II.* Vol. 5, *Victory and Occupation.* Washington, D.C.: U.S. Marine Corps Headquarters, 1968.

Friedman, Edward. *Backward Toward Revolution: The Chinese Revolutionary Party.* Berkeley: University of California Press, 1974.

Frillman, Paul and Graham Peck. *China: The Remembered Life.* Boston: Houghton Mifflin, 1968.

Fu Chueh-chin. *Tung-pei hsin sheng ch'ü chih hua-ting* (The Boundaries of the Northeast's New Provinces and Districts). Nanking: Hsing-cheng-yuan hsin-wen chü yin-hang, 1947.

Fulton, Austin. *Through Earthquake, Wind and Fire: Church and Mission in Manchuria, 1868–1950.* Edinburgh: Saint Andrews Press, 1967.

Gaddis, John Lewis. *The United States and the Origins of the Cold War, 1941–1947.* New York: Columbia University Press, 1972.

Garthoff, Raymond L., ed. *Sino-Soviet Military Relations.* New York: Praeger, 1966.

Gillin, Donald with Charles Etter. "Staying On: Japanese Soldiers and Civilians in China, 1945–1949." *Journal of Asian Studies* (May 1983), 42(3):497–518.

Gittings, John. *The Role of the Chinese Army.* London: Oxford University Press, 1967.

Glunin, Vladimir I. *Tret'ia grazhdanskaiia voina v Kitae (1946–1949): ocherk politicheskoi istorii* (The Third Civil War in China 1946–1949: A Political History). Moscow: Izdatel'stvo vostochnoi literatury, 1958.

Goldstein, Steven M. "Chinese Communist Policy Toward the United States: Opportunities and Constraints, 1944–1950." In Dorothy Borg and Waldo Heinrichs, eds. *Uncertain Years: Chinese-American Relations, 1947–1950,* pp. 235–278. New York: Columbia University Press, 1980.

Goldstein, Steven M. and Kathleen J. Hartford, eds. *Single Sparks: China's Rural Revolutions.* Armonk: M. E. Sharpe, 1986.

Grajdanzev, Andrew. "Manchuria: An Industrial Survey." *Pacific Affairs* (December 1945), 18(4):321–339.

Grajdanev, Andrew. "Manchuria as a Region of Colonization." *Pacific Affairs* (March 1946), 19(1):5–19.

Grew, Joseph C. *Turbulent Era: A Diplomatic Record of Forty Years, 1904–1945.* Boston: Houghton Mifflin, 1952.

Griffin, Patricia E. *The Chinese Communist Treatment of Counterrevolutionaries, 1924–1949.* Princeton, N.J.: Princeton University Press, 1976.

Gupta, D.C. *United States Attitude Toward China.* Delhi, 1969.

Halperin, Morton et al. *Bureaucratic Politics and Foreign Policy.* Washington, D.C.: Brookings Institution, 1974.

Harriman, W. Averell and Elie Abel. *Special Envoy to Churchill and Stalin, 1941–1946.* New York: Random House, 1975.

Harrison, James Pinckney. *The Long March to Power: A History of the Chinese Communist Party, 1921–1972.* New York: Praeger, 1972.

Heilungkiang sheng shc-hui k'o-hsueh-yuan ti-fang tang-shih yen chiu so and Tung-pei lieh-shih chi-nien kuan, eds. *Tung-pei k'ang-jih lieh-shih chuan* (Biographies of Northeast Anti-Japanese Martyrs). 3 vol. Harbin: Heilungkiang jen-min ch'u-pan she, 1980, 1981.

Herz, Martin F. *Beginnings of the Cold War.* New York: MacGraw Hill, 1969.

Hess, Gary. "The Iranian Crisis of 1945–46 and the Cold War." *Political Science Quarterly* (March 1974), 89(1):117–146.

Hinton, William. *Fanshen: A Documentary of Revolution in a Chinese Village*. New York: Random House, 1968.

Hittle, Lt. Col. James D. "On the Peiping-Mukden Line." *Marine Corps Gazette* (April 1946), no., 30.

Ho Hsi-ya. *Tao-fei wen-t'i chih yen-chiu* (A Study of the Bandit Question). Shanghai, 1925.

Ho Pao-lu. *O-kuo ch'in-lueh tung-pei chi-shih* (A Record of Russia's Invasion of the Northeast). Hong Kong: Tzu-yu ch'u-pan she, 1955.

Hofheinz, Roy M. *The Broken Wave: The Chinese Peasant Movement, 1922–1928*. Cambridge: Harvard University Press, 1977.

Hsiao Hung. *The Field of Life and Death and Tales of Hulan River*, Howard Goldblatt and Ellen Yeung, trs. Bloomington: Indiana University Press, 1979.

Hsieh Kuo-chen. *Ch'ing-ch'u liu-jen k'ai-fa tung-pei shih* (A History of the Opening of the Northeast by Migrants in the Early Ch'ing). Shanghai: Kaiming shu-tien, 1948.

Hsing-huo liao-yuan (A Single Spark Can Start a Prairie Fire). Peking: Jen-min wen-hsueh ch'u-pan she, vol. 4, 1961, vol. 7, 1963.

Huai-nien Chang Wen-t'ien t'ung-chih (Remembering Comrade Chang Wen-ti'ien). Changsha: Hunan jen-min ch'u-pan she, 1981.

Huai-nien Liu Shao-ch'i t'ung-chih (Remembering Comrade Liu Shao-ch'i). Changsha: Hunan jen-min ch'u-pan she, 1980.

Huang Jung-jae. "K'ua-hai pei-shang." (Leaping Across the Sea, Northward Bound). In *Hsing-huo liao-yuan*, 7:456–463. Peking: Jen-min wen-hsueh ch'u-pan she, 1963.

Huang Tsao. *T'u-ti ho ch'iang* (Land and a Gun). Harbin, 1948.

Hung Huang. *Tsui-hou ti ch'a-tzu* (The Last Dregs). Shenyang, 1949.

Iriye, Akira. *The Cold War in Asia*. Englewood Cliffs, N.J.: Prentice Hall, 1974.

Iriye, Akira. "Was There a Cold War in Asia.' In John Chay, ed. *The Problems and Prospects of American-East Asian Relations*, pp. 3–24. Boulder, Colo.: Westview Press, 1977.

Israel, John and Donald W. Klein. *Rebels and Bureaucrats, China's December 9ers*. Berkeley: University of California Press, 1976.

Jacobs-Larkcom, Dorothy. *As China Fell: The Experiences of a British Consul's Wife, 1946–1953*. Ilfracombe, Devon: Arthur H. Stockwell, 1976.

James, H. E. M. *The Long White Mountain or a Journey in Manchuria*. London: Longmans, Green, 1888.

Johnson, Chalmers. *Peasant Nationalism and Communist Power*. Stanford: Stanford University Press, 1962.

Jones, F. C. *Manchuria Since 1931*. London: Royal Institute of International Affairs, 1949.

Jordan, Donald A. *The Northern Expedition: China's National Revolution of 1926–1928*. Honolulu: University Press of Hawaii, 1976.

Kalinov, Cyrille. *Les Marechaux sovietiques vous parlent*. Paris: Librairie Stock, 1950.

Kalyagin, Aleksandr Ya. *Along Alien Roads.* New York: East Asian Institute, Columbia University, 1983.

Kang Chao, *The Economic Development of Manchuria: The Rise of a Frontier Economy.* Ann Arbor: Center for Chinese Studies, University of Michigan, 1982.

Kao Hsi-p'ing. *Yuan-tung huo ch'ien-yin hou-kuo* (Cause and Effect of the Catastrophe in the Far East). Taipei: Fan-kung ch'u-pan she, 1950.

Kataoka, Tetsuya. *Resistance and Revolution in China: The Communists and the Second United Front.* Berkeley: University of California Press, 1974.

Keeley, Joseph. *The China Lobby Man: The Story of Alfred Kohlberg.* New Rochelle, N.Y.: Arlington House, 1969.

Kennedy, Joseph P. "The U.S. and the World." *Life* (March 18, 1946), p. 107.

Kim, Ilpyong. *The Politics of Chinese Communism: Kiangsi under the Soviets.* Berkeley: University of California Press, 1973.

Kinney, Ann Rasmussen. *Japanese Investment in Manchurian Manufacturing, Mining, Transportation and Communications, 1931–1945.* New York: Garland, 1982.

Klein, Edward. "Situation in North China." *Marine Corps Gazette* (April 1946), no. 30.

Kolko, Gabriel, *The Politics of War: The World and United States Foreign Policy 1943–1945.* New York: Random House, 1968.

Kovtun-Stankevich, A. I. "Komendant Mukdena" (Mukden Commander). In *Na Kitaiskoi zemle: vospominaniia sovetskikh dobrovol'tsev 1925–1945 (On Chinese Soil: Memoirs of Soviet Volunteers, 1925–45), pp. 416–437.* Moscow: Nauka, 1977.

Kuan-yü ch'eng-shih cheng-ts'e ti chi-ko wen-hsien (Some Documents on Urban Policy). N.p.: Huapei Hsinhua shu-tien, 1949.

Kuhfus, Peter M. "Die Risiken der Freundschaft: China und der Jalta-Mythos." *Bochumer Jahrbuch zur Ostasienforschung 1984,* pp. 248–286.

Kuhn, Philip A. *Rebellion and Its Enemies in Late Imperial China: Militarization and Social Structure, 1796–1864.* Cambridge: Harvard University Press, 1970.

Kung-chan-tang yuan ti pang-yang (The Model of a Communist Party Member). N.p.: Tung-pei min-chu lien-chün tsung-cheng hsuan-ch'uan pu, 1947.

LaFeber, Walter. *America, Russia and the Cold War, 1945–1966.* New York: John Wiley, 1967.

Lao She. *Rickshaw.* Jean M. James, tr. Honolulu: University Press of Hawaii, 1979.

Lattimore, Owen. *Manchuria: Cradle of Conflict.* New York: MacMillan, 1935.

Lauterbach, Richard E. *Danger from the East.* New York: Harper & Row, 1947.

Leary, William M., Jr. *The Dragon's Wings: The China National Aviation Corporation and the Development of Commercial Aviation in China.* Athens: University of Georgia Press, 1976.

Leary, William M. *Perilous Missions: Civil Air Transport and CIA Covert Operations in Asia.* University: University of Alabama Press, 1984.

Lee, Chong-Sik. *Counterinsurgency in Manchuria: The Japanese Experience, 1931–1940.* Santa Monica: Rand, 1967.

Lee, Chong-Sik. *Revolutionary Struggle in Manchuria: Chinese Communism and Soviet Interest, 1922–1945.* Berkeley: University of California Press, 1983.

Lee Chong-Sik. "Witch Hunt Among the Guerrillas: The Min-Sheng-T'uan Incident." *China Quarterly* (April–June 1966), 26:107–117.

Lee, Frank C. "Land Redistribution in Communist China." *Pacific Affairs* (March 1948), 21(1):20–33.

Lee, Robert H. G. *The Manchurian Frontier in Ch'ing History.* Cambridge: Harvard University Press, 1970.

Lensen, George A. *The Damned Inheritance: The Soviet Union and the Manchurian Crises, 1924–1935.* Tallahassee: Diplomatic Press, 1974

Lensen, George A. *The Strange Neutrality: Soviet-Japanese Relations During the Second World War.* Tallahassee: Diplomatic Press, 1972.

Lensen, George. "Yalta and the Far East." In John Snell, ed., *The Meaning of Yalta,* pp. 126–166. Baton Rouge: University of Louisiana Press, 1956.

Leong, Sow-theng. *Sino-Soviet Diplomatic Relations, 1917–1926.* Honolulu: University Press of Hawaii, 1976.

Lew, Daniel. "Manchurian Booty and International Law." *American Journal of International Law* (April 1946), 40(3):584–591.

Lewis, John W., ed. *Peasant Rebellion and Communist Revolution in Asia.* Stanford: Stanford University Press, 1974.

Li, Lincoln. *The Japanese Army in North China 1937–1941: Problems of Political and Economic Control.* London: Oxford University Press, 1975.

Li T'iao-sheng and Lu Chung-chieh. *Ts'ung chiang-nan tao tung-pei* (From Kiangnan to the Northeast). N.p.: Shih-shih jen-chiu hui ch'u pan, 1946.

Liang Ching-tung. "The Sino-Soviet Treaty of Friendship and Alliance of 1945: The Inside Story." In Paul K. T. Sih, ed., *Nationalist China During the Sino-Japanese War, 1937–1945,* pp. 373–397. Hicksville, N.Y.: Exposition University Press, 1977.

Liang Ching-tung, ed. *Chung-mei kuan-hsi lun-wen chi* (Collection of Essays on Sino-American Relations). Taipei, 1982.

Lieberthal, Kenneth G. *Revolution and Tradition in Tientsin, 1949–1952.* Stanford: Stanford University Press, 1980.

Lin, C. T. "Mukden-Yangtze." *China Digest* (March 9, 1948), pp. 4–6.

Lin Feng. "Kuan-yü san-nien lai ti cheng-fu kung-tso pao-kao." (Report Concerning Government Work During the Past Three Years). In *Tung-pei jen-min tai-piao hui-i chung-yao wen-hsien* (Important Documents of the Northeast People's Representative Conference). N.p., 1950.

Lin P'eng, ed. *Hsin tung-pei chieh-shao* (Introducing the New Northeast). N.p.: Tung-pei jen-min ch'u-pan she, 1951.

Lindsay, Michael. *The Unknown War: North China 1937–1945.* London: Bergström and Boyle books, 1975.

Little, Richard. *Intervention: External Involvement in Civil Wars.* Totowa, N.J.: Rowman and Littlefield, 1975.

Liu, F. F. *A Military History of Modern China, 1924–1949.* Princeton: Princeton University Press, 1956.

Liu Pai-yu. *Shih-tai ti yin-hsiang* (Contemporary Impressions). Harbin: Kuanghua shu-tien, 1948.

Liu Shao-ch'i. *Collected Works of Liu Shao-ch'i, 1945–1957.* Hong Kong: Union Research Institute, 1969.

Liu Yu. *Rabochee dvizheniie v Kitae 1945–1949 gg. dokumenty i materialy* (The Workers Movement in China 1945–1949, Documents and Materials). Moscow: Nauka, 1969.

Liu Yun-an. *Demokraticheskoe i sotsialisticheskoe stroitel'stvo v severo-vostochnom Kitae* (Democratic and Socialist Construction in Northeast China). Moscow: Gosudarstvennoe izdatel'stvo politicheskoi literatury, 1957.

Lo Ta-yu, ed. *Wu-erh-san meng-nan erh-shih chou-nien chi nien wen-chi* (A Collection of Reminiscences of the Twentieth Anniversary of the Great Disaster of May 23). Taichung: Wu-erh-san chi-nien wen-chi p'ien-chi wei-yuan-hui, 1965.

Lun kung-shang-yeh cheng-ts'e (On Policy Towards Industry). N.p.: Hsinhua, 1949.

McCagg, William. *Stalin Embattled, 1943–1948.* East Lansing: Michigan State University Press, 1978.

McCormack, Gavan. *Chang Tso-lin in Northeast China, 1911–1928: China, Japan, and the Manchuria Idea.* Stanford: Stanford University Press, 1977.

McDonald, Angus W. Jr. *The Urban Origins of Rural Revolution: Elites and the Masses in Hunan Province, China, 1911–1927.* Berkeley: University of California Press, 1978.

McLane, Charles. *Soviet Policy and the Chinese Communists, 1931–1946.* New York: Columbia University Press, 1958.

McNeill, William H. *Plagues and Peoples.* Garden City, N.Y.: Anchor Press, 1977.

"Mao Tse-tung's Oral Report to the Seventh Party Congress: Summary Notes (April 24, 1945)." *Chinese Law and Government* (Winter 1977–1978), 10(4):3–27.

Mao Tse-tung. *Selected Works.* 4 volumes. Peking: Foreign Languages Press, 1967–1969.

Mao Tse-tung ssu-hsiang wan-sui (Long Live Mao Tse-tung Thought). Taipei: Institute of International Relations, 1974.

Marine Corps Gazette, 1946–1949.

Mastny, Vojtech. *Russia's Road to the Cold War: Diplomacy, Warfare, and the Politics of Communism, 1941–1945.* New York: Columbia University Press, 1979.

Melby, John F. *The Mandate of Heaven: Record of a Civil War, China 1945–1949.* Toronto: University of Toronto Press, 1968.

Meng Nan. *Chung-kuo t'u-ti kai-ko wen-t'i* (China's Land Reform). Hong Kong: Hsin min-chu ch'u-pan she, 1948.

Metzger, Thomas A. "Chinese Bandits: The Traditional Perception Re-evaluated." *Journal of Asian Studies* (May 1974), 33(3):455–458.

Migdal, Joel S. *Peasants, Politics, and Revolution: Pressures Toward Political and Social Change in the Third World.* Princeton: Princeton University Press, 1974.

Millis, Walter, ed. *The Forrestal Diaries.* New York: Viking, 1951.

Min-chu ti tung-pei (The Democratic Northeast). N.p.: Liao-tung Hsin-hua shu-tien, 1946.

Moise, Edwin E. *Land Reform in China and North Vietnam: Consolidating the*

Revolution at the Village Level. Chapel Hill: University of North Carolina Press, 1983.

Moorad, George. *Lost Peace in China.* New York: Dutton, 1949.

Moorad, George. "The Rape of Manchuria." *American Mercury* (March 1947), 64:278–286.

Moore, Harriet L. *Soviet Far Eastern Policy, 1931–1945.* Princeton: Princeton University Press, 1945.

Mou Yuan. *Hsin-yen: hsien chi tung-pei t'ung-pao* (Words from the Heart for My Northeast Compatriots). N.p., 1946.

Murzaev, E. M. *Severo-vostochnoi Kitai: fiziko-geograficheskoe opisanie* (Northeast China: A Physical-Geographical Description). Moscow: Izdatel'stvo akademii nauk SSSR, 1955.

Myers, Ramon H. *The Chinese Peasant Economy: Agricultural Development in Hopei and Shantung, 1890–1949.* Cambridge: Harvard University Press, 1970.

Myers, Ramon H. "Cooperation in Traditional Chinese Agriculture and Its Implications for Team Farming in the People's Republic of China." In Dwight Perkins, ed. *China's Modern Economy in Historical Perspective,* pp. 261–277. Stanford: Stanford University Press, 1975.

Myers, Ramon H. "Farm Production and Marketing in a Rural Economy of Surplus Land: Northeast China During the Republican Period." In Hou Chiming and Tzong-Shian Yu, eds. *Modern Chinese Economic History: Proceedings of the Conference on Modern Chinese Economic History,* pp. 221–250. Taipei: Institute of Economics, 1979.

Myers, Ramon H. "Socioeconomic Change in Villages of Manchuria During the Ch'ing and Republican Periods: Some Preliminary findings," *Modern Asian Studies* (1976), 10:(4):591–620.

Myers, Ramon H. "The Soviet Union and Nationalist China's Attempt to Recover the Northeast, August 15, 1945 to December 31, 1945." In Compilation Committee of Symposium on the History of the Republic of China, *Symposium on the History of the Republic of China,* 5:264–278. Taipei, 1981.

Na Kitaiskoi zemle: vospominaniia sovetskikh dobrovol'tsev, 1925–1945 (On Chinese Soil: Memoirs of Soviet Volunteers, 1925–1945). Moscow: Nauka, 1974.

Nagai, Yonosuke and Akira Iriye, eds. *The Origins of the Cold War in Asia.* New York: Columbia University Press, 1977.

Nathan, Carl F. *Plague Prevention and Politics in Manchuria 1910–1931.* Cambridge: East Asian Research Center, Harvard University, 1967.

Pak Hyobom, "Chinese Communists in the Eastern Three Provinces, 1918–1935." *Contributions in Asian Studies* (January 1971), 1:28–48. Leiden: E. J. Brill, 1971.

Pauley, Edwin W. *Report on Japanese Assets in Manchuria to the President of the United States.* July 1946, Washington, D.C., 1946.

Peng Ming. *Istoriia Kitaisko-Sovetskoi druzhby* (History of Chinese-Soviet Friendship). Moscow: Izdatel'stvo sotsial'no-ekonomicheskoi literatury, 1959.

Pepper, Suzanne. *Civil War in China: The Political Struggle, 1945–1949.* Berkeley: University of California Press, 1978.

Pepper, Suzanne. "The Student Movement and the Chinese Civil War." *China Quarterly* (October–December 1971), 48:698–735.

Perry, Elizabeth J. *Rebels and Revolutionaries in North China 1845–1945*. Stanford: Stanford University Press, 1980.

Popkin, Samuel L. *The Rational Peasant: The Political Economy of Rural Society in Vietnam*. Berkeley: University of California Press, 1979.

Pospelov, P. N., ed. *Istoriia velikoi otechestvennoi voiny Sovetskogo Soiuza 1941–1945* (History of the Great Fatherland War of the Soviet Union 1941–1945). Vol. 5. Moscow: Voennoe izdatel'stvo Ministerstva Oborony SSR, 1963.

Powell, John W. "Japan's Germ Warfare: The U.S. Cover-up of a War Crime." *Bulletin of Concerned Asian Scholars* (Oct.–Dec. 1980), 12(4):2–17.

Price, Jane L. "Chinese Communist Land Reform and Peasant Mobilization, 1946–1948." In F. Gilbert Chan, ed. *China at the Crossroads: Nationalists and Communists, 1927–1949*, pp. 217–253. Boulder, Col.: Westview Press, 1980.

Quester, George. *Nuclear Diplomacy: The First Twenty-Five Years*. New York: Dunellen, 1970.

Race, Jeffrey. "Toward an Exchange Theory of Revolution." In John W. Lewis, ed. *Peasant Rebellion and Communist Revolution in Asia*, pp. 169–204. Stanford: Stanford University Press, 1975.

Reardon-Anderson, James. *Yenan and the Great Powers: The Origins of Chinese Communist Foreign Policy, 1944–1946*. New York: Columbia University Press, 1980.

Rigg, Robert. "Campaign for the Northeast China Railway System." *Military Review* (December 1947), 27(9):27–34.

Rigg, Robert. *Red China's Fighting Hordes*. Harrisburg, Penn.: Military Service Publishing, 1951.

Rinden Robert and Roxane Witke. *The Red Flag Waves: A Guide to the Hung-ch'i Piao-p'iao Collection*. Berkeley: Center for Chinese Studies, University of California, 1968.

Robinson, Thomas W. *A Political-Military Biography of Lin Piao, Part 1, 1907–1949*. Santa Monica: Rand, 1971.

Romanus, Charles F. and Riley Sunderland. *Time Runs Out in CBI*. Washington, D.C.: Department of the Army, Office of the Chief of Military History, 1959.

Rudolph, Vladimir. "The Agencies of Control: Their Organization and Policies." In Robert Slusser, ed., *Soviet Economic Policy in Postwar Germany*, pp. 18–36. New York: Research Program on the USSR, Columbia University, 1953.

Rush, Myron, ed. *The International Situation and Soviet Foreign Policy*. Columbus, Ohio: Charles E. Merrill, 1969.

Russet, Bruce. "Toward a Model of Competitive International Politics." In James Rosenau, ed. *International Politics and Foreign Policy*, pp. 119–130. New York: Free Press, 1969.

Saga of Resistance to Japanese Invasion. Peking: Foreign Languages Press, 1959.

Sapozhnikov, B. G. and V. V. Vorontsov. "Osvoboditel'naiia missiia SSSR na Dal'nem Vostoke v gody vtoroi mirovoi voiny" (The Liberating Mission of the USSR in the Far East During the Second World War). *Istoriia SSSR* (July-

August 1965). No. 4, pp. 28–48.

Sapozhinikov, B. G. and A. T. Yakimov. "Propaganda sredi Iaponskikh voisk i naselenii severo-vostochnogo Kitaiia i severnoi Korei" (Propaganda Among Japanese Troops and the Population of Northeast China and Northern Korea). *Narody Azii i Afriki* (1975), 5:40–49.

Sartori, Giovanni. "Concept Misinformation in Comparative Politics." *American Political Science Review* (December 1970), 54(4):1033–1053.

Schaller, Michael. *The U.S. Crusade in China, 1938–1945.* New York: Columbia University Press, 1979.

Schran, Peter. *Guerrilla Economy: The Development of the Shensi-Kansu-Ninghsia Border Region, 1937–1945.* Albany, N.Y.: SUNY Press, 1976.

Scott, James C. *The Moral Economy of the Peasant: Rebellion and Subsistence in Southeast Asia.* New Haven: Yale University Press, 1976.

Selden, Mark. *The Yenan Way in Revolutionary China.* Cambridge: Harvard University Press, 1972.

Service, John S. *The Amerasia Papers: Some Problems in the History of U.S.–China Relations.* Berkeley: Center for Chinese Studies, University of California, 1971.

Shaw, Yu-ming. "The Year of Fate: The Chinese Civil War and International Politics in 1946." In Compilation Committee of Symposium on the History of the Republic of China, ed., *Symposium on the History of the Republic of China*, 5:264–278. Taipei, 1981.

Sherwin, Martin. *A World Destroyed: The Atomic Bomb and the Grand Alliance.* New York: Knopf, 1975.

Shilin, Alan I. "Occupation at Tsingtao." *Marine Corps Gazette* (January 1946), 30(1):32–35.

Shillinglaw, Geoffrey. "Land Reform and Peasant Mobilization in Southern China, 1947–1950." In David Lehmann, ed. *Peasants, Landlords and Governments: Agrarian Reform in the Third World.* pp. 121–155. New York: Holmes & Meier, 1974.

Shtemenko, S. M. *General'nyi shtab v gody voiny* (The General Staff During the War Years). Moscow: Voennoe izdatel'stvo, 1968.

Shue, Vivienne. *Peasant China in Transition: The Dynamics of Development Toward Socialism, 1949–1956.* Berkeley: University of California Press, 1980.

Skinner, G. William. "Chinese Peasants and the Closed Community: An Open and Shut Case." *Comparative Studies in Society and History* (July 1971), 13(3):270–281.

Skocpol, Theda. *States and Social Revolution: A Comparative Analysis of France, Russia and China.* New York: Cambridge University Press, 1979.

Sladkovsky, M. I. *Znakomstvo S Kitaem i kitaitsami* (My Acquaintance with China and the Chinese). Moscow: Mysl', 1984.

Sladkovskii, M. I., ed. *Leninskaiia politika SSSR v otnoshenii Kitaiia* (The Leninist Policy of the USSR Toward China). Moscow: Nauka, 1968.

Slusser, Robert, ed. *Soviet Economic Policy in Postwar Germany.* New York: Research Program on the USSR, Columbia University, 1953.

Starobin, Joseph R. "Origins of the Cold War." In Fredric Fleron and Erik

Hoffman, eds. *The Conduct of Soviet Foreign Policy*, pp. 275–288. Chicago: Aldine, 1971.

Stavis, Benedict. *The Politics of Agricultural Mechanization in China*. Ithaca, N.Y.: Cornell University Press, 1978.

Stephan, John. *The Russian Fascists: Tragedy and Farce in Exile, 1925–1945*. New York: Harper & Row, 1978.

Stein, Gunther. *The Challenge of Red China*. New York: Whittlesey House, 1945.

Stewart, John. "Manchuria Today." *International Affairs* (January 1944), 20(1):68–79.

Strong, Anna Louise. *The Chinese Conquer China*. Garden City, N.Y.: Doubleday, 1949.

Suh, Dae-Sook. *Documents of Korean Communism, 1918–1948*. Princeton: Princeton University Press, 1970.

Suh Dae-Sook. *The Korean Communist Movement 1918–1948*. Princeton: Princeton University Press, 1967.

Sun Chieh. *Tung-pei k'ang-jih lien-chün ti-ssu chün* (The Fourth Army of the Northeast Anti-Japanese United Army). Paris: Chiu-kuo ch'u-pan she, 1936.

Tai Hsuan-chih. *Hung-ch'iang-hui* (The Red Rifles Society). Taipei: Shih-huo ch'u-pan she, 1973.

Takeuchi Minoru, ed. *Mao Tse-tung chi* (The Works of Mao Tse-tung). Tokyo, 1970.

T'ang Yün. *Tung-pei wen-t'i chih chen hsiang* (The True Face of the Northeast Question). N.p.: Shih-tai ch'u-pan she, 1946.

Thaxton, Ralph. *China Turned Rightside Up: Revolutionary Legitimacy in the Peasant World*. New Haven: Yale University Press, 1983.

Tong, Te-kong and Li Tsung-jen. *The Memoirs of Li Tsung-jen*. Boulder, Colo.: Westview, 1979.

Topping, Seymour. *Journey Between Two Chinas*. New York: Harper & Row, 1972.

Tsai Hsing-san. *Chiang Ching-kuo yü Su-lien* (Chiang Ching-kuo and the Soviet Union). Hong Kong: Shih-tai ch'u -pan she, 1976.

Tseng K'o-lin. "Ta-ti ch'ung kuang." (Fighting for the Northeast). In *Hsing-huo liao-yuan*, 7:446–455. Peking: Jen-min wen-hsueh ch'u-pan she, 1963.

Tsou Tang. *America's Failure in China, 1941–1950*. Chicago: University of Chicago Press, 1963.

T'u Chien et al. *Chung-kuo jen-min chieh-fang chün chien-shih* (A Short History of the Chinese People's Liberation Army). Peking: Chan-shih ch'u-pan she, 1982.

T'u-ti cheng-ts'e fa-ling hui-pien (Compilation of Laws and Regulations Concerning Agrarian Policy). Shenyang, 1950.

Tucker, Nancy Bernkopf. *Patterns in the Dust: Chinese-American Relations and the Recognition Controversy, 1949–1950*. New York: Columbia University Press, 1983.

Tung Ch'i-chun. *Chin pai-nien lai chih tung-pei* (The Northeast in the Last Hundred Years). N.p.: Cheng-chung shu shü, 1946.

Tung-pei hua-pao (Northeast Pictorial). Harbin, 1946–1948.

Tung-pei jen-min ying-kai tsou shen-mo tao-lu (What Road Should the People of the Northeast Take)? N.p., 1946.

Tung-pei t'ung-chi chien pien (Concise Edition of Northeast *Statistics*). N.p., 1945.

Tung-pei wen-t'i (The Northeast Question). N.p: Chien-kuo shu-tien, 1946.

Tung-pei wen-t'i hsuan-ch'uan ta-kang (Outline for Propaganda on the Northeast Question). N.p.: Ai-kuo t'ung-hsun she, 1946.

Tung-pei wen-t'i yen-chiu chuan-chi (Special Collection of Studies on the Northeast Question). N.p.: Chung-lien ch'upan she, 1948.

Tung Yen-p'ing. *Su O chü tung-pei (Soviet Russia's Invasion of the Northeast).* Taipei: Chung-hua ta-tien, 1965.

Ulam, Adam. *Expansion and Coexistence: The History of Soviet Foreign Policy 1917–1967.* New York: Praeger, 1968.

Ulam, Adam. *The Rivals: America and Russia since World War II.* New York: Viking, 1972.

United States Armed Forces, Far East Headquarters, Military History Section, Japanese Special Studies on Manchuria. *Strategic Study of Manchuria's Topography and Geography.* Tokyo, 1955; *Logistics in Manchuria.* Tokyo, 1959.

United States, Department of the Army, Office of the Chief of Military History. *The Civil War in China 1945–1950.* Taipei, n.d.

United States, Department of State. *The Far Eastern Commission, 1945–1952.* Washington, D.C.: 1953.

United States, Department of State. *Foreign Relations of the United States, 1945–1948.* Washington, D.C.: 1969–1973

United States, Department of State. *Foreign Relations of the United States: The Conference at Malta and Yalta 1945.* Washington, D.C.: 1955.

United States, Department of State. *United States Relations with China: With Special Reference to the Period, 1944–1949.* Washington, D.C.: 1949.

Van Slyke, Lyman P., ed. *The Chinese Communist Movement: A Report of the U.S. War Department.* Stanford: Stanford University Press, 1968.

Van Slyke, Lyman P., ed. *Marshall's Mission to China December 1945–January 1947: The Report and Appended Documents.* Arlington, Va.: University Publications of America, 1976.

Vladimirov, Oleg E. *Nezabyvaemye stranitsy istorii i maoistskie fal'sifikatory* (Unforgettable Pages of History and the Maoist Falsifiers). Moscow: Znanie, 1971.

Vladimirov, O. and V. Ryanzantsev. *Stranitsy politicheskoi biografii Mao Dze-dun* (Pages from the Political Biography of Mao Tse-tung). Moscow: Izdatel'stvo politicheskoi literatury, 1969.

Vladimirov, P. P. *Osobyi raion Kitaiia* (Special District of China). Moscow: Novosti, 1973.

Vneshniaia politika Sovetskogo Soiuza 1945 god (Foreign Policy of the Soviet Union 1945). Moscow: Gosudarstvennoe izdatel'stvo politicheskoi literatury, 1952.

Vneshniaia politika Sovetskogo Soiuza 1946 god (Foreign Policy of the Soviet Union 1946). Moscow: Gosudarstvennoe izdatel'stvo politicheskoi literatury, 1952.

Wakeman, Fredric Jr. "Rebellion and Revolution: The Study of Popular Movements in Chinese History." *Journal of Asian Studies* (February 1977), 36(2):201–237.

Wang Chin-mu. *Chung-kuo k'ang-chan shih yen-i* (A Popular History of the Chinese War of Resistance). N.p.: Hsin-ch'ao shu-tien, 1951.

Wang Hui-min. *Hsin tung-pei chih-nan* (Guide to the New Northeast). Chungking: Shang-wu yin-shu-kuan, 1946.

Wang Ta-jen, ed. Tung-pei yen-chiu lun-chi (Essays on Northeast China). Taipei: Chung-hua wen-hua ch'u-pan shih-yeh wei-yuan-hui, 1957.

Wang Wen et al. "Yung-heng ti yu-i" (Eternal Friendship). In *Hsing-huo liao-yuan*, 7:464–471. Peking: Jen-min wen-hsueh ch'u-pan she, 1963.

Wang T'ieh-han. *Tung-pei chün-shih shih-lueh* (Historical Outline of Northeast Military Affairs). Taipei: Ch'uan-chi wen-hsueh, 1972.

Wedemyer, Albert C. *Wedemyer Reports!* New York: Holt, 1958.

Wei, Henry. *China and Soviet Russia.* Princeton: Van Nostrand, 1956.

Wei tung-pei ti ho-p'ing min-chu erh tou-cheng (Struggle for Peace and Democracy in the Northeast). N.p., 1946.

Wei-man hsien-hsiang (Contemporary Manchukuo). N.p., 1945.

Whiting, Allen S. "The New Chinese Communist." *World Politics* (July 1955), 7:(4):592–605.

Whiting, Allen S. and Sheng Shih-ts'ai. *Sinkiang: Pawn or Pivot.* East Lansing: Michigan State University Press, 1958.

Whiting, Allen S. *Soviet Policies in China, 1917–1924.* New York: Columbia University Press, 1954.

Whitson, William with Chen-hsia Huang. *The Chinese High Command: A History of Cummunist Military Politics, 1927–1971.* New York: Praeger, 1973.

Wilkinson, David. *Revolutionary Civil War: The Elements of Victory and Defeat.* Palo Alto: Page-Ficklin, 1975.

Wilson, Dick. *When Tigers Fight: The Story of the Sino-Japanese War, 1937–1945.* New York: Viking, 1984.

Wolf, Eric R. *Peasant Wars of the Twentieth Century.* New York: Harper & Row, 1973.

Wong, John. *Land Reform in the People's Republic of China: Institutional Transformation in Agriculture.* New York: Praeger, 1973.

Yao Sung-ling, ed. "Chang Kung-ch'uan jih-chi chung yu-kuan tung-pei chieh-shou chiao-she ching-kuo" (Extracts from the Diary of Chang Kia-ngau Relating to the Negotiations Over the Takeover of the Northeast). *Chuan-chi wen-hsueh*, February 1980–January 1981.

Yeh Chien-ying. "The Great Decisive Battle of Strategy." *Hung Ch'i*, January 1961. In *Survey of China Mainland Magazines* (February 13, 1961), 248; 2–14.

Yen Ying. *Tung-pei i-yung-chün chan-shih* (Battle History of the Northeast Volunteer Army). Hong Kong, 1963.

Yu I-fu. *Tung-pei jen-min ying-kai tsou shen mo tao-lu* (What Road Should the People of the Northeast Take)? N.p., 1946.

Zimmerman, William. "Choices in the Postwar World (1) Containment and the Soviet Union." In Charles Gati, ed. *Caging the Bear: Containment and the Cold War.* Indianapolis: Bobbs-Merrill, 1974.

INDEX

STUDIES OF THE EAST ASIAN INSTITUTE

THE LADDER OF SUCCESS IN IMPERIAL CHINA, by Ping-ti Ho. New York: Columbia University Press, 1962.

THE CHINESE INFLATION, 1937–1949, by Shun-hsin Chou. New York: Columbia University Press, 1963.

REFORMER IN MODERN CHINA: CHANG CHIEN, 1853–1926, by Samuel Chu. New York: Columbia University Press, 1965.

RESEARCH IN JAPANESE SOURCES: A GUIDE, by Herschel Webb with the assistance of Marleigh Ryan. New York: Columbia University Press, 1965.

SOCIETY AND EDUCATION IN JAPAN, by Herbert Passin. New York: Teachers College Press, 1965.

AGRICULTURAL PRODUCTION AND ECONOMIC DEVELOPMENT IN JAPAN, 1873–1922, by James I. Nakamura. Princeton: Princeton University Press, 1966.

JAPAN'S FIRST MODERN NOVEL: UKIGUMO OF FUTABATEI SHI-MEI, by Marleigh Ryan. New York: Columbia University Press, 1967.

THE KOREAN COMMUNIST MOVEMENT, 1918–1948, by Dae-Sook Suh. Princeton: Princeton University Press, 1967.

THE FIRST VIETNAM CRISIS, by Melvin Gurtov. New York: Columbia University Press, 1967.

CADRES, BUREAUCRACY, AND POLITICAL POWER IN COMMUNIST CHINA, by A. Doak Barnett. New York: Columbia University Press, 1968.

THE JAPANESE IMPERIAL INSTITUTION IN THE TOKUGAWA PE-
RIOD, by Herschel Webb. New York: Columbia University Press,
1968.
HIGHER EDUCATION AND BUSINESS RECRUITMENT IN JAPAN, by
Koya Azumi. New York: Teachers College Press, 1969.
THE COMMUNISTS AND PEASANT REBELLIONS: A STUDY IN THE
REWRITING OF CHINESE HISTORY, by James P. Harrison, Jr. New
York: Atheneum, 1969.
HOW THE CONSERVATIVES RULE JAPAN, by Nathaniel B. Thayer.
Princeton: Princeton University Press, 1969.
ASPECTS OF CHINESE EDUCATION, edited by C. T. Hu. New York:
Teachers College Press, 1970.
DOCUMENTS OF KOREAN COMMUNISM, 1918–1948, by Dae-Sook
Suh. Princeton: Princeton University Press, 1970.
JAPANESE EDUCATION: A BIBLIOGRAPHY OF MATERIALS IN THE
ENGLISH LANGUAGE, by Herbert Passin. New York: Teachers Col-
lege Press, 1970.
ECONOMIC DEVELOPMENT AND THE LABOR MARKET IN JAPAN,
by Koji Taira. New York: Columbia University Press, 1970.
THE JAPANESE OLIGARCHY AND THE RUSSO-JAPANESE WAR, by
Shumpei Okamoto. New York: Columbia University Press, 1970.
IMPERIAL RESTORATION IN MEDIEVAL JAPAN, by H. Paul Varley.
New York: Columbia University Press, 1971.
JAPAN'S POSTWAR DEFENSE POLICY, 1947–1968, by Martin E.
Weinstein. New York: Columbia University Press, 1971.
ELECTION CAMPAIGNING JAPANESE STYLE, by Gerald L. Curtis. New
York: Columbia University Press, 1971.
CHINA AND RUSSIA: THE "GREAT GAME," by O. Edmund Clubb.
New York: Columbia University Press, 1971.
MONEY AND MONETARY POLICY IN COMMUNIST CHINA, by
Katharine Huang Hsiao. New York: Columbia University Press,
1971.
THE DISTRICT MAGISTRATE IN LATE IMPERIAL CHINA, by John R.
Watt. New York: Columbia University Press, 1972.
LAW AND POLICY IN CHINA'S FOREIGN RELATIONS: A STUDY OF
ATTITUDE AND PRACTICE, by James C. Hsiung. New York: Co-
lumbia University Press, 1972.
PEARL HARBOR AS HISTORY: JAPANESE-AMERICAN RELATIONS,
1931–1941, edited by Dorothy Borg and Shumpei Okamoto, with
the assistance of Dale K. A. Finlayson. New York: Columbia Uni-
versity Press, 1973.
JAPANESE CULTURE: A SHORT HISTORY, by H. Paul Varley. New
York: Praeger, 1973.

DOCTORS IN POLITICS: THE POLITICAL LIFE OF THE JAPAN MED-
ICAL ASSOCIATION, by William E. Steslicke. New York: Praeger,
1973.

THE JAPAN TEACHERS UNION: A RADICAL INTEREST GROUP IN
JAPANESE POLITICS, by Donald Ray Thurston. Princeton: Princeton University Press, 1973.

JAPAN'S FOREIGN POLICY, 1868–1941: A RESEARCH GUIDE, edited
by James William Morley. New York: Columbia University Press,
1974.

PALACE AND POLITICS IN PREWAR JAPAN, by David Anson Titus.
New York: Columbia University Press, 1974.

THE IDEA OF CHINA: ESSAYS IN GEOGRAPHIC MYTH AND THEORY,
by Andrew March. Devon, England: David and Charles, 1974.

ORIGINS OF THE CULTURAL REVOLUTION, by Roderick Mac-
Farquhar. New York: Columbia University Press, 1974.

SHIBA KŌKAN: ARTIST, INNOVATOR, AND PIONEER IN THE WEST-
ERNIZATION OF JAPAN, by Calvin L. French. Tokyo:Weatherhill,
1974.

INSEI: ABDICATED SOVERIGNS IN THE POLITICS OF LATE HEIAN
JAPAN, by G. Cameron Hurst. New York: Columbia University
Press, 1975.

EMBASSY AT WAR, by Harold Joyce Noble. Edited with an introduction
by Frank Baldwin, Jr. Seattle: University of Washington Press, 1975.

REBELS AND BUREAUCRATS; CHINA'S DECEMBER 9ERS, by John
Isreal and Donald W. Klein. Berkeley: University of California Press,
1975.

DETERRENT DIPLOMACY, edited by James William Morley. New York:
Columbia University Press, 1976.

HOUSE UNITED, HOUSE DIVIDED: THE CHINESE FAMILY IN TAI-
WAN, by Myron L. Cohen. New York: Columbia University Press,
1976.

ESCAPE FROM PREDICAMENT: NEO-CONFUCIANISM AND CHINA'S
EVOLVING POLITICAL CULTURE, by Thomas A. Metzger. New
York: Columbia University Press, 1976.

CADRES, COMMANDERS, AND COMMISSARS: THE TRAINING OF
THE CHINESE COMMUNIST LEADERSHIP, 1920–45, by Jane L.
Price. Boulder, Colo.: Westview Press, 1976.

SUN YAT-SEN: FRUSTRATED PATRIOT, by C. Martin Wilbur. New
York: Columbia University Press, 1977.

JAPANESE INTERNATIONAL NEGOTIATING STYLE, by Michael
Blaker. New York: Columbia University Press, 1977.

CONTEMPORARY JAPANESE BUDGET POLITICS, by John Creighton
Campbell. Berkeley: University of California Press, 1977.

THE MEDIEVAL CHINESE OLIGARCHY, by David Johnson. Boulder, Colo.: Westview Press, 1977.
THE ARMS OF KIANGNAN: MODERNIZATION IN THE CHINESE ORDNANCE INDUSTRY, 1860–1895, by Thomas L. Kennedy. Boulder, Colo.: Westview Press, 1978.
PATTERNS OF JAPANESE POLICYMAKING: EXPERIENCES FROM HIGHER EDUCATION, by T. J. Pempel. Boulder, Colo.: Westview Press, 1978.
THE CHINESE CONNECTION: ROGER S. GREENE, THOMAS W. LAMONT, GEORGE E. SOKOLSKY, AND AMERICAN-EAST ASIAN RELATIONS, by Warren I. Cohen. New York: Columbia University Press, 1978.
MILITARISM IN MODERN CHINA: THE CAREER OF WU P'EI-FU, 1916–1939, by Odoric Y. K. Wou. Folkestone, England: Dawson, 1978.
A CHINESE PIONEER FAMILY: THE LINS OF WU-FENG, by Johanna Meskill. Princeton University Press, 1979.
PERSPECTIVES ON A CHANGING CHINA, edited by Joshua A. Fogel and William T. Rowe. Boulder, Colo: Westview Press, 1979
THE MEMOIRS OF LI TSUNG-JEN, by T. K. Tong and Li Tsung-jen. Boulder, Colo.: Westview Press, 1979.
UNWELCOME MUSE: CHINESE LITERATURE IN SHANGHAI AND PEKING, 1937–1945, by Edward Gunn. New York: Columbia University Press, 1979.
YENAN AND THE GREAT POWERS: THE ORIGINS OF CHINESE COMMUNIST FOREIGN POLICY, by James Reardon-Anderson. New York: Columbia University Press, 1980.
UNCERTAIN YEARS: CHINESE-AMERICAN RELATIONS, 1947–1950, edited by Dorothy Borg and Waldo Heinrichs. New York: Columbia University Press, 1980.
THE FATEFUL CHOICE: JAPAN'S ADVANCE INTO SOUTHEAST ASIA, edited by James William Morley. New York: Columbia University Press, 1980.
TANAKA GIICHI AND JAPAN'S CHINA POLICY, by William F. Morton. Folkestone, England: Dawson, 1980; New York: St. Martin's Press, 1980.
THE ORIGINS OF THE KOREAN WAR: LIBERATION AND THE EMERGENCE OF SEPARATE REGIMES, 1945–1947, by Bruce Cumings. Princeton University Press, 1981.
CLASS CONFLICT IN CHINESE SOCIALISM, by Richard Curt Kraus. New York: Columbia University Press, 1981.
EDUCATION UNDER MAO: CLASS AND COMPETITION IN CANTON

SCHOOLS, by Jonathan Unger. New York: Columbia University Press, 1982.

PRIVATE ACADEMIES OF TOKUGAWA JAPAN, by Richard Rubinger. Princeton: Princeton University Press, 1982.

JAPAN AND THE SAN FRANCISCO PEACE SETTLEMENT, by Michael M. Yoshitsu. New York: Columbia University Press, 1982.

NEW FRONTIERS IN AMERICAN-EAST ASIAN RELATIONS: ESSAYS PRESENTED TO DOROTHY BORG, edited by Warren I. Cohen. New York: Columbia University Press, 1983.

THE ORIGINS OF THE CULTURAL REVOLUTION: II, THE GREAT LEAP FORWARD, 1958–1960, by Roderick MacFarquhar. New York: Columbia University Press, 1983.

THE CHINA QUAGMIRE: JAPAN'S EXPANSION ON THE ASIAN CONTINENT, 1933–1941, edited by James William Morley. New York: Columbia University Press, 1983.

FRAGMENTS OF RAINBOWS: THE LIFE AND POETRY OF SAITO MOKICHI, 1882–1953, by Amy Vladeck Heinrich. New York: Columbia University Press, 1983.

THE U.S.-SOUTH KOREAN ALLIANCE: EVOLVING PATTERNS OF SECURITY RELATIONS, edited by Gerald L. Curtis and Sung-joo Han. Lexington, Mass.: Lexington Books, 1983.

THE FOREIGN POLICY OF THE REPUBLIC OF KOREA, edited by Youngnok Koo and Sung-joo Han. New York: Columbia University Press, 1984.

JAPANESE CULTURE, third edition, revised, by Paul Varley. University of Hawaii Press, 1984.

JAPAN'S MODERN MYTHS: IDEOLOGY IN THE LATE MEIJI PERIOD, by Carol Gluck. Princeton: Princeton University Press, 1985.

SHAMANS, HOUSEWIVES, AND OTHER RESTLESS SPIRITS: WOMEN IN KOREAN RITUAL LIFE, by Laurel Kendall. Honolulu: University of Hawaii Press, 1985.

HUMAN RIGHTS IN CONTEMPORARY CHINA, by R. Randle Edwards, Louis Henkin, and Andrew J. Nathan. New York: Columbia University Press, 1986.

ANVIL OF VICTORY: THE COMMUNIST REVOLUTION IN MANCHURIA, 1945–1948, by Steven I. Levine. New York: Columbia University Press, 1987.